GOODBYE, DARKNESS

The author in 1945

GOODBYE, DARKNESS

A MEMOIR
OF THE PACIFIC WAR

William Manchester

Birlinn

This edition published in
Great Britain in 2001 by
Birlinn Limited
West Newington House
10 Newington Road
Edinburgh
EH9 1QS

www.birlinn.co.uk

First published in 1980 by Little, Brown & Company

ISBN 1 81458 125 9

British Library Cataloguing-in-Publication Data
A catalogue record for this book is available from the British Library

Lines from 'We'll Build a Bungalow' by Betty Bryant Mayhams and Norris the
Troubadour copyright © Robert Mellin Music Publishing Corp. Used by permission.
Lines from 'On the Sunny Side of the Street' by Dorothy Fields and Jimmy McHugh,
copyright © by Shapiro, Bernstein & Co., Inc. Used by permssion.

Photographs on pp. 2, 8, 14, 158, 214, 348 and 392, US Marine Corps photos; p. 118,
Mark Kauffman © copyright 1951 by Time Inc., p. 36 US Navy photo; p. 54, United Press
International; p. 76, J. R. Eyerman, copyright © 1980 by Time, Inc.; p. 190, Bruce Adams;
p. 254, 7th AFF; p. 304, US Army photo; p. 323, Robin Moyer; p. 394, copyright © 1980
by George Silk. All other photographs are courtesy of Willam Manchester.

Printed and bound by
Antony Rowe, Chippenham

To
Robert E. Manchester
Brother and Brother Marine

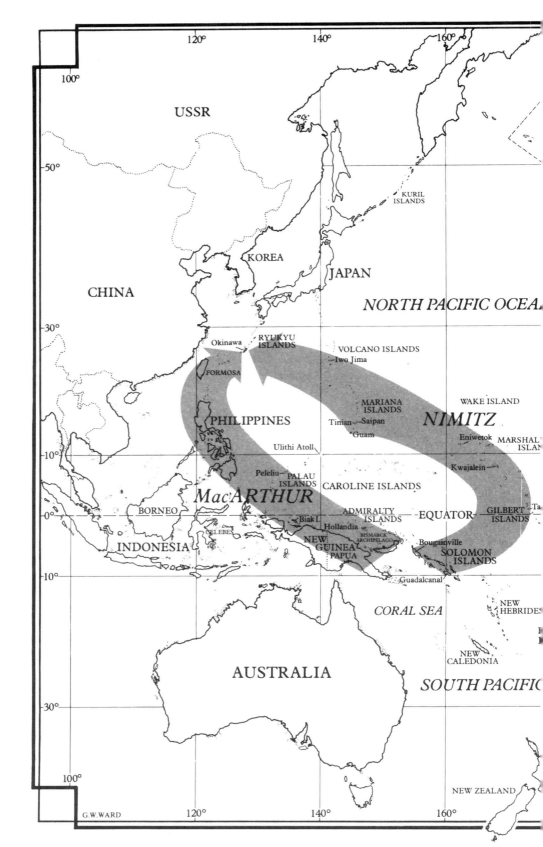

100°

120° 140° 160°

USSR

50°

KURIL
ISLANDS

KOREA

JAPAN

CHINA

NORTH PACIFIC OCEA

30°

Okinawa RYUKYU
ISLANDS VOLCANO ISLANDS
Iwo Jima

FORMOSA

MARIANA
ISLANDS WAKE ISLAND

PHILIPPINES Tinian Saipan *NIMITZ*
Guam

Ulithi Atoll Eniwetok MARSHAL
ISLAN

10°

Peleliu PALAU Kwajalein
ISLANDS CAROLINE ISLANDS

MacARTHUR

BORNEO ADMIRALTY EQUATOR GILBERT Ta 0°
Biak I. ISLANDS ISLANDS

CELEBES Hollandia
BISMARCK
INDONESIA NEW ARCHIPELAGO Bougainville
GUINEA SOLOMON
PAPUA ISLANDS

10°
Guadalcanal

CORAL SEA NEW
HEBRIDE

NEW
CALEDONIA

AUSTRALIA SOUTH PACIFIC

30°

100°

G.W.WARD 120° 140° 160° NEW ZEALAND

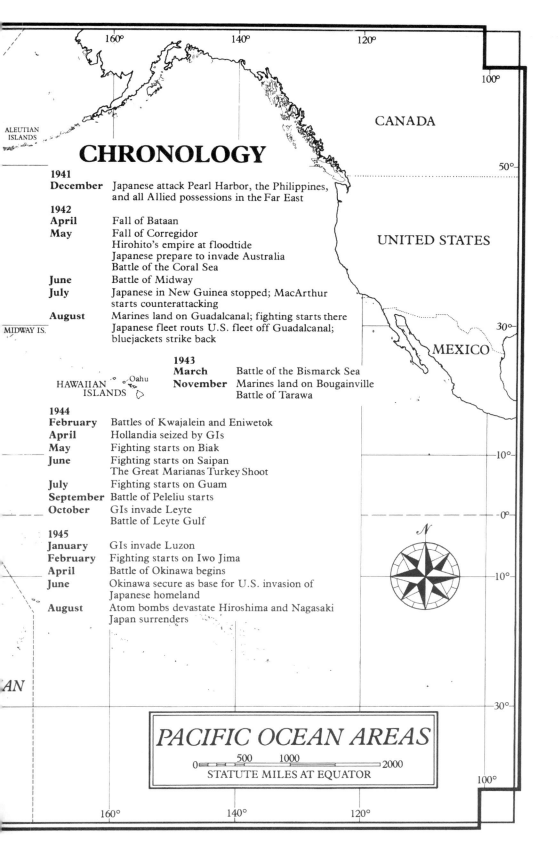

160°   140°   120°

100°

ALEUTIAN
ISLANDS

CANADA

CHRONOLOGY

50°

1941
December   Japanese attack Pearl Harbor, the Philippines,
and all Allied possessions in the Far East

1942
April   Fall of Bataan
May   Fall of Corregidor
Hirohito's empire at floodtide
Japanese prepare to invade Australia
Battle of the Coral Sea
June   Battle of Midway
July   Japanese in New Guinea stopped; MacArthur
starts counterattacking
August   Marines land on Guadalcanal; fighting starts there
Japanese fleet routs U.S. fleet off Guadalcanal;
bluejackets strike back

UNITED STATES

MIDWAY IS.

30°

MEXICO

1943
March   Battle of the Bismarck Sea
November   Marines land on Bougainville
Battle of Tarawa

HAWAIIAN   Oahu
ISLANDS

1944
February   Battles of Kwajalein and Eniwetok
April   Hollandia seized by GIs
May   Fighting starts on Biak
June   Fighting starts on Saipan
The Great Marianas Turkey Shoot
July   Fighting starts on Guam
September   Battle of Peleliu starts
October   GIs invade Leyte
Battle of Leyte Gulf

10°

0°

1945
January   GIs invade Luzon
February   Fighting starts on Iwo Jima
April   Battle of Okinawa begins
June   Okinawa secure as base for U.S. invasion of
Japanese homeland
August   Atom bombs devastate Hiroshima and Nagasaki
Japan surrenders

N

10°

AN

30°

PACIFIC OCEAN AREAS

0   500   1000   2000
STATUTE MILES AT EQUATOR

100°

160°   140°   120°

Your old men shall dream dreams,
your young men shall see visions.

— JOEL 2:28

War, which was cruel and glorious,
Has become cruel and sordid.

— WINSTON CHURCHILL

But we . . . shall be remembered:
We few, we happy few, we band of brothers;
For he to-day that sheds his blood with me
Shall be my brother; be he ne'er so vile,
This day shall gentle his condition.

— *Henry V*, Act IV, Scene iii

Route March

Illustrations

Maps

GOODBYE, DARKNESS

Blood That Never Dried

Our boeing 747 has been fleeing westward from darkened California, racing across the Pacific toward the sun, the incandescent eye of God, but slowly, three hours later than West Coast time, twilight gathers outside, veil upon lilac veil. This is what the French call *l'heure bleue*. Aquamarine becomes turquoise; turquoise, lavendar; lavendar, violet; violet, magenta; magenta, mulberry. Seen through my cocktail glass, the light fades as it deepens; it becomes opalescent, crepuscular. In the last waning moments of the day I can still feel the failing sunlight on my cheek, taste it in my martini. The plane rises before a spindrift; the darkening sky, broken by clouds like combers, boils and foams overhead. Then the whole weight of evening falls upon me. Old memories, phantoms repressed for more than a third of a century, begin to stir. I can almost hear the rhythm of surf on distant snow-white beaches. I have another drink, and then I learn, for the hundredth time, that you can't drown your troubles, not the real ones, because if they are real they can swim. One of my worst recollections, one I had buried in my deepest memory bank long ago, comes back with a clarity so blinding that I surge forward against the seat belt, appalled by it, filled with remorse and shame.

I am remembering the first man I slew.

There was this little hut on Motobu, perched atop a low rise overlooking the East China Sea. It was a fisherman's shack, so ordinary that scarcely anyone had noticed it. I did. I noticed it because I happened to glance in that direction at a crucial moment. The hut lay between us and B Company of the First Battalion. Word had been passed that that company had been taking sniper losses. They thought the sharpshooters were in spider holes, Jap foxholes, but as I was looking that way, I saw two B Company guys drop, and from the angle of their fall I knew the firing had to come from a window on the other side of that hut. At the same time, I saw that the shack had windows on *our* side, which meant that once the rifleman had B Company pinned down, he could turn toward us. I was dug in with Barney Cobb. We had excellent defilade ahead and the Twenty-second Marines on our right flank, but we had no protection from the hut, and our hole wasn't deep enough to let us sweat it out. Every time I glanced at that shack I was looking into the empty eye socket of death.

The situation was as clear as the deduction from a euclidean theorem, but my psychological state was extremely complicated. S. L. A. Marshall once observed that the typical fighting man is often at a disadvantage because he "comes from a civilization in which aggression, connected with the taking of life, is prohibited and unacceptable." This was especially true of me, whose horror of violence had been so deep-seated that I had been unable to trade punches with other boys. But since then life had become cheaper to me. "Two thousand pounds of education drops to a ten rupee," wrote Kipling of the fighting on India's North-West Frontier. My plight was not unlike that described by the famous sign in the Paris zoo: "Warning: this animal is vicious; when attacked, it defends itself." I was responding to a basic biological principle first set down by the German zoologist Heini Hediger in his *Skizzen zu einer Tierpsychologie um und im Zirkus.* Hediger noted that beyond a certain distance, which varies from one species to another, an animal will retreat, while within it, it will attack. He called these "flight distance" and "critical distance." Obviously I was within critical distance of the hut. It was time to bar the bridge, stick a finger in the dike — to do *something.* I could be quick or I could be dead.

My choices were limited. Moving inland was inconvenient; the enemy was there, too. I was on the extreme left of our perimeter, and somehow I couldn't quite see myself turning my back on the shack and fleeing through the rest of the battalion screaming, like Chicken Little, "A Jap's after me! A Jap's after me!" Of course, I could order one of my people to take out the sniper; but I played the role of the NCO in Kipling's poem who always looks after the black sheep, and if I ducked this one, they would never let me forget it. Also, I couldn't be certain that the order would be obeyed. I was a gangling, long-boned youth, wholly lacking in what the Marine Corps called "command presence" — charisma — and I led nineteen highly insubordinate men. I couldn't even be sure that Barney would budge. It is war, not politics, that makes strange bedfellows. The fact that I outranked Barney was in itself odd. He was a great blond buffalo of a youth, with stubby hair, a scraggly mustache, and a powerful build. Before the war he had swum breaststroke for Brown, and had left me far behind in two intercollegiate meets. I valued his respect for me, which cowardice would have wiped out. So I asked him if he had any grenades. He didn't; nobody in the section did. The grenade shortage was chronic. That sterile exchange bought a little time, but every moment lengthened my odds against the Nip sharpshooter. Finally, sweating with the greatest fear I had known till then, I took a deep breath, told Barney, "Cover me," and took off for the hut at Mach 2 speed in little bounds, zigzagging and dropping every dozen steps, remembering to roll as I dropped. I was nearly there, arrowing in, when I realized that I wasn't wearing my steel helmet. The only cover on my head was my cloth Raider cap. That was a violation of orders. I was out of uniform. I remember hoping, idiotically, that nobody would report me.

Utterly terrified, I jolted to a stop on the threshold of the shack. I could feel a twitching in my jaw, coming and going like a winky light signaling some disorder. Various valves were opening and closing in my stomach. My mouth was dry, my legs quaking, and my eyes out of focus. Then my vision cleared. I unlocked the safety of my Colt, kicked the door with my right foot, and leapt inside.

My horror returned. I was in an empty room. There was another door opposite the one I had unhinged, which meant another room, which meant the sniper was in there — and had been warned by the crash of the outer door. But I had committed myself. Flight was impossible now. So I smashed into the other room and saw him as a blur to my right. I wheeled that way, crouched, gripped the pistol butt in both hands, and fired.

Not only was he the first Japanese soldier I had ever shot at; he was the only one I had seen at close quarters. He was a robin-fat, moon-faced, roly-poly little man with his thick, stubby, trunklike legs sheathed in faded khaki puttees and the rest of him squeezed into a uniform that was much too tight. Unlike me, he was wearing a tin hat, dressed to kill. But I was quite safe from him. His Arisaka rifle was strapped on in a sniper's harness, and though he had heard me, and was trying to turn toward me, the harness sling had him trapped. He couldn't disentangle himself from it. His eyes were rolling in panic. Realizing that he couldn't extricate his arms and defend himself, he was backing toward a corner with a curious, crablike motion.

My first shot had missed him, embedding itself in the straw wall, but the second caught him dead-on in the femoral artery. His left thigh blossomed, swiftly turning to mush. A wave of blood gushed from the wound; then another boiled out, sheeting across his legs, pooling on the earthen floor. Mutely he looked down at it. He dipped a hand in it and listlessly smeared his cheek red. His shoulders gave a little spasmodic jerk, as though someone had whacked him on the back; then he emitted a tremendous, raspy fart, slumped down, and died. I kept firing, wasting government property.

Already I thought I detected the dark brown effluvium of the freshly slain, a sour, pervasive emanation which is different from anything else you have known. Yet seeing death at that range, like smelling it, requires no previous experience. You instantly recognize the spastic convulsion and the rattle, which in his case was not loud, but deprecating and conciliatory, like the manners of civilian Japanese. He continued to sink until he reached the earthen floor.

His eyes glazed over. Almost immediately a fly landed on his left eyeball. It was joined by another. I don't know how long I stood there staring. I knew from previous combat what lay ahead for the corpse. It would swell, then bloat, bursting out of the uniform. Then the face would turn from yellow to red, to purple, to green, to black. My father's account of the Argonne had omitted certain vital facts. A feeling of disgust and self-hatred clotted darkly in my throat, gagging me.

Jerking my head to shake off the stupor, I slipped a new, fully loaded magazine into the butt of my .45. Then I began to tremble, and next to shake, all over. I sobbed, in a voice still grainy with fear: "I'm sorry." Then I threw up all over myself. I recognized the half-digested C-ration beans dribbling down my front, smelled the vomit above the cordite. At the same time I noticed another odor; I had urinated in my skivvies. I pondered fleetingly why our excretions become so loathsome the instant they leave the body. Then Barney burst in on me, his carbine at the ready, his face gray, as though he, not I, had just become a partner in the firm of death. He ran over to the Nip's body, grabbed its stacking swivel — its neck — and let go, satisfied that it was a cadaver. I marveled at his courage; I couldn't have taken a step toward that corner. He approached me and then backed away, in revulsion, from my foul stench. He said: "Slim, you stink." I said nothing. I knew I had become a thing of tears and twitchings and dirtied pants. I remember wondering dumbly: *Is this what they mean by "conspicuous gallantry"?*

The Wind-Grieved Ghost

THE DREAMS STARTED AFTER I FLUNG MY PISTOL INTO THE CONNECT-
icut River. It was mine to fling: I was, I suppose, the only World
War II Marine who had had to buy his own weapon. My .45 was
stolen and hidden by a demented corporal the day before we shoved
off for Okinawa, and the battalion commander regretfully told me
that there was no provision for such a crisis. He promised me the
rifle of the first man to fall on the beach. Somehow unreassured, I
bought a Colt from a supply sergeant who would never be close
enough to the front line even to hear the artillery. The transaction
was illegal, of course, but I had a receipt for thirty-five dollars, and
afterward I kept the gun. It lay, unloaded and uncleaned, in the
back of a file cabinet for twenty-three years, until Bob Kennedy
was killed. Then, on impulse, in a revulsion against all weapons, I
threw it away. That, I thought, severed my last link with the war.
Kilroy, for me, was no longer there.

Then the nightmares began. I have always had an odd dream life.
I can waken, interrupting a dream; go to the toilet, return to bed,
fall asleep, and pick up the same dream from where I left off. I can
dream of playing tennis and wake up with tennis elbow. I seldom
have more than one drink, yet sometimes I dream I am roaring
drunk and waken with a hangover. It lasts less than twenty seconds, but I am reaching for the aspirin bottle when I come to my
senses. Once, after dreaming that I had climbed the Matterhorn, I
awoke exhausted. My new, recurrent nightmares were unique,

however. Ordinarily I dream in color; these incubi were chiaroscuros, stark black and white, like old movies. Under a Magellanic Cloud, the stars like chipped diamonds, stood a dark, shell-torn hill, its slopes soggy with gobs bearing the unmistakable clotting pattern of fresh blood. The air was rank with the stench of feces and decomposing flesh, and the cratered surface looked like hell with the fire out. Two men were trudging upward from opposite sides. One, wearing muddy battle dungarees and the camouflaged helmet cover that we wore to distinguish us from army infantrymen, was the scrawny, Atabrine-yellow, cocky young Sergeant of Marines who had borne my name in 1945. The other was the portly, balding, Brooks-Brothered man who bears it today.

They met on the crest, facing each other in the night like mirror and object. But their moods were very different. The older man, ravaged by the artillery of time, the outside corners of his eyes drawn down with the hooded lids of age, was diffident, unsure of himself. The Sergeant's eyes, on the other hand, flamed like wildfire. He angrily demanded an accounting of what had happened in the third of a century since he had laid down his arms. Promises had been made to him; he had expected a nobler America and, for himself, a more purposeful career than the pursuit of lost causes: Adlai Stevenson, John Kennedy, Bob Kennedy, Martin Luther King — all of them irretrievably, irredeemably, irrevocably gone. So the Sergeant felt betrayed. He hadn't anticipated that his country would be transformed into what it has become, nor his generation into docile old men who greedily follow the Dow-Jones average and carry their wives' pocketbooks around Europe. As in most dreams, his wrath was implied, not said, but the old man's protestations were spoken. Indeed, that is how each nightmare ended, with me talking myself awake. Then I would lie in darkness, trembling beneath the sheet, wondering who was right, the uncompromising Sergeant or the compromiser he had become. Here was the ultimate generation gap: a man divided against his own youth. Troubled, I saw no way to heal the split. Kilroy had returned, and this was his revenge.

It was ironic. For years I had been trying to write about the war, always in vain. It lay too deep; I couldn't reach it. But I had known it must be there. A man is all the people he has been. Some recollections never die. They lie in one's subconscious, squirreled away, biding their time. Now mine were surfacing in this disconcerting manner. It had, I knew, happened to others. Siegfried Sassoon wrote of his "queer craving to revisit the past and give the modern world the slip," and Sassoon's remembrances of World War I had been, if anything, gorier than mine. I also knew that, like most of my countrymen, I am prone to search for meaning in the unconsummated past. "America," John Brooks observed, "has a habit of regretting a dream just lost, and resolving to capture it next time." One thinks of Scott Fitzgerald, Robert Frost's "road not taken," Willa Cather's lost lady, and Thomas Wolfe: "Remembering speechlessly we seek the great forgotten . . . lost lane-end into heaven, a stone, a leaf, an unfound door. Where? When? O lost, and by the wind grieved, ghost, come back again."

I could think of but one solution. I had to revisit the Pacific. One motive was a yen to see the sights in the South Seas I had missed before, which means almost all of them; Napoleon said that his soldiers' only view of Russia was the pack of the man in front, and that was pretty much the case with me. (The only native woman I saw on Guadalcanal had a figure like a seabag. She was suffering from an advanced case of elephantiasis. Hubba hubba.) But the chief reason for going was to try to find what I had lost out there and retrieve it. Not only would I go back to my islands; I would visit all the major battlefields to discover, if possible, what we had done there and why we had done it, the ultimate secrets of time and place and dimension and being. I felt rather apprehensive, for I knew that most of it would be irrational. War is literally unreasonable. Today's youth cannot understand it; mine, I suppose, was the last generation to believe audacity in combat is a virtue. And I don't know why we believed it. The mystery troubled me and baffled me, for some of my actions in the early 1940s make no sense to me now. On Okinawa, on Saturday, June 2, 1945, I suffered a superficial gunshot wound just above my right kneecap and was shipped back to a field hospital. Mine was what we called a "million-dollar wound." Though I could hear the Long Toms in the distance, I was warm, dry, and safe. My machismo was intact; I was simply *hors de combat.* The next day I heard that my regiment was going to land behind enemy lines on Oroku Peninsula. I left my cot, jumped hospital, hitchhiked to the front, and made the landing on Monday.

Why had I returned to terror? To be sure, I had been gung ho at the outbreak of war. But I had quickly become a summer soldier and a sunshine patriot. I was indifferent toward rank, and I certainly sought no glory. "We owe God a death," wrote Shakespeare. So we do, but I hoped God would extend my line of credit indefinitely. I was very young. I hadn't published a short story, fathered a child, or even slept with a girl. And because I am possessed, like most writers, by an intense curiosity, I wanted to stick around until, at the very least, I knew which side had won the war.

So, craftily, I became the least intrepid of warriors, a survivor, not a hero, more terrier than lion. If there was a coward's way I took it. The word *hero,* to me, is redolent of Nelson Eddy in his Smokey Bear hat, with Jeanette MacDonald shrieking in his ear, or of John Wayne being booed in a Hawaiian hospital by an audience of wounded Marines from Iwo Jima and Okinawa, men who had had macho acts, in a phrase of the day, up their asses to their armpits. To be sure, I was not an inept fighter. I was lean and hard and tough and proud. I had tremendous reserves of stamina. I never bolted. I was a crack shot. I had a shifty, shambling run, and a lovely eye for defilade — for what the Duke of Wellington called "dead ground," that is, a spot shielded from flat-trajectory enemy fire by a natural obstacle, like a tree or a rock — coupled with a good sense of direction and a better sense of ground. To this day I check emergency exits immediately after registering in a hotel, and in bars you will find me occupying a corner table, with my flanks secure.

But that was the sum of my military skills. I had walked through the valley of the shadow of death and had been terribly frightened. Afterward, those few of us in my unit who had survived received a document from Secretary of the Navy James Forrestal citing us for "gallantry," "valor," "tenacity," and "extraordinary heroism against enemy Japanese forces," but those shining words didn't really apply to me. Indeed, at times it seemed to me that they applied to no one except the dead. I agreed with Hemingway: "Abstract words such as glory, honor, courage, or hallow were obscene beside the concrete names of villages, the numbers of roads, the names of rivers, the numbers of regiments and the dates." For us, they had been Buna and Suribachi; the Kokoda Trail and Tarawa; the First Marine Division and the Eleventh Airborne; the Kumusi and the Asa Kawa; December 7, 1941, and V-J Day. I honored them while hating the whole red and ragged business of war.

By the summer of 1978 I knew that I had to return to the islands. I had to find *out*, and the fact that I couldn't define what I sought merely made the journey inevitable.

So: once more unto the breach.

But first let me introduce myself to myself.

ABLE

From the Argonne
to Pearl Harbor

AT DAYBREAK ON FRIDAY, NOVEMBER 1, 1918 — ALL SAINTS' DAY
— the American Expeditionary Force in France launched its
final offensive of World War I, sending a huge wedge of fifty-six
thousand doughboys to break the back of Erich Ludendorff's
last-ditch defenses on the west bank of the Meuse River. At the
point of the wedge crouched its spearhead, the Fifth Marines.
After five days of waiting in the wilderness of the Forêt d'Argonne,
cloaked and soaked in a blinding fog, the leathernecks sprang forward behind a creeping artillery barrage and quickly overran the
main trench line on the heights overlooking the Meuse. The Germans fled; their scribbly ditches caved in; apart from stolid machine gunners, who kept their murderous barrels hot to the end,
the enemy soldiers became a disorderly mob of refugees. The army
commander of the AEF drive, Major General C. P. Summerall,
USA, praised the Marines' "brilliant advance," which had succeeded in "destroying the last stronghold in the Hindenburg
Line." He called it "one of the most remarkable achievements
made by any troops in this war. . . . These results must be attributed to the great dash and speed of the troops, and to the irresistible force with which they struck and overcame the enemy."
"Nothing," crowed the *New York Times*, "could stop our gallant
Devil Dogs."

That was not entirely true. It never is. Generals and war correspondents are preoccupied with the seizure of objectives, but at-

tacking troops, however victorious, take casualties, individual fighting men who are, in fact, stopped in their tracks. One of the Fifth Marines who fell in no-man's-land that morning was a twenty-two-year-old runner, Lance Corporal William Manchester of Attleboro, Massachusetts, the father of this writer. Lance Corporal Manchester had survived the drives on Soissons and the Saint-Mihiel salient, but this was his unlucky day.

Before dawn he and the rest of his company had stealthily crawled out of their trenches, advanced a thousand yards, and lain down in the mud. Then flares had burst overhead, opening the battle. In a letter dictated to a nurse, Manchester wrote his mother afterward: "At 6:30 A.M. we started, and believe me we had some barrage. . . . But the Heinies were chucking over a few themselves, and it was the worst they had — overhead shrapnel. We had advanced about two miles when one busted that had my initials on it. I say initials because it had a chap's name on it that was about ten feet away. He was killed instantly. The first that I realized I had been hit was when my arm grew numb and my shoulder began to ache. One piece went through the shoulder, just missing the shoulder blade. Another went in about 4½ inches below the other, but by some miracle missed my lung. The two wounds together are about eight inches long. The bones were missed but the cords and nerves were cut connecting with my hand." Later, in what he called a "left handed puzzle," he told his family that he would soon be sent "to a nerve hospital in Washington D.C. and have another operation. . . . The operation will be a very slight one for the purpose of tying the nerves when they were out of my shoulder."

Like many another casualty trying to spare his parents, he was putting a bright face on what was in reality a desperate business. Indeed, his entire Marine Corps career, beginning with his enlistment in Boston, had been a compendium of American military incompetence. He had spent less than four weeks as a recruit on Parris Island, the Corps' boot camp, and most of that had been occupied building a road. Somehow he had qualified as a sharpshooter with the Springfield 1903 rifle; otherwise he was untrained and unprepared for the fighting in France. Then his voyage across the

William Manchester, Sr., Fifth Marines, at age twenty-two, in 1919

Atlantic was interrupted when his troopship, the U.S.S. *Henderson,* caught fire three days out of New York; leaving all his personal possessions behind, he was transferred to the U.S.S. *Von Steuben.* As a replacement at Soissons and in the salient he learned something of combat on the job, but he still lacked the animal instincts of the veteran. His worst experience of official ineptitude, however, came after his November 1 wound. It was grave but not mortal; nevertheless, the surgeon at a casualty clearing station, following the French triage principle — concentrating on casualties who could be saved and abandoning those who couldn't — judged his case to be hopeless. Appropriately, on November 2, All Souls' Day, the Day of the Dead, his litter was carried into a tent known as the "moribund ward"; that is, reserved for the doomed. Gangrene had set in. He was left to die.

He lay there in his blood and corrupt flesh for five days, unattended, his death certificate already signed. Three civilians passed through the tent, representing the Knights of Columbus, the Red Cross, and the Salvation Army. The first, distributing cigarettes and candy, saw the Masonic ring on his left hand and skipped his cot. The Red Cross man tried to sell him — yes, *sell* him — a pack of cigarettes; Manchester had no money, so he got nothing. This outrageous exploitation of casualties was common in World War I. YMCA men were cigarette salesmen, too, though they had an excuse; at the request of the War Department, they were acting as agents of the army commissary, and the AEF gave nothing away to fighting men who had been so negligent as to get wounded. But millions of Americans had contributed to the Red Cross to ease the lot of the soldiers, and the conduct of some of its agents in hospitals behind the lines was nothing short of criminal. It was the Salvation Army man who finally gave the penniless, suffering lance corporal two packs of Lucky Strikes and tried to cheer him up. As long as he lived, Manchester reached for coins when he passed a Salvation Army tambourine. But he never forgave the Red Cross. Long after his death, his eldest son and namesake, lying in a Saipan hospital, was lent ten dollars by the Red Cross and given specific instruction on how it should be repaid. The son repaid none of it. He felt he owed this default to his father.

On the sixth day in the Argonne a team of navy medical corpsmen, carrying out the dead, found that Lance Corporal Manchester
was still alive. They expressed astonishment; much vexed, he testily
replied that he had no intention of dying and wanted to be removed
from this canvas charnel house. But by now there was no chance of
saving his right arm. Although amputation proved to be unnecessary, the limb would be almost useless, a rigid length of bone
scarcely covered by flesh, with a claw of clenched fingers at the end.
The hole through his shoulder, surrounded by hideous scar tissue,
could never be closed.

Transferred to an evacuation hospital and then a base hospital, he
was carried aboard the transport *Princess Matoika* in the first week
of February 1919, and carried off it in Newport News, Virginia, on
February 12. That same day he was admitted to the Norfolk naval
hospital. On April 11 a physician noted that "there is complete pa-
ralysis and atrophy of the muscles of the right forearm." On May
30 the Marine Corps reduced him to his precombat rank of private
and discharged him as No. 145404, "unfit for service." Note was
made that his eyes were blue, his hair light brown, his vision 20/20,
and his height 68 and ¾ inches. His weight was unmentioned; he
had hardly any. Because his signature bore no resemblance to that
on his enlistment papers, he had to make his mark, *X*, like an illiterate. Regulations also required that he impress upon his discharge
certificate the prints of his right fingers. That being impossible, he
had to write awkwardly: "My right hand is paralyzed because of
wound received in France, and therefore I cannot make plain
fingerprints, so I am using my left hand for this." In a typical touch
of Corps gracelessness, his papers carried the final comment: "Not
thought likely to become a public charge."

The small but plucky Manchester clan is one of New England's
oldest, though certainly not richest, families. Thomas Manchester
arrived from Yorkshire, England, in 1638, and three generations
later, on August 16, 1723, in Little Compton, Rhode Island, Ben-
jamin Manchester married Martha Seabury, a great-granddaughter
of John Alden and Priscilla Mullens, who, as every schoolchild
knows, told her future husband to "speak for yourself" when he

came to speak for Myles Standish. Thereafter candor became a family trait, together with piety, belief in the Protestant work ethic, and a powerful sense of sin. Over the next two centuries the tribe produced a score of clergymen, historians, and educators. During the Revolutionary War eighteen Manchesters served under George Washington, including *two* William Manchesters. In the early 1800s the bloodline took to the sea. Its most extraordinary skipper was Amos Manchester, who plied the China trade, walked across Russia on a bet, amassed eighty thousand dollars in 1810, lost it all in a swindle, and wound up digging clams for a living in Bristol, Rhode Island.

Gambling was a family weakness and eventually its undoing. Between them, Richard and his brother Seabury Manchester, grandfather of the World War I Marine and therefore my great-grandfather, owned two stagecoach routes, most of what is now downtown Attleboro, Massachusetts, and a stable of racing horses. They were fascinated by cockfights, however, and they lost their shirts as a result; Seabury's son Raymond inherited nothing. With Raymond the family touched bottom. He was a tubercular manual laborer at the Attleboro railroad depot. Entering this world during the Franco-Prussian War and leaving it during World War II, he spent most of his life putting away a fifth of Scotch a day and warring with his wife, Mary Logan Manchester. He never had a chance against Mary. No one did, not even the Pope. She was one of ten Roman Catholic sisters who emigrated from Ireland during the potato famines. After reading a tract by Mary Baker Eddy, she became a Christian Scientist, never saw a doctor, and buried all her sisters. She lived to be ninety-nine. At the age of ninety-five she was found shingling the roof of her farmhouse. A little Irish blood, like Irish whiskey, goes a long way; her drive was the saving of the family. She passed it along to her four sons, the third of whom was the Argonne casualty.

But — there are always buts when you deal with the Irish — there was another side to her. Today she would be a radical feminist, an executive in a large firm. Caged in the Victorian concept of what a wife should be, she expressed her hostility in attacks on her husband and in what my father described as the worst cooking in New England. He never complained about Marine Corps chow. It was the best he had ever had. Moreover, though she rejected her sisters' religion, Mary didn't reject them; after his graduation from high school in 1914 she hadn't permitted my father to work his way through Brown because every cent he made was sent to the other Logan girls. He was heartbroken. Brown wanted him, if only because he had been a second baseman at Attleboro High and had won an "A" as a star halfback. Instead, he became a costume jewelry salesman for the Watson Company. On his return home in 1919 his former employers took one look at his arm and suggested that he try another line of work. He did: taking advantage of veterans' preference for civil servants, he became a state social worker, and, ultimately, one of Massachusetts' leading advocates of birth control. That may have been his mother's influence. Possibly it may also be traced to the Knight of Columbus in that ghastly tent. At all events, his name was frequently denounced at Catholic masses across the state. Both his sons became enthusiastic users of contraceptives and are vigorous advocates of Planned Parenthood today.

My father's attitude toward the Marine Corps was highly ambivalent. He was sensitive about his handicap — God help the stranger who tried to give him a hand with his overcoat — and though he rarely discussed what had happened in France, he saw through the Corps scam. He didn't want me to join up if another war broke out. At the same time, he was proud to have been a leatherneck himself. My earliest memories are of Memorial Day parades, with him in his dress blues leading the procession. (I didn't notice that they always marched through the cemetery.) He taught me the "Marines' Hymn," the idiom — scuttlebutt, pogey bait, slopchute, skivvies — and the discipline: each week I stood at attention while he gave my bedroom a white-gloves inspection. But my admiration for the military mystique had another strong root. Just as Jesus was Jewish only on his mother's side, I was Yankee only on my father's. As a boy I frequently played the "Marines'

Hymn" on my harmonica, but I played another tune more often. It was "Dixie."

During his hospitalization in Norfolk, my father and other wounded men from France were visited by young women whose paths they would never have crossed under other circumstances. These were the heavily chaperoned daughters of the Virginia aristocracy. Among them was Sallie Elizabeth Rombough Thompson, a shy, beautiful twenty-year-old girl whose father, a Norfolk cotton broker, was a nephew of Stonewall Jackson, and whose mother was a Wilkinson, one of *the* Wilkinsons, who, on May 11, 1862, as a three-week-old infant, had been moved out of her home on Duke Street because a Union major on the staff of General George B. McClellan wanted to use it as his headquarters. The location of the mansion was a strategic asset; two months earlier the babe's Great Aunt Phoebe had watched from her bedroom window as the C.S.S. *Virginia,* née *Merrimack,* steamed out to battle the U.S.S. *Monitor* eleven miles northwest of the residence, in Hampton Roads, off Fort Monroe. It was the highlight of Phoebe's life. The family and everyone they knew were totally engrossed in the war, and later legions of Confederate widows would pass along their fervor, and their bitterness, to their children, their children's children, and, in my case, to their children's children's children's children. A half-century after Appomattox my mother would wear black on Confederate Memorial Day, study Washburn's incredibly biased *History of Virginia* in class, and stand while her headmistress led the school's singing of the stirring "Sword of Lee" ("Forth from its scabbard, pure and bright, flashed the sword of Lee . . ."). J. E. B. Stuart had died at Yellow Tavern in 1864, but his young widow lived into the twentieth century and taught my mother at Sunday school, not confining herself to the Scriptures; she loved to describe her husband's spectacular raid around the entire Union army in the fall of 1861. She and the rest of the Virginia Establishment regarded McClellan's occupation of Norfolk as particularly scurrilous and "ungentlemanly" — the ultimate transgression — because he had, they told one another, taken advantage of the absence of Norfolk's men. Every Wilkinson, every Jackson, every cousin, including

some in their fifties, were away fighting under Lee in three Virginia
regiments and the Dinwiddie Grays. Their ranks were decimated,
and their women plunged into lifelong grief, when Pickett's heroic
charge failed. On the night of July 3, 1863, that last terrible day at
Gettysburg, my grandmother's Aunt Margaret Wilkinson, accompanied by a slave holding a lamp aloft, combed the battlefield, turning over corpses, searching for her husband, John. She found him
alive, but he died after the amputation of his arm. His comrades
were stricken; they had left him for dead. *Respice, adspice, prospice.*
It happened at Gettysburg, it happened in the Argonne, and it
would happen again, to Aunt Margaret's great-great-nephew, first
in childhood and then on a remote Pacific beachhead of which he,
and his parents, for that matter, had never heard.

Like Douglas MacArthur, whose grandfather, father, brother,
and son were *all* christened Arthur MacArthur, my family's Christian names are somewhat confusing. My brother, Robert, practices
law with another attorney who is named Robert Manchester. Until
my father's death I was "Billa," or, more formally, "William Manchester, Jr." I hated that — I have always regarded "Jr." as a sly
boast of legitimacy — and throughout my early life I was mortified
by people telephoning our house who had to be asked whether they
wanted "Big Bill" or "Little Bill." Similarly, both my mother and
her mother (who, once the hated Yankees had left, returned to her
Duke Street home and matured into a stately woman, always
dressed like Queen Mary, toque hat and all) were called Sallie. The
daughter was "Baby Sallie," but after her marriage that became absurd, and introductions were often awkward. I called my grandmother "Nanny," which increased the confusion when we were in
Virginia because there I was turned over to a real nanny.

The Union officer who had liberated the first Sallie's birthplace
felt remorseful later and appeared at the threshold of a nearby family mansion to which the Wilkinson women had moved, bringing
with him a bowl of fresh strawberries. A maid consulted her
mistress and returned to tell him what he could do with his strawberries. His anxiety to make amends was more expedient than generous, for he had found that he had offended a family whose power

reached north of the Mason-Dixon line, and who, had they deigned to use it, could have given him problems. Unlike most of the South's great families, they were not left destitute when their Cause was Lost. They had forfeited a lot, especially blood, but a great deal was left. My grandmother Sallie attended a finishing school where only French was spoken, and she spent each year's social season in Manhattan with her Aunt Mattie, whose husband had a seat on the New York Stock Exchange. After her wedding the Thompsons and their children occupied a front-row pew in Saint Andrew's, Norfolk's fashionable Episcopalian church, with a polished brass plaque on the little swinging door to remind others that Thompsons, and nobody else, were entitled to pray this close to God. Given the sad estate into which the Manchesters had fallen, and the fact that Baby Sallie's fiancé was a Yankee, she would obviously be marrying Down. She didn't look at it that way, however; neither did he; and neither, once they had met the prospective groom, did her relatives. Whatever the Watson Company thought, to Southerners a wound was a badge of honor. And my father was handsome, tactful, and charming. He was an instant success in Norfolk society. On Flag Day, June 14, 1921, he and my mother were wedded in the bride's family's summer home on Willoughby Beach, Virginia, by two Episcopalian priests, from Saint Andrew's Church and the Church of the Advent in Ocean View. Their marriage became the happiest I have ever known.

I may have startled them. For once in my life I was prompt, arriving nine months, two weeks, and four days after they left the altar. True to the tradition of both families, I held my first deathbed scene just eleven months later. On the bleakest day of February 1923, in a cold Attleboro flat, I came within a breath of death from double pneumonia. The doctor — they all made house calls in those days — departed under the impression that I was gone, and my mother, in whose arms I lay, saw my eyes capsize until only the whites were visible. My throat actually began to rattle. Then I shuddered, stifling the rattle, and my eyes rolled back. The resummoned physician darted back into the room and reexamined me. No doubt about it, he said with astonishment; I was still on this side of the river. But little Bill remained a feeble Bill. A more hospitable climate was necessary, so each winter we boarded the Norfolk boat in Providence, Rhode Island, returning to Massachusetts in the spring.

Thus I grew to be a mild, fragile boy. "He's like Ed," said Grandma Manchester, referring to an ectomorphic uncle. As a Christian Scientist Grandma frowned on the doctors in my life. When I was prostrate with whooping cough, she kept telling me, "It's all in your mind, Billa." Then she caught it from me and *I* hung over *her* bed, saying, "It's all in your mind, Grandma," until, with a sickly smile, she agreed and struggled to her feet. But despite her disapproval of physicians, I was too delicate to forgo them. And this had powerful implications for my emerging character. My physical problems led to social problems. Recently an old friend of the family wrote one of my aunts: "What an unusual childhood Bill had. I remember Billa going to Farmers School. . . . Sallie brought Billa up very, very polite, real Southern — not blunt like the Yankees of the north. The big boys of Featherville" — a tough neighborhood — "just did not mean to give Billa any peace."

My incapacity for violence became a family issue. Both my father and my grandfather had spent their grammar-school years in the three-room Farmers School. In addition, I was the son of a Marine; it was inconceivable that I should be a sissy. Yet I was. "Hit back," my father sternly told me. "Never forget that you are a Manchester." But my mother said, "Always remember that you are a gentleman," and I couldn't reconcile the two, thereby failing Scott Fitzgerald's test of a first-rate intelligence: "the ability to hold two opposed ideas in the mind at the same time, and still retain the ability to function." Civility triumphed. Swapping punches made no sense to me. I simply couldn't see the point of inflicting pain on another boy. Word of my vulnerability circulated swiftly, and was passed around just as quickly when we moved to Springfield, Massachusetts, in my eighth year. My father's pension was small; he was becoming a pioneer in social work and, like most pioneers, he was poorly paid; in the late 1920s and early 1930s we lived in some tough neighborhoods. The Springfield equivalents of Featherville were the Columbus Avenue gang, the Acushnet School gang, and the Plumtree Road gang. Any member of any of them who had lost face knew he could regain it by giving me a bloody nose.

It would be good to report that I accepted this punishment stoically, but I didn't. Somebody was always "after" me; I was in a state of more or less continual terror, a fugitive from punishments I did not understand. What I couldn't grasp was that it was my refusal to hit back which enraged them, not my physical frailty. I was a milksop, but other milksops escaped unscarred. My difficulty was that my tormentors knew that, despite my fear, I was too proud to solicit their good opinion. Yet they never gave up. Two of them I remember vividly. The first bore the Dickensian name of Art Loosemore; he was the first to knee me in the groin. The other persecutor also evokes pelvic memories, though of a very different nature. To inflict the ultimate humiliation upon me, one gang decided to let a girl beat me up. Her name was Betty Zimmerman. At eleven she already had the build of a bull dike. Flattening me with a single blow, she straddled me in what Masters and Johnson call the female-superior position, swatting away until she had given me two shiners. I recall with amazement that I felt aroused. I was glad when she stopped pummeling me, but I missed her toiling loins. It wasn't masochism. Already I had the libido of a flaming heterosexual and not, as one might expect, given my temperament, the other.

But I knew that I was different from other boys: skinny, lacking coordination or small-muscle skills, inept with marbles, easily found in relievo, and a flop on sandlots — after the captains of two teams had picked the rest of the players, they had to choose up all over again, to determine which side would be burdened with me. During luncheon recess we would all sit on the school steps, and the others would vie in identifying the makers or models of passing cars. I couldn't tell a Packard from a Ford; I still can't. I simply didn't *fit*. I didn't even like popular songs, because I felt that the lyrics insulted my intelligence. Later, as an adult, my strong sense of individuality would be an advantage, but in my early years it was a heavy cross to bear. The chasm between me and my peers was revealed one day when I asked a boy if he knew the last words of Stonewall Jackson. "He didn't say nothing," the boy replied. "It was some kid who said, 'Say it ain't so, Joe.' " He thought Stonewall Jackson had played center field for the 1919 Chicago White Sox.

By the time I reached my teens, I had found a way to thwart bullies, striking up a friendship with a strong boy who shared my curiosity about the world beyond Springfield. Meanwhile, however, I had retreated from the playground to the library, from camaraderie to introspection and the written language. My mother has doggerel I scribbled at the age of seven. At eleven I was typing short stories, derivative of Poe, on the Underwood my father used for case reports, and I cannot remember a time in my life, excepting combat, when I was not deep in a book. In our bookcases at home, brought from Virginia, and in the Forest Park branch of the Springfield Public Library, I was introduced to writers rarely known to young boys: Ruskin, Macaulay, Thomas Huxley, Matthew Arnold, and those touchstones of every intellectual son of New England, Thoreau on civil disobedience and Emerson on forbearance and self-reliance. Of course, their concepts were beyond me, as, later, I would founder over Joyce and Pound. These writers attracted me, and delighted me, by the skill with which they used the language. Their reasoning eluded me, but I learned style from them long before the public school system apprenticed me to Howells and Hawthorne.

The Ruskins and the Macaulays were the cream of an odd crop. I also devoured Wyss's *Swiss Family Robinson, Treasure Island, The Little Colonel, The Trail of the Lonesome Pine*, Swift on Gulliver, Lamb on roast pig, *Tom, the Water Baby*, a translation of Malory's *Morte d'Arthur*, and, on a descending scale, William Ernest Henley, Sir Henry Newbolt, G. A. Henty, Franklin W. Dixon, Burt L. Standish, Edward Stratemeyer, and Horatio Alger, Jr. My appetite for juvenile junk was enormous. One summer on Cape Cod I read twenty Frank and Dick Merriwells in less than a week. But a pattern was forming; I was being drawn to Victorian authors and those who followed the Victorian mode. (I was a throwback in other ways; I scorned saddle shoes and reversible raincoats and loathed Swing.) This slanting toward the last century was most striking, and most significant, in books about war. Here I passed Scott Fitzgerald's test. My vision of martial splendor, both ours and that of our allies, could withstand all threats of disillusionment; I was transported by dreams of leathernecks sweeping all before them, and the glint of moonlight on the sabers of French cavalry, and British squares standing firm with the Gatling jammed and the colonel dead. It wasn't difficult. Millions had done it before me. Their equivocal view of battle can be summed up in a single word. At Waterloo Pierre Cambronne commanded Napoleon's Imperial Guard. When all was lost, a British officer asked him to lay down his arms. Generations of schoolboys have been taught that he replied: "The Guard dies, but never surrenders." Actually he said: "*Merde!*" ("Shit!") The French know this; a euphemism for *merde* is called "the word of Cambronne." Yet children are still told that he said what they know he did not say. So it was with me. I read Kipling, not Hemingway; Rupert Brooke, not Wilfred Owen; *Gone with the Wind*, not Ambrose Bierce and Stephen Crane.

The pacifism of the 1930s maddened me. I yearned for valor; I wanted the likes of Lee and the Little Colonel to be proud of me. To show my contempt for the Yankees, I fashioned a homemade Stars and Bars from a sheet and watercolors, and sneeringly flaunted it at school recess. My classmates were confused; they didn't know what it was. Once my mother had screwed up her courage and told her father-in-law that she supposed his father had fought her grandfathers. Grandpa sat in confused silence for a while; when drunk, he always looked extremely puzzled. Then he realized that he had been insulted. He raised his chin and gave her a stare of hauteur. "*Manchesters,*" he said, "sent *substitutes.*" My mother didn't know what he was talking about. Luckily for my hide, I was experiencing a similar failure of communications. It was ludicrous. Here was a ninety-eight-pound weakling, an unsuccessful

Charles Atlas client whom even Betty Zimmerman could beat the shit out of, dreaming of glory under banners furled long ago in dusty attics. Most of the rest of my generation believed in appeasement, at least when it came to war, but I was an out-and-out warmonger, a chauvinist dying for the chance to die. As it happened, my daydreams were translated into reality by the emergence of a wicked genius bearing a black Swastika, a Teutonic monster unmatched in all the books I read, who could be destroyed only on the battlefield. Long afterward I flattered myself that I had been prescient, that like Churchill I had seen the gathering storm. It is true that I wept over Nanking and Munich, and that, once I had learned a little German, I rose early to rage at Hitler's wild speeches. But the fact is that I was really an eager Saint George looking for a dragon. I'm not sure that, or something like that, wasn't true of Churchill, too.

Henry V was naturally my idol, and here we skirt one of the central events of my life: my discovery of Shakespeare. I was now fifteen. For years I had been plagued by a vocabulary of words I could understand but not pronounce because I had never heard them spoken. "Anchor" had come out "an-chore," "colonel" as "ko-low-nall," and I had put the accent on the third syllable of "diáspora." But I could no longer ignore diacritical marks in dictionaries; Shakespeare cried to be read aloud. And as I did so I was stunned by his absolute mastery. In Johnson's secondhand bookstore in Springfield I found a forty-volume set of his works, with only *Macbeth* missing, for four dollars. I knew where I could get a *Macbeth* for a dime, so I paid a dollar to hold the set, and returned with the rest two months later. I have it yet, tattered and yellowing. It was the best bargain of my life.

I memorized the role of Hamlet, then Marc Anthony in *Julius Caesar*, and then long soliloquies from *Macbeth*, *Lear*, *Othello*, and *Romeo and Juliet*. In high school I produced, directed, and starred in *Hamlet* and, looking like a minstrel-show end man, in *Othello*. My stage career ended in 1938, when the Smith Club of Springfield brought Orson Welles to the Municipal Auditorium. This was a few weeks after his Martian broadcast. The place was jammed. But after sneaking into countless concerts, I knew every room in the building, including the one where Welles would rest during the intermission between his lecture and his readings. I appeared on the threshold, immaculate in my double-breasted blue-serge suit. "Mr. Welles," I said in my reedy adolescent voice. He looked up from his text. I piped, "I am the president of the Springfield Classical High School Dramatic Club." His eyes bulged. His jaw sagged. In a hollow voice he gasped: *"No!"*

My father had taken a lively interest in my stage career, though he had vetoed my plan to enter the American Academy of Dramatic Arts. "Actors are bums," he said, and that was the end of that. He was determined to save me from debauchery. To New Englanders of his stock, the worst blow that could fall on a youth was acquiring "a Record," that is, a police record; it was as great a stigma as Jean Valjean's yellow passport. (I took a different view. Later, in college, when I was arrested for being drunk and disorderly on the Amherst green and fined ten dollars, I passed the hat at my fraternity and never gave the matter another thought.) One day when I was about fifteen I was one of several boys lolling on a lawn like Restoration rakes with two girls who were notorious for going, as we put it, all the way. We were playing "under the sheet," adding that phrase to song titles and thus giving them giggly double entendres. A nosey Parker looked out her window, saw our orgy, and called my father, who fetched me home and clouted me. Shortly afterward I heard about masturbation and asked him for the real lowdown on it. He gave me the old malarkey about brain damage and how he had never done it, hadn't even heard about it until a sex hygiene lecture in the Marine Corps. Then he gave me the keeping-yourself-pure spiel and explained the facts of life. I bought it all; I tried hard (and unsuccessfully) to follow his advice and think pure thoughts. He had assumed that I would. Somehow he kept his faith in me, affectionately calling me "Bozo" and always looking for sources of pride there, just as I was trying to please him. His favorite song was "I'm Always Chasing Rainbows." He was of that generation that believed in the pot of gold at the end of the rainbow — my generation knows that if it's there, it belongs to the government — and he believed that if I shaped up I could lick the world.

Yet I was a discouraging son. He didn't really expect much of me: just that I be a normal American boy, fleet of foot, handy with a mitt and a bat, a tinkerer who could fix things like warped storm doors, defective lawn mowers, light switches, and running toilets. I could do none of these. On one memorable July 4 I dropped a whole bag of "torpedoes," fireworks which exploded upon impact, on my feet, and had to be rushed to the hospital. The following year I picked up a live sparkler from the wrong end. Given my love of prose, I should have at least been a good student. I wasn't; lessons bored me. I preferred books which teachers didn't assign or, in most cases, hadn't even read. Once I brought home a report card with three D's. Seeing my father's disappointment and then feeling it — he believed in corporal punishment for that, too — I finished the next marking period with straight A's, which, as he rightly pointed out, proved that I could do it. Then I failed Shop, which was considered impossible. We were all building little short-legged, hinged tables for people who breakfasted in bed. The instructor turned the legs for me on a lathe. All I had to do was drive the nails straight. I couldn't do it, not once. My father took one look at my efforts and groaned, like the Giant Despair in *Pilgrim's Progress*.

My one success in his eyes, and I did it for him, was in Scouting. I became a junior assistant scoutmaster and an eagle scout. In a formal ceremony I pinned a little silver eagle on my mother's dress and my father pinned my badge on me with his one hand. Our picture was in the papers. I have it still, and looking at it I can see only that hand. He could do almost anything with it, even build a cold room and a fruit cellar, and I, with my two hands, could do so little.

At. the dinner table my mother always cut his meat into small pieces. It was his only concession to his handicap. He gardened, painted, and defeated me with effortless ease in Ping-Pong and horseshoe pitching. No one could beat him at anything. He was direct, forceful, incapable of compromise. Once a landlord flirted with my mother and sent her flowers. My father came home, took the flowers back to the landlord, and crammed them down his throat. Later, thanks to a small inheritance from one of his Manchester aunts, he made a down payment on a suburban home. The local Communist party decided to picket it. They wanted to see the public welfare rolls, a likely source of future party members. My father had decided that those unfortunate enough to be on relief should not be embarrassed and exploited; their names would be kept in confidence. Compared with what was to come thirty years later, the Communist demonstration was almost charming. (One placard read: "Mr. Manchester, servant of the people, does not serve the people.") But on the first — and last — evening, they boasted to reporters and neighbors that we were cowering in our darkened house. As they were about to break up, our Chevy turned in to the driveway. My father had taken us to Sam's Diner and then to a Jeanette MacDonald–Nelson Eddy double feature.

He was such a beautiful man, with such a beautiful rainbow of a laugh. Later as a newspaperman I came to know many world figures, from Churchill and Eisenhower to Stevenson and the Kennedys. I never met a man with more charisma than my father. He ruled us like a pasha. Yet in retrospect I wish he had been a shade less competent. He was the only member of the family who knew how to drive a car, or write a check, or negotiate a loan. Inexplicably he had permitted half of his national serviceman's insurance to lapse; only five thousand dollars of it, and the shrinking equity in our home, seemed to stand between us and eligibility for those same relief rolls should he die. And he was dying. He suffered from migraines, ulcers, hypertension, and most of all from the wounds of 1918, which had never really healed. One frightening evening he was carried, bleeding internally, out of the house, to an ambulance, and thereafter he was in and out of Springfield Hospital and veterans' hospitals.

The end approached as World War II approached, but I knew far more about what the Germans were doing than what was happening to the man who supported my mother, my four-year-old brother, and me. I stood by his bed for the last time on Sunday, January 19,

1941. He knew he had only a few days to live, but the possibility that he might cease to exist never entered my mind. Mute and un-comprehending, I kissed him upon the lips, held his good hand while he said that I was a genius (that being a common excuse for daffiness then) and reminded me once more that I was a Man-chester (with all that that entailed). But his strongest message was unspoken. His eyes said: *Avenge me!*

I was eighteen by the calendar, fourteen or less in knowledge of the world. He hadn't even permitted me to apply for part-time employment, because he said I would be taking jobs from the poor. Somehow I had reached the extraordinary conclusion that we were rich. Actually I knew nothing about money; I had heard, in the course of one conversation between my parents, that our house was worth either eighty-five thousand dollars or eighty-five hundred, I didn't know which; to me the second figure, which was correct, was essentially no different from the other. So, in the autumn of 1940, I had left for Massachusetts State College in Amherst, cocky in my newfound masculinity and increasingly sure of my flair for the lan-guage. During the Christmas vacation I had rattled away on my typewriter, aware that my father lay ill in the hospital but kept in ignorance of what the doctors had told my mother: that it was a matter of time, and of very little time, before he left us. I returned to Amherst for the end of my first semester. In the middle of final exams the call came from an uncle: "Your dad has passed away." He was forty-four years old.

I remember the funeral. It was savagely cold, an iron cold; the ground had to be jackhammered open to receive the coffin. A little sapling stood at the foot of it. Today it is a beautiful tree, and he lies in its lovely shade, but then it offered pitifully small protection from the weather. We were all shivering, then shaking. The others were weeping, but I just stared down at the grave. I wondered: *Where has he gone?* Then a curtain falls over my memory. It is all a dark place in my mind. I recall nothing that happened in the next four months. It was my first experience of traumatic amnesia, or fugue. I was in deep shock. My mother later told me how helpful I was in selling the car and house, in moving us to a tenement and taking in a roomer. None of it has ever come back to me. Apparently I returned to college and completed the year. The dean's office has a record of my grades. I have looked at the textbooks I studied that semester. It is as though I were seeing them for the first time.

When I returned to conscious life I was working as a grease monkey in a machine shop at thirty-five cents an hour, eighty-four hours a week. If I made five hundred dollars between that job and another job in the college store — thirty cents an hour there — I could, with a scholarship, stay in school. My mother told me that whatever happened, I must not think of dropping out. I was dumbfounded. Such a thought had never crossed my mind. Like Chekhov's perennial student, I could imagine no life away from classes and books.

But the perennial student's cherry orchard came down, and my undergraduate years were abruptly interrupted on December 7, 1941. In the spring of 1942, guided by the compass that had been built into me, I hitchhiked to Springfield and presented myself at the Marine Corps recruiting station, a cramped second-story suite of rooms with a superb view of a Wrigley's billboard and the Paramount Theater parking lot. The first test was weight, and I flunked it. There wasn't enough of me. The sergeant, or "Walking John," as the Corps called recruiting NCOs, suggested that I go out, eat all the bananas and drink all the milk I could hold, and then come back. I did. I made the weight. Immediately thereafter I was sick. My liver, colon, and lungs — all my interior plumbing — fused into a single hard knot and wedged in my epiglottis. The sergeant held my head over a basin as I threw up banana after banana, and he said, not unkindly, "Just keep puking till you feel something round and hairy-like coming up. Keep that. That's your asshole." I recovered and continued with the exam. Meanwhile all that milk was working its way through my system. My back teeth were floating. At last the end was in sight. A pharmacist's mate nodded at a rack of twenty-four test tubes and told me to go over in the corner and give him a urine specimen. But once I started, I couldn't stop. I returned and handed him twenty-four test tubes, each filled to the brim with piss. He looked at the rack, looked at me, and then back at the rack again. An expression of utter awe crossed his face. It was the first misunderstanding between me and the Marine Corps. There would be others.

Arizona, I Remember You

DURING THE INTERVAL BETWEEN MY FATHER'S DEATH AND THE OUT-
break of war in the Pacific, my loss of perception had been matched
by American ignorance of the threat in the Far East. The United
States was distracted by the war in Europe, with Hitler's hammer
blows that year falling on Yugoslavia, Greece, Crete, and — the
greatest crucible of suffering — Russia. Virtually all Americans
were descended from European immigrants. They had studied Con-
tinental geography in school. When commentators told them that
Nazi spearheads were knifing here and there, they needed no maps;
they all had maps in their minds. Oriental geography, on the other
hand, was (and still is) a mystery to most of them. Yet the Japanese
had been fighting in China since 1931. In 1937 they had bombed
and sunk the U.S. gunboat *Panay* on the Yangtze and jeered when
the administration in Washington, shackled by isolationism, had
done nothing. Even among those of us who called ourselves "inter-
ventionists," Hitler was regarded as the real enemy. It was Hitler
Roosevelt had been trying to provoke with the Atlantic Charter, the
destroyer swap with Britain, Lend-Lease, and shoot-on-sight convoys, each of which drew Washington closer to London. Europe,
we thought, was where the danger lay. Indeed, one of my reasons
for joining the Marine Corps was that in 1918 the Marines had been
among the first U.S. troops to fight the Germans. Certainly I never
dreamt I would wind up on the other side of the world, on a
wretched island called Guadalcanal.

Roosevelt never changed his priorities, but when the Führer re-fused to rise to the bait, the President found another way to lead us into the war — which was absolutely essential, he felt, if the next generation of Americans was to be spared a hopeless confrontation with a hostile, totalitarian world. On September 27, 1940, the Japa-nese had signed the Tripartite Pact with Germany and Italy. That opened the possibility of reaching the Axis through Tokyo. And Roosevelt knew how to do it. During the four months before the pact, the fall of France, Holland, and Belgium had wholly altered the strategic picture in Asia. Their colonies there were almost de-fenseless, but FDR let it be known that he felt avuncular. Even before the Tripartite Pact he had warned the Japanese to leave French Indochina alone. Once the Nipponese tilted toward the Axis, he proclaimed an embargo on scrap iron and steel to all na-tions outside the Western Hemisphere, Great Britain excepted. He reached the point of no return in the summer of 1941. On July 24 Jap troops formally occupied Indochina, including Vietnam. Two days later the President froze all Japanese credits in the United States, which meant no more oil from America. Britain followed suit. This was serious for the Japanese but not desperate; their chief source of petroleum was the Netherlands East Indies, now In-donesia, which sold them 1.8 million tons a year. Then came the real shock. The Dutch colonial government in Djakarta froze Japanese assets there — and renounced its oil contract with Dai Nippon ("Dai" meaning "Great," as in Great Britain). For Prince Fumi-maro Konoye, Emperor Hirohito's premier, this was a real crisis. Virtually every drum of gas and oil fueling the army's tanks and planes had to be imported. Worse, the Japanese navy, which until now had counseled patience, but which consumed four hundred tons of oil an hour, joined the army in calling for war. Without Dutch petroleum the country could hold out for a few months, no more.

Konoye submitted his government's demands to the American ambassador in Tokyo: If the United States would stop arming the Chinese, stop building new fortifications in the Pacific, and help the emperor's search for raw materials and markets, Konoye promised not to use Indochina as a base, to withdraw from China after the situation there had been "settled," and to "guarantee" the neutrality of the Philippines. Washington sent back an ultimatum: Japan must withdraw all troops from China and Indochina, withdraw from the Tripartite Pact, and sign a nonaggression pact with neighboring countries. On October 16 Konoye, who had not been unreasonable, stepped down and was succeeded by General Hideki Tojo, the fiercest hawk in Asia. The embargoed Japanese believed that they had no choice. They had to go to war unless they left China, a loss of face which to them was unthinkable. They began honing their ceremonial samurai swords.

All this was known in Pennsylvania Avenue's State, War, and Navy Department Building. The only question was where the Nips would attack. There were so many possibilities — Thailand, Hong Kong, Borneo, the Kra Isthmus, Guam, Wake, and the Philippines. Pearl Harbor had been ruled out because Tojo was known to be massing troops in Saigon, and American officers felt sure that these myopic, bandy-legged little yellow men couldn't mount more than one offensive at a time. Actually they were preparing to attack *all* these objectives, including Pearl, simultaneously. In fact, the threat to Hawaii became clear, in the last weeks of peace, even to FDR's chiefs of staff. U.S. intelligence, in possession of the Japanese code, could follow every development in Dai Nippon's higher echelons. On November 22 a message from Tokyo to its embassy on Washington's Massachusetts Avenue warned that in a week "things are automatically going to happen." On November 27, referring to the possibility of war, the emperor's envoy to the United States asked, "Does it seem as if a child will be born?" He was told, "Yes, the birth of a child seems imminent. It seems as if it will be a strong, healthy boy." Finally, on November 29, the U.S. Signal Corps transcribed a message in which a functionary at the Washington embassy asked, "Tell me what Zero hour is?" The voice from Tokyo replied softly: "Zero hour is December 8" — December 7 in the United States — "at Pearl Harbor."

The Americans now knew that an attack was coming, when it would come, and where. The danger could hardly have been greater. Japan's fleet was more powerful than the combined fleets of America and Great Britain in Pacific waters. U.S. commanders in Hawaii and the Philippines were told: "This dispatch is to be considered a war warning. . . . An aggressive move by Japan is expected within the next few days." That was followed on December 6 by: "Hostilities may ensue. Subversive activities may be expected." The ranking general in Honolulu concluded that this was a reference to Nipponese civilians on Oahu. Therefore, he ordered all aircraft lined up in the middle of their airstrips — where they could be instantly destroyed by hostile aircraft. The ranking admiral decided to take no precautions. Put on constant alert, he felt, his men would become exhausted. So officers and men were given their customary Saturday evening liberty on December 6. No special guards were mounted on the United States Fleet in Pearl Harbor — ninety-four ships, including seven commissioned battleships and nine cruisers — the only force-in-being which could prevent new Japanese aggression in Asia. Only 195 of the navy's 780 antiaircraft guns in the harbor, and only 4 of the army's 30 antiaircraft batteries, were manned. And most of them lacked ammunition. It had been returned to storage because it was apt to "get dusty."

In the early morning hours of Sunday, December 7, 1941, as Americans slept off hangovers in Waikiki amid the scent of frangipani, the squawk of pet parrots, and the echo of surf on Diamond Head, two hundred miles north of them a mighty Japanese armada steamed southward at flank speed. Altogether there were 31 pagoda-masted warships, but the thoughts and prayers of all the crews were focused on the 360 carrier-borne warplanes, especially those in the lead attack squadron aboard the flattop *Akagi*. The squadron leader was told that if he found he had taken the enemy by surprise, he was to break radio silence over Oahu and send back the code word *tora* (tiger).

In darkness the pilots scrambled across the *Akagi*'s flight deck to their waiting Nakajima-97 bombers, Aichi dive-bombers, and Kaga and Mitsubishi Type-O fighters — the swift, lethal raiders which the Americans would soon christen "Zeroes." Zooming away, they approached Kahuku Point, the northern top of Oahu, at 7:48 A.M. and howled through Kolekole Pass, overlooking the U.S. Army's Schofield Barracks, thirty-five miles from Honolulu. Luck rode with them: an overcast cleared and the sun appeared in a rosy satin dawn, sending warm pencils of light shining down on the green valleys and green-and-brown canebrakes, the purplish spiny mountain ridges, and the brilliant blue sea, rimmed by valances of whitecaps. Dead ahead, on Oahu's southern coast, lay their targets: Wheeler, Bellows, Ewa, and Hickam airfields and, most important, the magnificent port which the ancient Hawaiians had christened *Wai Momi* — "water of pearl." There American battlewagons lay anchored in groups of two off Ford Island, in the center of the harbor: the *California, Maryland, Oklahoma, Tennessee, West Virginia, Arizona, Nevada*, and the thirty-three-year-old *Utah*, now retired from active service.

At the Japs' height, ten thousand feet, they looked like toy boats in a bathtub. Swinging at chains around them, hemming them in and making an escape almost impossible, were eighty-six other vessels, concentrated in an area less than three miles square. Even if the men-of-war could maneuver around them, the one channel to the sea and freedom was barred by a torpedo net. The Japanese commander signaled his squadron: *"To-, to-, to,"* the first syllable of *totsugeki*, "Charge!" Then he signaled the *Akagi: "Tora, tora, tora!"* Then, back to his air fleet: *"Yoi!"* ("Ready!") and *"Te!"* ("Fire!"). Flying at treetop level and defying the pitifully few dark-gray bursts of flak polka-dotting the serene sky, successive waves of Nip aircraft skimmed in over Merry Point, attacking and wheeling to return again and again. Zeroes strafed; dive-bombers and torpedo bombers dropped missiles and sticks of dynamite through the roiling, oily, reeking clouds of smoke, knocking out 347 U.S. warplanes and 18 warships, among them all the battleships, the cruisers *Helena* and *Honolulu*, and the destroyers *Cassin* and *Downes*. At a cost of 29 planes the Nips killed or wounded 3,581 Americans, nearly half of them on the sunken *Arizona*.

The destruction of the *Arizona*, which had been moored in tandem with the repair ship *Vestal*, was the most spectacular loss. A

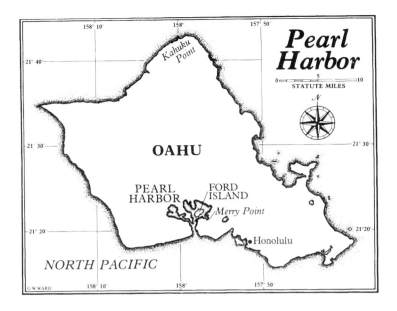

Pearl Harbor

OAHU

bomb set off fuel tanks, which ignited eight tons of highly volatile black powder — stored against regulations — and that, in turn, touched off vast stocks of smokeless powder in a forward magazine before it could be flooded. Instants later three more bombs, including one right down a funnel, found their targets. As over a thousand U.S. bluejackets were incinerated or drowned, the 32,600-ton battlewagon sent up 500-foot-high cascades of flame, leapt halfway out of the water, broke in two, and plunged to the muddy bottom, her vanishing forecastle enshrouded in billowing clouds of black fumes. Not even Kukailimoku, the war god of ancient Havai'i, had envisioned such a disaster. "Remember Pearl Harbor" became an American shibboleth and the title of the country's most popular war song, but it was the loss of that great ship which seared the minds of navy men. Six months later, when naval Lieutenant Wilmer E. Gallaher turned the nose of his Dauntless dive-bomber down toward the *Akagi* off Midway, the memory of that volcanic eruption in Pearl Harbor, which he had witnessed, flashed across his mind. As the *Akagi* blew up, he exulted: "*Arizona, I remember you!*"

Like Merlyn in *The Once and Future King*, the old man in my dreams knows the future; it is the past that is unrevealed to him. Thus, in the waning months of 1978 I don my old Raider cap and board a United Airlines flight to Hawaii, the first leg of my journey back to the islands. The huge plane receives us into its belly like some fantastic modern Trojan horse, and presently we rise, effortlessly, above the smog, to a sky as blue as a kingfisher's wing. Eastward, as we turn, I glimpse a range of heavily jowled mountains. Below lies dense L.A., threaded by freeways. Then we glide down the bleak concrete and cinder-block sleeve of Watts and out past Cabrillo Beach. Below, the tide restlessly gnaws at the shore; up here, in pristine cleanliness, I am cosseted with pillows, steak, champagne, a movie if I want it (I don't), and a pretty, young, boisterous, outrageously outspoken stewardess who has my number. Serving me dinner, she drops a fork and mutters, "Shit." The Sergeant in me says, "Nice girls don't talk dirty." Her eyes lick at me merrily. She grins and says, "I'm a woman, not a girl. Anyway, you should talk. I saw you giving me the once-over, you dirty old man." I say, "I'm not a dirty old man, I'm a sexy senior citizen." She: "Where'd you get that?" I: "Some bumper sticker at the Old Folks' Home." But the game stops there. She passes on, a member of the Pepsi generation who has deduced that I am on the wrong side of fifty-five, a senescent old-timer, laden with medication for hypertension, antibiotics for rotting teeth, and tricyclics for endogenous depressions — a walking drugstore in no condition for any strenuous activity. Which is as it should be. At my age I ought to feel calm, untroubled, unchallenged by any female or, for that matter, anybody. Yet I am uneasy. A few Japanese soldiers, I have read, still lurk in the bush on the islands; every now and then one emerges. It would be just my luck to be the victim of the last banzai charge. That is ridiculous, of course; still, I am nervous. The fact is that I have no idea of what I shall find Out There.

Then the old war songs begin in my head. All my life I have had one tune or another running through my mind, and I have never been able to control them. Since our takeoff, this internal Muzak has been playing the appropriately assuasive "I'll Be Seeing You." But now there is a change on the brain's record player. Lyrics stifled long ago come crowding back, first, to the tune of "Mac-Namara's Band":

> *Just now we're all rehearsing for another big affair,*
> *We'll take another island, and the Japs'll all be there . . .*

And:

> *Bless 'em all, bless 'em all,*
> *As back to our foxholes we crawl . . .*

Then, to the same air, mispronouncing the name of a shocking battle:

> *Oh, we sent for MacArthur to come to Tarawa*
> *But General MacArthur said no,*
> *He gave as the reason, it wasn't the season,*
> *Besides there was no U.S.O.*

Then, to the tune of "Embraceable You":

> *Replace me, I can't go home without you . . .*

And:

> *I don't want no more Marine Corps*
> *Gee, Mom, I wanna go*
> *Right back to Quantico*
> *Gee, Mom, I wanna go home . . .*

And the haunting:

> *Say a prayer for your pal*
> *On Guadalcanal,*
> *He needs God's help, it's true . . .*

What, I suddenly wonder, am I *doing* here? I am headed toward places I vowed never to see again, toward excessive vegetation, away from gentle New England's forsythia, pussy willows, laurel, lilac. I could be deep in the leather chair by my Connecticut fireplace, reading Muriel Spark or Peter De Vries, or listening to Tchaikovsky's musical euphemism of 1812 combat. I don't *need* this, says the old man in me; yes, you *do*, the Sergeant says grimly. And as our silvery tube climbs above rough weather at thirty-five thousand feet, the Sergeant takes over.

Hawaii was the destination of my first airplane ride, but we were coming from the opposite direction, from Saipan, with stops at Guam and Johnston Island. It was a long flight — about four thousand miles — and the best our C-54 could do, with all four engines toiling a-whump, a-whump, a-whump, was under 265 miles per hour. There were twenty-five of us, all on litters. Apparently this had always been a flying ambulance; the bulkheads of its long, cigar-shaped ward were whitewashed, the deck was rubber, trays bearing tubes and syringes were screwed in place, and everything had that unmistakable smell of medicinal chemicals. At least, that is my recollection. I wasn't an altogether reliable witness. I was weaning myself from morphine. The weaning hadn't been my idea in the beginning. I had been on a half grain a day; then an army medical officer had cut it off completely, leaving me to cold turkey. I could have returned to the drug here. But having gone this far without it, I was determined to finish the job. The Doc on the plane knew all this; he thought the cold-turkey decision had been a mistake; he kept asking me if I needed "something." I shook my head each time and turned my face into the pillow. After he had left, the withdrawal routine would start again: yawning, shaking, sweating, cramps, nausea, tears, gooseflesh, a runny nose, and the chuck horrors. Every hour one of the four corpsmen aboard would check my systolic pressure and my rectal temperature, tracing the rising curves on my chart with his rubber finger. If they went too high the Doc might give me a fix despite my protests.

"Do you need something?"

"No, I'm fine."

The Doc looked like an Arab. He had that swarthy complexion and ropy mustache. He was balding and trying to hide the fact by brushing his hair where it didn't want to go. The result was that he looked as though he had just risen hastily from bed. His skin was coarse and pitted with acne scars. When he leaned over me I could see the shadowy hollows and recesses in his face and the network of veins around his irises. At less than a foot my vision was fine. Past that it blurred; the bandages had been removed from my eyes just before we took off, and in addition I suffered from the dilation of all addicts. Any bright light made the pupils smart. Luckily the lights here were dim. I could see enough to know that I wasn't the sickest man aboard. Aft of me was a man with a head wound. It was tightly bandaged, but blood was seeping through the gauze; I could hear the unsteady dripping on the gizmo that was feeding him intravenously. On the port side of the aisle a lieutenant had a chest wound; he was raggedly sucking in air. Below him was the victim of a kamikaze, a chief petty officer bound up like a mummy. His hands were free, however. Each had an anchor tattooed on the back of it. The anchors kept clawing at one another, as though trying to link up.

My blindness had been from shock, and it was passing. My biggest problems just then were a splitting headache and several pieces of shrapnel deep in my back. Shrapnel and something else. The Doc studied my X ray and gave a little cry:

"Why, that looks like a piece of tibia — a shinbone!"

"It is."

"Jap?"

"One of my men."

He moved on. Then the real pain in the ass would prowl up, a fat corpsman who seemed to think we all ought to be clowns.

"C'mon, Sarge, grin! Let's see that old grin! That's it! Grin!"

He would go on like that, on and on. The only way to get rid of him was to force a miserable smirk. Then he would depart, beaming himself, his mission accomplished.

Another corpsman, gaunt and lugubrious, spoke in tones of prac-

ticed pity. He tried to be cheerful; I found him unbearably depressing.

"You'll make it, Sarge. You're a fighter, I can tell."

"Yeah."

"In a month you'll be back giving those yellow bastards hell."

But I had no hell left to give anyone. My head throbbed as the
Douglas engines throbbed. I lay in the half-light, fighting the pain
where the fragments of shrapnel and bone were, yearning for the
drug, my cigarette tracing glowing trajectories in the air, my stomach churning as I wiped my eyes, my nose, and my brow with the
length of gauze dressing they had given me, wondering how many
aboard would, in fact, make it. Not all, I knew; too many were in
critical condition. Head Wound went first. We had just crossed the
International Date Line northeast of Wake when he moaned heavily. Swift shapes darted up, but before they could reach him he
sobbed, "Mom!" and was gone. The blood kept dripping, however,
until Fatso cleaned up. He drew the sheet over the dead man's face
and folded it over in a straight new margin. I dozed off. The Doc
awoke me, peering at me from a range of about three inches.

"Have a good nap?"

"Sure."

"How do you feel?"

"I'm OK."

"Do you hurt much?"

"Nope."

"Do you need something?"

"Nope."

I looked around. Chest Wound had gone, too; there was only a
lump under the sheet where his head had been. The next time
Fatso appeared I asked how many other men we had lost. He tried
to change the subject, but Mummy heard us, and his voice, a rich
baritone, rose through his bandages. He said: "Three others, all at
this end." Fatso looked distressed, maybe because he couldn't tell
whether Mummy was grinning under all those layers of grease and
plaster. Then he brightened and said there wouldn't be any more
deaths.

Actually there was another, a man at the far end I hadn't seen. By the time we entered our glide pattern over Hickam Field, I had almost mastered the geography of our C-54 quarters, with one exception. Down near the tail, to starboard, there was a dark place. Squint as I might, I couldn't make it out. I assumed that the lights had burned out there, or that it was used to store gear. But as we touched down, two of the corpsmen entered the place, and when the door opened they emerged carrying a litter — another corpse, hidden under its temporary shroud. As the Doc passed, I called to him. He paused. I asked him who else had died.

"The poor fellow," he sighed. "He was so quiet that most of the other patients didn't even notice him."

"Who was he? What was his outfit?"

"He was a private in the Fifth Marines."

I felt queer. I said, "My father was in the Fifth."

"Your *father?*"

"A long time ago. Another war."

He said, "Do you want this poor fellow's name?"

"No," I breathed. "*No!*"

He looked at me closely. "You *do* need something."

"Shove it, Mac."

Mummy chuckled.

United flight 005 touches down at Honolulu International Airport at precisely 7:35 Hawaiian time, and as I emerge I am instantly wrapped in sheets of hurrying rain, torrents slanting down diagonally, at intervals coming down in waves, like surf. I am unsurprised. It *always* rains when I arrive in the Pacific. If there is ever a drought, they can cable me; I'll come out and fix it. Expecting just such a storm, I have fastened all the intricate buttons in the collar of my Burberry. No protection against cloudbursts can match a Marine Corps poncho, but ponchos are unacceptable in the Halekulani, the last of Waikiki's great prewar hotels, where I am soon dining with Jean and Bob Trumbull. In the early 1950s Bob and I were foreign correspondents in India, he for the *New York Times* and I for the *Baltimore Sun*. I have friends scattered through the Pa-

cific, and a fairly good working knowledge of Asia, but Bob's is en-
cyclopedic. On December 7, 1941, he was city editor of the *Honolulu Advertiser* and a stringer for the *Times*. Then the *Times* hired
him full-time, and he has been with the paper ever since, mostly
around the Pacific basin. He is the last of the *Times* World War II
correspondents still on the job.

Hawaii, he tells me, is, for the first time in its pluralistic history,
gripped by racial tension. The problem is the Japanese. Although a
minority, they are tightly organized, and as a result they control the
local Establishment — the politics, industry, unions; even the presi-
dency of the university. The other inhabitants, and particularly the
white Americans who have retired here, resent all this. But, Bob
adds, Nipponese affluence is not confined to Hawaii. That, or
something like it, will appear almost everywhere on my journey. In
peace Hirohito's subjects have achieved what eluded them in war:
dominance of a Greater East Asia Co-Prosperity Sphere. I tell Bob
that the Germans have done the same thing in Europe. The victors
of V-E and V-J days, we agree, have been outmaneuvered, outsold,
and outsmarted by the vanquished.

My own feeling the next morning is that whoever is in charge
here has appalling taste. This is a community of honky-tonks.
High-rise condominiums, uncannily like Puerto Rico's, have put
the famous beaches northwest of Diamond Head in perpetual
shade. Aiea Heights Hospital, where I once lay with thousands of
other Marine casualties from Iwo and Okinawa, has been razed and
replaced by CINCPAC headquarters, but the military seems no
longer able to correct pernicious practices of civilian tradesmen. On
Hotel Street electric guitars are turned up to incredible sound levels. Aloha shirts are offered at preposterous prices. Muscular transvestites accost you under a marquee which bears the announcement
BOYS WILL BE GIRLS. Prostitution is illegal, but the bars and strip
joints on Hotel Street are crowded with hookers who, if a man
pauses within arm's reach, will caress his crotch with a gentle
squeeze. There are more massage parlors, strip joints, and por-
nographic shops than cafés. Signs ballyhoo DOUBLE-BEDROOMAN-
TICS! MALE-FEMALE SEXANTICS! WATCH ORAL SEX LIVE! Japan's De-

cember 7 raid thirty-eight years ago was an outrage, but one feels that the destruction of Honolulu's tenderloin would be less outrageous today.

The route followed by the Japanese fliers that long-ago Sunday may be traced with some precision. Kolekole Pass, overlooking Schofield Barracks, is a quiet canyon in the steep mountains; one hears no roaring planes there now, only the rustling of leaves in a soft breeze and the murmur of high-tension wires. The barracks below are virtually unaltered since James Jones wrote of them in *From Here to Eternity:* the quadrangles, the orange buildings, the banyans are redolent of Jones's tale, though they are more sparsely populated; where twenty-five thousand soldiers were based at Schofield in 1941, there are fewer than four thousand today. No scars of the raid are visible here. To find them, one must drive to Hickam Field — where strafers' .50-caliber bullets are still embedded in a peach-colored concrete wall — and, of course, to the harbor itself.

Historical shrines often become diminished by mundane surroundings. One thinks of Saint Peter's in Rome and Boston's Bunker Hill. Still, it is jarring, when driving to the port where the United States entered World War II, to find a prosaic green-and-white freeway sign, exactly like those on the American mainland, directing drivers to:

90 EAST

PEARL HARBOR

Following it, and instructions phoned to me at the Halekulani by CINCPAC, I come to a naval complex of moors and piers, fringed by palms warped by millennia of offshore winds. Elsewhere commercial launches leave hourly for tours of the harbor, but I am booked on a military VIP junket. Judging by my fellow passengers, almost anyone can be a VIP. There are young boys in T-shirts chewing bubble gum; middle-aged, hennaed, hairnetted women; gross men in riotous aloha shirts. They all seem to be carrying Polaroids or Instamatics. A pretty blonde, whose parents must have been teenagers, if not younger, at the time of the great attack here, appears wearing a petty officer's rating chevrons and calls us to order. Before we leave, she says, we are going to see a short motion picture. She leads us into a Quonset hut and the lights go down.

The movie, an NBC documentary, is suggestive of the March-of-Time style and was probably spliced from film clips shortly after the war. The narrator's voice is stentorian; the crashing score is by Richard Rodgers; there is a lot of Japanese footage captured after the war. Its chief interest is in what it omits. There isn't a single reference to U.S. bungling. Much is made of the fact that the Japs missed U.S. oil reserves, enough for two years, and dockyard repair facilities. At the end, with Rodgers's music soaring triumphantly, American warships steam out into the twilight to wreak vengeance on the deceitful enemy. As the lights are turned up, one almost feels that the Pearl Harbor raid was an American victory. Judging by their comments as we file out, the other VIPs are impressed. One recalls that the American navy has always been attentive to its reputation. Especially remembered is the alacrity with which, after the raid, the title of the commanding admiral here was changed to Commander in Chief, Pacific (CINCPAC), from Commander in Chief, United States (CINCUS).

Shepherding us aboard the VIP launch, our blond seawoman warns us that no pictures may be taken of the port's nuclear submarines, lest they fall into the hands of unfriendly powers. Then we shove off, and she begins her spiel. Little of it is new to me, so I let my attention wander. Ford Island is lush and unpopulated, its runway too short to accommodate today's jets. Floating markers show where each battleship was anchored that December 7. A wood-and-rusted-iron relic pinpoints the location of the *Utah*, which went bottom-up at 8:12 A.M. on the morning of the raid. The chief point of interest is the *Arizona* memorial. It is quite lovely, a graceful dipping concrete arch honoring the 1,102 U.S. bluejackets who lie entombed below. (Why wasn't the ship raised? They tried. Two navy divers went down and applied acetylene torches to the hull; accumulated gases within exploded, killing both of them.) Peering down, you can see the rusting forecastle, over whose jutting mast, above the water, the colors are raised and lowered each day.

The VIP passengers swarm around, babbling excitedly. This is distasteful, but not peculiarly American. I have seen the same twittering at European war memorials. It is absent in civilian cemeteries. But scenes where men died violently are somehow stimulating.

The nuclear submarines which we cannot photograph are, in fact, unphotogenic. They are indeed ugly, looking uncannily like sharks. Swinging at anchor in various coves are slate-gray guided-missile cruisers and fast frigates, none of them interesting to a necromancer like me. But I jerk upright as we dart by one inlet. Moored there are the last ships I expected to see in Pearl Harbor — two spanking-new destroyers flying the Rising Sun battle ensign of the Empire of Japan. Ashore, I make inquiries and am told that, yes, I saw what I thought I saw. In fact, Japanese naval officers in dress whites are frequent guests at Pearl's officers' mess. And, my informant adds, they are very polite. Naturally. They always were. Except, of course, for that little interval there between 1941 and 1945.

At 3:00 A.M. in my comfortable Halekulani bed, my eyes pop open. The lean, hard, dreamland Sergeant in me has been leering sardonically, recalling the loudmouthed tourists, Hotel Street's smut, the navy's cover-up movie, and the welcome mat for Hirohito's seafarers. That will be the Sergeant's attitude every night — and he will come every night — during the early stages of my trip. If I rarely mention him, it is because his performance has become as unvaried as a cult rite. He gloats and glares and smirks cynically. I have begun to realize that it will take a great deal, a fire storm of passion, to exorcise him.

In Honolulu the old man has no answer for the Sergeant. His experiences here have shaken him. Somehow Hawaii hasn't stirred memories of the blows inflicted on that distant day of infamy. And I think I know why. The answer, I believe, is that there was virtually no opposition to the Japanese, and therefore no fight. Like Fort Sumter, like Sarajevo, the disaster at Pearl is best remembered as a curtain raiser, largely irrelevant to the drama which followed. We were prepared to visit retribution on the enemy tenfold, but we didn't identify with the victims. Few had fought back. And as professionals they should have been ready to fight. Now we, the amateurs, had to do the job. And though we mourned them, the very brevity of the December 7 attack meant that there hadn't been time to hang breathless on their fate.

The Philippines, however, was another story.

CHARLIE

Ghastly Remnants
of Its Last Gaunt Garrison

MY ARRIVAL AT MANILA INTERNATIONAL AIRPORT, IN THE SMALL hours of a Thursday morning, is hilarious. Carlos Romulo, a friend of mine and a legend to the Filipinos, has sent word from the UN that he wants his countrymen to treat me with "our traditional hospitality." Traditional hospitality, to one of the Spanish patricians who rule the Philippines, stops just short of offering a guest his place in the marriage bed. One moment I am standing before an officious little airport bureaucrat, arguing with him over the validity of a health form. In the next moment this unfortunate clerk is whisked away, possibly to penal servitude, and I am being greeted by a delegation of ten high officials, headed by a cabinet minister. As I slide into an air-conditioned limousine, a siren commences to wind in a police cruiser directly in front of us, and we are off, following it to the Manila Hotel, where General Douglas MacArthur lived before Pearl Harbor. My schedule, I am told, has been prepared. President Marcos will receive me. His First Lady, the beautiful Imelda Romualdez Marcos — a.k.a. "the Iron Butterfly" — will also grant me an audience, and on the last evening of my visit the Romulo family will hold a reception in my honor.

This sort of thing hasn't happened to me since the Turkish general staff mistook me for an envoy from President Eisenhower. My feelings are mixed. Official sanction opens many doors, but it closes others. The Philippines have been under martial law for seven years; Marcos is a dictator; anxiety over his image abroad has, I'm sure, been one of his motives in staging this fantastic welcome for me. Luckily I haven't arrived unprepared; I have the names of the underground leaders who oppose him, and I know how to reach them. My mission, however, is neither to flatter nor to expose the present regime. I am digging into the past, and the past, in the Philippines, is littered with booby traps. Many members of Manila's present Establishment bear names of men who collaborated with the Japanese during the war; one must be careful with them. In addition, as Teddy White has observed, the journalist who becomes a celebrity has special problems. Those whom he interviews know that their replies to him may be quoted by historians. So they become bland at best, or, at worst, self-serving.

In Manila a prosperous American may quickly acquire the feeling of having become an honorary member of a very small upper class, all of whom recognize one another anywhere. I am unastonished to encounter Imelda Marcos in a public building. We chatter idly about her coronation as Miss Manila '53 — there had been no Miss Manila until then, but her family's powerful friends created the title when she wasn't chosen Miss Philippines — and we hardly notice her guard of honor, twenty-two uniformed Filipinos with fixed bayonets, standing at present arms. In czarist Russia noblemen called the masses "the dark people." Here they are more like an endless bolt of gray cloth, every thread exactly like the others. It would be so easy to retreat into one of the patricians' mansions, but the rules of the writer's trade forbid that. So I cancel appointments and, instead, ride on "jeepneys" and explore the city. Jeepneys are minibuses, jeeps roofed with gaudy awnings and decorated, on their bonnets, with silvery Catholic icons. Recognizing my nationality, passengers call me "Joe," and some ask for money, the shiny barrier between all Americans and the world's have-nots. Its presence is felt most keenly when one wanders into the Tondo, Manila's equivalent of San Juan's Perla, a vast slum of huts and cardboard cartons, where, one is told, strangers may be slain by poison dart guns. I emerge unharmed but glad to be out of it. I wouldn't venture into the Tondo after dark.

Next morning I rise before dawn. My room overlooks Manila

Bay, and in the first olive moments of day I sense a hulk of land to my right. Then the land becomes visible, a peninsula floating in a smoke-colored vapor, and the jungly land rises harshly to two five-thousand-foot mountains whose torn, ragged edges, even in that opaque haze, betray their volcanic origin. I am looking at Bataan.

Beginning at 2:00 A.M. on Monday, December 22, 1941, three shopping days before Christmas, some forty-three thousand troops of Lieutenant General Masaharu Homma's Fourteenth Army began wading ashore at Lingayen Gulf, 120 miles north of Manila. They had been expected for two weeks. Guam had fallen to the Japs in a few hours, and although the U.S. Marine garrison still held Wake Island, after a forty-five-minute battle in which a handful of Marines had routed a Nipponese invasion fleet, Wake was also doomed. But everyone knew that the real struggle would come in the Philippines. Allied troops were commanded by a sixty-year-old general who had retired from the U.S. Army in 1937 and had been recalled to active service by President Roosevelt the same day Roosevelt shut off Tokyo's oil spigots. Douglas MacArthur's great years lay ahead, but no one could have known that in the tumultuous days which followed Pearl Harbor. Despite nine hours' warning from Pearl, the general's air force was destroyed on the ground at Clark Field. Moreover, he had failed to move his rice stocks to defensible positions. And now, with Homma ashore, most of MacArthur's green, undisciplined Filipino troops broke and ran for the hills. Over ten thousand Jap assault troops, spreading like a vast stain over northern Luzon, merged into three columns and came thundering down Route 3, the old cobblestoned military highway that led to Manila.

Then MacArthur recovered. The Japanese expected him to defend the capital. Instead, he abandoned it and executed a series of dazzling moves which stunned and bewildered Homma. Soldiers call a retreat a "retrograde maneuver." MacArthur was carrying out a *double* retrograde maneuver, extricating both the surviving troops which were still fighting Homma and the smaller force defending southern Luzon, uniting them and thereby foiling the enemy's attempt to split his command. Leapfrogging his divisions backward, holding positions until the last possible moment and then twitching down barriers for their pursuers to stumble over, he withdrew his forces across the twin-spanned Calumpit Bridge, twenty miles northwest of Manila, just south of the San Fernando rail junction. Then, with his forces intact, he ordered the bridge blown. Looking like "a tired hawk"— the phrase is Romulo's — MacArthur had succeeded in forming an army of sixty-five thousand Filipinos and fifteen thousand Americans within the sheer green ridges and deep valleys of Bataan Peninsula. On January 6, 1942, they sowed mines, dug trenches, and wired themselves in, awaiting the enemy's assault on their line.

It came and they held. And held. And held. To the amazement of the world, which had seen resistance to Dai Nippon crumble everywhere else — the siege of Singapore had lasted just seven days when the British general surrendered eighty-five thousand Empire troops to thirty thousand Japanese — MacArthur's men, ridden by malaria, beriberi, smallpox, dysentery, hookworm, dengue fever, and pellagra, repulsed Homma's January offensive and, when he attempted two amphibious landings behind their lines, flung the invaders into the sea. Again and again the American regulars and their Filipino allies barred the enemy from penetrating deeper than the midriff of the peninsula. They thought they could retake Manila, which, at the time, seemed a distinct possibility. Homma was a bumbling commander, and his troops, also afflicted by diseases, were second-rate; Japan's elite divisions were attacking the Malay Barrier, south of Singapore. All MacArthur's men needed was help from the United States. And therein lies a tragic tale.

They had every reason to believe that convoys were on the way. Roosevelt cabled Manuel Quezon, president of the Philippine Commonwealth, then on Corregidor: "I can assure you that every vessel available is bearing . . . the strength that will eventually crush the enemy. . . . I give to the people of the Philippines my solemn pledge that their freedom will be retained. . . . The entire resources in men and materials of the United States stand behind that pledge." General George C. Marshall, FDR's army chief of staff,

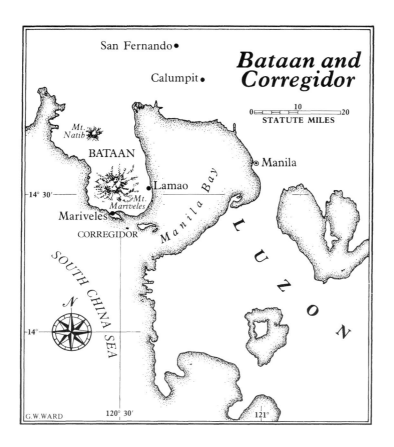

San Fernando•

Calumpit•

Bataan and Corregidor

0 |10| 20
STATUTE MILES

Mt. Natib

BATAAN

Manila

14° 30'

•Lamao

Manila Bay

Mt. Mariveles

Mariveles•

CORREGIDOR

SOUTH CHINA SEA

LUZON

N

14°

G.W.WARD

120° 30'

121°

radioed MacArthur: "A stream of four-engine bombers, previously delayed by foul weather, is enroute. . . . Another stream of similar bombers started today from Hawaii staging at new island fields. Two groups of powerful medium bombers of long range and heavy bomb-load capacity leave this week. Pursuit planes are coming on every ship we can use. . . . Our strength is to be concentrated and it should exert a decisive effect on Japanese shipping and force a withdrawal northward."

All this was untrue. Not a plane, not a warship, not a single U.S. reinforcement reached Bataan or Corregidor. The only possible explanation for arousing false expectations on the peninsula was that Washington was trying to buy time for other, more defensible outposts. As the truth sank in, the men facing Homma became embittered. Unaware that MacArthur had to remain on the island of Cor-regidor — "the Rock" — because its communications center provided his only contact with Washington, they scornfully called the general "Dugout Doug." That was cruel, and unjust. But if ever men were entitled to a scapegoat, they were. Quite apart from the Japanese, they faced Bataan's almost unbelievable jungle. Cliffs are unscalable. Rivers are treacherous. Behind huge *nara* (mahog-any) trees, eucalyptus trees, ipils, and tortured banyans, almost im-penetrable screens are formed by tropical vines, creepers, and bam-boo. Beneath these lie sharp coral outcroppings, fibrous undergrowth, and alang grass inhabited by pythons. In the early months of the year, when the battle was fought, rain poured down almost steadily. The water was contaminated. MacArthur's men ate roots, leaves, papayas, monkey meat, wild chickens, and wild pigs. They sang, to the tune of "The Battle Hymn of the Republic":

> *Dugout Doug MacArthur lies ashakin' on the Rock*
> *Safe from all the bombers and from any sudden shock . . .*

And one soldier wrote:

> *We're the battling bastards of Bataan:*
> *No mama, no papa, no Uncle Sam,*
> *No aunts, no uncles, no nephews, no nieces,*
> *No rifles, no planes, or artillery pieces,*
> *And nobody gives a damn.*

Yet they fought on, with a devotion which would puzzle the gen-eration of the 1980s. More surprising, in many instances it would have baffled the men they themselves were before Pearl Harbor. Among MacArthur's ardent infantrymen were cooks, mechanics, pilots whose planes had been shot down, seamen whose ships had been sunk, and some civilian volunteers. One civilian was a saddle-shoed American youth, a typical Joe College of that era who had been in the Philippines researching an anthropology paper. A few months earlier he had been an isolationist whose only musical interest was Swing. He had used an accordion to render tunes like "Deep Purple" and "Moonlight Cocktail." Captured and sentenced to be shot, he made a last request. He wanted to die holding his accordion. This was granted, and he went to the wall playing "God Bless America." It was that kind of time.

Only in early spring, when Homma was strengthened by twenty-two thousand fresh troops, howitzers, and fleets of Mitsubishis and Zeroes, did the Filipinos and Americans on Bataan Peninsula surrender. Then Corregidor, the bone in the throat of Manila Bay, held out for another exhausting month. Even so, Marines and bluejackets entrenched on the island's beaches killed half the Nipponese attack force. And it wasn't until June 6 that formal resistance ended, when a Jap hauled down the last American flag and ground it under his heel as a band played "Kimigayo," his national anthem.

Nevertheless, the capitulation was the largest in U.S. history. For those who had survived to surrender on Bataan, the worst lay ahead: the ten-day, seventy-five-mile, notorious Death March to POW cages in northern Luzon. Jap guards began shooting prisoners who collapsed in the sun and suffocating dust beneath the pitiless sky. Next they withheld water from men dying of thirst. Beatings followed, and beheadings and torture. No one knows how many Allied soldiers perished during this Gethsemane, but most estimates run between seven and ten thousand. After the war the Filipinos decided to pay tribute to these martyrs with signposts marking each kilometer on Route 3, which was paved and rechristened MacArthur Highway. Each sign bore a silhouette of three stumbling Allied infantrymen trying to help one another, and travelers were told how far the Death Marchers had struggled at that point. It is sad to note that over half the signs have vanished, lost through neglect or taken by sightseers. This is *that* kind of time.

But other memorials are intact, though not always where one might expect to find them. The airstrip where MacArthur lost most of his B-17 air force is merely another B-52 runway. The vital Calumpit Bridge is identifiable only by an odd reference point: a soft-drink bottling factory surrounded by weeds. There are no plaques or shafts in the rainforests where the beleaguered Filipinos and Americans counterattacked Homma's troops, driving them back and back. However, in the village, or *barrio*, of Lamao, which lies on the bay side of the peninsula, a stone identifies the spot where Major General Edward P. King, Jr., the Bataan commander, capitulated on April 9, 1942, and in Mariveles, on the southern tip, an American rifle is cemented into a block, with a GI helmet welded to the butt of the gun. If you charter a helicopter, monuments may be found on the slopes of the peninsula's towering heights, Mount Mariveles and Mount Natib. One inscription reads, "Our mission is to remember"; another, in Tagalog, the native tongue, marks the "Damabana Nang Kagitingan" — the "Altar of Valor." A relief map with colored red and blue lights shows successive Japanese and Allied positions on the peninsula. It is interesting to note that the altar is the work of Ferdinand E. Marcos, who, as a junior officer here (he was a *third* lieutenant), was awarded two Distinguished Service Crosses, two Silver Stars, and two Purple Hearts, making him the war's most decorated Filipino. If Mussolini made trains run on time, it can at least be said that Marcos lets the dead lie in style. There is just one happily discordant note. Chiseled letters bear the democratic message "To Live in Freedom's Light Is the Right of Mankind." Above it stands a crucifix formed of two parallel uprights and two horizontal bars. It can only be described as a double cross.

The easiest way to see Bataan, if you can afford it, is by helicopter; next easiest is by rented launch, which can take you from Manila to Mariveles — where tadpole-shaped Corregidor is visible, three miles from the peninsula — in less than two hours. But if you really want to steep yourself in Bataan's synoptic past, you must go by land. Since there is no rail service and buses are unreliable, this means in a car, preferably with four-wheel drive, because ruts and potholes pit MacArthur Highway. Lack of maintenance characterizes the Pacific's adoption of occidental modes almost everywhere. It may even be found in the tiny central Pacific Republic of Nauru, whose precious phosphate deposits are said to give its six thousand people a per capita income of over forty thousand dollars a year. If a car breaks down on Nauru, it is ditched and replaced with another.

There are no limousines on Bataan, and very few cars. The typical vehicle is a wagon drawn by a horse or a bullock. To park and enter a *barrio* is to move back to the Stone Age. Until MacArthur retreated into the peninsula, the inhabitants lived as their ancestors had, content in their insularity. After the war most of them returned to it. There are a few signs of the twentieth century there — an Exxon refinery at Lamao and a few tiny huts with rusting tin roofs where Hollywood films are shown. Even so, none of the natives seems to grasp what a refinery is, and the favorite recreation is watching cockfights. The government in Manila has outlawed them, but the peasants here don't know it; inland, they haven't even heard of Manila. Or, for that matter, of Bataan. It is their universe; they need no name for it. Except for the inhabitants of New Guinea and the northern Solomons, I know of no people more isolated from the outside world than the Bataanese. Here, on mountainous slopes within sight of the Philippines' capital, warriors hunt game with bows and arrows. Lithe Filipinas, striding past rice paddies with hand-carved wooden pitchforks balanced on their lovely heads, pass backdrops which might be taken from a Tarzan movie — waterfalls cascading in misty rainbows, orchids growing from canyon walls, and, from time to time, typhoons lashing the palm-fringed beaches.

Driving from the site of the Calumpit Bridge to Mariveles, you leave your car from time to time for excursions beyond the bayside *barrios*. The villages are all pretty much alike. There is no electricity — generators must be brought in for the rare movies — and virtually no line of communications to the world outside. Fishermen live in little straw shacks atop stilts. Their boats are outriggers. Inland, bullocks tug hand-hewn implements through rice paddies; the green sprouts are reaped by stooping women wading in the ankle-deep water. Their husbands climb palm trees to toss down coconuts, whose dried meat, copra, is their one export — the largest export, indeed, of the entire Philippines. An acrid scent bites the air; following it, you come upon a sugarcane field being burned off. Somehow the jungle seems friendlier to those who inhabit it. Men sing as they hammer away with rough mauls; women gossip while sitting in a circle, peeling leaves from cabbage plants; children hoot cheerfully as they play tag between lumbering water buffalo in shallow, muddy streams crowded on their banks with huge green shrubs whose wide leaves dip gracefully in all directions.

Twice, in the memory of their patriarchs, outsiders have arrived uninvited to use this as a killing ground: in the 1942 struggle and again when the victorious Americans returned three years later. No one knows how many peasants were slain by random shots and artillery bursts, but certainly more of them died than American civilians at home, who had a stake in the war yet were out of danger. And what, the Sergeant in me asks, did we give them in return? Well, there was venereal disease, hitherto unknown here. And insensate hatred between aliens, and efficient ways to destroy those you hated. Most cruelly, they were left with an uneasy feeling that these monstrous strangers had, for all their brutality, found clever ways of making life more tolerable and interesting. It was cruel because that way of life can never coexist with theirs. One recalls a prescient passage in the journal of Captain James Cook, the first European to discover the South Seas, in 1769: "I cannot avoid expressing it as my real opinion that it would have been far better for these poor people never to have known our superiority in the accommodations and arts that make life comfortable, than after once knowing it, to be again left and abandoned in their original incapacity of improvement. Indeed they cannot be restored to that happy mediocrity in which they lived before we discovered them if the intercourse between us should be discontinued."

I am aboard a helicopter, descending through a blue mist between Corregidor's sheer cliffs toward the old Fort Drum parade ground. From this height the island seems larger than expected — about the size of Manhattan — and attractive. Of course, that was not always true. "Why, George," Jean MacArthur said to

George Kenney, her husband's air commander, when she returned to Manila Bay at the end of the war, "what have you done to Corregidor? I could hardly recognize it, when we passed it. It looks as though you had lowered it at least forty feet." Certainly it had been lowered some. Between Japanese artillery in the first months of the war and Kenney's B-24s dumping four thousand tons of bombs on it later, the Rock had been changed beyond belief, denuded, among other things, of all vegetation. Today neither Jean nor Kenney would recognize the Rock. Two years after the war American troops reforested it, populated it with monkeys and small deer, and presented it to the Philippines as a national park. Only park police and caretakers live there now, though there is a small guesthouse on a bluff overlooking the North Dock for tourists who want to remain overnight. Like the picnics at Verdun in the 1920s, turning the Rock into a recreational spot may be an attempt to exorcise the desperate past.

If so, it fails, for despite the view from the helicopter, once you step upon the parade ground you feel yourself caught by a slipped cog of time, transported back in a thirty-seven-year time warp. Especially is this true in Malinta Tunnel. The tunnel is a short ride from the parade ground in a park bus, or, if you have taken the two-hour ferry from Manila, a short winding walk from the North Dock. Twin sets of rails lead into Malinta, but they are useless now; a recent typhoon loosened an avalanche on the craggy hill overhead, which slid down the seventy-foot beetling outcropping over the east entrance, partly blocking it and reducing the carved legend there to NNEL. Inside the 826-foot shaft are twenty-four 30-foot laterals, short passages branching off the main corridor. There is no electricity, and you have to step carefully to avoid stumbling over old crates of eight-inch-gun ammunition, but with a flashlight you can read signs identifying which laterals were used for casualties, for religious services, for messing, for nurses' quarters (a wooden barrier across the maw here; the memory of their virginity is honored by Filipinos, who still think maidenhood important), and — Lateral Number Three — for MacArthur's headquarters.

In the dim light and dank, musty air, one feels like an intruder.

The remains of Malinta Tunnel, Corregidor

You are surrounded by some eleven thousand ghosts, the number of men Jonathan Wainwright surrendered to the Japanese on May 8, 1942. A sense of individual loneliness survives them. Here they had wept, moaned, sworn, slept fitfully, dreamed, quivered with fear, bled, and died. In these laterals each had endured his or her special kind of illness — the women terrified of rape, Filipino Catholics (four of every five) of dying without last rites; Romulo in anguish for his family, now in Jap hands; Quezon coughing away his tubercular life; MacArthur pacing in his cramped quarters and threatening to disobey Washington's repeated order that he abandon his command and try to break out to Australia, saying, as he paced, that he would rather resign his commission, cross to Bataan, and enlist there as a private. The general's prose was dramatic, as always, but Corregidor's last stand was nothing if not melodramatic. After Corregidor had fallen he said of it: "Intrinsically it is but a barren, war-worn rock, hallowed as so many places [are], by death and disaster. Yet it symbolizes within itself that priceless, deathless thing, the honor of a nation. Until we claim again the ghastly remnants of its last gaunt garrison, we can but stand humble supplicants before Almighty God. There lies our Holy Grail."

American sophisticates mocked such empurpled rhetoric, but there was no laughter in the Philippines. To Filipinos the Rock is still sacred ground. Leaving Malinta one discovers, around a corner to the left, a thirty-foot stone shaft with a simple plaque identifying this as the spot where Wainwright displayed the white flag. A mounted diagram shows who was where during the siege. On Topside, Corregidor's highest point, a marble dome is suspended above a white memorial; once a year the sun shines through the hole in the dome, turning white to gold. Nearby an eternal flame flickers, and torn pieces of shells and strips from wrecked aircraft have been welded into a cathedral spire. Walls alongside bear the names of the great Pacific battles. The Japanese remember Corregidor, too. Nipponese Christians have erected a cross, with the inscription, in Japanese and English: "May the bodies of the dead soldiers of the Philippines, the U.S., and Japan rest in peace."

War monuments have never stirred me. They are like the reconstructed buildings at Colonial Williamsburg, or elaborate reproductions of great paintings; no matter how deft the execution, they are essentially counterfeit. In addition, they are usually beautiful and in good taste, whereas combat is neither. Before the war I thought that Hemingway, by stripping battle narratives of their ripe prose, was describing the real thing. Afterward I realized that he had simply replaced traditional overstatement with romantic understatement. War is never understated. Combat as I saw it was exorbitant, outrageous, excruciating, and above all tasteless, perhaps because the number of fighting men who had read Hemingway or Remarque was a fraction of those who had seen B movies about bloodshed. If a platoon leader had watched Douglas Fairbanks, Jr., Errol Flynn, Victor McLaglen, John Wayne, or Gary Cooper leap recklessly about, he was likely to follow his role model. In crises most people are imitative. Soldiers received "Dear John" letters copied from those quoted in the press. The minority who avoided Hollywood paradigms were, like me, people who had watched fewer B movies than we had read books. That does not mean that we were better soldiers and citizens. We certainly weren't braver. I do think that our optics were clearer, however — that what we saw was closer to the truth because we weren't looking through MGM or RKO prisms.

Thus my most moving moments on Corregidor are neither in the tunnel nor before the shrines. They are more mundane, coming amid the island's surface relics, where men like me fought against impossible odds to defend the yawning AA batteries and the huge, 360-degree, 12-inch coastal batteries, with their 17-mile range, which still leer across Manila Bay. Particularly evocative are the gaunt stone dun-colored skeletons of the ruined Fort Mills barracks, now overgrown with lichen and *dalakorak* vines. Here, rusted but still recognizable, is the homely debris of military housekeeping, the canteens and mess gear, the hastily discarded .30- and .50-caliber shells, the old-fashioned straight razors and steel combs and mops used in preparing for formal inspections in the last days of peace. And as I poke and prod among these souvenirs of anguish, my mind drifts back to the tunnel's rail track. It troubles me, something there. I once saw rails like that before.

Of course! It had been that single, narrow-gauge set of tracks at the Asa Kawa. I had skulked along its embankment on my way to . . .

Abruptly the poker of memory stirs the ashes of recollection and uncovers a forgotten ember, still smoldering down there, still hot, still glowing, still red as red.

The name of the little rise was Amike Ridge. The Japs held it; we needed it. But enemy guns on adjacent hills kept driving us off. The last time there had been any large-scale action here, an attacking company had been reduced to one officer and nineteen men. Now Bob Fowler, Fox Company's CO, was being told to take the crest late that afternoon. I carried the message to him in the shadow of that railroad embankment. His SCR-536, his hand-talkie, wasn't working — they never did when you needed them — and his SCR-300, his backpack radio, had also broken down, cutting his only wireless tie with battalion. So I had been sent. Had I known I was carrying a sheaf of death warrants, I would have ducked into the company command post (CP), left Fowler's order with any one of his several lieutenants or senior noncoms, and made myself scarce. Runners like me were transients, subject to hijacking by any commander who needed an extra hand. Sure enough; moments after I rambled in, smeared with mire from the embankment, the corporal who was supposed to lead the right-hand squad took a bullet in the shoulder. Fowler, recognizing me, told me to replace the corporal. I was, I realized, in deep peril. One squad, twelve men, would be looking out for each other. And who was going to look out for their strange new three-striped leader? Since Fowler himself was later killed, I can't be bitter. But God knows I felt ill-used before that night was over.

As it happened we weren't part of the assault. There was a little draw just west of the ridge, pitted with shell holes. Fowler wanted it cleared out; Japs hidden there could turn his flank. It was uninhabited, but lethal all the same, for the enemy was encircling the entire ridge with a tremendous concentration of artillery. As my father had found, the worst shells are those that burst overhead. That was what the Nips were sending over. I remember hearing the chargers braying on the left as the men went up the slope, the Southerners among them yip-yipping their rebel yells, while I carefully probed the length of the draw, my .45's safety off, my finger ready to squeeze at the slightest sound or movement. My exaggerated, combat-wise, high-knee gait was like the strides of a man wearing new bifocals and unsure of how far away the ground might be. I was seasoned now, scared but in control provided I wasn't pushed too hard. I didn't anticipate trouble once I saw the draw was empty. No shells were arriving there just then.

Actually I was about to be shoved and decked. I was returning to the squad on the double when I tripped on a strand of communications wire and fell headlong into a large muddy crater left by an earlier bombardment. At that instant a Jap shell shimmied in and exploded about fifteen feet above the draw. My fall saved me. The others were all killed instantly, though I had no way of knowing that at the time. Fowler's attack was clearly failing; the shouts were fading, dying down. I had no intention of moving till night fell. When it did, I crawled around to find whether there were any of my people still alive. There weren't; no one moaned; everywhere I groped I felt only gobs of blood, shards of shattered bones, ropy intestines, and slimy brains. A flare burst overhead. I saw none of the squad had made it. There wasn't even the form of a human body. I slid back into the crater and lay there for a while in a numb stupor, trying to wipe the offal from my hands. Suddenly I half turned into the muck, a victim of survivor's guilt, pounding and pounding and pounding my fist, sobbing, *It isn't fair, it isn't fair, they're dead, why can't I be dead, it isn't fair*. Twelve men had been entrusted to me and I had lost them. Still weeping, I passed out.

There are no clocks on battlefields. Time is seamless there. I haven't the faintest idea how long I was out. As I regained consciousness in the darkness a fly was drawing Zs around my head. There was no other sound, only an enormous stillness without echo. Apparently rain had fallen; I was drenched, and there were new puddles around me. I felt paralyzed. It was so bleak in that hole, so lonely and so forever. I wondered vaguely if this was when it would end, whether I would pull up tonight's darkness like a quilt and be dead and at peace ever more. Again I passed out, and as I came to, I felt the skin prickling on the backs of my hands and the nape of my neck. A fresh fear was creeping across my mind, quietly, stealthily, imperceptibly. I sat up, my muscles rippling with suppressed panic, stared across the shell hole, now dimly lit by moonlight and a descending flare, and saw that I had company, a creature somehow familiar, who flickered in and out of sight, an adumbration on the fringes of my awareness.

Hallucinations, as Robert Graves and Siegfried Sassoon recalled in their memoirs of World War I trench warfare, are common in war. If you lie in a dark hole, listening to the sound of your own breathing, dead objects may rise and live, bald rocks may be transformed into men's pates, pinnacled stones may become witch's fingers. One of the commonest delusions is to see in the distance a buddy you know is dead, one you actually saw die, now very much alive. He is smiling at you. You run over and, of course, he isn't there. Then there are appearances of phantom Nips. I knew a major who dropped his pants in the bush on Guadalcanal and squatted to defecate. A shot rang out. Another Marine had spotted a Nip sniper in a coconut tree overhead. The dead sniper dropped thirty feet and plopped right in front of the major. Starting right then he developed an extraordinary case of constipation. Every time he tried to empty his bowels he saw Japs above him. Three weeks later he was flown to Nouméa for surgery, but meanwhile his value in combat had been wiped. Similarly, a man in our 81-millimeter mortar platoon awoke in his foxhole one night and saw himself ringed by Japs with fixed bayonets. He grabbed his carbine, tried to turn off the safety, and hit the magazine release instead. The magazine fell out. He had a weapon but no ammunition in it. He grabbed the barrel by the stacking swivel, turning the butt into a club, and swatted away in all directions, crying for help. He was lucky he wasn't killed by the Marines around him. They wrestled him to the ground and convinced him he was out of danger, but to the end of his life, three weeks later, he stubbornly insisted that those Japs had been real. And, of course, to him they were.

So it was with me that terrible night. Another flare revealed that my visitor was feminine. That was startling: what was a woman doing up here? My heart welling with pity, I thought she must be a native, one of the innocent civilian bystanders who were dying in the struggle for the island. Then the shock of recognition hit me. She wasn't harmless. She was evil. I was in the presence of the Whore of Death. Since killing my first Japanese soldier I had been one of her many pimps, leading Jap after Jap into her brothel. Now she wanted me as her next trick.

Her identity might have puzzled others. She lacked the grace and movements of a geisha; she wasn't even oriental. Nor was she the stereotypical slut of the Occident. She wore no black-net stockings, no flimsy negligee. She knew her mark too well for that. Corrupted innocence, not candid wickedness, was the right bait for an inhibited New Englander. She was, instead, dressed like the girls I remembered at Smith and Mount Holyoke: a cashmere twin-sweater set, a Peter Pan collar, a string of pearls, a plaid skirt, bobby socks, and loafers. Her dirty-blond hair fell in a shoulder-length pageboy coiffure, and when she turned her head abruptly to glance at her watch, she tossed her tresses like a young goddess. Her legs were crossed, her skirt demurely below her knees. Judging by her silhouette in the dim moonlight, her figure was superb, her breasts high and firm beneath the cashmere, her legs magnificent. Glowing phosphorescence, a kind of inner light, revealed the lure of her sexuality, and flashes of translucence allowed me to see through her clothes intermittently.

But she wasn't from the Seven Sisters. The moonlight and a closer flare betrayed her. Indeed, to a healthy imagination she was the most improbable of sex objects. Her flesh was anything but appealing. It was deathly white, like a frog's belly, and covered with running sores. Twin lines of vile maggots appeared on her upper lip, entering her nostrils in endless, weaving columns. Gray fungus grew up her arms. Gaunt, prehensile hands restlessly clutched at each other, like fingers stitching a shroud. When she grinned lewdly, as she presently did, she revealed vicious jagged teeth sharp enough to rip out your throat, as those of Java rats are said to lunge through your cheeks to reach the morsel of your tongue. She exhaled a foul stench. But it was her eyes, eyes as old as tombs, which were most phenomenal. A direct stare is the boldest way to invade the sheath of privacy which envelops each of us, and she was using it devastatingly, diminishing the distance between us to the intimacy of a membrane. Her wide pupils were in turn stony, reptilian, shameless. She trembled suggestively. She was soliciting me, beckoning me toward cathexis.

None of this sounds inviting, let alone seductive. But the shell which had wiped out my squad had barely missed me. So close a call with death is often followed by eroticism. It is characteristic of some creatures that they are often very productive before their death and, in some cases, appear to die in a frenzy of reproductive activity. Desire is the sequel to danger. That is the reason for the recruitment, in most of history's great armies, of camp followers. At a wink from the soiled Whore of Death I became semihard; she knew that and stretched herself, accentuating her bust and her slender waist and increasing my tumescence. I simultaneously loathed and craved her. She was an enchantress in an old tale whom men have loved to their destruction. She wouldn't sigh or swoon or feign affection. Love was the last thing she had to offer. Her coarse, blurred, sepulchral voice, just audible, rasped obscenities and spoke of the bargain she proposed to strike in the language she had used for a thousand years of warfare. The key words were *lust* and *blood* and *death*. She had been in business a long time. Her face was eroded by a millennium of whoring. The traffic around her lunging crotch had always been heavy, but the number of customers in this century had dwarfed all those before.

Abruptly she hoisted her skirt to her hips and spread her legs. My pulse was hammering, my sexual craving almost overwhelming. That was my moment of maximum temptation. For the first and only time in my life I understood rape. I have never been more ready. Then, from her sultry muttering, I learned her fee. I couldn't mount her here. She gestured toward the Japanese lines. I shrank back, shaking my head and whispering, *No, no I won't, no, no, NO.* Just then a random shell rustled over and landed a few yards away. In the flash she disappeared. But my yearning for sexual release remained. I unfastened my dungarees and touched myself. I came in less than five seconds. I was that close.

After crawling out of the hole I was, for the only time in combat, quite lost. It wasn't until the sky was lightening that I saw the hunchback of the ridge against the eastern sky and, taking bearings from it, crept slowly toward Fox Company's wire. My situation was still extremely perilous — Fowler had dug in for the inevitable counterattack. I was about five yards from safety when a deep voice with a Bronx accent challenged me, ordering me to halt. I gave the password. The voice said gently, "Come on in, Mac." I reported to Fowler, omitting my vision. He grieved for his lost squad and asked anxiously, "Were you hurt?" I shook my head and said, "Not a scratch." I believed it.

I leave Corregidor for Manila aboard a steamship, a rusting, lumbering vessel. As we pull away from the Rock's North Dock the captain tugs the whistle cord, and I am distracted by its lonely shriek, sadder than the wails of steam locomotives I remember from my boyhood. Seen from the second deck, where I perch in a plastic chair outside a plastic lounge, the water is calm and blue. Throughout the two-hour voyage the air is humid, and as we approach the dock just off Roxas Highway the capital is partly obscured by smog. I observe all this, and write it down, because that is my trade. But my mind is elsewhere. I am thinking of Christmas Eve, 1941, when MacArthur and his party abandoned Manila to Homma and sailed to the Rock on the small interisland steamer *Don Esteban*. They were on Corregidor thirteen weeks. Once he grasped the staggering fact that he would receive no reinforcements, the general knew the Japanese would take the island. He intended to die there and expected his wife and his four-year-old son to die with him. After he had balked at Washington's order that he leave, he was vulnerable to a court-martial. Still he held back. Then his staff, reviewing the cables from the War Department, persuaded him that a great army awaited him in Australia, ready to return under his leadership and reconquer the Philippines.

His breakout through three thousand miles of enemy waters, first by PT boat and then aboard a decrepit plane, is one of the greatest escape stories in the history of war. But when he reached the little Australian town of Kooringa, he was stunned to learn that the country was virtually defenseless. He had fewer troops Down Under than the garrison he had left on Bataan and Corregidor. Australia's divisions were in Egypt, fighting Rommel. "God have mercy on us," MacArthur said hollowly when he was told. Turning away, he clenched his teeth until his jaw was white. "It was," he later wrote, his "greatest shock and surprise of the whole war." But the Diggers took heart when he appeared in Melbourne. They knew how exasperating he could be; every civilian who had dealt with him was aware of his vanity, his megalomania, and his paranoia. But his military genius was already a legend. And genius was required by the Allies at this point in the Pacific war, for Australia faced imminent invasion by the triumphant armies of the Empire of Japan.

DOG

The Rim of Darkness

IN THE SPRING OF 1942, WHEN CORREGIDOR FELL AND I JOINED
the Marines, a glance at a global map would have convinced an
impartial observer, were there any left, that our side was losing the
war. Indeed, one could have argued persuasively that the Allies had
already lost it. Hitler was master of Europe. He ruled an empire
larger than the United States, with conquests stretching from the
Arctic waters in the north to the Libyan Desert in the south, from
the English Channel in the west to within a day's march of the Cas-
pian Sea in the east. It seemed that nothing could stop Erwin Rommel from seizing Cairo and the Suez Canal. Certainly the Americans
couldn't. Thus far they had been an ineffectual ally. They had no
troops in the field. They couldn't even serve, in their President's
phrase, as a valuable "arsenal of democracy." U.S. merchantmen
were being torpedoed nightly in the Atlantic — 1,160 that year —
often within view of their Atlantic seaboard. Too few were reaching
Murmansk or English ports with tanks or munitions to tip the
scales. An imminent linkup between German and Japanese armies,
probably in India, appeared to be inevitable.

American eyes were riveted on Europe. Asia and Oceania, on the
other hand, mystified them. They mistook Singapore for Shanghai
and thought it was a Chinese city. Most of them were unaware that
Hawaii is closer to Japan than to the Philippines. Later, men on
Iwo Jima would get V-mail from relatives who thought they were
fighting in the "South Pacific," although Iwo, like Lower Califor-

nia, is over seventeen hundred miles north of the equator. To this day, few GIs and Marines have the remotest idea of where they fought. Even Australians, whose very survival was threatened by Hirohito's legions, are baffled by the geography of the Pacific.

Allied commanders had some knowledge of it, however, and they were almost overwhelmed by the task confronting them. They estimated that recapturing lands lost to the foe would take at least ten years. The Rising Sun was blinding. The Japanese empire dwarfed Hitler's. It stretched five thousand miles in every direction and included Formosa; the Philippines; Indochina, Thailand, and Burma; Malaya, Sumatra, Borneo, Java, and the Celebes; the Kuril Islands, the Bonins, Ryukyus, Marianas, Carolines, Palaus, Marshalls, and Gilberts; northern New Guinea; two Alaskan islands; most of inhabited China; and almost all of the Solomons. In less than six months the Nipponese had taken a gigantic leap toward a *Pax Japonica,* conquering lands which had resisted penetration by the Western powers for over a century. Like the tsunamis, those undersea tidal waves which break with unpredictable force upon distant shores, the Nipponese blitz had swept up a million square miles, almost a seventh of the globe, an area three times as large as the United States and Europe combined.

These were golden days for the conquering soldiers of Dai Nippon. A neutral onlooker writes that they found "lush realms, with snow-white beaches, frond huts, coconut palms and dark-skinned people who wore sarongs, grass skirts and loincloths called lap-laps. . . . The [Japanese] went fishing in the lagoons or streams, using camouflage nets as seines. They played cards and swam. They climbed palm trees to gather coconuts, and exchanged cigarettes and canned goods for fresh fruit — bananas, papayas and mangoes. Until the shipping lanes were cut off . . . vessels from Japan brought news, letters, movies, dancers, singers, and packages filled with snacks and other amenities. Particularly welcome were the socalled 'comfort women,' prostitutes who volunteered for service in the battle zones to help ease the tensions and improve the morale among the troops." To the Japanese, Southeast Asia was a treasure house, "the land of everlasting summer."

Their leaders were dazzled. They had never anticipated such successes. At the time of Pearl Harbor they had expected to lose a quarter of their naval strength in their first offensives. Instead, they had won their new imperial realm at a cost of twenty-five thousand tons of shipping, less than that of the *Arizona* alone. The largest Nipponese warship to go down had been a destroyer. In Tokyo, Hirohito — who had acquired 150 million new subjects — told his Lord Keeper of the Privy Seal: "The fruits of war are tumbling into our mouth almost too quickly." His elated generals and admirals had no such misgivings. They knew they had broken the myth of white supremacy. They had surpassed the Allies on every level. Their strategy was superior, their tactics more skillful, their navy and air force larger and more efficient, their infantry better prepared and more experienced. In amphibious operations, as Gavin M. Long has pointed out, "their landings of whole armies on surf beaches were of a magnitude only dreamt of in the West."

Now they confronted an unimagined, stupendous choice: whether to lunge eastward toward Hawaii or southward into Australia. They tried both. The eastward drive was turned back at Midway. Down Under was another matter. As early as February 1942 an armada of 243 carrier-borne Japanese planes had demolished the Australian port of Darwin. The next Jap step would be to acquire enough island airstrips to throw up an umbrella covering massive landings on the heavily populated southeastern coast of Australia. The Diggers were desperate. Having underestimated the Nipponese before Pearl Harbor, they now swung the other way. To the average Australian, glued to his Philips radio and listening to reports that enemy hordes were coming closer and closer, the Japs looked invincible. MacArthur was in Melbourne because Australian Prime Minister John Curtin had asked FDR for a symbol of U.S. commitment to protect his country. There, and in New Zealand, terrifying posters showed a bestial, snarling Jap soldier hurtling across the sea, the rising sun at his back, and in one hand, a crumpled map of Australia. Across the poster was printed: "The word now is MUST."

The chances that it could be done seemed slight. Never had a nation been more naked to aggression. Apart from seven Wirraways, training planes resembling Piper Cubs, its defensive air force — Kittyhawks and Gypsy Moths, with fabric-covered wings and wooden propellers that could be started only by spinning them by hand — had been almost annihilated by Zeroes over Malaya. Defending infantry were middle-aged men carrying .303 bolt-action, single-shot rifles, with magazines holding five cartridges, originally issued during the Boer War. Primitive machine guns resembled nineteenth-century Gatling guns, and where the Japanese were expected, there were two old naval six-inch guns and three obsolete three-inch guns.

Except for one brigade of the Sixth Division, crack Anzac troops were still in the Middle East. These veterans of Greece, Crete, and North Africa were frantically boarding transports and would soon be homeward bound, but the Japanese were much closer; the crisis would have to be resolved without them. MacArthur found the Australian government crippled by defeatism. In Melbourne its generals were wedded to what they called "the Brisbane Line," which would be fixed along the Tropic of Capricorn, actually just above Brisbane. Beyond the line, the great western and northern regions of the continent would be sacrificed. Plans had been drawn up to scorch the earth there — destroying military installations, blowing up power plants, and burning docks. This would have left the Australians with the settled southern and eastern coasts. But MacArthur correctly guessed that the southeast was precisely where the Japanese intended to come ashore. He again threatened to resign his commission unless the concept of the Brisbane Line was scrapped. Prime Minister Curtin yielded, but his people despaired, believing that the last hope of saving their homes had been lost.

Before the invasion, the Nipponese needed to sever Australia's supply lines to the United States and build a staging area. To achieve the first, they were building airfields in the Solomon Islands. The staging area would be New Guinea's Port Moresby, three hundred miles from the Australian coast. The Battle of the Coral Sea — actually fought on the Solomon Sea — had turned back a Jap fleet which had been ordered to capture Moresby by sea. Then the Japs seized a beachhead at Milne Bay, halfway to their objective. MacArthur pored over maps and decided that Moresby would be the key to the campaign. He said: "Australia will be defended in New Guinea," and: "We must attack! Attack! Attack!"

But where? In the tangled, uncharted equatorial terrain, the two suffering armies could only grope blindly toward each other. Some offshore isles were literally uninhabitable — U.S. engineers sent to survey the Santa Cruz group were virtually wiped out by cerebral malaria — and subsequent battles were fought under fantastic conditions. One island was rocked by earthquakes. Volcanic steam hissed through the rocks of another. On a third, bulldozers vanished in spongy, bottomless swamps. Sometimes the weather was worse than the enemy: at Cape Gloucester sixteen inches of rain fell in a single day. And sea engagements were broken off because neither the Japanese nor the American admirals knew where the bottom was.

The Allies were slow to comprehend the Solomons threat, but by the late spring of 1942 they had brought New Guinea into full focus. The world's second largest island (second to Greenland), New Guinea stretches across the waters north of the Australian continent like a huge, fifteen-hundred-mile-long buzzard. As you face the map, the head is toward the left, southeast of the Philippines. The tail, to the right — at about the same degree of latitude as Guadalcanal in the Solomons — is the Papuan Peninsula. Both armies had come to realize that whoever held this peninsula would command the northern approaches to Australia. In taking Milne Bay the enemy had nipped the tip of the tail. That troubled MacArthur, but didn't alarm him; he could count on the Australians to dislodge them; the threat wasn't immediate. Meanwhile, however, another Jap force had anchored off Buna and Gona, villages on Papua's upper, or northern, side. Their purpose was obscure. Between Buna and Gona on the north and Port Moresby on the south loomed Papua's blunt, razor-backed Owen Stanley Range, the Rockies of the Pacific, rising tier on limestone tier, its caps carrying snow almost to the equator and its lower ridges so densely forested that some spurs resembled paintings by Piero della Francesca. To send an army over these forbidding mountains, upon

which more than three hundred inches of rain falls each year, was regarded as absolutely impossible. MacArthur sent two of his ablest officers to Moresby, directing them to study its defenses. They came back full of assurances. The city was surrounded by water and impenetrable rainforest, they said. They omitted one detail. Either because they hadn't seen it or because they regarded it as insignificant, they failed to mention a little track that meandered off into the bush in the general direction of the Owen Stanleys. Soon the world would know that winding path as the Kokoda Trail.

Anyone trying to grasp the nature of the fighting which now lay ahead must first come to grips with its appalling battlefields and the immensity of the Pacific Ocean. The first task is difficult, the second almost impossible. It is a striking fact that you could drop the entire landmass of the earth into the Pacific and still leave a vast sea shroud to roll, in Melville's words, "as it rolled five thousand years ago." Geographers usually divide Oceania into three parts — Melanesia, Micronesia, and Polynesia — but these terms are confusing and largely irrelevant to the campaigns of World War II.

The foci of action in 1942 were New Guinea, the Solomons to the east, and, between them, the Bismarck Archipelago, whose two chief islands, New Britain and New Ireland, resemble the letter *J* inverted and on its back, with New Britain as the shank and New Ireland as the hook. In the Allied grand strategy, the Pacific would ultimately be divided into two theaters of war. On the left, MacArthur would drive north through New Guinea to the Philippines. Meanwhile Chester Nimitz and his fellow admirals, having stopped the Japs in the Solomons, would lunge across the central Pacific, hopping over a chain of islands: Tarawa, the Marianas, Iwo Jima, to Okinawa. At that point the twin offensives would merge. Okinawa would be the base for an American invasion of the Japanese home islands, with Nimitz commanding the fleet and MacArthur sending the GIs and Marines ashore. None of this, however, was envisaged in that first desperate year of the war. The geography must be mastered first.

Names on maps of the southwest Pacific, where the first battles were fought in 1942, are deceptively familiar, for most of them are those of Western explorers, European statesmen, and their European homelands, such as the Owen Stanleys (for an English voyager of the 1840s); the Shortland Islands (after John Shortland, a sixteenth-century British sailor); Bougainville (for Louis Antoine de Bougainville, a Frenchman after whom the bougainvillea creeper was also named); Finschhafen and the Bismarcks (German); and, more obviously, New Georgia, Hollandia, and New Hanover. New Guinea was christened by a Spaniard, Ortiz de Retes, and Papua — originally "Ilhas de Papuas" — by a Portuguese, Antonio de Abreu. Now and then a native name, like Kapingamarangi, Mangareva, or the Solomon isle of Kolombangara, suggests the primitive force in the greenery, in the dazzling glare of liquid sunshine that conceals a shimmering Senegalese blackness which, in turn, in its very quiddity, gleams with an ultraviolet throb. Conrad, writing of Africa, put it well. It is the heart of darkness, the lividity at the core of the most magnetic light.

In the view of World War II GIs and Marines, most of what they had heard about the South Seas was applesauce. They had expected an exotic world where hustlers like Sadie Thompson seduced missionaries, and Mother Goddam strutted through *The Shanghai Gesture*, and wild men pranced on Borneo, and Lawrence Tibbett bellowed "On the Road to Mandalay" while sahibs wearing battered topees and stengah-shifters sipped shandies or gin pahits, and lovely native girls dived for pearls wearing fitted sarongs, like Dorothy Lamour. Actually, such paradises existed. They always have. Tahiti, forty-six hundred miles east of New Guinea, is one of them. In 1777 Captain Cook's surgeon's mate wrote of seeing there "great number of Girls . . . who in Symmetry & proportion might dispute the palm with any women under the Sun." Another visitor noted the plays enacted by Tahiti's *arioi* sect, in which "the intimacies between the sexes were carried to great lengths." These dreamy islands could have been matched elsewhere in 1942. What young Americans in the early 1940s could not understand was that the local cultures, delicate and ephemeral, could not coexist with engines of death and destruction. GIs put down natives as "gooks." To the Diggers they were "fuzzy-wuzzies." White men who live among them, or have traveled widely in the islands, call them "indigenes," or sometimes "blackfellows," names of simple dignity to which they are surely entitled. It is true that theirs was, and for the most part still is, a Stone Age culture. The first wheel many of them saw was attached to the bottom of an airplane. It is equally true that their simple humanity would prevent them from even contemplating a Pearl Harbor, an Auschwitz, or a Hiroshima, and that their devotion to wounded Australians during the war won them the altered name of "fuzzy-wuzzy angels."

Before the war, before the great colonial empires began to come unstuck, indigenes were ruled by lordly Europeans who called themselves Residents and lived in enormous Residencies. Some of these buildings survive. In central Java, for example, you can find the ruins of what was once a Dutch Resident's Residency, a huge bungalow on the brow of a hill with a high thatched roof supported by Doric and Corinthian pillars, so as to form a broad veranda. Once the householder answered to the name of "Tuan." Today, in his abandoned, walled-in, wildly overgrown garden are areca palms, fruit trees, and roses, a blowsy tribute to one man's faith in white supremacy.

It was a mighty force in the floodtide of imperialism. Here, "Out East," as the British put it, a European who would have been a clerk or a shopkeeper at home could become, because of the color of his skin, an absolute monarch. His native vassals — and he had swarms of them — were each paid four cents a day. He wore a pith helmet and immaculate white ducks, and dined well; in Sumatra's thirty-two-dish rice banquet, each successive dish bore a ball of rice topped by a different delicacy, among them fried bananas, grated coconut, duck, sausages, chicken, and eggs. If he was single, he hired a mistress by the week, and if he was permissive, he allowed her to use his private bidet. His sports were polo, golf, and tennis — in Singapore alone there were six golf courses and two thousand tennis courts. On vacation he could visit "B.N.B." (British North Borneo), "F.M.S." (Federated Malay States, also a crown colony), Hanoi's opera house, which was large enough to seat every European who might want to come, or Saigon's famous theater, the most celebrated in the Far East, where a young entertainer named Noel Coward made his dramatic debut in *Journey's End*, a play which, had his audiences but known it, foreshadowed the end of their way of life. In Saigon, now Ho Chi Minh City, the French are not, of course, remembered with affection. Neither are the Dutch in the Malay Barrier. During World War II Sukarno was a Japanese puppet, and his seventy million fellow Indonesians thought none the less of him for it.

On the other hand, New Guinea's indigenes have warm recollections of Caucasians and treat them with great respect. In 1942, even before the triumphant Japanese had settled in, one black tribe from the interior crossed two hundred miles of hills and strand forest to join the thin line of Australians defending Moresby. Had the Japs been friendlier, they might have converted some of the Papuans. Instead, like the Nazis in the Ukraine, they alienated potential friends by barbaric policies. Islanders who failed to bow deeply to all Japanese were slapped in the face — a custom in the Nipponese army, but a mortal insult in New Guinea. Moslems' skullcaps were knocked off with rifle butts. Use of the English language, or even pidgin, was forbidden. Blackfellows had to carry ID cards and armbands signifying Nipponese ratings of their degrees of trustworthiness. The Japanese language and Greater East Asia propaganda were compulsory in schools. So ruthless were Hirohito's secret police in pulling out the fingernails of uncooperative natives that their jeering query, "Do you need a manicure?" triggered fear and resentment throughout Papua. The Japanese simply did not understand these people. They thought they could gain face by humiliating their European and American POWs. Nips carried a pamphlet written by one Colonel Masanobu Tsuji which told them: "When you encounter the enemy after landing, think of yourself as an avenger come at last face-to-face with his father's murderer. Here is the man whose death will lighten your heart of its burden of brooding anger. If you fail to destroy him utterly you can never rest in peace." The consequence of this was a brutal treatment of prisoners beyond any laws of war — the 1957 film *Bridge on the River Kwai* was based upon a real incident — which aroused the compassion of the gentle natives around Port Moresby.

Americans seem to have a special place in native hearts. When the Japs had conquered Manila, General Homma ordered a victory parade, the music to be provided by a local band. An audience of natives was rounded up. The tunes were greeted with scattered applause until the last one, which triggered a standing ovation. Homma, startled, smiled in all directions. He didn't know the Filipino musicians were playing "Stars and Stripes Forever."

So there are still parts of the black world where the white man is welcome. Nevertheless, anyone who wants to know the lay of the land in the islands needs a key friend, who has other friends, who have friends here and friends there — a cordial net of human relationships which makes all things possible. The first friend is the important one. Finding him in Papua New Guinea is not easy. The inhabitants speak 760 languages, not counting dialects. During my recent visit to Port Moresby a defendant and a string of interpreters had to go through seven languages to enter his plea; the horrified judge, foreseeing what this would mean in a trial, dismissed the prisoner. Often communication can be achieved only in bastardized pidgin. If a blackfellow wants to say "my country," it will come out "kantri-bilong-mi" (country-belong-me). And he will be right; since 1975 Papua New Guinea has been an independent nation, though economically it is still a colony, with an Australian sitting beside virtually every key official, making recommendations which are almost always accepted.

My first friend of a friend in New Guinea is barrel-chested Sir John Guise, the independent country's first native governor-general, now retired and living in Moresby. He receives me in his modest four-room home of cinder block painted light green. The chairs are plastic; the floor, linoleum; the only appliances in sight are a stereo, a Banks radio, and a floor fan, all powered by batteries. This is the life-style of a man who presided over a nation as large as New England, the Middle Atlantic states, and West Virginia combined, populated by three million Papuans. Unless they are living in old European Residencies, the political leaders in the emerging nations of the southwest Pacific live more frugally than the mayor of a typical American city. Sir John waves me to a chair and takes one himself. He is chewing betel nut, which, if you are unaccustomed to it, is an unsettling experience for the spectator; every time the chewer opens his mouth his gums appear to be hemorrhaging. I first encountered it in India. The effect on the user is much like marijuana's. Under its influence, Sir John looks in my direction with what we in the Marine Corps called a thousand-yard stare; then the stare shortens until his eyes are locked into mine. He speaks of his people and their lands, and his voice is incredibly deep, like thunder rolling down the vault of heaven. His complexion is cordovan, skin rippling over knotted tendon and stretched muscle. The impression is of an immensely powerful paterfamilias; and as word of his visitor spreads through the neighborhood, his home, and then his chair, are in fact surrounded by indigenes, all of whom are related to him.

Our mutual acquaintance has warned me to be neither obsequious nor condescending toward Sir John; either will bring a curt dismissal. But the warning is unnecessary. Empathy is the first gift of a successful interviewer. In the Marine Corps men who picked up the ways of the Orient were said to have gone "Asiatic." I went Asiatic with the ease of a chameleon shifting from San Diego brown to Guadalcanal green. Similarly, I have an imitative ear. At one time or another I have picked up a dozen accents as quickly as a born linguist picks up languages, and my pidgin is workable, but the thought of 760 languages stuns me. I cannot cope with them. That is one reason why I have come to Sir John.

He understands, and asks how he can help me. I tell him I want to see the old battlefields of Kokoda, the Kumusi, Buna, Gona, Lae, Salamaua, Madang, Aitape, and also Rabaul, the Japanese stronghold which MacArthur bypassed. "Forget Buna and Gona," he advises me. "There's nothing there now." The other visits can be arranged, he says. I make my second request, for a night trek in the jungle, to compare it with similar bush I have seen in the Solomons, India, and Indochina. I want to understand what fighting in it was like. He replies that one rainforest is like another. Not so, I counter; the others lacked mountains. He grins and asks, "Do you really think you can climb the Owen Stanleys at your age?" I am startled. The thought that I couldn't had never occurred to me. I say uncertainly, "I stay in shape." He laughs heartily, and I hollowly. Then he speaks briefly to his flock, starting a chain of events which takes me into deep jungle and exceeds all my expectations but one. The exception, of course, is the one Sir John spotted. I simply cannot make it up the ridges. Burdened with equipment in a creel on my back, drenched with sweat, my thighs afire, I repeatedly take breaks in the heat and watch, mortified, while my guides, and even native women and children, scamper effortlessly to the top. I remember that during the war we all vowed that if we lived through it we would bury our weapons in our backyards, sit in rocking chairs on our porches, watch the rain, and tell the guns, "Rust, you son of a bitch, rust." And here I am again, ten thousand miles from my rocker, staggering under the weight of other gear. Oh, Lord, how could I have forgotten?

If the trails are wide enough I ride in a rented Land Rover. But I prefer traveling by sea. My companions, who vary in number from two to five, conjure up ancient launches, praus, and, on a memorable overnight trip, an outrigger powered by a square sail overhead. Among my two hosts that day is a *pawany*, a kind of witch doctor who has given me a feathered juju to ward off evil spirits. In a Walter Mitty mood I remember Frank Buck and "Bring 'em Back Alive." Actually I could bring back a large zoo if there were some way to capture the species I see in the bush and the savannas of Papua and the Bismarcks, but perhaps it would be wise here to put the fauna in its proper setting, which is quite as spectacular as the creatures it supports.

One begins at the beach, where the light is so silvery that if the sun is overhead you cannot look directly at the sand, and where, at sundown, the deep blue water turns briefly to liquid gold and then to a Homeric wine red. If you are gliding in aboard a native boat, the only offshore sound is the splash of scurrying flying fish arrowing in on their prey. Below our canoe, myriad creatures, easily visible in the lucid water, provide an endlessly changing kaleidoscope: giant turtles, jewellike banded angelfish, translucent jellyfish waving their tentacles, slimy water snakes, minnows clustered like butterflies, squirrelfish, groupers, lionfish, pipefish, lungfish — the liquid spectrum widens and deepens, like the heaven here at night beneath the Southern Cross. Then there are the colors of the underwater rock: amethyst, scarlet, emerald, salmon pink, heliotrope, lilac, all as pale and delicate as those in the wardrobe of an eighteenth-century marchioness. The very air has the sensuous feel of a rich, soft fabric. You sense that you are approaching Eden, or an Eden run amok, a land so incredibly fertile that its first heady scents, as you wade through the restless, lacy surf, have the effect of a hallucinatory drug.

The coconut trees, lithe and graceful, crowd the beach in their ordered rows like a minuet of slender elderly virgins adopting flippant poses, simpering in the zephyr that never quite dies while sunlight, piercing their leaves with the playful malice of a Persian cat, splashes the ground in ever-changing patterns of light. Inland from the endlessly pounding surf, depending on the beach you have chosen, are sago swamps, fronds of shade acacias, flaming yellow cannas, aromatic white calophyllums, and the slender elegance of incredibly tall bamboo forests, or great mango trees, their fruit purplish red or yellow among the massive leaves. (On the northern shores are rubber trees, each with a tap to catch its milky sap, displaying their chevroned bark in cool columns and green silence. In Rabaul, once a name which terrified a million Allied fighting men, one sits in the Kaivanu bar on Mango Avenue and tries to count the hundreds of varieties of sprays of spider orchids and other magnificent herbaceous epiphytes that crowd the shade trees with pink and white frostings of thick blossoms.)

It is like a romantic mirage. Traveling is part of my trade, and I have seen more of the world than most men. Western Europe, which most Americans want to visit, is, I think, a disappointment. I have lived in the Ruhr; it is like Pittsburgh without jaywalkers. My rooms in London were a half-block from George Raft's gambling casino in one direction and, in another direction, a few blocks from Hugh Hefner's local Playboy Club. In Paris I passed an American drugstore on the Champs-Élysées every day. But except for India I know of no land so enchanting as the beaches and lagoons of the South Pacific. Among the mangroves in the lowlands, each trunk sheathed in vines, one hears an endless concert from screaming cockatoos, crowned pigeons booming through the leaves on their whirring wings, and clamoring myna birds. A staggered swarm of fifteen-inch-wide butterflies hangs in the air like a dazzling mobile. In the red hibiscus one glimpses a spectacular bird of paradise, Papua New Guinea's national emblem. Over a nearby stream a kingfisher squats on an overhanging nipa branch, the bird's vivid blue reflected in the water. As you approach, it darts away with a flashing glitter of jeweled wings, and you move on, drawn by the feathered rapids of white water upstream. The rivers of the South Seas are a marvel in themselves. Inland on Guadalcanal's Kokumbona there is a liquid cascade which we called Mydick Falls — christened by Blinker Reid, the point man on one of my patrols, who saw it first and gasped, "My dick!" — but that torrent is dwarfed by the roaring current of Papua's Fly River, navigable for 560 miles, whose volume of water is so great that it could provide hydroelectric power for all Papua *and* Australia.

Streams, the arteries of commerce, support villages at their mouths, often within sight of the beaches. The typical village has a score of bell-shaped huts on stilts to provide coolness and protection from floods, the thatched roofs rising high, like hives. Approaching one of them, crossing the Yumi River over a shaky bamboo bridge, my companions and I find beached canoes, dugouts, and frail sampans with rattan hoods. Next we hear the squealing of little black pigs and then the sounds of men and women, all of whom, we discover, are wearing lap-lap shorts. The fishermen, their day's catch in, are asleep on woven mats. Other men, and children, are planting taro, pandanus (screw pines), yams, and sago palms, chanting as they do so. Two young women are nourishing baby pigs. Beside a pile of tropical fruit, which resembles a Ghirlandajo picture, a group of older women are busy sorting out huge bunches of bananas, bolts of tapa, kava bowls, and necklaces of shells, beads, bones, dogs' teeth, sharks' teeth, and, incredibly, Pepsi-Cola bottle caps. Other women are working on stalks of the very useful sago palm; the trunk provides flour for cakes and porridge, and the fabric from the huge, branching single flower, twelve feet across, will make bunchy skirts which, dyed in rich, deep colors, are worn for festive occasions.

One of the indigenes, sleeping in the feathery shade of acacias, stirs, yawns, and approaches his visitors. Evidently he is the headman, or "big man." He is a tall, striking figure, his wiry hair dyed with lime, his satin skin the color of coffee, a string of red berries at his throat, and, behind one ear, a flower like a tongue of crimson flame. Alas, there is no way to communicate with him. The visitors cannot speak his tongue, and he has no pidgin. One would like to ask why anyone bothers to work at all here. This is the ultimate *dolce far niente* existence. There is no need for clothing or shelter; the breeze from the water is perpetually steady; and an exotic diet is always within reaching distance. Apart from the yams, pandanus, and sagos, there are fruit and paste from the spreading green breadfruit trees, coconuts, dried green bananas, sugarcane, arrowroot, dried skipjack (tuna), dried akule (reef fish), and assorted nuts and gourds.

Of course, the Papuans do not think of themselves as blessed. People never do. Everyone wants something that others have. Rousseau's "noble savage" craves the comforts and appliances of Western technology. Beginning in 1942, Moresby natives have seen what they, with their belief in sorcery, can only interpret as magic rituals. They have observed white men open refrigerator doors and remove delightful containers. So they build imitation refrigerators of wood, paint them white, and peek inside from time to time, looking for snacks and tinned beer. It doesn't work? Never mind; they remember Australians or Americans ordering them to fetch a batch of papers quickly: "Hurry up, chop-chop, me kickee ass bilong you." Then the white man would riffle through the papers, pick up a tube, and say a few words. As a result, a plane soon landed bearing marvelous freight. The native is no dummy. He can imitate any rite. He puts together a facsimile of a telephone with tin cans and string. He shuffles papers and speaks into the can; then he searches the sky, predicting, "Moni i kam baimbai" ("Money he come by and by"). But the moni doesn't kam, and neither does the plane. So he tries to perfect his ceremonies, building more replicas of refrigerators and phones, convinced that sooner or later he will get it right. Frustrated, a New Hanover tribe formed a "Lyndon B. Johnson cult" in the 1960s. Even in New Guinea people knew that nobody was more effective with gadgets and telephones than Lyndon Johnson. They adopted a motto, "Yumi Lakim Johnson" ("We Like Johnson"). They wanted the President to become their "numbawan bikpela long kantri" — "number one big fellow of the country," meaning chieftain of their own country. Somehow they amassed sixteen hundred dollars for a one-way ticket from Washington to Moresby and sent the ticket to the White House. Johnson didn't arrive. "Basman ino kam" ("Bossman he no come"), their leader regretfully told them. It seems a pity. LBJ would have made a marvelous king of the blackfellows, and he would have enjoyed the job immensely. There would have been no antiwar demonstrations, no prickly congressmen, no Bobby Kennedy. And like every other foreigner to visit the narrow shelves of land along the beaches of the South Seas, he would have been enchanted by the closest thing to paradise on earth. Even pidgin, once it has been mastered, can be a source of constant delight. The Lord's Prayer begins: "Papa bilong yumi Istap Antap" ("Father on top belong you and me"). Apollo 14 was "tupela igo daun wokabout long mun" ("two fellow he go down walk along moon"). A woman's vagina is "bokis ilong missus" ("box belongs to girl"). Johnson would have loved that, too.

Why, then, does the mere mention of the southwest Pacific cause the men who fought there to shudder? Why does so genteel an author as Herman Wouk, whipped into a white-lipped rage at the mere thought of Guadalcanal, write that it "was and remains 'that fucking island' "? Why was combat there considered — correctly — worse than Stalingrad? These days Peace Corps volunteers on the islands, believing they are dwelling in an idyll, are baffled by the area's reputation. Over and over they ask me for an explanation. But my words are inadequate. Plainly they are unconvinced. Therefore I tell them to do what I did in my Papuan explorations: "Move a thousand yards inland. Just be sure you take a compass and leave a Hansel-and-Gretel trail behind you. If you don't you will die."

That is literally true. Indeed, the distance may be, not a thousand yards, but fifty feet. You lose all sense of direction, and the chances of a successful return are virtually nonexistent. In the 1960s an airliner crashed in Puerto Rico's celebrated rainforest, which was used to film the Tarzan movies. It took three years for search planes to find the wreckage. If the jungle has seduced you into entering it — and it *is* seductive — you are so bewildered by the masses of green enfolding you that you are, in effect, blinded. During the war infantrymen sat between the buttresses of banyan roots and watched Japanese patrols passing within eight feet. Unless Japs stumbled over them, they were quite safe. The jungle was helpful then, but there is little else to be said for it. Having lived in it, I can understand why Papuans believe in witchcraft and seek to ward off evil spirits by wearing enormous headgear with bird of paradise feathers, or tattoos, or tusks in their pierced noses, or by plastering themselves from head to toe in gray mud, or by painting their faces in red and blue stripes with dyes extracted from New Guinea shrubs. One will do most anything to put a hex on the jungle. And the Papuans, of course, have lived in it all their lives. One of their valued wartime skills was the gift of telling, from the snap of a twig, whether an intruder was an animal or a Jap. Australians swore, and still swear, that the natives are born with this sixth sense. At all events, they had it in 1942 and the Allied soldiers didn't.

Leaving a Grimm brothers' spoor in our wake, blazing a trail, so to speak, for the time when we shall retrace our steps, my two companions and I plunge into the wild verdure and presently find ourselves in a green fastness. I am struggling through festoons of vines and the bramble hooks of creepers which reach as high as my bush jacket and ensnarl me, again and again, while I wade between soaring kanari trees overgrown with vines and moss. The sunlight can barely filter through the foliage to the rotting leaves and mud beneath my boots. The luxuriant, entangled undergrowth is both pestilential and sinister. The Yumi is somewhere near — I can hear echoes of its rapids, but cannot guess where they are coming from. As we blunder onward, one of the indigenes steers me away from the quicksands of a herbaceous swamp. The heat is unbelievable. Rain falls briefly, only making the air steamier. As the sun reappears you have the impression of being in a hothouse, sultry, humid, breathless, and seething. You have the feeling that everything around you is growing rapidly, with a savage violence.

This is virgin jungle, the climax forest, the primeval slime. In the time of Tacitus all Germany was covered by a vast Hercynian forest, so dense that a man could walk from Poland to the Rhine without once glimpsing the sun, but wooded Germany at least had a net of trails. There are few here, and if unattended they are quickly reclaimed by the relentless foliage. In Papua the pathless green masses stretch in all directions among the mangroves, nipas, and kanaris. We progress slowly through the buttressed grandeur of the trees, cross a little glade of scrub and sharp kunai grass — less humid here, but the sun is brutal — and take a break in the shade of a bamboo marsh, where shoots rise in their slender elegance to great heights, and the green filtered light speckles the riotous growth. Then, having caught my breath, I become conscious of the rainforest's endless noise.

There is the inevitable myna bird, of course, making a terrific commotion. Next comes the harsh chatter of the insects, kept out of reach by our smelly Cutter ointment but buzzing and snapping just the same. In nearby treetops I hear the twittering of sunbirds delicately coquetting with the parasitic flowers that grow upon the boughs of the kanaris. Cicadas are singing their grating song. Bullfrogs croak. The chik-chak gives its harsh, penetrating, and chillingly human cry. Finally the chorus is led by the shriek of a feverbird, rising like an endless oriental melody to which one listens with growing exasperation.

We hoist our packs and tunnel onward under the breathless flush of the late afternoon. By now my bush jacket is drenched, my vision obscured by my own sweat. The stench of rotting vegetation is nauseating. Progress is slow; the effort it exacts is exhausting. Again and again I pass gigantic trees swathed in luxurious ferns and lichen like bridal veils cascading down, and echoing, wind-haunted ravines, and wet green ridges, and treacherous morasses. The jungle is mysterious, trembling. I become obsessed with the illusion that some evil animal is six feet to my left, crashing as I crash, awaiting his chance to pounce. Since one of my guides would have heard any creature there, my fear is probably groundless, but it is not entirely unreasonable. Stealthy cannibals still flourish in Papua. And New Guinea's animal life would give the bravest man pause. Hideous crabs scuttle underfoot. Reptiles are coiled around tree limbs. And somewhere in this green hell lurk scorpions, bats, baboons, spiny anteaters, ratlike bandicoots, cassowaries, wild boars, and crocodiles: an awesome menagerie which seems to justify the irrational conviction that a menacing beast is close, and coming closer. This is the kind of jungle I learned to fear and hate in my youth, a soggy miasma of disease-bearing insects, snakes, precipitous slopes, mire, swamps, heat, humidity, landslides of falling rock, and rushing rivers to cross, rivers whose creatures include bloodsucking leeches with circles of tiny teeth, like lampreys, who feast on your anus and your genitals. There is horror everywhere, everywhere, and angst.

And thirst. Above all, thirst. Ordinarily it is odors that are most evocative of the past, but here, with me, it is a raging obsession with water. We always left on patrol with two full canteens hanging from our web belts. During breaks, when you could have gulped down a quart, you had to limit yourself to two sips. That was called "water discipline." I didn't forget it in planning this return to the Pacific. Abercrombie and Fitch having chosen this extremely inconvenient time to go out of business, I assembled my equipment at Hunting World and L. L. Bean, and I included canteens. But a man in a rainforest, unable to collect more than a few drops during cloudbursts, can never fully slake his thirst. So now I beg my two guides to lead me to "wara," and after a heroic surge through a prickly thicket of ferns, we approach the banks of the Yumi.

Already I am swallowing dryly, anticipating relief; if I try to speak, I think, I will bark. But first I must master a little piece of tricky footwork. Sharp rocks stand between me and the rapids. One misstep, one misplaced grasp, could mean a slide down to oblivion on the land side, or into the torrent on the other. Helped by one Papuan in front and one behind, I make it, drop prone, and plunge my face into a turbulent eddy, drinking and cooling my face at the same time. I feel foolish until I see that my blackfellows are doing the same. Then I loll wearily against a sheet of stone, gasping and enjoying my first real view since entering the forest. The creek is pleasant, restless, rippling. In the distance I can see what was obscured in the bush, a blue outline of the mountains, lying range upon range, as far as the eye can see. Our rest here, as vitality once more surges through me, is enhanced by a diversion. One of the Papuans chuckles and points. On the far bank, in a patch of muck, a drove of Leaping Lennies has assembled to entertain us. These bizarre creatures, resembling pancakes with big eyes, are the color of the muck they live in. They scuttle about, gamboling on their flappers like an unorchestrated parody of Busby Berkeley choreography. There is just one problem. The comic relief leaves a bitter afterthought. You turn away with the queer feeling that the mud itself has come alive, and that eerie impression lingers and lingers.

Overhead three puffs of cloud grow, merge, and darken. Huge drops of rain begin to pelt us. Scarcely dry from our perspiration, we are soaked as, at my urging, we continue upstream. The water, which until now has been throwing back a thousand flickering reflections of sunlight, is gray, turbid, rocketing over its stony bed with tremendous force. Dusk is almost upon us. Soon we must camp. But our progress is interrupted by the lead guide, who holds up a warning hand. Around the bend an enormous kanari tree is swaying. Its roots having been undercut by the current, it is held tipsily erect by a weakening cradle of creepers. Approaching it at this point is out of the question, so we watch for an hour, riveted, until the creepers give way and the massive trunk crashes through puny bush and scrub and hits the Yumi with a booming roar, forming a shallow dam. Behind it the water builds and builds, and, in minutes, flows over the bole. The indigenes take a deep, hissing breath, then laugh. I don't laugh. At Cape Gloucester we lost a hundred Marines to huge falling kanaris. I wondered then, and still wonder, how this was phrased in Marine Corps records. "Killed in action" was an honorable end, meaning that a Marine had died for something, but how do you officially describe the end of a man who died because a tree fell on him?

On the bank about a hundred yards upstream, among nipa palms, mangroves, and sagos like huge bunches of ostrich feathers, we find a shelf of moss and break out our packs. My gear includes a waterproof sleeping bag, and after bolting down a prepared meal of curried rice — cold, but vastly preferable to C rations — I change clothes under the shelter of a beetling rock. The blackfellows don't mind the wet. Sogginess is a norm for them. Darkness falls swiftly in the tropics; I am still squirming in my bag, beneath jury-rigged mosquito netting, searching with my haunches for hip holes in the lichen, when we are abruptly plunged into total night. I cannot even find my pipe, but I am too tired for that anyway. In my weariness I expect to drift off quickly, but the day has brought back too many bad memories, each to be sorted out, rewrapped, and tucked back in its sheaf of sorrow and rationalization. And then, just as I am beginning to doze, the moon appears and the jungle's night shift starts to waken. At first the only sound was the quick water of the serpentine river below and the dripping rain among the trees overhead. Otherwise I lay in the silence of centuries, undisturbed even by a breeze in the cassias. Now the rain stops. The sky clears. I spot the Southern Cross and a three-quarter moon tracing its broad path on the river. A tree is delicately silhouetted against the sky. The air is fragrant with the scents of flowers on boughs, and fireflies, sparkling dimly, dart here and there in their silvery flight.

Suddenly my whole body is whipped taut in a single spasm: nearby some marsupial, probably seized by a snake, shrieks in panic. The shriek is succeeded by the loud singing of a bird, mellifluous and rich, and for an instant, with a catch at the heart, I think of a New England thrush. Moments later a humming grows around me: cicadas and mosquitoes are testing my netting. In the lunar light a huge cockroach stalks leisurely among them. Unalarmed, they continue trying to home in on me, pitiless and menacing, their cumulative drone having the effect of a note drawn out on a distant organ. Above them, night birds pass with a whirring of wings. One of them settles on a nearby branch. It is again a fever-bird, and from its perch it starts its solo, first blaring three notes in a descending chromatic scale, then four, then five. The varying notes of the scale succeed one another with infuriating persistence. Against my will I feel I must count them, and because I have no way of knowing how many there will be, listening becomes an ordeal, filing my nerves. Then, running under this psychic agony, there is a growing awareness of something hotly passionate in the jungle, a sense that the whole rainforest is watching me, that just a few yards away in the lush wilderness a macabre war is being waged, and that I, defenseless, will be the winners' prize. Suddenly I recall my Virginia nanny threatening me with the bogeyman — "the yama-yama man" — in a Victorian music-hall song:

If you don't watch out, he'll catch you without a doubt,
If he can!

Maybe he's hiding under that chair, ready to pounce on you anywhere;
Oh, run to your mama, here comes the yama-yama man!

The child within us never vanishes. And neither does man's atavistic fear of the dark. Buried in our memory banks, too deep to reach by reason, lies the conviction that hideous, hairy specters, black robed and carrying bloody scythes, lurk beneath treetops, writhing in the night, waiting for the dark of the moon, when they will pounce, and shred with their jagged teeth, and devour. And this barbaric apprehension grips me here, in peacetime, in the company of friendly Papuans. In battle, darkness can strip men of their sanity. With a start I remember that it was on just such a night as this that Sergeant Major Michael J. Powers, USMC, lost his mind.

Periodically our skipper, Captain "Buck" Rogers — an Englishman whose parents had been tortured to death by Japs in Hong Kong, and who bore an astonishing resemblance to the comedian Terry-Thomas — would break out the company, and, while we stood at rigid attention in the compound, would read us the findings of certain courts-martial arising from sexual indiscretions in the U.S. Navy, of which, of course, the Marine Corps is a part. Typically he would inform us that, "in violation of Specification Seventeen, Chapter Two, Naval Courts and Boards, one John Smith, boatswain's mate first class, U.S. Navy, did indecently, lewdly, and lasciviously convey to one William Jones, a private, U.S. Marine Corps, an indecent, lewd, and lascivious proposal, as a result of which the said John Smith did take the penis of the said William Jones in his, the said John Smith's, mouth."

At about this time a balloon would appear over our heads, inside of which a saw was being thrust through a log of wood, with the caption "Zzz." We knew nothing about said John Smith and said William Jones or any of the others whose shame was described to us in those formations. Their felonies would have been committed somewhere far away, perhaps on the North Atlantic or in the United States. It didn't matter where; the findings had to be proclaimed in ringing tones to every navy man around the world, and the offenders packed off to Portsmouth Naval Prison. The punishments were staggering: the usual sentence was eighty-five years in prison. As unsubtly as possible, we were being warned that no matter how horny we got, we couldn't go down on each other. It mystified us. Youth is more sophisticated today, but in our innocence we knew almost nothing about homosexuality. We had never heard of lesbians, and while we were aware that male homosexuals existed — they were regarded as degenerates and called "sex perverts," or simply "perverts" — most of us had never, to our knowledge, encountered one. (The battalion surgeon, a urologist in civilian life, did nothing to enlighten us. He was a strange man. He worked constantly on his memoirs, to be called *Troubled Waters*.) There were stories about students hitchhiking home from campus and being picked up by men who, once the car was again under way, would try to stroke their thighs. But these accounts were usually second- or thirdhand hearsay. There was so much excitement (and apocrypha) about heterosexuality that we seldom gave its inversion a second thought. Had we been told that practitioners of oral sodomy wanted to live together openly, with the approval of society, and insisted on being called "gay," we would have guffawed. That just wasn't one of the rights we were fighting to protect. We weren't exactly prejudiced. It was, literally, mindlessness. We hadn't thought about it. That didn't make it unique. We weren't fighting for the emancipation of housewives, either, or for the right of blacks, who performed menial, if safe, tasks far behind the lines, to bleed alongside us. Like most soldiers in most wars, we were fighting for the *status quo ante bellum*. And like the others we were doomed to disappointment.

On one point we were clear: perverts were limp-wristed, effeminate, and, when they could get away with it, transvestites. Before we sailed for Guadalcanal, when we were billeted stateside in Linda Vista, California, we were solemnly told that all queers in California wore red neckties and hung out at the corner of Hollywood and Vine, a myth we all accepted. Finally — and there were no exceptions — they always lisped. Therefore the other NCOs and I laughed when our sergeant major told us, in a drunken moment (and an unusual one, because liquor was generally reserved for officers; enlisted men, including sergeants, got beer), that he had slept with men. Mike Powers was in the regular Marine Corps, a professional soldier; he had served in Nicaragua, Haiti, and on Gibraltar. It was at Gibraltar that he had, by his soused account, violated Chapter Two's Specification Seventeen almost nightly. His lovers had been civilians, he said, some of them distinguished European civilians. When he retired from the Corps he was going to write a book about his affairs with them. Like the battalion surgeon he had a working title. It was *Famous Cocks I Have Sucked.*

We didn't take him seriously, partly because in the Marine Corps there was a constant rivalry to see who could be the coarsest. His behavior was in many ways regrettable, but always in macho ways which, we thought, were the exact opposite of homosexuality. Six feet two, blond and virile, he was heavily muscled and deep-voiced. As a soldier he seemed to have just one flaw. He seemed to suffer from a sense of unreality, as did so many regulars of the Old Corps. Otherwise he was a poster of a Marine. His strength was extraordinary. He could juggle a twenty-pound Browning automatic rifle (BAR), tossing it from hand to hand as though it were a drum-majorette's baton. He laughed easily, drank gallons of beer, told entertaining (if unbelievable) stories about his coal-mining family in Kentucky's Harlan County, and was very tough on the men. He was a great one for corporal punishment. If he disliked a private, he would bloody his nose, and sometimes knock him out, with his huge fist. He had a sadistic streak, too. He would take a man down to the beach and order him to fieldstrip his M1, bury the parts in the sand, then reassemble them — whereupon Mike would put him under arrest for having a dirty rifle. Another of Mike's tricks was to break out a platoon and order one rifleman to climb a tree and toss down the apples. But the tree was a Samoa palm; it had no apples. So Mike would tell the rest of the platoon to help the poor guy up there by throwing stones to dislodge the apples — in other words, to stone their buddy.

A grizzled gunnery sergeant in the Twenty-second Marines told us that our sergeant major had been a Parris Island drill instructor in the early 1930s and had been busted for ordering his platoon to masturbate by the numbers (hut! two! three! four!). So he was peculiar, but hardly depraved. He seemed to be a born leader. Thomas Aquinas once raised the issue of choosing between a proud man and a pusillanimous one. Take the proud one every time, he advised, because you will be sure that he will at least do something. Powers certainly did things. He seethed with energy. On a long march he would dart from the head of the battalion to the tail and back, running easily while the rest of us could hardly trudge slowly under the weight of our packs and equipment, rumbling threats at the weary and later putting them on report. The most dreaded sentence was "P and P" — "Piss and Punk"; that is, bread and water. Those who got it were sealed in a one-man privy for seventy-two hours. Quite apart from the diet, such confinement in the equatorial heat was both cruel and unusual, but when Mike recommended it, Lieutenant Colonel Krank, the battalion commander, always saw to it that it was imposed.

Some of us correctly guessed that Mike had a hold on Krank. Later, on Okinawa, we learned what it was. The colonel was an alcoholic, and Mike had a friend in a port battalion up at the Point Cruz dock who provided him with whiskey by the case. On Okinawa our supply dump took a direct hit from enemy artillery. The colonel had to fight the rest of the battle sober. It was hard on him, and he saw to it that it was hard on us, too, though no worse than under Mike at his worst. Afterward, wiser to the ways of deviates, I marveled that we hadn't taken Mike at his boozy word. We should have known by experience that all mesomorphs didn't prefer women. The most spectacular example was a colonel who had been one of the great heroes of Guadalcanal. This exemplar of heroism was caught *flagrante delicto*, his penis rammed to the hilt in the anus of a corporal. Because of his fame (and perhaps his rank) he was spared imprisonment. He was allowed to resign and, the last I heard of him, was a major general in Chiang Kai-shek's army. Maybe that was worse than Portsmouth.

Mike's departure from the battalion had nothing to do with his sex life, unless you believe that all sodomites are cowards, a bit of apocrypha which is discredited by, among other evidence, the colonel's decorations. Our strutting, bullying, powerfully built sergeant major just couldn't stand the strain of concentrated enemy shellfire. He could take small-arms fire, and once he demolished a Nambu light-machine-gun nest with a grenade. But artillery turned his bowels to water. Here, up to a point, he had my sympathy. There is a certain fairness — if anything in battle can be fair — in one rifleman fighting another. Each has a chance, and can improve his luck with skill and suppression of natural fear. But there is something grotesque and outrageous about a man safely behind fortifications, miles away, pulling a lanyard and killing other men who cannot see him, let alone reach him. Most artillerymen are at least vulnerable to counterbattery fire. Even "Pistol Pete," as we called the big Jap cannon on Guadalcanal, had been reached by the 105-millimeter howitzers of the Eleventh Marines. But as the war progressed, the number of enemy fieldpieces multiplied.

The climax approached when we moved on Dakeshi. Our problem there was complicated by the preoccupation of our gunners with their own ideas about how their huge weapons should be used. One of them bragged to me that they had mastered TOT — time-on-target — fire. Each morning at dawn they hit eighty-two road junctions behind enemy lines simultaneously. I asked why. "Well," he said, "at least we take out eighty-two Jap MPs every day." But what needed taking out were those big Nip guns. Our guys eventually did it, but meanwhile we were being pounded around the clock, especially after dark, the enemy theory being that men deprived of sleep are sluggish fighters.

During one of the worst nights I was dug in behind a natural parapet, a long, yard-high ridge of earth, in so deep a hole that my greatest worry was of being buried alive. Barney was on one side of me and Rip Thorpe on the other. Behind us, to our rear, was a large field of mud. For once I welcomed rain. That field's slimy porridge absorbed a lot of the shell bursts. Dry ground would have been worse, and exposed rock the worst of all, because a projectile landing on rock shatters it into splinters which are as lethal as shrapnel. It wasn't really heavy stuff that night; their batteries were firing the Kyunana Shiki Kyokusha Hokeiho, or "97 model high-angle infantry gun." It actually could fire our 81-millimeter mortar shells. In fact, we were told, during a daring shore-to-shore raid behind our lines three days earlier, the Nips had stolen crates of our shells from the Eleventh Marines supply dump. And so, infuriatingly, we concluded that we were being punished by our own ammo. Despite the fact that we had been hit by much bigger slugs, this barrage was ghastly because it never stopped. Incoming mail warbled overhead almost without pause, and the concentration was so accurate that I had to dig myself out seven times. I kept calling to Barney and Rip, passing the word for every man to sound off so his buddies could hear him. There wasn't much I could do for a casualty, but a corpsman had given me sulfa powder, morphine syringes, and dressings. I couldn't expect him to move up in this. Besides, the battalion aid station was taking a beating, too.

At 2:00 A.M. by my watch the firing stopped, like great tolling bells that are suddenly silenced. That was predictable. The Japs were giving us a respite, not out of pity, but in the hope that we would emerge, move around, and empty our bowels and bladders outside our foxholes. Then their next fusillade would catch us in the open. The Germans had introduced that tactic in World War I, and it was typical of our racism that we believed the Germans were responsible for this piece of professionalism, too. Just as Mac-Arthur thought the planes that attacked him on the first day of the war were piloted by Nazis, so were we convinced that Nazi artillerymen were commanding the Jap batteries. Anyway, we weren't deceived by the lifting of barrages. We shored up the walls of our holes, lit cigarettes, and muttered words of encouragement to each other. It was during this lull that we realized something was wrong to our right. A hysterical voice, like the sound of flawed chalk on a blackboard, sang out: "Halt! Who goes there, friend or foe?" Rip whispered, "Jesus, are we being infiltrated?" But that was impossible. The Japs had been shelling the fields in front of us, too. And just then a flare blossomed overhead. I peered over my little parapet. I had a good field of fire, and nothing stirred there.

Then the voice was raised again. It had dropped a register and sounded like Mike's, though that seemed impossible. The voice cried again, "Who goes there?" One of my wags — I think it was Bubba — answered, "Benedict Arnold." Nervous laughter rippled along the line. Next the shrill voice said tremulously, but with rising volume, "Knock off beating the bishop, guys; get ready to charge." That was followed by a giggle which turned into a gale of laughter. This was trouble. I had seen combat fatigue, and recognized the signs, but couldn't believe they were coming from an Old Corps sergeant major. And I couldn't think what to do. I decided to do nothing. I wasn't going to risk my life, certainly not when the rationale for it appeared extremely dubious. But moments later I realized that I had to act. Muttering voices came from my right, and Barney, after listening to a mumble from the man on his other side, told me: "Fix bayonets. Powers is going to attack. Pass the word." Rip said, "Powers is snapping in for a survey" — "survey," in this context, being the Marine Corps equivalent of an army "Section Eight": a discharge on grounds of insanity.

I was in a fix. In this sector I was next senior to Powers, but the gap between a buck sergeant and a sergeant major is roughly comparable to that between a platoon leader and a lieutenant colonel, and I was notoriously insubordinate. Yet this was an illegal order if there ever was one. Only an officer could make such a decision, and there were no officers on our starboard flank. That's why Mike was there, the seasoned NCO capable of dealing with any replacements who panicked. No one had foreseen that Powers himself might panic. Nevertheless, that was the only explanation, and when I heard another babble of shrill giggling coming from him, I knew I had to take over, meanwhile reaching somebody with enough rank to end this madness. I told Rip: "Pass the word, but add that I'm countermanding the order." Then I told Barney: "Pass the word. We're not going to attack." The two muttered messages went off, the first to port and the second to starboard, diminishing as they moved away and picking up volume as the replies came back. Barney's arrived first. He said tersely, "Powers says you're yellow and you're to put yourself under arrest." Then Rip picked up the word coming from the other direction: "Mister Murphy says to relieve Powers and get him back to battalion." That solved one problem and raised another. It meant moving a six-foot-two, 230-pound six-striper when the Japs were going to lay another volley on us any minute. I crouched there behind the parapet, trying to think. Barney asked, "What are you going to do?" I said, "Nothing until after the next delivery."

And here it came, rumbling overhead and sounding like the old Superchief, dropping in the mud and detonating with a great roar, spattering everyone from the mortarmen to us with muck. The next one fell short. They had us bracketed again, and after that the shit hit the fan, with screams from the wounded which could scarcely be heard under exploding shells, with men praying at the top of their voices, presumably in the hope that God could hear them if they were loud enough, with Rip and Barney and me checking with each other after each close burst, and they then checking those on the sides away from me. Briefly I forgot Powers. The only life I wanted to save was my own. When I did remember him, I savagely hoped that he'd gone off on his crazy charge alone. Maybe it would work. Maybe a hundred thousand Japs would lay down their arms at the sight of him and he'd win the war single-handed. The President of the United States would personally award him the Congressional Medal of Honor. *Yowzah.*

Then the barrage died again and I could hear him. He was sobbing now. I priggishly disapproved; a Marine is supposed to cry inside; he can be afraid but can't bring shame upon himself by showing his fear. The fact is that I wanted to weep myself, and I wondered whether I could ignore the word from Murphy and let things drift. But Murphy hadn't forgotten me; word again came down, repeating his order, and then a green flare burst overhead, lighting my path to Mike. No excuse now. I wiggled out of my hole and scooted along our line till I got to him. He was spread-eagled on the ground outside his foxhole, shaking uncontrollably, first shrieking as I once heard a horse shriek, then blubbering and uttering incomprehensible elementary animal sounds. Next to him was a three-man hole: kids; boots just off the boat. "What's the matter?"

one of them asked anxiously. I said, "You people give me a hand." I told each which arm or leg to hold. I said, "We're going to put him away."

It was a slippery, confused trip through the muck. Twice we got lost; the blooming flares, which were signals to the howitzers, saved us each time. Powers bawled on, a broken, maundering hulk of a man. Just as the Jap gunners started working us over again, we rounded a little mound of earth and stumbled into the dimple on the reverse slope which served as the battalion aid station. A Coleman lantern gleamed faintly. It was like a grotesque scene from a Durrenmatt play: bodies, severed limbs, and gouts of blood everywhere. The noise of our loudmouthed sobber attracted the attention of the battalion surgeon, who came over, wiping his bloody hands on his bloody apron. He stared, incredulous. I doubt that he had ever seen waters more troubled than the sergeant major's tears. He asked, "That's Mike Powers?" I said, "It was." He said, "I thought you'd crack before he did." I said, "So did I." Then a gentle, shy corpsman named Bobby Winkler came over, a sloe-eyed, fawnlike youth with the longest lashes I have ever seen on a boy. He stooped over the sergeant major, stroked his forehead, and said soothingly, "There, there." Powers whimpered. I felt sorry for him, the prick. His mewling died away. Winkler said to us, "I'll take care of him." I said to my three replacements, "Let's take off." We made it back to our holes just as the new deliveries began to soar in.

I never saw Powers again, but I know what happened to him. Long afterward I was bedridden in San Diego's Balboa Park Naval Hospital. Every morning a doctor and two nurses made their rounds accompanied by a wheeled cart we called the "agony wagon" because the doctor took various glittering steel instruments from it to probe your wounds. Mercifully, the reading of official proclamations — when we were supposed to "lie at attention" — immediately followed doctors' rounds, the tedious ritual thus coming while we were too distracted by pain to care. Usually I could tune it out entirely, but one day, through a red haze of suffering, I heard the officer of the day declare that one Michael J. Powers, a sergeant major in the Marine Corps, had been sentenced to eighty-five years in Portsmouth Naval Prison for indecently, lewdly, and lasciviously taking into his mouth the penis of one Robert F. Winkler, medical corpsman second class. Winkler was also sentenced, but I cannot remember his term. So that, I thought bitterly, is how Powers had repaid him. The stories Mike had told us while plastered had been true. He really had been a sodomite at Gibraltar. Now he would have plenty of time to write that book. I wondered whether he would include Winkler in it.

In a many-colored vision of splendor, the waters of the Yumi gleam with the rays of sunrise. "Tulait [dawn]!" cries one of the blackfellows, greeting it, and though I try to roll over for another forty winks I am jolted into a sitting position by the hammering of a woodpecker and its sardonic laugh as it darts from tree to tree, mocking my sluggishness. We break camp quickly and return to the village, our boat, the sea, and Port Moresby. After a day's rest I am ready to tackle this end of the slimy, zigzagging, seventy-eight-mile-long Kokoda Trail. As I wait for my Avis Land Rover a betel-nut-chewing Papuan, striking up a conversation, tells me, "Mipela Niugini i laik kisim planti ren" ("We New Guineans like to get a lot of rain"). I tell him, "Gut," and it is in fact a good thing, because whether he likes it or not, even here, at the driest spot, the annual rainfall is seldom less than 180 inches. At a junction here called MacDonald's Corner one can see what appears to be an ingenious monument to seventy Australians still missing in action nearly forty years after the fighting. It is a sundial so constructed that as the sun moves overhead, a shaft of gold shines directly on each engraved name. The concept, like the similar memorial on Bataan, is moving, but the cloud masses overhead mock it. Few rays reach here.

If you hire a sturdy vehicle with four-wheel drive, you can turn north from Moresby's Island Hotel, turn right at MacDonald's Corner, and writhe through quagmires until you reach a bump in the road known as Owers Corner. There you park in a checkerboard of puddles, for there, ten miles from Moresby, the trail begins. "The

Track," GIs called it; to the Diggers it was "the Bloody Track." You find it today much as it was then. In slippery ravines you stumble over tree roots, and for every two steps forward, you slip back one. One battalion took seventeen hours to hack its way through a third of a mile, all the time under such heavy fire that the mud was bloodstained along its entire length. At Ioribaiwa Australian engineers built what they mordantly called the "Golden Staircase," which survives today — four thousand twenty-inch steps, held together by roots, up a twenty-five-hundred-foot ridge and down and up again, each step hacked into clay, much as mountaineers cut traverses in ice. Now, as then, the air here is hot and extremely humid. Overhead, shrouded in clouds, loom jagged peaks, one, Mount Victoria, as high as 13,368 feet. Below, the jungle is studded with bottomless bogs. Often the trail is covered with waist-deep slop.

Presently you come upon relics of the war: rusting bulldozers sprawled along the way, corroded helmets, the disintegrating remains of Caribou transport planes and Mitsubishi bombers, and gas masks. The Japanese gas masks were used to diminish the stench of the rotting corpses they piled up to form barricades of flesh. (We sliced sections from the masks' rubber tubing to rim our dog tags, so the clash of metal on metal couldn't be heard at night.) Abruptly you are aware of a reedy, singing sound nearby. You can't place it; you have never heard anything like it. A thinly forested plateau edges westward here, and you struggle through it, toward the source of the odd sound. Then, weirdly, you come upon it. Evidently there was once a grassy airstrip on the plateau. Parked there in tidy rows, worthless since V-J Day, are thirty P-38 Lightnings and B-24 Liberators, wingtip to wingtip. Their thin skins deteriorated long ago. What you hear is a breeze singing through the naked struts and ribs of the abandoned fuselages.

Back on the trail, you realize that the jungle is opening up. Obviously others have beaten this track recently, and in large numbers. Signs of civilization appear: repaired Quonset huts, a hydroelectric installation, and a bridge formed of Marsden matting, those steel links, like gigantic erector-set strips, which we used to lay down landing fields in the bush. Around a corner, you come upon a Salvation Army hut. There are other such hostels along the trail; on weekends Papuans like to fly to Kokoda, a more negotiable clearing near the middle of the path, for hikes. What was Gethsemane for soldiers is recreation for native youths. One wonders whether they can grasp 1942's excruciation here. Probably not; like the Peace Corps volunteers, they avoid the rainforest itself and are rewarded by the pleasures on its periphery. You can tell them about the horrors at the heart of the jungle, but words are inadequate. You cannot show them photographs, because photographs of the bush are meaningless. One picture here is not worth a thousand words; it is not even worth one. So they gambol along the Bloody Track, sublimely ignorant of what was, in Samuel Eliot Morison's words, "the nastiest fighting in the world."

Shortly after sunset on Tuesday, July 21, 1942, Japanese troopships began landing 14,430 Nipponese infantrymen on the northern coast of the Papuan Peninsula. They were watched from the hills by the "Maroubra Force," a handful of native militiamen led by Basil Morris, an Australian who had remained behind to radio news of developments around Buna and Gona. Each Jap, Morris reported, wore a camouflaged uniform, a steel helmet plumed with leaves, and green paint smeared on his face; each carried, in addition to his weapon, a machete and a sharp shovel punctured with holes to stop damp earth from sticking to it by suction. The Australian noted that about two thousand of the Nips were stripped for action. Although Morris had no way of knowing it, these were Colonel Yosuki Yokoyama's shock troops, the elite of Major General Tomitaro Horii's South Seas Detachment. When they began climbing toward him, Morris assumed that they were merely patrolling. To his astonishment he saw them manhandling mortars, machine guns, and fieldpieces up the slimy, zigzagging Kokoda Trail.

In Brisbane, MacArthur's headquarters, it was still an article of military faith that no army could cross the Owen Stanley Range. George H. Johnson, perhaps the shrewdest war correspondent there, had assured his readers that an enemy offensive over the mountains was out of the question: "The track is impossible for mechanized transport, and so it seems unlikely that the Japs can hope to attempt an overland invasion of Moresby by pushing southward through the mountains." Johnson was chided by MacArthur's staff for even raising the possibility. The handful of Australians stationed on the trail seemed unnecessary. The steep, slippery, root-tangled path, flanked by seven-foot-tall blades of kunai grass, was drenched by torrential downpours. The few plateaus were fields of reeking mud. The very air savored of rot and stink lilies. The track was the width of a slim man's shoulders; at places, such as the cold, twenty-seven-hundred-foot "Gap" in the Owen Stanleys, it ceased, in effect, to exist. Donkeys couldn't climb it; neither could mules. Even if successful, an army would have to advance single file. Then there were the rivers. The Kumusi River would drown the strongest swimmer; natives called its intersection with the path "Wairopi" — pidgin for the wire rope from which a precarious footbridge was suspended. The trail, what there was of it, was grim all the way. One Australian officer called it a "track through a fetid forest grotesque with moss and glowing phosphorescent fungi."

But the Japanese, having conquered Malaya, Borneo, Java, Sumatra, the Philippines, and the Solomons, believed that no terrain was impassable. And they were contemptuous of the defenders. At that time only a few hundred Australians stood between them and Port Moresby. They had routed ten times as many Diggers at Rabaul. Preceded by Yokoyama's crack jungle troops, Horii's men leapfrogged their battalions forward, trading lives for progress. How many of them perished in this heroic endeavor will never be known. Many succumbed in the rivers, and others disappeared in quicksand or plunged into gorges. Sometimes it would take an hour to cut through a few yards of vegetation. The first man in a file would hack away with his machete until he collapsed of exhaustion; then the second man would do the same, and so on. In that climate the life expectancy of the men who lost consciousness and were left behind could often be measured in minutes.

Once the two forces collided, the Australians were no less heroic.

They knew that every day, every hour they held the enemy in check brought reinforcements closer — their fellow countrymen from the Mideast and the Americans racing toward Port Moresby from the opposite direction. The Diggers did what they could. In the fourth week of the campaign an Australian lieutenant colonel, William T. Owen, destroyed the Wairopi bridge by ripping out the locknuts that secured its cables; then he dug in with a single company to make his stand. The Nips built a bridge of their own, and on August 7, the day the Marines landed on Guadalcanal, Owen was killed while throwing a grenade. The Maroubra Force, beefed up to 533 men, fell back on the village of Deniki. Here the Diggers actually threw the foe back, but, vastly outnumbered, and running low on rations and ammunition, they then retreated another five miles, to Isurava. After three days of fruitless banzai charges, the Japanese again did the impossible. Until now fighting had been confined to the trail, the problems of advancing through the jungle on either side being considered insuperable even by them. But at Isurava Jap volunteers slipped into the trackless rainforest and penetrated the Diggers' flanks. The defense cracked. The Australians fell back through the frigid Gap, and back farther, until on September 17 the Nipponese seized Ioribaiwa, within sight of Port Moresby. There their commander decided to pause. Six hundred miles to the east, on Guadalcanal, the plight of the U.S. Marines was even more desperate than the Australians'. Once the leathernecks had been driven into the sea — and Horii had no reason to doubt that would be their fate — the Japs on that island could be shipped across the Solomon Sea to reinforce him here.

By now the condition of his troops was almost indescribable. "Let the jungle beat the Japs," said the Australian general Sir Thomas Blamey, and the jungle had just about done it. Riddled with scrub typhus and dysentery, their bloodstained uniforms torn to pieces, the Nipponese were no longer the superb force which had begun to mount the Owen Stanleys in July. One of them wrote in his diary: "The sun is fierce here. We make our way through a jungle where there are no roads. . . . Thirst for water, stomach empty. The pack on the back is heavy. My arm is numb like a stick. 'Water, water.' We reach for the canteens at our hips from force of habit, but they do not contain a drop of water." Horii, issuing his last rice ration to his fevered, emaciated troops, said of them that "no pen or words can depict adequately the hardships suffered." A Japanese war correspondent wrote of Jap "infantrymen without rifles, men walking on bare feet, men wearing blankets of straw rice bags instead of uniforms, men reduced to skin and bones plodding along with the help of a stick, men gasping and crawling on the ground."

In the 1870s Count Luigi Maria d'Albertis, a European explorer, had written that it was easier to climb a Swiss alp than an ordinary hill in Papua. Now both armies had crossed, not ordinary hills, but the worst of the Owen Stanleys, and along the way they had, when not fighting, built machine-gun nests, dug mortar pits, and climbed trees to snipe at the enemy. The Japanese were starving, cannibalizing their dead comrades, whose bones were then picked clean by jungle ants. One of these skeletons lay half-buried beside the trail, with its hand thrust out. It says much about the hardening impact of such combat that when the Australians passed this horror on their way back to Buna, each grasped the dead hand and said, "Good on you, sport."

They, too, were hungry, with as many as twenty men sharing a single tin of bully beef. One new officer later wrote of them: "Physically, the pathetically young warriors . . . were in poor shape. Worn out by strenuous fighting and exhausting movement, and weakened by lack of food and sleep and shelter, many of them had literally come to a standstill." Johnson described them as "thin, haggard, undernourished, insect-bitten, grimy, and physically near the end of their tether. They were fighting on fighting spirit alone." In the dense terrain of matted vegetation, marshland, and steep gorges, constantly threatened by ambush, flanking, infiltration, and treetop snipers, they aged rapidly and came to look more like tramps than soldiers. Their helmets had rusted red. Their dashing, broad-brimmed felt hats were caked with mud. Sores erupted on their genitalia. Their uniforms rotted on their backs. The flesh on their feet, swollen by endless slogging, peeled away when they removed their socks. And American GIs, now arriving at last and entering the lines, shared their fate. In the sodden, suffocating heat they fell prey to jungle rot, dysentery, dengue fever, and malaria. They hadn't been issued tents or proper weapons. Like the Diggers and the Japs, they lived on short rations.

Yet they and their Australian allies retained their sense of humor, one of the best indexes of morale. They joked about the five M's — mosquitoes, mud, mountains, malaria, and monotony. The first, the "mozzies," as Aussies called them, were considered the worst. It was at Templeton's Crossing, where the trail was nothing but a steep, greasy clay ravine, down which soldiers slid, braked by vines they gripped as they went, that a Digger first spun the yarn about the Bofors AA gunner who caught a mosquito in his sights, mistook it for a Zero, and opened fire. And it was in the piercing chill of the Gap — fires were forbidden — that another Aussie told the tale of two mosquitoes lifting the netting over a tasty mess sergeant, studying his dog tag to identify his blood group, and debating whether or not to eat him on the spot or take him into the jungle, an argument which ended when one said he should be devoured here: "If we take him into the bush the big chaps'll grab him."

Allied leaders were grimmer. "It looks at this moment," President Roosevelt wrote MacArthur, "as if the Japanese Fleet is heading toward the Aleutian Islands or Midway and Hawaii, with a remote possibility that it may attack Southern California or Seattle." In his reply, the general correctly stated that the Nips' chief goal now was "New Guinea and the line of communications between the United States and Australia. . . . If serious enemy pressure were applied against Australia . . . the situation would be extremely precarious. The extent of territory to be defended is so vast and the communication facilities are so poor that the enemy, moving freely by water, has a preponderant advantage." As MacArthur saw it, he himself had no choice. He had to push Horii's army back across the Owen Stanleys in head-on fighting, with none of the brilliant sweeps and double envelopments which were to establish him as the war's greatest commander. This would be his bloodiest drive: 8,546 Allied soldiers lost. It was small consolation that the Japanese lost 10,000 men, and that Horii, their leader, drowned in attempting to recross the Kumusi, though MacArthur did take satisfaction in what he called Horii's "ignominious death."

After two weeks of deadlock at Ioribaiwa, the momentum shifted to the Allies. On the fifth day of toe-to-toe slugging, Horii disengaged north of the Imita Ridge and began withdrawing. The terrain was just as merciless going the other way, with the additional handicap that the worst of what Australians call "the Wet" — the rainy season — was upon them. The orderly retreat of the Japanese suddenly turned into a rout. Abandoning their weapons and trampling one another underfoot, they fled northward. Elsewhere the Diggers of the Seventh Division and the American GIs of the Forty-first and Thirty-second divisions might have fallen on their rear, but the precipices of the Owen Stanleys made that impossible. And at the end, at Buna, Gona, and, between them, Sanananda Point, the regrouping Nips made a savage, murderous last stand. MacArthur's men, having hacked their way through Papua's dense rainforests, forded its deep rivers, shinnied up its banyan trees for observation, scaled its cliffs, and descended the slopes of the foothills on the far side of the mountains, debouched on a low, flat coastal plain of coconut plantations, missionary settlements, and clusters of thatched shanties. Awaiting them was a desperate army — seventy-five hundred Japanese in front of Buna alone — trained bush fighters at home in the tangled swamps and kunai patches of the Buna plain, entrenched in coconut-log bunkers sheltering Nambus with interlocking fields of fire. Enjoying good lateral communications, they were easily reinforced by fleets of destroyers from Rabaul. In the early weeks of the battle American warplanes from Moresby were turned back over the Owen Stanleys by prodigious cloudbursts in the mountains. Japanese pilots faced no such obstacle; swarms of them flew down from Rabaul's teeming airdromes, making life even more miserable for the drenched Allied soldiers. It says much of the terrain that at one point one of MacArthur's field commanders, a two-star general, had to swim two miles to reach his troops.

Gona was overrun in the second week of December 1942, and Buna and Sanananda in January 1943. "No more Bunas!" MacArthur vowed. The key fight, however, was for the air overhead. In early March B-24s and B-17s of the U.S. Army Air Corps won the Battle of the Bismarck Sea, sinking at least eight transports bringing enemy reinforcements from Rabaul to Papua. The few Japanese who reached New Guinea from the lost ships had to swim ashore. Tokyo wrote off Papua. Having retaken Milne Bay, MacArthur now seized one Japanese stronghold after another: Wau, Salamaua, Lae, Nadzab, Madang, Aitape, Wewak — bastions which the enemy had thought could hold out for years. Part of the reason for the Allied successes was superior generalship and improved aircraft. But neither of these was responsible for the victory in the Owen Stanleys. That was the feat of MacArthur's finest military weapon, the unsung infantryman, the GI and Digger who endured the cruel jungle and outfought the Japanese man for man. The Allies were, quite simply, better soldiers than the enemy's.

Those of us who fought in the Pacific believed we would be remembered, that schoolchildren would be told of our sacrifices and taught the names of our greatest battles. But we didn't anticipate the velocity of postwar history; didn't realize that events would succeed one another more and more rapidly, in a kind of geometric progression, swamping the recent past in an endless flood of sensationalism; didn't know that instant celebrities would glitter blindingly and then disappear overnight. One of them, Andy Warhol, has prophesied: "In the future, everybody will be famous for fifteen minutes." The fame of most Papuan clashes didn't last even that long. Readers ignorant of New Guinea, preoccupied with the European theater, flipped past newspaper stories of the remote struggle and remembered only the name of MacArthur, who had seen to it that his own name dominated communiqués from the southwest Pacific.

It would be inaccurate to say that names of the old battlefields mean nothing out there today. The truth is more ironic. Incredibly, tourism has become a major industry in New Guinea. Places which were dreaded in the early 1940s have acquired new identities. In tourist brochures Lae, for example, has become a city offering every visitor "an air-conditioned fun time"; one brochure reveals that it now "feasts both the eye and the heart with its abundant evidence of prosperity and civic pride" in "a lush tropical setting" which "encourages golfers to both enjoy and practice their favorite sport." Rabaul is also endowed with an eighteen-hole golf course; the former Japanese stronghold is "beautiful and spectacular . . . with its magnificent harbor" that "could hardly be more spectacular," and visitors are encouraged to explore the twelve miles of Rabaul caves which once sheltered crack Nipponese regiments. Madang "looks like everyone's dream of a Pacific Island resort — and when you land, you are not disappointed." Milne Bay offers "idyllic atolls" and "sun fun." Truk, beneath whose waters Hirohito's Fourth Fleet lies rusting (it may be viewed through glass-bottomed tourist boats), offers "air-conditioning in Eden . . . the waters of the vast lagoon are smooth and clear, a skin-diver's dream, a water skier's delight, a fisherman's paradise."

It is as though European veterans were invited to "Ski at Bastogne!" or "Surf at Anzio!" The circular for Wewak, where MacArthur bypassed thirty-five thousand Japanese troops, is more evocative; it is said to possess "one of the most remarkable reservoirs of animal, reptile, insect and bird life anywhere." New Guinea's overall recreation slogan comes even closer — "Papua: it's like every place you've never been" — though in my case even that is inapplicable. New Guinea is very much like another place I have been, a Solomons island which James Michener described as "that godforsaken backwash of the world"; which was known as Pua Pua to the natives; which the Japanese called Gadarukanaru, "KA," or "The Island of Death"; which Americans knew as Guadalcanal; and which we Marines who served there simply referred to as The Canal.

EASY

The Raggedy Ass Marines

IN THOSE DAYS ALL MARINE CORPS RECRUITS WERE ASSIGNED TO one of the Corps' two boot camps. Those enlisting west of the Mississippi River were sent to San Diego; those who joined up east of the Mississippi went to Parris Island, South Carolina, an isle whose reputation was just marginally better than those of Alcatraz and Devil's Island. So I was going to see the Deep South after all. Having signed up for four years, or more if the war lasted longer; having sworn that "I will bear true faith and allegiance to the United States of America; that I will serve them honestly and faithfully against all their enemies whomsoever; and that I will obey the orders of the President of the United States, and the orders of the officers appointed over me, according to the Rules and Articles for the Government of the Army, Navy, and Marine Corps of the United States" — having, in short, put my life in hock to the most fearsome and hazardous of the country's armed forces — I boarded a special train occupied by other young men who had done the same. We had hardly begun to roll from Springfield when I made a friend in Lawrence Dudley, of Bowdoin. Dudley was heavy, flaxen-haired, and round-shouldered. He knew that once his poor posture had caught the eye of our drill instructor ("DI," we later learned, was the salty term), he would be in for a hard time. But becoming a Marine was important to him. During his college summers he had worked in the Springfield arsenal as an assistant to John Garand, who had invented the Garand, or M1, rifle, which had replaced the

Springfield '03 as America's basic infantry weapon. I had fired the '03 in an ROTC course. Dudley said the M1 was better (he was wrong) and felt, as a testament to his faith, that he should carry one in combat instead of tinkering away the war years in the arsenal, which could have been easily arranged by his friends there.

In Washington we paused for three nighttime hours and were told we could go "ashore" instead of waiting in Union Station. Dudley and I repaired to a nearby nightclub. Neither of us had ever been in one before, and we were appalled. All I can remember is a drunken brunette, apparently a customer, who insisted on taking off all her clothes, and a comedian with a voice that grated like a file who kept breaking himself up by saying: "Damon went out and got Pythias drunk." It was an introduction to the kind of wartime entertainment available to American enlisted men. Back on the train we slept, and I awoke, trembling with anticipation, in the sacred soil of the old Confederacy. I rushed for the rear platform. Everything I had been told had led me to expect plantations, camellias, and darkies with banjos strumming "Old Black Joe." Instead I looked out on shabby unpainted shacks and people in rags, all of them barefoot. No Taras, no Scarletts, no Rhetts; just Tobacco Road. And this was *Virginia*, the state of Robert E. Lee. I felt cheated; disinherited; apprehensive. What awaited me on Parris Island, which was grim even by Southern standards? Despair swept me as we reached our destination, heard departing, newly graduated sea soldiers yelling, "You'll be sorreeee!" and saw noncoms in field hats carrying menacing swagger sticks. The NCOs stared at us as though we were some low and disgusting form of animal life. They spat tobacco at our feet and kept calling us "shitheads."

Astonishingly, I adored Parris Island. Boot camp is a profound shock to most recruits because the Corps begins its job of building men by destroying the identity they brought with them. Their heads are shaved. They are assigned numbers. The DI is their god. He treats them with utter contempt. I am told that corporal punishment has since been banned on the island, but in my day it was quite common to see a DI bloody a man's nose, and some boots were gravely injured, though I know of none who actually died. I recall being baffled later when Patton was reprimanded for slapping a GI. All of us had endured much more than that. The gentlest punishments were those for dropping a rifle (sleeping on eight of them) and for eating candy (carrying an oozing mass of chocolate for two days). If the boot called it "candy" he would have been punished further, the proper expression being *pogey bait*. The Corps had its own language, and boots were required to learn it, just as the inhabitants of an occupied country must learn the conqueror's tongue. A bar was a *slopchute*, a latrine a *head;* swamps were *boondocks*, and field boots, *boondockers*. A rumor was *scuttlebutt*, because that was the name for water fountains, where rumors were spread; a deception was a *snow job*, gossiping was *shooting the breeze*, information was *dope*, news was *the scoop*, confirmed information was *the word*. You said "Aye, aye, sir," not "Yes, sir." The nape of the neck was the *stacking swivel*, after a rifle part. An officer promoted from the ranks was a *mustang*. Your company commander was *the skipper*. You never went on leave; you were *granted liberty*, usually in the form of a *forty-eight* or a *seventy-two*, depending on the number of hours you could be absent. If you didn't return by then, you were *over the hill*. Coffee was *Joe;* a coffeepot, a *Joe-pot*. Battle dress was *dungarees*. A cleanup of barracks, no matter how long it lasted, was a *field day;* a necktie was a *field scarf*, drummers and trumpeters were *field musics*. Duffle bags, though indistinguishable from those used by GIs, were *seabags*. To be *under hack* meant to be under arrest. To straighten up was to *square away;* a tough fighter was a *hard-charger;* underwear was *skivvies;* manipulating people was called *working one's bolt*. *Lad* was a generic term of address for any subordinate, regardless of age. One of my people, a twenty-eight-year-old Vermont school principal, was known, because of his advanced age, as "Pop." An officer five years his junior would summon him by snapping, "Over here, lad."

Some of these terms have crept into the language since World War II, but no one outside the service knew them then. Boots had to pick them up fast. They were courting trouble if they described their combat hardware as anything but 782 *gear*, that being the number of the form you had to sign as a receipt. It was equally unwise to call a deck a "floor," a bulkhead a "wall," an overhead a "ceiling," a hatch a "door," or a ladder "stairs." Every Marine was "Mac" to every other Marine; every U.S. soldier was a "doggie" and was barked at. The Corps' patois was astonishingly varied. To "sight in" or "zero" was to determine, by trial and error, the sight setting necessary to hit a bull's-eye with a given weapon. "Snap in" could mean sighting and aiming an unloaded rifle; it could also mean breaking into, or trying out for, a new job, somewhat like the army's "bucking for." As a noun, "secure" described an outdated movement in the manual of arms; as a verb, it signified anchoring something in place or ending an activity — thus, when the Battle of Tarawa was won, the island was "secure." "Survey" was even more flexible. It could mean, not only a medical discharge from the Corps (anyone feigning combat fatigue was "snapping in for a survey"), but also retirement from the Corps, disposing of worn-out clothing or equipment, or taking a second helping of chow. There was even a word for anything which defied description. It was "gizmo."

On Parris Island these and all other customs of the boot's new way of life were flouted at great risk. You were told that there were three ways of doing things: the right way, the wrong way, and the Marine Corps way. The Corps way was uncompromising. Failure to salute your superiors — including privates first class — brought swift retribution. The worst discipline I saw came during floodlit midnight calisthenics. In one common exercise we paired off; each boot hoisted his rifle as you would hoist a battering ram and placed the butt against his buddy's forehead. The buddy would touch the butt and duck. The man with the rifle was supposed to try to strike his forehead before the other man could drop, but since you knew you were going to reverse roles, the sensible course was to let him get out of the way. Enter the vengeful noncom. *He* put a rifle butt against the offender's forehead and slugged him before there was time to dodge. The boot who merely suffered a concussion was lucky.

How could I enjoy this? Parts of it, of course, I loathed. But the basic concept fascinated me. I wanted to surrender my individuality, curbing my neck beneath the yoke of petty tyranny. Since my father's death I had yearned for stern discipline, and Parris Island, where he himself had learned discipline a quarter-century earlier, gave it to me in spades. Physically I was delicate, even fragile, but I had limitless reservoirs of energy, and I could feel myself toughening almost hourly. Everything I saw seemed exquisitely defined — every leaf, every pebble looked as sharp as a drawing in a book. I knew I was merely becoming a tiny cog in the vast machine which would confront fascism, but that was precisely why I had volunteered. Even today, despite the horrors which inevitably followed, I am haunted by memories of my weeks as a recruit. It is almost like recalling a broken marriage which, for one divorced partner, can never really end.

Our platoon was number 618, and our DI was a leathery corporal from Georgia named Coffey. The Marine Corps had always recruited a disproportionate number of men from the South, where the military traditions of the early 1860s had never died. Later I met many Raiders like that, and Coffey was typical: tall, lanky, and fair haired, with a mad grin and dancing, rain-colored eyes full of shattered light. They were born killers; in the Raider battalions, in violation of orders, they would penetrate deep behind Japanese lines at night, looking for two Nips sacked out together. Then they would cut the throat of one and leave the other to find the corpse in the morning. This was brilliant psychological warfare, but it was also, of course, extremely dangerous. In combat these Southerners would charge fearlessly with the shrill rebel yell of their great-grandfathers, and they loved the bayonet. How my father's side defeated my mother's side in the Civil War will always mystify me.

Yankee boys were just the kind of meat this Georgian Caesar fed upon. His appetite was further whetted by the fact that many of us had been university students, a fact which triggered the anti-intellectual in him. He himself was illiterate and, apart from his training duties, startlingly ignorant. Even there he sometimes skidded; while specifying the rigors of our calling, he was supposed to teach us a synoptic history of the Corps, and it turned out that he thought the American Revolution had occurred in "nineteen and ten" and World War I in "nineteen and thirty-four," with the French as our enemies. After this last, a Dartmouth man unwisely laughed. Our DI flushed and declared his own war on all "wisenheimer college eight balls." He invented sobriquets, most of them scatological, for boots from New England campuses. For some reason — perhaps because I obviously felt that I had found a home in the Marine Corps — I got off lightly. I was merely "Slim," a *nom de guerre* which stuck to me throughout my forty-month cruise and was vastly preferable to my fraternity nicknames; I happened to be damned, or blessed, with outsize genitalia, so in college I had been called first "Tripod," and then "Sashweight." It embarrassed me then. Not until I joined the Marines did I learn that hefty equipment along that line was admired in some quarters. One day I found myself hip-to-hip at a trough urinal with a former Reno gigolo. He gazed down at me for a long moment and then asked thoughtfully, "Slim, what did you do in civilian life?"

As expected, Coffey's favorite target of opportunity was slope-shouldered, potbellied Larry Dudley. This was partly Dudley's fault. He couldn't help his figure, but he was remiss in other ways, too. The DI liked to say, "God gave you the face you were born with, but I'll give you the face you'll die with." That was untrue of Dudley. His expression never changed. Even when he was out of step, which was often, he looked bland, nonchalant, slightly pained. His greatest blunder, however, was a spectacular feat of tactlessness. On the evening of the day we were issued our 782 gear, Coffey stood in the doorway of a Quonset hut, facing us vassals, who ranged in a semicircle outside. The only light came from the interior of the hut, at the DI's back. He was holding an M1, fieldstripping it as he talked, naming the parts. Then he reassembled the rifle. "Now," he said triumphantly, "let's see one of you college kids do it." He thrust the weapon at the most intent member of his captive audience — Larry Dudley, lately of Garand and Dudley. *Oh, God,* I prayed; *don't let him do it.* But Dudley did it. He took that M1 apart so fast we could hardly see the blur of his moving hands; then he put it back together with the same blinding speed and handed it to the DI. There were a few stifled chuckles for the avenged shitheads of Platoon 618. Coffey turned the color of a song then popular: deep purple. His loss of face was immense, but being a DI he could strike back in many ways. He swiftly chose one. "OK, wisenheimers," he said in a pebbly voice, balancing the weapon on the palm of his hand. "If he can do it, you can all do it. Fall out here at 0500 with your pieces, ready to fieldstrip."

We were stunned. Our asses were in a sling. None of us had the faintest idea of what Dudley had been doing. We couldn't even tell the difference between the trigger-housing group and the barrel-and-receiver group. Fortunately Dudley, for all his faults, had also learned ingenuity from Garand. Though taps sounded twenty minutes after Coffey had dismissed us, and illumination of any kind was forbidden thereafter, we carried on a night-long seminar with flashlights under blankets. Dudley taught three men, each of them taught three more, and so on. By dawn we were exhausted, but we could do it. At 0450 our DI shrilled his whistle and strode down our line of bunks yelping his usual morning greeting: "OK, shitheads! Drop your cocks and grab your socks!" When we fell out he had already adopted a tragic expression. Clearly he expected us to fail and had rehearsed one of his sinking spells, which were as memorable as the *Titanic*'s. Then, as he blinked in disbelief, each of us in turn took his rifle apart, identifying the bolt camming lug, hammer springs, sears and lugs, and the rest, put the piece back together, and smartly brought it to port arms for inspection. Cheated and smarting, Coffey put us through a grueling day: an hour of calisthenics, a second hour of close-order drill, a third hour of lunging, with fixed bayonets, at straw-stuffed dummies; a session of throwing live hand grenades and then rolling out of a fall (never creep), another session of instruction in how to use short-bladed Kabar knives in hand-to-hand combat (always ripping *up*, into the gut; a downward thrust can be blocked more easily); a cruel hundred-yard sprint wearing gas masks, suffering from inadequate oxygen; and the most idiotic drill of all, snapping in with simulated rifle fire at an imaginary enemy warplane flying overhead. Perhaps this had been practical in World War I, when Fokkers drifted lazily over no-man's-land, but since then strafing fighter planes had developed the speed to flash by before an infantryman could set his feet. Yet we were being taught to aim at the horizon, leading hypothetical Zeroes as hunters lead quail. Long before the sunset gun sounded we all knew we were being punished for Dudley's virtuoso performance. He lost a lot of popularity that day.

None of us, I think, comprehended how all this training would end on battlefields, why we were being taught monstrous things. Our thoughts and our life-style were still largely civilian. Flaked out before lights out, or standing around the lister bag, a container of pure water which resembled a seabag suspended from three tepeed poles, we whistled popular songs — the current hits were "Chattanooga Choo-Choo" and "Blues in the Night" — and shot the breeze much as we would have done at home. I remember us talking about a news item reporting America's annual consumption of seventeen billion cigarettes a year, none of us suspecting that it might be unhealthy, and what it would be like to shack up with Betty Grable or prong Hedy Lamarr. We scorned conscientious objectors and other hambos. We said inane things like, "Hello, Joe, whaddya know?" "I just got back from the vaudeville show." We laughed at pink-toothbrush ads and cartoonist Frank King's frenzied press conference, called to scotch rumors that Gasoline Alley's Skeezix Wallett would be killed in action. The more sophisticated of 618's boots yearned for a roll of moola and a seventy-two in New York, where they could wander along West Fifty-second Street and hear, at spots like the Famous Door, the Onyx Club, and Kelly's Stable, a tumultuous crash of drums heralding "In the Mood" or Harry James leading a wickedly fast "Sweet Georgia Brown," the brass section on their feet, horns swinging like cannon out across the ballroom.

Yet here, as so often, I dissented from the majority of my generation. Swing's orchestration, its utter lack of improvisation, still bored me; I preferred the brilliant riffs of Wild Bill Davidson, Muggsy Spanier, Eddie Condon, J. C. Higgenbotham, and Jack Teagarden. Neither could I share the growing nostalgia, among my fellow former undergraduates in the Quonset, for suburban New England's trellised verandas and croquet lawns. Sometimes memories of my grandmother's ancient homestead, with its wine-red sumac, its fire-red barberries, and its split silver-birch fence, tugged at my heart, but mostly I wanted to be where I was. And so, I think, did the rest, or at any rate the best, of the other boots. Without having the haziest idea of what combat would be, we wanted, in a phrase which sounds quaint today, to fight for our country. Subsequent generations have lost that blazing patriotism and speak of it, if at all, patronizingly. They cannot grasp how proud we were to be Americans.

Because of that pride, we survived jolts like our DI's torments and the sobering realization that citizen-soldiers are very different from professional soldiers. The peacetime Marine Corps assumed that enlisted men were brutes and treated them accordingly. I recall my shock the first time I saw a private being led away in chains. And I remember our collective horror when we all became suspects in a rape case. The victim was the daughter of a garrison officer. At one point in her struggle, she said, she had bitten her assailant's penis. Therefore, the commanding general decided, every man on the island must submit to a "short-arm inspection." The inspection was a massive logistic undertaking, involving thousands of loins. We stood in line hour after hour, awaiting our turn. Along the way, several oddities turned up. One exhibitionist, anticipating an inspection of his short arm sooner or later, had submitted to excruciating pain for the sake of a practical joke. He had caused the words "Hi, Doc!" to be tattooed on the inside of his foreskin. He was immediately put under hack — on what charges I neither know nor can imagine. The complex operation, as complicated in its way as an amphibious landing, produced no evidence whatever. Later I learned that the son of another officer had been arrested and charged. Still later, I met a corpsman who had served as one of the inspectors. He said it had been a shattering experience. It still haunted him. "I have these nightmares," he said hollowly. "All I can see is cocks, cocks, millions of cocks, all of them swarming around me."

My Parris Island triumph came on the rifle range. On Record

Day we fired sixty-six shots, all but ten of them rapid-fire, at targets two hundred, three hundred, and five hundred yards away. Each shot was worth a maximum of five points, for a bull's-eye. Riflemen could qualify in three categories: marksman, sharpshooter, and — very rare, requiring 305 points out of a possible 330 — expert rifleman. I knew I would do well. My M1 was zeroed in to perfection. I had steady hands; I could hold my breath indefinitely, steadying the muzzle; I could fold my right ankle under my buttocks for kneeling shots; and I had 20/10 vision, meaning that what was visible to a man with 20/20 vision at one hundred yards was just as sharp and clear for me at two hundred yards. I was also clever in adjusting my sling. The sling is the leather strap on a rifle, which looks useless to a civilian; it can be extended and looped around the left arm, locking the butt to the right shoulder. Record Day was clear and windless. I hardly missed anything. My score was 317. A colonel congratulated me and told me that 317 was unprecedented. Because of it, because of my adjustment to the Corps, and because of my college education, I was sent directly to the Corps' OCS in Quantico, Virginia. My world brightened a little, as though there were a rheostat on the sun and someone had turned it up a notch. Later I realized that was an illusion — that I wasn't meant to be an officer, at least not by Quantico standards, and that the attempt to make one of me was a grave error.

At Quantico we were quartered, rather grandly, in permanent red-brick barracks, each company with its own squad bays. The chow was excellent. Our rank was private first class, but we wore small brass insignia on our shirt collars, each reading simply "O.C." Weekends we were usually given liberty in Washington, and the departure of the Saturday noon train from Quantico to D.C. was always bedlam; it was said that the only people to wind up on board were those who had come to see their friends off. In the capital there were about six girls for every man. Saturday night a dollar admitted you to the weekly singles dance on the lowest floor of the Washington Hotel. Girls ringed the walls; a bold Marine O.C. could cruise the ballroom slowly, picking the cutest girl and, if he was really insensitive, firing questions about which had cars and apartments. Back at the base, weekday classes were conducted by decorated officers who spoke lucidly, wittily, and always to the point; a single phrase from one of them was worth more than all of poor Coffey's ramblings. There were courses in mapping, leadership, and tactics. Field exercises included forced marches, perimeter defenses, protection of platoon flanks, and how to deal with such crises as unexpected mortaring. Nobody called you a shithead. Some enlisted men on the streets even sirred you.

It was hell.

Parris Island had been an excursion into an exotic world, tolerable even at its worst because you were all in it together, and you knew that together you would all make it. But an officer candidate at Quantico had few friends. The system set each man against the others. If you could artfully make another man look like a fool, you did it; you were diminishing the competition. Everybody was on the muscle. "Shape up here or ship out" was the slogan heard most often. It meant that if you weren't commissioned here as a second lieutenant, and sent on to advanced training, you would be consigned to the serfdom of an enlisted man. But I liked enlisted men, and I wasn't at all sure that I liked these officers-to-be. I recognized their type. I had known many of them, if distantly, in college. They were upper-middle-class snobs, nakedly ambitious conservative conformists, eager to claw their way to the top. In another ten years their uniforms would be corporate gray-flannel suits. Now they yearned to wear officers' dress greens; some were already learning to fieldstrip Sam Browne belts. The thought that they might fail in their pursuit of gold bars turned them into quivering jelly. It would mean, they thought, that they had disgraced themselves in the eyes of their families and friends.

In this setting I was, if not lost, certainly misplaced. At first my dissidence was not apparent. Merits and demerits were awarded with "good chits" and "bad chits" written up by our officer-instructors and noncom-instructors. These brought elation or despair to aspirants, and — this soon became important — affected the stature of each man in the eyes of other candidates. I began accumulating good chits from the first day. In a week I was my company's "first sergeant"; two weeks after that I became "company commander." Thus my stock was high when we were confronted by the school's shabbiest custom, known as "fuck-your-buddy night." Every candidate was required to fill out a form rating his fellows, applying to each the school's ultimate test: "Would you want this man as your kid brother's commanding officer?" At first glance this sounds sensible, but a second thought exposes infamy. The men were rating *themselves*. They were to be judged as judgers of others. Thus those who had been publicly scorned, derided, and baited by our instructors were doomed. The process was discussed with appalling frankness in the squad bays. If a sergeant-instructor had torn a strip off John Doe, then Doe was clearly incompetent to lead kid brothers. Worst of all, Doe, unaware of the ax suspended over him, was playing the same game, putting Richard Roe at the bottom of his list because a major had chided him for tucking his field scarf into his shirt, a doggie practice and therefore unacceptable in the Marine Corps. Thus men suffered the fate of vultures; when one falls sick, the others eat him.

I remembered Thoreau: "Public opinion is a weak tyrant compared with our own private opinion. What a man thinks of himself, that it is which determines . . . his fate." My self-esteem could not survive this process. I thought of putting Doe and Roe at the top, but that would have been irresponsible, and I would have failed to make my point. So I turned in a blank form. The captain who commanded our teachers — an Amherst man whom I had met before the war — summoned me for "office hours," the Marine Corps' equivalent of the navy's "mast," a disciplining ritual. I was asked for an explanation. I gave it. I was warned that disobedience of orders was a grave offense and then coldly dismissed. Overnight my Niagara of good chits dried up. I was being watched. There was one consolation; I was not alone. A mustang-to-be Marine regular named Lacy, a winner of the Navy Cross, had done the same thing for the same reason. Denying a commission to a hero was unthinkable, however. Denying me one was a real possibility. And presently I made it inevitable.

I had already been measured for my officer's uniforms when I came to grief. At Quantico, unlike Parris Island, there was an undercurrent of malice, almost of sadism, in the discipline imposed by noncommissioned instructors. They knew we were fresh youths, most of whom would soon outrank them, and they can hardly be blamed for getting in a few last licks. But sometimes they went too far. On the last Saturday before commissioning, most candidates had arranged weekends in Washington, phoning parents and girls to meet them in Union Station. The last event before our noon dismissal was a rifle inspection. It was an absurd ritual. The basement of our barracks was equipped with steam hoses, guaranteeing immaculate bores. A lieutenant-instructor went down our ranks, peering at our M1s; he congratulated me on mine, the first good chit I'd had since fuck-your-buddy night. He then departed for his own weekend. But we weren't dismissed. A corporal-instructor reexamined our rifles, told us a third of them were filthy, and canceled our weekend liberty. Instead of enjoying the nation's capital we would clean our rifles properly and then roll up our sleeves for a two-day field day. Catholics would not be permitted to go to confession or attend mass. And phone calls were forbidden, which meant that the girls and parents in Union Station would mill around in confusion and anxiety.

Something snapped within me. I had no plans for the weekend; having been thwarted in my inept search for a pushover, even in the hotel ballroom where the odds were six-to-one in my favor, I had decided to stay on the base. But I considered the corporal's order an atrocity. It was like turning over a smooth rock and seeing a leggedy thing scuttle away into darkness. I decided to make what would now be called a nonviolent protest. The corporal found me sitting on my bunk, childishly pouting, staring mulishly at nothing, my rifle across my knees. "Why aren't you cleaning your weapon?" he asked. "Because it's already clean," I said. "Says who?" said he. "The lieutenant," said I. The fact that this was true did not diminish my insubordination. The subsequent proceedings could end only in my dismissal. I knew that. But even when Lacy begged me to go through the motions of obedience for my own sake — not to mention the sake of those who, having rated me high on their fuck-your-buddy sheets, were afraid their judgment would be questioned — I refused.

Thus I was hailed before a hastily assembled court-martial Monday morning. I still wouldn't budge. I told the kindly, troubled lieutenant colonel who presided over the court that I had joined the Marines to fight, not to kiss asses and wade through the very sort of chickenshit we were supposed to be warring against. That, I'm afraid, is exactly how I put it. I made but one request: I asked to be sent to my father's regiment, the Fifth Marines. That was denied me. I was warranted as a corporal, to be jumped to sergeant when I reached my new post in Tent City, New River, North Carolina, where new battalions were forming for imminent transport overseas. Thus I departed Virginia, an immature knight in tin armor. The rheostat was turned down several notches. But I still had my petty pride, not to mention the fact that I now outranked my father.

It was in North Carolina's Tent City that Marine General Alexander A. Vandegrift had assembled the men whom he was to lead on Guadalcanal. Samuel B. Griffith, my old commanding officer, recalls: "Headquarters Marine Corps now began pumping personnel into New River to bring Vandegrift's command to war strength; odd lots arrived almost daily. They were a motley bunch. Hundreds were young recruits only recently out of boot camp at Parris Island. Others were older. . . . These were the professionals, the 'Old Breed' of United States Marines. Many had fought 'Cacos' in Haiti, 'banditos' in Nicaragua, and French, English, Italian, and American soldiers in bars from Shanghai, Manila, Tsingtao, Tientsin, and Peking. They were inveterate gamblers and accomplished scroungers, who drank hair tonic in preference to post exchange beer ('horse piss'), cursed with wonderful fluency, and never went to chapel ('the God-box'). . . . They knew they were tough and they knew they were good. There were enough of them to leaven the Division and to impart to the thousands of younger men a share of both the unique spirit which animated them and the skills they possessed."

I remember one of them, Master Gunnery Sergeant Lou Diamond, as a rumpled old man in soiled dungarees, with an untidy goatee and a pronounced starboard list when he was drunk, which was often. In Tent City he looked like a bum; he reminded me of some cynical old chimpanzee who goes through the motions for the sake of the bananas. But the scatological excesses of a Genet tell us more about a man's fiber than the closely reasoned insights of a Gide. If there had been such a thing as a black belt for mortarmen, Lou Diamond would have won it. On Guadalcanal his accuracy with his 81-millimeter piece was extraordinary. There was a myth that he had sunk a Japanese destroyer by manipulating increments and lobbing a mortar shell down its stack — apocryphal, but the very fact that it was widely believed suggests Lou's immense reputation.

My own reputation was quite different. I became what was called an "intelligence man." In World War II our Table of Organization (TO) provided that the Headquarters Company of each Marine Corps line battalion include a curious unit called an "intelligence section." I was informed that I would lead such a section in my battalion. The unit's duties were defined as "scouting, mapping, interrogation of prisoners, and other normal duties of the intelligence section." Mapping in the middle of battle? Questioning POWs whose language we didn't speak? And what were "other normal duties"? I was told that we were to estimate enemy strength on the battalion's front, to identify enemy units by the flashes on the tunics of their dead, to patrol deep behind enemy lines, to advise our junior officers who were having trouble reading maps, and to carry messages to company commanders whose field radios — SCR-536s and SCR-300s — were out of order.

Only the last three of these — patrolling, reading maps, and carrying messages — proved to be practical. No Marine in the middle of a firefight, however clever he may have been, knew any more about the foe than the rifleman in the next foxhole. Even then the Marine Corps seemed to sense this, for we were being taught other roles: wiring, mortaring, replacing fallen men in our battalion's three companies — D (Dog), E (Easy), and F (Fox). Our section had the additional, grim responsibility of clipping dog tags from the necks of Marines killed in action. To allow for this, five men were added. At times I had as many as nineteen lads on our roster. We called ourselves "the Raggedy Ass Marines." The rest of the battalion called us "the bandits." Whatever the name, I was this odd lot's honcho.

We were in fact very odd. Most of us were military misfits, college students who had enlisted in a fever of patriotism and been rejected as officer candidates because, for various reasons, we either despised the OCS system openly or did not conform to the established concept of how officers should look, speak, and act. For example, Chet Przyastawaki, who had been a running back for Colgate, had a build like Charles Atlas but the voice of a Wagnerian soprano; if he shouted the effect was that of Kirsten Flagstad screaming. Beau Tatum of the University of Virginia had no sense of direction. At Quantico he not only flunked map reading; he repeatedly led patrols into Virginia swamps never penetrated before.

Many, like Przyastawaki, lacked command presence. There was always something lacking the Marine Corps wanted and they didn't have. Rip Thorpe came from Fordham; he had been on the first-string basketball varsity. He would have made a far better section leader than I did, and in fact I went to our battalion officer and told him so. The lieutenant threw me out of his tent. Rip, it developed, had a very black mark beside his name. He thought military traditions, close-order drill, and the rest of it, absolutely ridiculous. So he laughed at them. Not only that; he actually sought out solemn occasions for their comic relief. Let one sergeant of the guard be formally relieved by another and here came Thorpe, roaring up through a cloud of whaleshit, grinning from ear to ear. He was, in a word, a menace to established customs.

So it was with all of us. Bubba Yates of Ole 'Bama, whose accent was clotted with moonlight and magnolias, was walleyed. Dusty Rhodes of Yale was painfully shy; if summoned for any reason, he blushed to the roots of his silky black hair. Barney Cobb of Brown had been insubordinate, like me, and suffered the added stigma of openly admiring Japanese culture. Lefty Zepp was the son of a Louisville physician and had himself been a Harvard premed. He wore his father's .38 Smith and Wesson suspended from his web belt and a fancy pair of custom-made boondockers, and he carried an ivory swagger stick and expensive binoculars. Enlisted men often saluted him. He returned the salutes crisply but said nothing. Like Przyastawaki he had a treacherous voice. It had been arrested in midpuberty, trapped in a sad croak. He sounded like Mickey Rooney playing Andy Hardy; some of the machine gunners began calling him "Andy," but he was still Lefty to us. Probably the brightest of us was an MIT physicist named Wally Moon, a pallid lad with a face like a bleached mole. Wally suffered from exophthalmia, protruding eyeballs, and in addition he wore horn-rimmed glasses that gave him a look of perpetual surprise. He was built close to the ground, like a cabbage — had, in fact, the lowest center of gravity of anyone I've ever seen — and with that and his vision, Quantico had tossed him out. Yet he was the only man I've known who could do the *New York Times* crossword puzzle in ink. The other collegians were equally unusual. Among them was a hypnotist, a midget who had somehow evaded the height requirement at a recruiting depot, and a man with Saint Vitus's dance, or something very like it — grotesque facial tics which, when he was excited, would pursue each other across his features like snipe. Inevitably he was christened "Whipeye," though I tried to see to it that no one in the section called him that to his face, and eventually it was changed to "Blinker." Yet surely that would not have disabled him in combat. Indeed, the only ex-student whose OCS dismissal made sense to me was Shiloh Davidson III, a sly, vulpine Princetonian who was absolutely untrustworthy. Davidson never forgave the Marine Corps for not commissioning him. He nursed an almost pathological hatred of all officers. He was just waiting to give it malevolent expression. Sooner or later his time would come, but I could think of no way to anticipate it.

The rest of my people had never seen a campus but had scored very high on the Corps' aptitude tests. Izzy Levy was from Chicago. He had been a stock boy in a factory; he had told the Walking John that he was a salesman because that, to his knowledge, was the civilian job with the most status. He could, when he chose, look like a half-wit. Yet the tests revealed him as a genius. I have never met anyone else who could add a column of four-digit figures from the *left*. My most supportive lad in those early days was the huskiest and, we all thought then, the most honest man in the section. Although we did not know it, in civilian life Whitey Dumas had been a confidence man. Jailed in Portsmouth on charges of impersonating an officer, he had talked his way out by telling the warden that he could read and speak fluent Japanese. He could do neither, but the lie was so enormous that no one challenged it, and Whitey, knowing that the chances of his encountering a genuine Japanese were minimal, invented a language which looked like, and sounded like, the real article. Our colonel was proud to have an interpreter in the regiment. He ordered Whitey to give Japanese lessons to officers and senior NCOs every day. Whitey did it convincingly, with a blackboard and chalk. I still remember his Jap equivalent for "Voulez-vous coucher avec moi?" It was "Naka-naka eeda koodasai?" It is meaningless, but we all committed it to memory. His hoax went unsuspected until the last months of the war, when, impersonating an officer once more, he was unmasked by a captain, a graduate of one of the Japanese language schools that had been set up after Pearl Harbor and were finally — too late — bearing fruit.

All that lay ahead as we trained in North Carolina, where already there was a widespread awareness in the battalion that the Raggedy Asses were unsuitably bookish, slack on the drill field, and generally beneath the fastidious stateside standards established in the Corps' 169-year history. If there had been such a thing as a military quotient, the spit-and-polish equivalent of an intelligence quotient, our MQ would have been pegged at about 78. It is fair to add that this rating would have been confined to our parade-ground performance. We were regarded as good combat prospects. All of us, I believe, had qualified as sharpshooters, and one other, like me, was an expert rifleman. It was thought (and, as it proved, correctly thought) that we would be useful in battle. Our problem, or rather the problem of our leaders, was that we lacked what the British called Quetta manners. We weren't properly starched and blancoed, weren't martially prepossessing — weren't, in a word, good for the regiment's image.

We were rarely given liberty, because the skipper was ashamed to let civilians see us wearing the Corps uniform. We looked like a slack-wire, baggy-pants act out of a third-rate circus. Shirttails out, buttons missing, fore-and-aft (overseas) caps down around our ears — these were signs that we had lost our initial enthusiasm for being crack troops, either in OCS or on bases elsewhere, and were playing our roles of incorrigible eccentrics to the hilt. We looked like caricatures in the *Leatherneck*, the Marine Corps equivalent of *Yank*, and the only reasons our betters allowed us to stay together, setting a bad example for one another and damaging battalion élan, were our scores on intelligence tests and our special training. Between our arrival in New River and our assignment to Tent City, we had all attended something called intelligence school. It was largely a repetition of Quantico classes. Theoretically we emerged from the school as experts in identifying enemy units, recognizing the silhouettes of enemy planes (Japanese *and* German; we still didn't know where we were going), reconnoitering behind enemy lines, and so on. It was all very vague. In Tent City we carried out exhausting exercises in the Carolina boondocks, inflating black rubber boats and silently guiding them toward beaches, carrying out simulated missions at night, and becoming snarled in bales of communications wire.

I remember one gigantic ball of wire, about fifteen feet in diameter. The lieutenant commanding the communications platoon, also a part of Headquarters Company, came over and stared at it in utter amazement. He had been an AT&T executive in civilian life, and he told me in an almost reverential voice that never, not even when serving as an adviser to one of Central America's banana republics, had he ever seen such an inextricable tangle. "It would take twenty years for a man to straighten that out," he said. "Let me get my camera." He sent the developed prints back to his company's New York office, where, he later told me, they were dismissed as fakes. That was one of our minor disasters. Whenever it was Beau Tatum's turn to keep the map, we were an even greater trial. Our patrols would disappear into the piney woods, subsisting there on K and C rations, utterly lost, until we were found thrashing around in the bush and led back by a rescue party from the battalion's 81-millimeter mortar platoon, our long-suffering neighbors in Tent City.

This sounds, I know, like an American version of Jaraslov Hasek's *Good Soldier Schweik*. It wasn't, really. In our own odd way, we loved the Marine Corps; it was the emperor's clothes, not the emperor himself, that we ridiculed. At the time we thought of this training period as a waste of time. Actually, it was a useful shakedown cruise. Like couples in forced marriages, we were compelled to explore one another's traits. On the whole we liked what we found. Discovering common tastes, our morale rose. Part of the section formed a quintet, built around Przyastawaki; they sang songs like "Moonlight Bay," "The Old Apple Tree," "Someone to Watch Over Me," and "Let the Rest of the World Go By." Another part, with some overlapping from the singers, played hearts night and day. (Barney, Zepp, and I, intellectual snobs, played chess.) We developed an affected jargon; we said, not "shit," but "fecal matter from a desiccated yak." Because, despite the TO, we were after all just heavily laden infantrymen, we groaned, "My aching back," or, simply, "My back." Not long before we boarded troop trains for the West Coast, we were all offered seventy-two-hour passes. There would be no second chance, we were warned, but I nevertheless declined, believing my case for leave later would be stronger without it; I was hoping for a few days with my mother and didn't want to jeopardize that. Most of the others took off for New York in an incredible automobile they had bought for twenty-five dollars. It broke down repeatedly on both the trip up and the return — they had just five hours in Manhattan — but afterward it sounded like so much fun that I wished I'd gone.

Meanwhile I was trying to learn to be a leader. It would never be easy for me. I felt bogus. But by giving my people a free rein, and arguing their cases with the skipper and staff NCOs, I was slowly building a reservoir of goodwill. During our North Carolina weeks I had just two problems: Hunky O'Banion and Shiloh Davidson. Hunky thought I was soft. He was a born griper. He was forever threatening to write his congressman, whose name, unfortunately, he didn't know. Though he was naturally bright, his values were those of the Philadelphia slum in which he had grown up. He expected an iron hand; when I refused to flex one, he kept trying to incite me. Since I knew he had been a Golden Gloves boxer, I was wary of him. I sought appeasement. It didn't work; soon he was taunting me openly, calling me "Priscilla." The others were enjoying the spectacle, so finally, reluctantly, I invited him to join me in the boondocks. He knocked me down. I rose and he knocked me down again. And again. And again. My nose felt dented and my mouth was full of blood, but with the help of a nearby sapling I labored back upright each time. In the beginning Hunky enjoyed himself, but then it became too easy. After I had been flattened five times, he muttered, "Ah, screw it," and strode back to camp. I cannot say I gained anything from this one-sided bout, but clearly he had lost something. He started showing up in sick bay each morning, complaining of a strained sacroiliac. Back problems were known as the surest way to a survey; they always puzzled physicians. (Later, whenever we were headed for combat, Whitey Dumas, the con man, would moan and wiggle his shoulder muscles until the sighing corpsman sent him to a base hospital.) So Hunky returned to Philadelphia, to the vast relief of one scrawny sergeant of Marines.

Shiloh Davidson was another matter. He was, and plainly considered himself to be, at the opposite end of the social spectrum from Hunky, though Hunky was too isolated in his own cultural cage to be touched by Shiloh's snubs. The Davidsons were in the Social Register, members of the New York Yacht Club, and given to annual tours of Europe. Shiloh had nothing against me, provided I didn't throw my genealogy at him, but his feelings toward officers continued to border on the homicidal. One day he was routinely assigned to police duty in Officers' Country. This entailed picking up debris, squaring away tents, cleaning up the head, and filling the lister bag. At some point that day he was struck by a mad flash of inspiration. Since officers regarded enlisted men as numbskulls, he reasoned, he would offer them proof of it. Water and gasoline were kept in almost identical green five-gallon "jerry-cans," distinguished by the color of the X's on the outside, white for water and

yellow for gasoline. The lister bag was empty, so Shiloh filled it —
with gas. A first lieutenant, returning parched from a training patrol, filled his canteen cup, swallowed once, and spluttered fuel all
over himself. The strange thing is that Davidson's assumption was
proved right. No one reproached him except me; for the first time
in my life I threatened another man and meant it. Lieutenant Colonel Krank, very upset, vented his wrath on the innocent platoon
leader. The lieutenant was declared a fire hazard, confined to his
tent for three days, forbidden visitors, and ordered to give up cigarettes for a week. The poor victim was a chain-smoker. I thought
he, at least, might give me a hard time. He never mentioned it to
me. Nobody expected much from the Raggedy Ass Marines then.

Our regimental commander, Colonel Horace F. Hastings,
USMC, a.k.a. the Old Turk, was the kind of colorful hard-charger
that the Marine Corps has always valued highly. The years had
shrunk his slabs of muscle to gristle, and he had a grooved, wind-
bitten face with wattles that turned crimson when he was enraged,
which was often. I remember his brooding eyes, corded neck, sinewy hands, veined nose, the touch of crimson at his temples, and
the way his lips nibbled at each other, like those of a nervous horse.
It was reported that he was a native of Vulture's Gulch, Arizona, a
community which, I later discovered, does not exist. If the town
was bogus, so, in part, was he. Our colonel, though doubtless
brave, was not very bright. Inside his second-rate mind, one felt,
a third-rate mind was struggling toward the surface. But on
one point officers, NCOs, and privates were in full agreement:
he was a terrific swordsman. The evening before we sailed for
the Solomons I saw him surrounded by young women in the lobby
of San Diego's U. S. Grant Hotel, wearing dress blues and all
his decorations, striking the lordly pose of a czar carefully choosing tonight's bedmate. (Recently I learned he is living in London,
an octogenarian pleasuring English girls who hadn't been born
when we fought under him.) In the field he adopted a piratical
stance, wearing a bleached khaki fore-and-aft cap pushed rakishly
to the back of his head, his hands on his lithe hips, his chin tilted

up aggressively. He looked every inch the gifted commander. Alas, he wasn't. He was relieved in the middle of his first battle for incompetence.

He was the most redundant man I have ever known, forever saying things like "Eat lots of food and plenty of it," "Here in Dixie we're in the Deep South," and "Keep fit and healthy." In San Diego he announced: "We're going to sail tomorrow aboard ship." Our elusive Japanese language interpreter would, he told me, meet officer and senior noncoms on the *General C. G. Morton*'s "fantail, in the stern." On Guadalcanal he predicted: "Sunrise will come at dawn."

The Marine Corps was his whole life. The Corps birthday is November 10. On such occasions, even when in the jungle, he would wear all his medals — not just the ribbons, but the actual medals — and preside over an officers' banquet. The high moment was always his toast to the Corps, during which he recited all Corps victories, including, erroneously, Bull Run, where leathernecks broke and ran. (Most of their officers had defected to the Confederate Marine Corps.) The United States went unmentioned, and though the regimental colors were there, the Stars and Stripes was conspicuously absent.

The Old Turk had had a strange career. Bit by bit we pieced it together from Old Salts, thirty-year men who had fought with him in World War I. Hastings was a mustang. In 1918 he had been a First Soldier, a Topkick. At the height of the Saint-Mihiel offensive he had misunderstood an order; the word was passed to fall back, but he thought it meant the opposite. So while the others withdrew — he thought they were bolting — Hastings plunged ahead. As it happened, the Germans had just decided to retreat. So he seemed to have taken the position single-handed. He won a Navy Cross and put up second-lieutenant bars. Between wars he picked up a Silver Star and two Purple Hearts in the banana republics. Until he was appointed our commanding officer, he had never led a large body of troops. Indeed, his most notable professional accomplishment was the invention of a device designed to catch insects.

A wit in the Third Battalion spread the rumor that Hastings's middle initial stood for "Flytrap." Truth is often veiled in myth, and so it was here. Bedeviled by bugs in his Caribbean campaigns, he had devised a complicated cage, with many tunnels, chambers, and mazes, which, he believed, would ensnare flies faster than the stickiest flypaper. The result was a celebrated field manual. Featuring detailed drawings and precise instructions (". . . the prey form a cone of dispersion, a beaten zone, with the slope of Plane 'A' determining the approximate curve of the trajectories . . ."), it was adopted by the Navy Department as the "M1-A1 Flytrap." All the information necessary to put the contraption together was in the manual, but until he became our leader, neither the inventor nor anyone else had actually built one. Now he ordered it done. Our company constructed a snare, faithfully following the directions, and we were told that the colonel would inspect it at 0900 the following Saturday to count the number of flies ambushed. A day passed, then another. The trap was empty. The regiment confronted its first crisis. If we stayed on course, Saturday would bring catastrophe. It would be as though Odysseus, having said his farewells before leaving for a historic journey, went down to the sea only to find that the boat had left without him. Foreseeing this, Hastings's executive officer grimly ordered that enlisted personnel capture ten flies each and put them in the trap. Mike Powers gave me this appalling directive and threatened to strangle me when I asked for it in writing. I told the section to think of it as a challenge. It was; we barely beat the Saturday deadline, but we did make it. The colonel was obviously pleased. Heartened, he told the exec that if that many bugs could be enmeshed by a trap with one opening, why not catch twice as many with two openings? The exec — for the first, and to my knowledge, the only, time — made a genuine contribution to the war effort. If there were two entries, he discreetly suggested, the quarry could fly in one and out the other. Hastings pondered this. At last he said it was a good idea with lots of merit. A week later the trap was quietly dismantled.

Except for his dismissal — I was present when he was fired, and was embarrassed by his humiliation — that was my worst experience under the colonel. It was not, however, the worst for certain collegiate ex-jocks. Athletes tended to join the Marine Corps; their values and skills were appreciated there. One morning Hastings and Colonel Branch Packard, commander of the Fourth Marines, discovered that each could form a complete all-American football team from the men on his roster. Born competitors, they decided to have a football game. The fact that the temperature was 103 degrees in the shade didn't discourage them. Neither did the absence of a field; that was what enlisted men were for. So we cleared a more or less level area 120 yards long and 60 yards wide. Goalposts were erected. Then we tried to remove all the stones, an insuperable task. The players, most of them junior officers, had suggested they play touch, but both colonels indignantly rejected the idea; *Marines* wouldn't settle for sissy stuff. The day of the big game dawned hot and muggy. A little podium had been erected at the fifty-yard line, protected from the sun by a huge green parasol. There the two regimental commanders stood erect, like sahibs at a durbar, while the sweating, gasping jocks, wearing only camouflaged skivvy shorts, toiled and grunted. Most of the rest of us encircled the field, cheering mechanically, though I left in disgust after the first few plays. Later I learned that the navy doctors, alarmed at the incidence of heat prostration on the field, had demanded that the contest end after the first quarter. It was a scoreless tie.

Nevertheless, the notion that good athletes make good fighters persisted. Had our leaders paid closer attention, they would have found that ectomorphs and endomorphs fight just as well on the battlefield as mesomorphs. Whatever Wellington said about Waterloo being won on the playing fields of Eton, it didn't apply in the Pacific. The war against Japan was won by the muscular, the skinny, the fat, the long, the short, and the tall. It was won in the gut.

Once we boarded our troop train for California, I knew my expectations of fighting the Nazis were a pipe dream. Now I would have to learn to hate the Japanese, a people whom at the moment I hated less than, say, I hated the troop train. We slept there in built-in tiers of bunks, like those in SS concentration camps, and we all swore that no one could be confined in closer quarters and survive. (We were wrong. Troop transports — APAs — followed the same principle and were even more cramped.) Like Lenin in his sealed train we rolled swiftly and unheralded across the Deep South, Arkansas, Oklahoma, the Texas panhandle, New Mexico, Arizona, and, finally, California, where we bivouacked under canvas in Linda Vista, a few miles north of San Diego. The First Marine Division had sailed for Guadalcanal from San Francisco, Norfolk, and New Orleans, but our port of embarkation would be Dago. This was my introduction to southern California, and my first impression was that it was wonderful. At dawn we would rise in a gentle mist, which would burn off by midmorning. The rest of the day was fresh, sunny, and glorious. The harbor was sapphire blue, the shore rocks emerald. At dusk ribbons of purple streaked the hills inland, the western sky reddened, and the sun's drop was spectacular. Most evenings we had liberty in Dago. Nights we slept beneath blankets.

Recently — some thirty-five summers later — I returned to San Diego. Everyone had told me I wouldn't recognize it, but I did. The smog was new, and Linda Vista had vanished beneath weeds and new construction, but the part of the city I knew best was still familiar. The Grant Hotel, though seedy and dwarfed by the gleaming Little Americana Westgate Hotel across the street, looks as it did from the outside, which is mostly how I saw it then. The uniform store still stands on Broadway, four blocks from the waterfront, though it now provides uniforms for nurses, chauffeurs, doormen, orderlies, elevator operators, and policemen. Balboa Park is largely unchanged. A short walk from there takes you to the enormous Marine Corps parade ground, where with a little tug you watch field-hatted DIs chewing out trembling boots. Across the water an immense aircraft carrier looms grayly. The gaping docks at the foot of Broadway are unused, but if you close your eyes you can recall boarding an APA wearing a field marching pack, your seabag on your shoulder, saluting the ensign on the fantail even though you couldn't see him. And a brief stroll from the transport bays takes you to the railroad station, where I — or, more correctly, Barney — met my mother.

This was a terrible time for her. She had already lost her husband; my baby brother and I were all she had. To support herself, she had taken a secretarial job at the Federal Reserve Bank in Oklahoma City. We had both assumed I would have at least a few days' leave before sailing. As it turned out, the only way she could say goodbye to me was to come to Dago. That day, for unexplained reasons, all liberty was canceled, so I went over the hill, climbing a wire fence. Barney went with me. By now we were skilled in the arts of evasion; we could almost enter a phone booth and leave by a side door. And we were deft improvisers. We didn't know whether my mother would be arriving by train or by bus — actually she was aboard a train, standing up for most of the thirty-six-hour trip — so he covered one depot while I covered the other. We met every batch of arrivals for twelve hours. Then he found her, and I embraced her and took her to the Grant, where I had hired a room. The manager intercepted us outside the elevators. She has always looked much younger than she is. He misunderstood our relationship, and I was about to fly at him when he recoiled, hopping, and apologized.

We ate at a little red waterfront sandwich shop, strolled around the square outside the hotel, and returned to her room. For the first time since leaving for Parris Island I could take a real bath; like Blanche DuBois, in my youth I felt deprived without frequent soaks in a hot tub. And then the two of us talked hour after hour. The mother-child dyad is central to any man's development, and this was especially true of me, for I had always been more anima than animus, more "feminine" in the Jungian sense — sensitive, poetic, creative, warm — than "masculine": direct, orderly, logical, assertive. I had begun to change since putting on a uniform, but my mother was still the sun around whom I orbited. We reminisced about my childhood, about nursery stories from those days, even sang some nursery songs. We didn't talk much about my father. That wound was too recent even to have begun healing. Later I remembered those hours of tender talk when I read why

MacArthur, in writing postwar Japan's constitution, gave Nipponese women the vote. It was, he said, the most effective way of
curbing samurai militarism. Men make war, he told his staff.
Women hate it. Certainly my mother did, and no one had better
reason. This frail, loving woman, incapable of hurting a soul, had
been raised by the fierce Confederate Valkyries and shattered by the
death of the war-crippled man she loved. Now she had to see her
son off to even more terrible fighting.

She gave me a watch, which miraculously survived the war and
still keeps good time. Then she rode down to the lobby with me
and we embraced. Outside on Broadway I looked back through a
window. She was still where I had left her, standing alone, crying.
Our eyes locked. I turned away, my eyes also damp. In many ways
I was still a boy.

But I wanted to be a man, and an essential step in the process —
one my mother wouldn't have understood — was the forfeiture of
my own virginity. To every thing there is a season, and a time to
every purpose under the heaven; a time to be born, and a time to
die; a time to kill, and a time to heal. There is also a time to get
laid, and I was due. We weren't going to be stateside much
longer — there was ominous activity around the APAs by the
docks — but my prospects for strange purple sins were improving.
I was surer of myself, readier to take charge; being a sergeant had
done that for me, too. And I had a couple of good leads. The best
one came from an unlikely source, a fellow sergeant named Bareass
Miller. Even by Marine Corps standards, Miller was crude. If he
felt horny and no relief was in sight, he said, he would "walk into a
crowd of women, pull out my cock, and burst out crying." That
hadn't been necessary here, he said, because a girl named Taffy
Meredith, from his Midwest hometown, was working for the government in a town south of Dago. She had lined up a bombshell for
him. He had screwed Taffy herself before enlisting. "She puts
out," he said, "and she's classy." Her father was a judge. She had
been a coed at Michigan State; now she had a defense job. She
thought it patriotic. Besides, all the boys had left the campus.

Bareass had told her he'd try to find someone suitable for her here. "Lovely tail, more your type than mine," he said. He'd phone her, tell her I was collegiate, and set up a tryst.

We met in the San Diego Zoo. The lioness was pissing at the time. There I was, as agreed, and just as I heard a feminine rustle approach, this coarse beast ejected a stream of urine like water from a garden hose. I stared at it, enthralled and blushing, wondering darkly whether Bareass could have arranged this — it would have been just like him. Then I heard the girl giggling. She touched my sleeve and said softly, "Slim?" The lioness finished and I turned, doffing my barracks cap and saying, "Taffy?" Neither of us spoke for a long moment. She was giving my fraternity ring a sidelong glance, and I was speechless. In a lifetime a man may encounter three or four young women with such extraordinary figures, and hers was my first. But there was more to her than that, an indefinable air of breeding. Bareass was right; Taffy had class. Her upper lip was long and aristocratic; her neck high; her smallest movements dainty; her spill of hair just the right shade of light auburn. Altogether she was beautiful in a hieratic, mystic way. Her dress was designed along classic Greek lines: white matte silk crossed cleverly at her throat and then fell away in liquid folds. Her arms were bare. Earrings were her only jewelry. On my initiative — I *think* it was mine; in our generation a girl like that always made you believe it was yours — we impulsively held both hands, face to face, and rocked back on our heels like a couple in a square dance, appraising each other in a growing silence. At that time less than 1 percent of the population had a college background — a tenth of today's. We paired off, speaking almost simultaneously: Michigan State and Massachusetts State, Chi Omega and Lambda Chi, varsity swimmer and cheerleader. Simultaneously we both burst into laughter, as though we had heard a marvelous intramural joke. In less than a minute we found that back east we had three mutual friends, and in another minute, still laughing but holding just one hand now, her right and my left, we were frolicking through Balboa Park naturally and easily and, we thought, as gracefully as Fred Astaire and Ginger Rogers, pausing to sing the old songs, so recently heard on campuses across America but already dated:

We'll build a bungalow big enough for two,
Big enough for two my honey, big enough for two,
Tua-luma-lumma . . .

Please do to me what you did to Marie
Last Saturday night, Saturday night,
First you caressed her, then you undressed her . . .

And words which still haunt me, though my college students today tell me they are sexist:

A man without a woman is like a ship without a sail,
Is like a boat without a rudder, is like a kite without a tail . . .

On a park bench she raised her hands to her hair, and the movement did something for her. I asked her about her work, and we were howling before she could finish: ". . . in the data-analysis group of the aptitude-test subunit of the worker-analysis section of the division of occupational analysis and manning tables of the bureau of labor utilization of the War Manpower . . ." We dried our eyes after that one, and she said seriously that she had heard scuttlebutt about the Women Marines. She intended to join up. Later I heard more about these female leathernecks. The men in the Corps called them "BAMs," for "broad-assed Marines," and they called the men "HAMs," for "hairy-assed Marines." Men like Bareass enjoyed such exchanges, but whatever Taffy and I were, we weren't vulgar. I know what we thought we were. We thought we were in love. Already on the bench, once the giggling stopped, we were caressing each other, our bodies arching, yearning for each other. It seemed remarkable at the time, but of course it wasn't. In peacetime we wouldn't have reached this point until the eighth or ninth date, but the clock and the calendar were moving relentlessly, and it seemed a millennium since either of us had met someone from the same background.

In my next incarnation I may choose not to fall in love in war-time, not unless I am at least a major and can afford a room of my own. Taffy and I had literally nowhere to go. Already other couples were passing slowly, eyeing the bench. We parted then, but the next night I took her to a movie, *Mrs. Miniver,* during which I established that Taffy had an active tongue, wore Munsingwear, and responded to my restless foreplay with the normal prickling of erectile tissues, labial weights, and thickenings. As the last reel spun she explored me. I was fully tumescent. My fingers entered her — two of them, then three, then four. She whispered: "Girls are sort of elastic."

All this was wrong, and I think it was jarring for both of us. Such a poem of a girl deserved to be wooed by candlelight, with gentle reassurances and Debussy in the background. At the very least I should have given her a whirlwind courtship, with gifts and flowers and, above all, a mattress. We were not this kind of people. But they were that kind of times. And I had to keep glancing furtively at my watch. I was due back at Linda Vista in a half hour. Payday was two days away, and I wanted to reach an understanding *now.* After the show, in a rundown diner which advertised "Scotch-type" whiskey and "hamburger-type" meat — one of those places with two price lists, servicemen paying more — I took my courage *à deux mains* and made a puerile remark, one I'd been rehearsing during the movie, about the taste of the original apple remaining in our mouths. Again she made it easy for me. She eyed me, then dropped her eyes, sighed, and said, "I guess I'm kind of roundheeled." I looked blank. The expression was new to me. So she said, "You know — a pushover. Miller probably told you. I've been naughty, really *bad,* a couple of times. I was nervous about this blind date." She took my hand and looked up again. "But now I'd like to be with you if you want."

In those days hotel clerks gave couples a hard time if the woman wasn't wearing a wedding ring. She said she could borrow one. I stammered something about reserving a room at the Grant right now, and after a telephone call there, we were all set for Saturday night. There was a bad moment when I came out of the phone booth. She was nursing her elbows. She bowed her head and mumbled, "I feel dirty." But when I kissed her she kissed back, hard. I was elated. I knew Powers would cover for me. We would have the whole night. As we parted her eyes widened, then looked heavy. Her mouth softened. Her lips silently said, "Slim." She rose and left, her walk slow and swaying.

Back at the camp, in the NCO slopchute, Bareass leered and demanded, within hearing of a half-dozen other sergeants, a full report on my patrol. I was angry, which was unreasonable of me. He, after all, had made my assignation possible. And although I was trying to keep my romantic feelings on a lofty plane, on another level they were quite primitive, even exploitive. Part of me wanted to tumble the girl out of sheer lewdness and male vanity. I wanted to be in like Flynn. Try as I might to suppress it, a crude tabloid headline kept flashing across my mind: MANCHESTER GETS ASHES HAULED / PUTS BLOCKS TO KNOCKOUT COED. I wanted to take out bragging ads, rent billboards, buy air time to announce that I had hit the mother lode.

Nevertheless there *was* more to our relationship than that. I believed that I had adored her at first sight, that I wanted more than carnal knowledge of her. I felt sure that each of us could live joyously in the other. Subconsciously, I suppose, I wanted to leave my seed in her before sailing. Subconsciously, perhaps, she wanted to receive it. Our time together had been cruelly brief — though thousands of others had made wartime marriages after a few hours' acquaintance — but already I had an idealized image of her, and I believed that was true of her image of me, too. I had to be tender with her, and selfless. Coupling would mean more to her than it meant to, say, the lioness. I was right. To my everlasting sorrow, I was right.

Paydays were erratic in the Marine Corps, but liturgical. The paymaster sat behind a little desk in the company compound, and we formed a line in front of him. I thought he would never get to me. I was at the end of the line; I had been packing my gear. Taffy and I were to meet three hours later, outside the uniform shop, as soon as she could leave work and take the Ramona bus to Dago. Actually I had no idea how much dough I would get. My sergeant's pay was seventy-eight dollars a month, but because the paymaster's visits were irregular, and there were deductions for war bonds, I had never given cash much thought. I only knew that since my mother's visit I had been stone broke; I'd had to borrow to take Taffy to the pictures. Had I been better informed, I might have anticipated the monstrous injustice which was about to be visited upon me. It happened, from time to time, that the Marine Corps would discover that it had been systematically overpaying a man. In that event, the account would be squared on the next payday. The paymaster patiently explained this to me as I stood, baffled and then apprehensive, before him. At last I said, "How much do I get?" Wordlessly he slapped a quarter on the desk. "That's *all?*" I cried. He nodded. And I knew that there was no appealing a paymaster's decision.

Frantically I ran around the camp, trying to lay the sleeve on friends. All the Raggedy Ass Marines were gone. There was Bareass, but he and his girl had a date at the Grant, too. In his tactful way he suggested I take it up with the chaplain. So I was left with an erection and two bits. Twenty-five cents bought exactly three minutes of conversation between Linda Vista and Ramona. I called Taffy, but it was impossible to explain such a situation to a girl, any girl, in three minutes. She was at first startled, then subdued — her voice so low that I could hardly hear her. I promised to get the money together somehow. Would she meet me outside the uniform store next Saturday? She mumbled; I didn't understand her and said so, and she said in a slightly higher register, "No, Sunday. At the zoo, where we were." I was about to tell her I would change the reservation at the Grant, but then my time was up. The line went dead.

During the next week I raised every nickel I could. I borrowed shamelessly from the Raggedy Asses when they returned from liberty that night. I would have robbed a bank if I had known where one was. Altogether I amassed over a hundred dollars, enough to rent the hotel's honeymoon suite. In the zoo I waited a long, long time. Darkness was coming down upon the park when she arrived in a dull frock, with a haggard, heartbreak look and eyes which avoided mine. She wore no ring. I studied the dress. "Did you molt?" I asked with hollow cheeriness. Then I tried to take her in my arms. She turned her cheek and let me peck it. She was standing stiffly, her elbows at her sides, clasping her purse as though she were afraid someone might snatch it. Someone did; I did. Again I tried to embrace her. She folded her arms high over her shoulders and pivoted away in that way girls did then when they were embarrassed, or caught off balance. "Let's sit on the bench," she said. The weight of unshed tears hung in her voice. Feigning confidence, I told her I had made another reservation at the Grant and felt stunned when she shook her head decisively. We really didn't know each other, she said; we had been crazy to think of such a thing; she wasn't that kind of a girl; she didn't want her name to become a barracks joke. The words made no sense, but the bleak, funereal music was clear. She had been ready the other day, but she wasn't now. The wine had passed its point. She finally said that we mustn't see each other again.

Stricken, I just sat there, 140 pounds of bone, gristle, and dismay. I felt a gray, hopeless lassitude. Looking back across the years, I yearn to tell the Sergeant: *Play for time, you jerk. Take her to another movie; get back on the campus track; let her laugh and warm up and then take her; she'll want you then.* Instead I idiotically hummed a few bars of "Something to Remember You By," the broadest possible hint at the memorable something I wanted from her. She retrieved her purse and took a tighter grip on it. Fighting the pain in my chest, I looked over her shoulder at the night sky. A roving moon sailed through a white corridor of cloud; then a wind vexed the sky and stars were visible through rags of clouds. Taffy fell silent. I glanced down. A moonbeam rested on a long diagonal across her face, from eyes to lips. She had nothing more to say; neither did I. We left the park holding hands once more, but now as children walk hand in hand from a playground that has been closed, this one, for us, having just been closed forever. At the time I invested the scene with the dimensions of tragedy, silver rain slanting on cruel lilacs. In fact it was a temporary disappointment, like having to give up a good book before reading the last chapter.

It seems merely poignant now, regrettable but remote. I knew little about Taffy, and nothing about war. At that time I wasn't even aware of the naval hospital elsewhere in the park. Certainly I never dreamed that I would one day lie there, tormented by memories of horrors which, the day Taffy and I said goodbye, would have been incomprehensible to me.

After the war, when my first book was published, I heard from her. She had become a Pan Am stewardess and was living in Paris. I was newly married, so my reply was merely cordial. But I still have flickering memories of her. As we parted on Broadway a juke-box somewhere was playing, *We'll meet again, don't know where, don't know when.* It wasn't true, yet I think of Taffy whenever I hear the lyrics of those years, when the Dipsy Doodle was a thing to beware, and there was going to be a certain party at the station, when the lights went on again all over the world; when she wouldn't sit under the apple tree with anyone else but me, and would walk alone, and be so nice to come home to, till the end of time. Thanks for the memory, Taffy. Here's looking at you, kid.

That left Mae. Or May. I never learned how she spelled her name, and I'm not absolutely sure she knew, either. She was very dumb: a bleached blonde in her late twenties, a borderline alcoholic who would have turned pro if she hadn't had money coming in from another source and hadn't, rightly, feared the competition. Her problem was that her orifice was tight. But I had no inkling of that beforehand. All I knew was that a gunnery sergeant in Fox Company had met her in a dance hall south of the new Camp Pendleton and shacked up with her. The gunny had made a habit of passing on this sort of information — he was known, I groan to report, as the battalion's lay preacher.

So I went from Taffy to Mae, from the sublime to the ridiculous. Mae did have a certain gargoyle charm; she was a character out of George S. Kaufman by Ring Lardner, with Al Capp acting as accoucheur. I had never known such a woman. If Taffy was upper middle class, Mae was underclass. Her complexion was purpled by past pleasures, and after my second drink in the dance hall her mouth developed a disconcerting way of seeming to wander all over her features. She was wearing about twenty bracelets — she sounded like a light machine gun when she moved. From a distance she had a sepia thirties prettiness, but her mouth had been eroded by at least a decade of promiscuity. Her voice had the timbre of a saxophone. When she raised it, it sounded as if she was telling somebody to sack Troy. She accepted my assurance that I was a friend of the gunny without batting a false eyelash, and before I could even order new setups she had yanked me to my feet with a startling flex of muscle, crying, "Let's dance!" That was her first remark. Her second, after a half-dozen clumsy steps, was: "Just because I let you dance with me don't mean I'm going to let you get into my pants." Her third — by now her hips were really swatting me — was: "On the other hand, it don't mean I won't."

She had my riveted attention. Back at the table she chugalugged both our drinks ("Booze ain't good for a man, dear, it takes the lead out of his pencil"); then, at her instruction, I paid an outrageous price for a fifth of Southern Comfort and gripped my shrinking roll. "So much for prelims," she said practically, seizing the bottle, taking my arm, and kissing my cheek with slack, rubbery lips. "Now I guess you want to get your end wet. I got Freddy's car outside." Dazed, wondering who Freddy might be, I meekly followed her to a coupe in the lot behind the hall. I had hardly slipped behind the wheel when she was in my arms. Only the young and the short can achieve coitus under those circumstances; I had youth, but I was six feet tall, and after several acrobatic attempts Mae conceded that we couldn't make it here. We would have to go to her furnished room. I glided out to the highway, following her directions. "There's just this one thing," she said, powdering her nose and rattling on as I raced toward whatever nest she had. "I've got this new bed. One of them Murphy beds? It came new last week. I think they sold me a lemon." She patted my arm. "But you'll fix it for sure." I heard a liquid sound. She was gulping Southern Comfort from the bottle.

Chez elle was an incredible warren. Langley Collier couldn't have improved upon her spread: a snafu of clothes and jars and empty bottles, more bracelets, necklaces, a douche bag, shards of broken glass, unraveled toilet paper, and at least three mousetraps littered the floor. To an anal compulsive, it was shocking. The only illumination was provided by a bridge lamp which had fallen on its side. By this light I saw that Mae, between gulps from the bottle, was stripping. She looked at me with transomed eyes. She said, "Hurry up." She was naked now, and I saw what looked like a tattoo on her lower abdomen, just above her pelt. It *was* a tattoo. I held the lamp closer and incredulously read: "Abandon Hope All Ye Who Enter Here."

She was beaming down at me, obviously proud. "Oh, come *on!*" I said, disgust momentarily mastering lust. She pouted. "It was Freddy's idea." I asked who Freddy was. She said, "My husband." I cried, "You've got a *husband?*" "Oh, he's over in England, in the Eighth Air Force," she said casually. "Probably screwing one of them duchesses. Just think of it as lend-lease. The old switcheroo. Sometimes one of his buddies comes by and takes a poke at anybody I'm with. But you can't make an omelet without breaking eggs," she ended inanely.

So that was how she lived: on an allotment. And yet, against all sense, I too had undressed. She looked and gasped: "Jesus, I don't know, I'm on the tight side. . . ." But in the next instant our tongues were entwined. If it hadn't been for the broken glass, and uncertainty about what else lay underfoot, I think I would have floored her there. Instead, I looked around for the bed. She panted, "In the wall," and pointed to two straps dangling from what could only be the Murphy bed. "Take one and I'll take the other." She had been right; it *was* defective. The strength of the springs holding it upright was almost unbelievable. I stood back, wiping my brow. "Some Marine!" she jeered. I asked, "How do you get it down alone?" She said, "I can't. I sleep down the hall with my girl friend Mabel. I complained to the company. They're sending somebody down tomorrow A.M."

By a herculean effort, during which I expected a rupture any moment, and with ferocious tugging from Mae, the bed descended. Almost at once it started to rise again. We grabbed it. "That's the other thing," she said defensively. "It don't lock down good. The catch was put on wrong." She showed me. I tugged. It was like trying to pull a grenade pin with numb fingers. I skinned a knuckle and wiggled the gizmo back and forth until it held. Then, drenched with sweat and smelling of it, we boarded the mattress and I mounted her in the missionary position. I didn't fit. Mae reached around, groped in the debris below, and produced a jar of Vaseline. "We'll give you a grease job, that's what we'll do," she said confidently. I tried again. She started to moan, but I simply couldn't penetrate her. Then the bed began to rise again. Following the law of gravity, my knees slipped from her hips to her armpits, bringing my equipment over her chin. She shrieked: "I ain't gonna eat that thing!"

I apologized, explained, and told her we'd have to start again, by which I meant the bed; the rest would have to wait. Again we brought it down on the floor and worked on the catch. Mae, who had felt horny, was beginning to feel rage. She was hanging over me, her lank hair shaking and that mobile mouth slurring obscene invective. I told her I wasn't very good at that sort of thing. She heckled: "And you call yourself a man!" "But not a mechanic," I said, wincing as I lost skin to the damned catch. She said: "Wait a minute! I just remembered — I got instructions!" Bare, dripping perspiration, my desire slackening, I studied the leaflet she brought under the dim light bulb. It resembled the manual on detail-stripping a BAR, or the one for building the colonel's flytraps. Mae was gurgling Southern Comfort; I think she had already given up. But I felt challenged. Shafts, rods, gears — it completely baffled me. Still, I read on. Like Mount Everest for Mallory, the Murphy bed was There.

We made two more feeble attempts. If we had been physically compatible, I think I would have rolled us off the mattress and chanced the glass, the mousetraps, and whatever else lurked below. But it was useless. My strength was ebbing. By the time I grappled with my skivvies and khakis, I was not only frustrated, I was also suffering from motion sickness. I rolled off the levitating mattress and left Mae sprawled across the litter below, snoring and belching. The bottle was almost empty. I wanted to break it over either her head or the bedstead. But I was too tired, and too sore with lover's nuts, for either. Instead, I stumbled downstairs, found a pay phone, and called a taxi. Sexwise, my score was still zero to zero. And after paying the cabbie for the long trip, I was broke again. I couldn't even afford a tip. The driver was surly. I was surlier.

Nine hours later I led my section aboard the APA *Morton*, into a compartment below the waterline which would be our pent home throughout the seventeen-day voyage to Guadalcanal. Two light meals would be served each day; we would have to bolt each down, while standing, in a maximum of three minutes. We could expect to grow filthier each day; the only showers would be saltwater showers. We couldn't exercise — there was no room — or, for security reasons, remain on deck, where we might catch a breeze, after darkness. Already, as the winches shrieked and the transport built a welter of water beneath her hull, we were encountering one of the miseries of life on a transport: the deafening sound of the PA system, the blast of "The smoking lamp is out. Now sweepers, man your brooms! A clean sweep-down, fore and aft!"

But my thoughts were elsewhere just then. I wasn't thinking of Mae, or Taffy; not even of my mother. I was trying to make peace with my very personal, existential, Augustan faith, remembering Psalm 107, about men that go down to the sea in ships. Most fighting men cannot imagine their own deaths. All those I knew on that ship were confident that they would see America again. I wasn't; I had no premonition, but I knew the odds and was uncomforted by them. In any event, my destiny was nonnegotiable. I stood on the fantail, watching the California coastline recede as the *Morton* and the rest of the convoy began zigzagging to evade submarines. I was aware, and depressed by the knowledge, that this was probably my farewell to the United States. I hoped I would fight well. I felt ready; I felt that my men were ready. Then I made my way to the other end of the ship and peered westward across the gray expanse of water, superficially like my Atlantic but immeasurably larger and more vivid. Its name, considering the role it was about to play in our lives, was the ultimate irony. It was called Pacific.

FOX

The Canal

MY FIRST IMPRESSION OF GUADALCANAL IS SOMEWHAT BLURRED, BE-cause I began by looking in the wrong direction. The great battle was over — a source of disappointment to some, and, to me, of inexpressible joy — but we were proceeding with the combat landing drill just the same. Buckling on my chamberpot helmet that hot August morning, saddling up so my pack straps brought the padding to the exact place where the straps joined on the tops of my shoulders, I peered westward across a cobalt sea dancing with incandescent sunlight and saw a volcanic isle which looked as ominous as the hidden fire in its belly. It didn't bear the slightest resemblance to what we had been told to expect. Casually flipping my hands to my hips and sauntering to the rail, I smoothed the wrinkles out of my voice and said in my deepest, manliest, trust-the-Sarge manner: "So that's it. They gave us bad dope, as usual." Someone touched my forearm. It was little Pip Spencer, the chick of the outfit. He said: "It's on the other side, Slim." I had been looking at Savo Island. I turned southward, disconcerted, having lost face even before we boarded the Higgins boats — those landing craft with hinged ramps built in New Orleans by the flamboyant Andrew Jackson Higgins — and beheld a spectacle of utter splendor.

In the dazzling sunshine a breeze off the water stirred the distant fronds of coconut palms. The palm trees stood near the surf line in precise, orderly groves, as though they had been deliberately planted that way, which, we later learned, was the case; we were looking at plantations owned by Lever Brothers. (Their stock-holders were following the course of the Pacific war with great interest. Later the Allies settled nearly seven million dollars in damage claims. The Japanese, of course, paid nothing.) On the far horizon lay dun-colored foothills, dominated by hazy blue seven-thousand-foot mountains. Between the palms and the foothills lay the hogback ridges and the dense green mass of the Canal. Our eyes were riveted on it. We were seeing, most of us for the first time, real jungle.

I thought of Baudelaire: *fleurs du mal.* It was a vision of beauty, but of evil beauty. Except for occasional patches of shoulder-high kunai grass, the blades of which could lay a man's hand open as quickly as a scalpel, the tropical forest swathed the island. From the APA's deck it looked solid enough to walk on. In reality the ground — if you could find it — lay a hundred feet below the cloying beauty of the treetops, the cathedrals of banyans, ipils, and eucalyptus. In between were thick, steamy, matted, almost impenetrable screens of cassia, liana vines, and twisted creepers, masked here and there by mangrove swamps and clumps of bamboo. It was like New Guinea, except that on Papua the troops at least had the Kokoda Trail. Here the green fastness was broken only by streams veining the forest, flowing northward into the sea. The forest seemed almost faunal: arrogant, malevolent, cruel; a great toadlike beast, squatting back, thrusting its green paws through ravines toward the shore, sulkily waiting to lunge when we were within reach, meanwhile emitting faint whiffs of foul breath, a vile stench of rotting undergrowth and stink lilies. Actually, we had been told in our briefings, there were plenty of real creatures awaiting us: serpents, crocodiles, centipedes which could crawl across the flesh leaving a trail of swollen skin, land crabs which would scuttle in the night making noises indistinguishable from those of an infiltrating Jap, scorpions, lizards, tree leeches, cockatoos that screamed like the leader of a banzai charge, wasps as long as your finger and spiders as large as your fist, and mosquitoes, mosquitoes, mosquitoes, all carriers of malaria. If wounded, you had been warned, you should avoid the sea. Sharks lurked there; they were always hungry. It was this sort of thing which had inspired some anonymous lyricist among the 19,102 Marines in the first convoy to compose the lugubrious ballad beginning, "Say a prayer for your pal on Guadalcanal."

On the nineteen transports in the original force the Marine infantry had been subdued, and not just because of the air of foreboding gloom which spread like a dark olive stain over the entire island. Down below in the holds enlisted men had been quiet, though awake, writing letters, sharpening bayonets, blackening the sights of rifles and carbines, checking machine-gun belts to make certain they wouldn't jam in the Brownings, rummaging in packs to be sure they had C rations. They carried canteens, Kabar knives, and first-aid kits hooked to web belts; packs of cigarettes, Zippo lighters, shaving gear, skivvies, mess kits, shelter halves, ponchos, two extra bandoliers of ammunition for each man, clean socks, and, hanging from straps and web belts like ripe fruit waiting to be plucked, hand grenades. Some were literally whistling in the dark ("My momma done tole me . . .") or just milling around in the companionways. There wasn't much room to mill. Around the heads people were almost wedged against each other, a few inches from sodomy. There was no place to sit. Tiered in fives, and, where the overhead was higher, in sixes, the bunks were cluttered with helmets, helmet liners, knapsacks, pick and shovel entrenching tools, and 782 gear. During the long hours of waiting, the tension and frustration became almost unbearable. There was a myth, then and throughout the war, that this had been planned, that the Marine Corps wanted us infuriated when we hit the beach. But the Corps wasn't that subtle. And the men needed no goading. Morale was sky-high, reminiscent of Siegfried Sassoon's account of British esprit the week before the Battle of the Somme in 1916: "there was harmony in our company mess, as if the certainty of a volcanic future put an end to the occasional squabblings which occurred when we were on one another's nerves. A rank animal healthiness pervaded our existence during those days of busy living and inward foreboding. . . . Death would be lying in wait for the troops next week, and now the flavor of life was doubly strong. . . . I was trying to convert the idea of death in battle into an emotional experience. Courage, I argued, is a beautiful thing, and next week's attack is what I have been waiting for since I joined the army." If you were a green Marine fresh from civilian life, waiting to race ashore on Guadalcanal, vitality surged through you like a powerful drug, even though the idea of death held no attraction for you. Your mood was an olla podrida, a mélange of apprehension, cowardice, curiosity, and envy — soon to be discredited by events — of the safe, dry sailors who would remain on board.

The bluejackets who would come closest to your destination were the coxswains of the Higgins boats. At the signal "Land the Landing Force," their little craft, absurdly small beside the transport, bobbed up and down as you climbed down the cargo nets hanging over the APA's side. Descent was tricky. Jap infantrymen carried 60 pounds. A Marine in an amphibious assault was a beast of burden. He shouldered, on the average, 84.3 pounds, which made him the most heavily laden foot soldier in the history of warfare. Some men carried much more: 20-pound BARs, 45-pound 81-millimeter-mortar base plates, 47-pound mortar bipods, 36-pound light machine guns, 41-pound heavy machine guns, and heavy machine-gun tripods, over 53 pounds. A man thus encumbered was expected to swing down the ropes like Tarzan. It was a dangerous business; anyone who lost his grip and fell clanking between the ship and the landing craft went straight to the bottom of Sealark Channel, and this happened to some. More frequent were misjudgments in jumping from the cargo net to the boat. The great thing was to time your leap so that you landed at the height of the boat's bob. If you miscalculated, the most skillful coxswain couldn't help you. You were walloped, possibly knocked out, possibly crippled, when you hit his deck.

Judged by later standards, the Guadalcanal landing of August 7, 1942 — America's first offensive of the war, encoded "CACTUS" — was primitive. Amphibious techniques were in their infancy. The Marine Corps lacked essential information on tide, terrain, and weather. There were no reliable maps, no LSTs, and no DUKWs, those amphibian tractors, or boats with wheels, which were then still in the experimental stage. The heyday of underwater demolition teams lay ahead. World War I weapons were standard because the Corps, though part of the navy, used army equipment and didn't get new issue until the last GI got his. One curious weapon, which we came to loathe, was a machine pistol called the Reising gun; it rusted quickly, jammed at the slightest provocation, and was quite useless in the jungle. The twin-purpose entrenching tool hadn't reached the Pacific yet. Again, men were carrying 1918 relics: even-numbered men had little picks and odd-numbered men little shovels; once ashore, they dug in together. The Higgins boats were crude prototypes, and on shore-to-shore operations they were towed by "Yippies," or YP (yard patrol) craft, wide, smelly speedboats which emitted deafening chug-chugs and clouds of sparks, making stealth impossible. The landing force's chief job was to complete and use the unmatted twenty-six-hundred-foot airstrip the Japanese had already started, but there were shortages of cement, valves, pipes, pumps, prefabricated steel sections for fuel storage tanks, Marsden runway matting, and earth-moving machinery. (There was one small bulldozer. Only the operator was allowed to touch it. Under a standing order, anyone else approaching it was to be shot.)

But the basic attack concept, shelling a beach and then sending in waves of infantry, had been established. Marines were grouped thirty-six men to a boat. The boats for each wave formed a ring, circling until they fanned out in a broad line and sped the wave shoreward. Aboard, you crouched beneath the gunwales, seasick, struggling to keep from vomiting. There was no Dramamine then. Most men compared the seasickness to that on a terrible roller coaster ride, Mae's Murphy bed raised to the nth degree. Coxswains in later operations learned to give their wretched human cargo smoother rides, but none improved on the precise timing that August morning at the Canal. Zero hour had been set for 9:10 A.M. At 9:09 the first wave splashed ashore toward the quiet, shell-shredded palms on Red Beach, four miles east of the Lunga River. Lacking opposition, two battalions of the Fifth Marines, my father's old regiment, swiftly established a two-thousand-yard-wide beachhead.

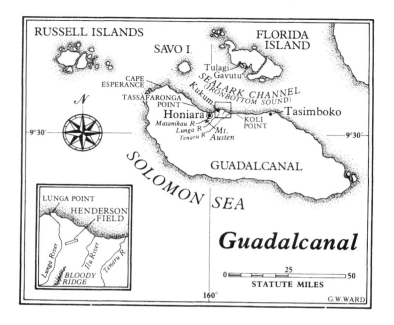

My own landing, much later, was typically inglorious. As our wave circled nauseously, a cloud no larger than a turd appeared in the sky. It grew. At the instant my boondocker hit the gray sand, the skies opened and ten inches of hard, driving, torrential rain began to pour down like that San Diego lioness pissing on a flat rock.

Guadalcanal is shaped like a paramecium, or a fat limp letter *S* on its side. Though different in dimensions, and though mostly uninhabitable, the Canal is about the size of Long Island. The right tip droops down toward New Caledonia, eight hundred miles away, then the closest Allied stronghold. The left end rises to a tip, Cape Esperance, which, on a map of New York, would put it in the vicinity of Long Island's Great Neck. North of the cape lies the volcanic isle I had mistaken for the Canal, Savo Island — White Plains on the New York map. To Savo's right are the Florida Islands, chiefly Tulagi, Gavutu, and Tanambogo — near Bridgeport, Connecticut, if the map analogy is held. The body of water between the Canal, Savo, and the Floridas may be compared to Long Island Sound. Before the fighting it was known as Sealark Channel. After more than thirty-five ferocious naval battles had been fought there, with, among others, sixty-five major warships sunk — roughly half American and half Japanese — Sealark was rechristened Ironbottom Sound. During my seven months on Guadalcanal the Sound and its surrounding islands became as familiar to me as an Amherst apple orchard. I especially remember one wreck. During a midnight, moonless, hull-to-hull slugging Samarra off Tassafaronga Point in which two of our fighting admirals were killed — Dan Callaghan and Norman Scott — three Jap transports were run aground. One day long afterward, I decided to board one of these hulks. It was not one of my brighter ideas. I dove through a shell hole beneath the waterline and found myself in a compartment full of water. My head hit the overhead: no air. My lungs were bursting when, by blind luck, I found the original shell hole and darted through it, bleeding from a half-dozen cuts. Then I remembered the warning about sharks. The Australian crawl was invented by a Solomon Islander, Alex Wickham, but I doubt that he could have matched my dash to shore.

The first European to sight these waters was Alvaro de Mendaña de Neyra in 1597. Looking for King Solomon's legendary islands and failing to find them, he named the archipelago "Islas de Salomón" and the Canal itself after his Spanish birthplace, Guadalcanal. It is an extraordinary fact that until our landing, the Japanese army's general staff hadn't even heard of the island; the Jap navy had been managing affairs in the Solomons, and the army-navy split was even greater in Tokyo than in Washington. But no one could really be expected to keep all of Mendaña's *islas* straight. There were archipelagos within archipelagos: 1,001 isles in the Russell subgroup alone, and even more in the New Georgias. Altogether, the Solomons sprawl across nine hundred miles, roughly forming two chains. The channel between these chains, leading down to the Canal, became known as the Slot. It was a natural funnel for planes and ships lunging southeastward from the great Nip bastion of Rabaul to the northwest. Even better, from the Japanese point of view, their approaching armadas coming down the Slot would be masked, for those defending our reconquest of the Canal, by Savo.

Informed that the Marines were ashore on the Canal, a senior colonel on Hirohito's general staff wondered aloud what the Americans could possibly want with "an insignificant island inhabited only by natives." The colonel's superiors and his opposite numbers in the Japanese navy could have told him. Their men had been on the Canal for six weeks, bossing Korean laborers — "termites" was our word for the Koreans — who were building the airfield. That field was what the Americans wanted. News of its construction by the Japs, radioed to New Caledonia by Australian coastwatchers who had stayed on their islands and gone bush, meant Australia itself was on the Jap hit list. It must be remembered that at the time Dai Nippon's troops had not once tasted defeat. Victories had become a Nip narcotic. Until Guadalcanal, their only encounters with the Marine Corps had ended in defeat for us: the loss of Wake Island, the surrender of the Fourth Marines on Corregidor, and an inept submarine-borne raid on the Gilbert Islands by Carlson's Raiders (Second Raider Battalion), where nine men left behind by Carlson were beheaded. "Where," Tokyo Rose jeered after that, "are the United States Marines hiding?" Convinced now that they were invincible, the Japanese were taking dead aim on the landing beaches nearest Brisbane, Sydney, and Melbourne, the population centers of the last surviving Allied power in the South Pacific. It was the threat to Australia that triggered American seizure of Guadalcanal. That audacious move was as desperate as Hitler's losing gamble that same year at Stalingrad. Its chances of success were dim at the outset. They were to grow dimmer.

The battle's architect was Admiral Ernest J. King, the U.S. chief of naval operations. The documents of that year indicate that King's fellow service chiefs could not decide whether their goal in the Solomons should be to stop the Japs there or merely to harass them. But the admiral was determined to drive them back. Unfortunately the old sundowner picked as his campaign commander Vice Admiral Robert L. Ghormley, a poor selection because Ghormley was convinced the situation in the Solomons was hopeless. Alexander A. Vandegrift, the soft-spoken Marine Corps general who would head the hodgepodge of leatherneck units making the landing, had been told that he needn't expect a combat assignment before January 1943. Various convoys were carrying his troops — reinforced regiments from two Marine divisions and miscellaneous battalions — toward New Zealand when Vandegrift was told he must recapture Guadalcanal and its surrounding islands — "denying the area to Japan" — on August 1. That was less than a month away. Appalled, the general begged for a postponement. King moved the date back to August 7, but that, he said, would be his last concession.

One difficulty in re-creating the past is that the reader knows how it will turn out, so that events have an air of inevitability. That was not true at the time, especially in the case of the Canal. Vandegrift's men were in wretched shape. Most were suffering from dysentery; rations condemned as unfit in Panama, and returned to the United States for destruction, had inexplicably been shipped to the Marines. In Wellington, New Zealand, where their advance echelon landed, the annual rains had begun. Wellington's longshoremen chose this astonishing moment to go on strike. Drenched, sick Marines — New Zealand was in the middle of a flu epidemic — had to load their own ships in eight-hour shifts under dim lights, wrestling with soaked cardboard cartons which frequently burst open, leaving a swamp of soggy cornflakes, beans, clothing, and miscellaneous debris. Because of the strike they would have to attack with only ten days of ammunition and, in the words of a divisional order, other "items actually required to live and fight." "All wharfees is bastards," one Marine wrote on the wall of a dockworkers' toilet. That wasn't the Corps' last quarrel with organized labor. After Ghormley had moved his flag to Nouméa, in New Caledonia, sixty American merchant ships dropped anchor there. They were carrying rations for the Marines, who by then were starving on the Canal. The crews, on the advice of their union leader, refused to sail to the Canal unless granted exorbitant pay for overtime and for service in "combat zones." Their demands were rejected. The Marines went hungry. If the ghost of Joe Hill had appeared on the Canal, he would have been shot again.

But the chief target of the men's resentment was the navy brass.

After the long battle was over, some veterans of it struck a medal showing an arm bearing admiral's stripes dropping a hot potato into the hands of a kneeling Marine. The motto was "Faciat Georgius" — "Let George do it." There was no need to identify the admiral. It was Frank Jack Fletcher. Fletcher had let the Corps down once before, when he had been sent to relieve the beleaguered men on Wake Island and had turned back pleading lack of fuel, though his own logs prove he had plenty. ("Always fueling," was Samuel Eliot Morison's judgment of Fletcher.) Now Ghormley singled out this dismaying man to direct America's first landing of the war. With the task force preparing to sail for the Solomons, Fletcher called a conference aboard his flagship *Saratoga* and asked how many days would be needed to put Vandegrift's men ashore. Told that about five days would be necessary, he said flatly that he would leave after two days "because of the danger of air attacks and because of the fuel situation . . . if the troops can't be landed in two days, then they should not be landed." Vandegrift, aghast, again pleaded for more time. The admiral said that he would entertain no objections. He then closed the conference. There were those in the Marine Corps who thought that Fletcher wanted to add a fourth color to the American flag.

Yet he and Ghormley were not alone in believing that the offensive was doomed. MacArthur, usually hawkish, said the plan was "open to the gravest doubts." Major General Millard F. Harmon, the senior army officer in Ghormley's area, reported to George Marshall after we had established our beachhead: "Can the Marines hold it? There is considerable room for doubt." At a time when a dozen high-altitude fighter planes would have saved Marine lives, Hap Arnold, the chief of the air force, refused to send any on the grounds that they would be sacrificed in vain. Delos Emmons, who was Arnold's air general in the South Pacific, reported categorically that the island could not be held. Ghormley, all but writing the campaign off, refused to strengthen the landing there, to the point of ignoring an order from King to do so. Even Vandegrift later said he himself could have listed "a hundred reasons why this operation should fail." Vandegrift's plight may be measured by his surprise and gratitude when Alexander Patch, commanding the American division in New Caledonia, withdrew twenty thousand pairs of shoes from his quartermaster's shelves and sent them to the Canal so Marines would no longer have to fight barefoot. It took a presidential order and a scrappy admiral — William Halsey, who replaced the timid Ghormley — before the troops began to receive real support from their rear echelon. FDR knew the risks; he had begun preparing Churchill and Stalin for the loss of the island. (He didn't know that the Marines had decided not to surrender — that rather than give the enemy "another Bataan" they were prepared to slip into the hills and fight on as guerrillas.) But Roosevelt also realized that the Canal was shaping up as one of those decisive battles, like Waterloo, Gettysburg, and Dien Bien Phu, in which both sides have resolved upon a showdown and prestige transcends strategic position. Forced to choose between New Guinea and the Canal, which were being fought simultaneously, the Japanese decided to try to hold the line in Papua and reinforce the Canal. Therefore the President wheeled his wheelchair into his White House map room, spent a half hour studying his charts of the South Pacific, and then directed his admirals and generals "to make sure that every possible weapon gets into that area to hold Guadalcanal."

In the Islamic world there is said to be one night, called the Night of Nights, upon which the secret gates of the sky open wide and the water in the jugs tastes sweeter. Conversely, in each of our amphibious convoys, once it had reached the open sea, there came a moment of moments when the human cargo in the holds learned of its destination, whereupon the water from the scuttlebutts tasted rancid and sour. We knew we would hate the answer to our questions, but, masochistically, we speculated endlessly on our fate. On Wednesday, July 22, 1942, when the Canal-bound seventy-five-ship expeditionary force sailed from Wellington, it was floating on rumors as much as on the Tasman Sea. The fleet was said to be headed for a half-dozen destinations; this being the first anniversary of Hitler's invasion of Russia, one story had it that the troops were going to join the Red Army and fight the Germans. As the coast of

New Zealand shrank and then vanished, all eyes were on the leading vessel, Rear Admiral Richmond Kelly Turner's flagship, the
U.S.S. *McCawley*, soon to become known to all Marines in the
South Pacific as "Wacky Mac." Then Wacky Mac hoisted the signal: the fleet was bound for Guadalcanal.

Nobody had ever heard of it. On the nineteen APAs the guys had
a thousand queries for their officers. What was the target island
like? Any bars? Any tail? They were told that it was part of a British Solomon Islands Protectorate. That sounded impressive; in
those days the British Empire still inspired respect. But that was
about all the men could be told. Turner himself knew little more.
The only figures on enemy strength came from reports radioed
about by coastwatchers, who, though on the spot, were hiding deep
in the bush and could therefore offer only the vaguest of estimates.
One of Vandegrift's colonels, desperate for intelligence, had studied
seventeenth-century sailing charts and interviewed missionaries,
traders, schooner captains, and Lever Brothers employees, all refugees from the Solomons. Based on what they had told him, he had
drawn a rough map of the Canal's northern coast, where the airfield
was being built. It proved to be unreliable, almost worthless, showing, among other things, 1,350-foot Mount Austen — which we
came to know as the "Grassy Knoll" — to be two miles inland
when in fact it was nearly four. Vandegrift had expected to seize it
the first day. In the Canal's tropical wilderness an Indian file of
husky men could cover less than four hundred yards a day even
without Japanese opposition, which, in the case of Mount Austen,
would mean over two weeks. Vandegrift changed his mind as soon
as he saw the island. (Austen and its adjoining ridges, Gifu, Sea
Horse, and Galloping Horse, would not fall until after more than
four months of fighting.) Two American officers had flown over the
island in a B-17. Jumped by three Zeroes, they flamed two, fled
back with the third on their tail, and reported that the airstrip was
almost finished and there appeared to be no obstacles on the landing beaches. Yet better sources of information were available, or
should have been. It is characteristic of relations between America's
armed forces at this time that MacArthur's G-2 (intelligence), hav-

ing completed a detailed photo-map of the Canal nearly three weeks earlier, mailed it to Ghormley. The package was improperly addressed and lost in the Auckland post office.

The Marines' first break was the weather. On Wednesday, August 5, and Thursday, August 6, squalls and overcast skies grounded the Rabaul-based Jap pilots of long-range Kawanishes who had been flying routine air searches over the Solomons. Three Nip planes did take off from Tulagi on Thursday, but with ceilings as low as a hundred feet they were back in an hour. They reported, "Result of searches: Negative." Thursday night the darkened American convoy glided through the strait between Savo and Cape Esperance, unseen by enemy crews manning howitzers on both sides. Friday morning coastwatcher Martin Clemens, in his remote jungle hideaway, heard the first roar of the U.S. naval bombardment. Two thousand sleeping Japanese on the north coast — Red Beach — were awakened by salvos from the U.S.S. *Quincy* bursting among them and demolishing forty of their warehouses. By the end of the afternoon 10,900 Marines were on the Canal and 6,025 on Tulagi, though most of their equipment was still aboard the ships. In me-fella-you-fella pidgin conversations with the natives, who had already been alienated by the Japanese, they quickly recruited guides. Fanning out professionally, the Marines dug their two- or three-man foxholes, wired themselves in for the night, and spread the password and countersign —"lollypop" and "lallygag," because the Japs were said to have trouble pronouncing the letter *l*. (I never understood that. I think their problem was the letter *r*. They called us "Malines.") The troops were all hyped up. Morison later wrote: "Lucky indeed for America that in this theater and at that juncture she depended not on boys drafted or cajoled into fighting but on 'tough guys' who had volunteered to fight and who asked for nothing better than to come to grips with the sneaking enemy who had aroused all their primitive instincts."

The palms on the beach were bent seaward, curtseying toward Tulagi, but inland they stood tall and straight. Because the soap company needed the ground beneath them kept clear for harvest-

Red Beach, Guadalcanal, 1978

ing the coconuts, the Marines had a clear run to the crushed-coral airstrip, which was swiftly taken and named Henderson Field after a Corps pilot who had died in the Battle of Midway. Repair sheds, hangars, and revetments were already finished. Obviously the enemy had expected to use the field within a week at the latest. The scoop was that the Japanese liked to fight in the dark, so Vandegrift expected a counterattack that first night. He was very vulnerable on Red Beach. Equipment had piled up alarmingly. When a Bougainville coastwatcher had radioed, "Twenty-four torpedo bombers headed yours," sailors manhandling the crates had had to dive for shelter. Luckily the bombardiers from Rabaul were wildly inaccurate, merely inflicting minor damage on one U.S. destroyer. But the only disturbance on the Canal after darkness was from land crabs, screeching tropical birds, and a stampeding herd of wild pigs. Men whispered hopefully to one another that now, with the beachhead secure, GIs would relieve them, letting them return to the bars of Wellington. They studied the unfamiliar stars in the sky and dreamt their wistful dreams.

Across Ironbottom Sound the situation was very different. There the Marines were encountering their first real combat. Tulagi, Gavutu, and Tanambogo were honeycombed with caves and the leathernecks were taking casualties. Hand grenades were almost useless; the enemy tossed them back. Merritt Edson's Raiders (First Raider Battalion) had forty-seven killed; the Marine Parachutists, eighty-four dead. It is a myth — inspired by the Iwo Jima flag raising — that every World War II Marine carried an American flag in his pack, but somebody on tiny Tanambogo had one of them, and for several hours the island resembled a nineteenth-century battlefield, with the Stars and Stripes snapping angrily over one end of Tanambogo and the Rising Sun over the other. After a noisy charge a Marine sergeant pulled down the Nip banner, and dynamiters sealed the caves one by one. That should have given the enemy's commanders pause — nothing like that had happened to them before — but their rear echelon was as overconfident as ours was fearful. Rabaul reassured Tokyo; the chief of the naval general staff donned his dress uniform and appeared at Hirohito's summer villa at Nikko to inform the emperor that there was no cause for worry. One banzai attack, he predicted, would drive the Marines into the sea. That Friday night four waves of crack Nip troops hit the Raider lines on Tulagi with mortars, grenades, and machine guns. A handful of attackers made it through the lines to the old British Residency but were killed back there when they were discovered hiding under the veranda. At dawn Pfc John Ahrens, an Able Company BAR man, was found covered with blood. He had been shot twice in the chest and bayoneted three times. Around him were the corpses of a Nip officer, a Nip sergeant, and thirteen Nip infantrymen. His huge company commander, Lewis W. Walt, picked up the dying youth and held him in his arms. Ahrens said, "Captain, they tried to come over me last night, but I don't think they made it." Walt said softly, "They didn't, Johnny. They didn't."

Five hours later Vandegrift boarded the Wacky Mac and was dealt another blow. An enemy fleet had been sighted leaving Rabaul. Fletcher was withdrawing three carriers from the Sound. Turner, who as a consequence would now lack air cover, had to weigh anchor and sail away with the transports bearing the Marines who had not yet debarked and most of the landing force's supplies — its sandbags, howitzers, coastal defense guns, most of its ammunition, and all but eighteen spools of its barbed wire. Vandegrift, deprived of his lifeline, would be left with a few days' rations, no more. He accused Fletcher of "running away," but to no avail. Of course, he was told, the transports would soon return. That was certainly the navy's plan, but that night brought catastrophe. The armada steaming south from Rabaul was bigger and closer than had been thought, and it was commanded by one of Hirohito's most gifted admirals, Gunichi Mikawa. Leading seven cruisers and escorting vessels down the Slot, Mikawa, concealed by the cone of Savo Island, appeared undetected at 1:43 A.M. and pounced on the Allied force which had been left to hold the Sound. He had already launched his torpedoes when a U.S. destroyer sounded the alarm. The forty-minute battle which followed was one of the most crushing defeats in American history. Of five Allied cruisers, four were sunk and the fifth crippled; of the American and Australian sailors in the water, 1,023 were killed, drowned, or eaten by sharks. The return of Fletcher's task force was postponed indefinitely, perhaps forever. The troops ashore were left bare-assed. Now the "Tokyo Express," as they called it, would come roaring down the Slot to land Jap troops on the island around the clock and shell the Marines on shore from ships beyond the range of the Americans' pitifully small mortars and guns.

Bastogne was considered an epic in the ETO. The 101st Airborne was surrounded there for eight days. But the Marines on Guadalcanal were to be isolated for over four months. There have been few such stands in history. Over the millennia of war certain crack troops must be set apart, elite units which demonstrated gallantry in the face of overwhelming odds. There were the Greeks and Persians at Thermopylae, Xenophon's Ten Thousand, the Bowmen of Agincourt, the Spanish *Tercios*, the French Foreign Legion at Camerone, the Old Contemptibles of 1914, the Brigade of Guards at Dunkirk. And there was the olio of leatherneck units who fought on the Canal under the name of the First Marine Division. All but abandoned by the vessels which brought them there, reduced to eating roots and weeds, kept on the line though stricken by malaria unless their temperature reached 103 degrees, dependent for food and ammo on destroyers and fliers who broke through the enemy blockade, always at great risk, they fought the best soldiers Tokyo could send against them, killed over twenty thousand of them, and won. In an author's note accompanying *The Thin Red Line*, his novel about the Canal, James Jones wrote that "what Guadalcanal stood for in 1942–43 was a very special thing," that he wanted to share with his readers the "special qualities which the name Guadalcanal evoked for my generation." James Michener compared the fighting on the island to Valley Forge and Shiloh. Morison wrote: "Guadalcanal is not a name but an emotion, recalling desperate fights in the air, furious night naval battles, frantic work at supply and construction, savage fighting in the sodden jungle, nights broken by screaming bombs and deafening explosions of naval shells." Winston Churchill, after studying the battle, simply wrote: "Long may the tale be told in the great Republic."

At the time, however, one wondered whether there would be anyone left to tell it. It should be added that, had it been told then, the teller's enthusiasm for Churchill's European war would have been tepid. One reason the struggles in the Pacific constantly teetered on the brink of disaster is that they were shoestring operations. At one point the United States was spending more money feeding and housing uprooted Italian civilians than on the Americans fighting the Japanese. The navy let the Marines on the Canal down because Washington was letting the navy down, devoting nearly all its resources to Eisenhower's coming invasion of North Africa. We knew that our theater was a casualty of discrimination, not because Tokyo Rose told us — though she did, again and again — but because our own government, appealing to its national constituency, which was almost entirely comprised of former Europeans and their descendants, boasted of it. The news about the Italian refugees, for example, was released by the State Department. It pleased Little Italys across the country. The Marines, MacArthur's GIs, and the bluejackets in the Pacific were less elated.

Slipping past the leering guns of the Nip cordon, American destroyers managed to meet the Canal's crying need for ammunition and, later, artillery. Food was another matter. The average leatherneck lost twenty-five pounds during the siege. Night blindness became a serious problem for the men on the line; they simply weren't getting enough vitamin A. To his Raiders, men of machismo who resembled the British commandos, Colonel "Red Mike" Edson gave a quintessential piece of Marine Corps advice. "There's plenty of chow," he said, grinning wickedly. "The Japs have it. Take it away from them." Red Mike's mordant wit became part of the Canal legend. So did the incident of Admiral Halsey's bully beef. When Halsey took over he changed the momentum of the battle with a few words. Visiting the Canal — something Ghormley had never done — he held up two fingers and told Vandegrift, "Give me two days. I'll have AKA's here in two days." A war correspondent accompanying him asked if he thought the Marines could hold on. Halsey jerked his thumb toward the Japanese lines. "How long do you think *they* can take it?" he asked. During his day on the Canal the island was bombed by Bettys and shelled by Jap cruisers firing eight-inch guns at a range of ten thousand yards. Vandegrift was anxious to get the admiral off the Canal after dark. He was worried, not only about Halsey's safety, but also about his digestion. Vandegrift knew how appalling the chow would be. The admiral wouldn't go. He dined, as Vandegrift and his officers dined, on thin, gummy bully beef. In an obvious attempt to boost morale, he said enthusiastically: "You know, this is the best bully beef I've ever tasted. I wish the men in my galley could do as well. Let me talk to your mess sergeant." The man appeared, trembling in the presence of so mighty an officer.

Halsey raved on and on about the bully beef. Then he stopped. Vandegrift nudged the mess sergeant. "Say something to the admiral," he whispered. Still quaking, the man stuttered: "Bul-Bullshit, Admiral. Bul-Bullshit."

Edson's joke about taking Japanese supplies proved to be wisdom in disguise. Fleeing into the bush, the enemy had left large stocks of soy sauce, rice, tinned sliced beef, canned Japanese seaweed, crab meat, canned vegetables, and beer, and Marines enthusiastically digested it all. Cooks preparing it warmed chow on field stoves burning Japanese kerosene. The meals were eaten from Jap bowls with Jap chopsticks. After the entrées the leathernecks sucked Jap hard candy and drank sake from delicate Jap cups. The enemy's cornucopia, in those early days, seemed inexhaustible. Red Mike himself found diversion in an English translation of a "Short History of Japan"; his mess was enlivened by Nip phonograph records played on a captured Victrola. Men were issued Japanese occupation money to buy Japanese souvenirs. At Henderson Field, two large Japanese air stations, an air-compression plant for torpedoes, machine shops, and two electric-light plants proved to be invaluable. Nip girders and Nip piles were used to build bridges and piers. Everyone smoked Japanese cigarettes. The chances of mailing letters were slight, but men wrote then anyhow — on Japanese rice paper. Some calculated the number of days left in their enlistments with Japanese abaci. Heads were built of Nip lumber and shielded from flies by Jap screening. Since Fletcher had fled with all the toilet paper, and since Tokyo Rose seemed to be the only reliable source of information, Marines completed their toilet rites at the head by wiping themselves with copies of the *New York Times* which had somehow made it through the blockade. One issue was so used with particular relish. It reported that the Marines were TIGHTENING THEIR GRIP on the Solomons AS NAVY KEEPS SUPPLIES FLOWING IN. On the strength of this dispatch, the troops were thrilled to learn, the Dow-Jones stock average had gained 4.93 points. But the most priceless news story, too precious for disposal in the head, appeared on page 25 of *Time*'s August 24 issue. Reporting on the Battle of Savo Island, it revealed: "Japanese cruisers and destroyers tried to smash the invasion fleet. Then came what U.S. tars had long prayed for: the first real gun-to-gun test of U.S. and Japanese surface sea power. Result: a licking for the Japs."

One Marine gunny taught a small class in Nipponese flower arrangement, using a superbly illustrated book recently published in Tokyo, and another NCO, who had liberated an ice plant which had been left in excellent condition by the departing enemy, erected two signs outside it. One read:

TOJO ICE FACTORY
UNDER NEW MANAGEMENT
— J. Genung, Sgt., USMC, Mgr.

The other sign was headed TODAY'S SCORE. On it, after each air battle overhead, he used a Japanese brush to write U.S. aircraft losses and the number of enemy planes stitched, flamed, and splashed. If you were cowering in a foxhole near Henderson, you could often hear the hot .50-caliber cases falling from the sky. After a lull, when Condition Red was lifted, someone would say: "Ain't getting any more cases; let's go up to the ice plant." The Seabees, whom every Marine adored, had arrived, extended and finished Henderson Field two weeks after the landing, and immediately started work on a two-hundred-yard grassy fighter strip parallel to it. On August 20, the first twelve SBD (Scott Bomber Douglas) Dauntless dive-bombers flew in from the east and landed on Henderson, followed by nineteen stubby-winged Wildcats. It was, Vandegrift later recalled, "one of the most beautiful sights of my life. I was close to tears and I was not alone." Enemy pilots led by Vs of arrowing Aichi 99s covered by Zeroes raced down from Rabaul to challenge them. The field, shelled every night, was in deplorable condition. If rain was falling it was a mire; if the day was dry the runway was obscured by clouds of dust. Maintenance crews were constantly cannibalizing downed U.S. planes; otherwise they had no spare propellers, wheels, windscreens, or tires. Also lacking were machines to belt ammunition, bomb hoists, dollies, and tank-ers. The pilots were dead on their feet and weakened by their grim diet of beans, rice, and hash. Nevertheless, as the weeks passed the statistics showed that our fliers were outscoring the Japs and their Zeroes, Bettys, and Zekes. The Marine airmen called themselves the "Cactus Air Force," after the code name for the Canal operation, and their aces — Pappy Boyington and Joe Foss especially — were heroes to the infantry.

Dogfights were daylight spectacles. The nights belonged to the Japanese fliers, chiefly two of them: "Louie the Louse," a float plane which nightly dropped two to four drifting pale green flares over the beachhead, and "Maytag Charlie" or "Washing Machine Charlie," so named for his whining toy engine, which sounded like an airborne Yippie. You could set your watch by Charlie. Each night he dropped his 250-pound bombs, too few to threaten the Marines' defenses, but enough to keep them awake, which was the idea. Colonel Robert Pepper's 90-millimeter antiaircraft guns sought Charlie in vain. Four American night fighters up there would have done the job in a few minutes, but somehow requests for them were always pigeonholed in Nouméa. So when he came, you jumped from your soggy blankets and dove into your foxhole, which held as much as six inches of water. In the hot zinging iron that fell, men said they found American nuts, bolts, and screws — scrap iron the United States had sold to Japan before Pearl Harbor. One corporal claimed he recognized Eleanor Roosevelt's false teeth. Nobody laughed. Louie and Charlie weren't funny. Nights were feared on the Canal. You watched the beautiful tropical sunsets with dread.

The salvos from Nip warships also banished sleep; so, later, did the shells from "Pistol Pete," a 15-centimeter enemy howitzer on the Grassy Knoll. Our counterbattery fire could never find him. Every time you tried to rest there would be a shot from Pete, the flashing guns of Nip destroyers, Louie's flares, Charlie's drone, or the wail of a siren — another item liberated from the Japanese — at Henderson. When coastwatchers on New Georgia warned that enemy aircraft were overhead there, the word was passed that Condition Yellow was in effect. When they approached the Sound, it was

Condition Red. These aerial pests were, and were meant to be, blows at morale. The men on the line couldn't even *see* the bastards. Even the guys on the beach rarely caught a glimpse of the enemy. If they did, it was usually because the Japs wanted to heighten Marine anxiety with an insolent procession of warships just beyond the reach of Pepper's old five-inch naval guns. Once a Jap move backfired, though. Two Higgins boats, on a mail run from Tulagi to the Canal, seemed doomed when a black Jap submarine, unseen by the men on the boats but clearly visible to those ashore, suddenly surfaced in the Sound behind them. Nip sailors sprang from the conning tower and manned the sub's forward gun. At that moment, to the horror of the men on the beach, blue smoke rose from a malfunction on one of our boats and the other slowed to pick up her crew. The Nips bracketed them in two shots. The men in the boats seemed as good as dead. Then, out of nowhere, a newly arrived battery of Marine 75-millimeter artillery opened fire. The sub lurched toward one side, damaged. The Japs piled into their conning tower, the black hull vanished, and the Higgins boat bearing the shaken Marines glided into its berth at Carpenter's Wharf.

At that time, when the Japanese infantrymen were attacking the Marine perimeter from all sides, our defensive arc was about four miles wide. Its eastern anchor was the juncture of the Ilu and Tenaru rivers and the sea. From there it ran down to a ridge a thousand yards south of Henderson and reached its other anchor at the mouth of the Lunga River to the west. This parabola may be roughly compared to a human face, with the Ilu at the left eye, the ridge at the nose, and the Lunga at the right eye. Generally this semicircular line clung to the high ground. Ideally it should have been an iron cordon, sandbagged and shielded by a double-apron barbed-wire fence with heavy reconnaissance patrols probing westward beyond the village of Kukum to the banks of the broad, ominous Matanikau River, about five miles from the Lunga. Later that was in fact done, but with so few Marines ashore in those first weeks, only heights could be strongly defended. There, on the jungly slopes, the men on the line would wire themselves in at night. Between them and the enemy were entrenched Marines in listening posts. The listening posts would report sounds of Jap movement. Nobody, to the best of my knowledge, volunteered to spend the night in a listening post.

But there was really no safe spot within the perimeter. Cooks, bandsmen, and runners were rushed into gaps when enemy breakthroughs seemed imminent. One night a Japanese officer brandishing a samurai sword came within a few yards of the pagodalike structure which served as Vandegrift's command post. The general, pacing the muddy wooden floor, turned, startled. "Banzai!" screamed the Jap, disemboweling a gunny. Nearby, Sergeant Major Shepherd Banta was giving one of his men unshirted hell. Banta drew his pistol, killed the Jap with one shot, and, turning back, continued his tongue-lashing. Anyone, anywhere on the beachhead, might, at any given moment, win a Purple Heart. Feverish or not, if men could walk then they were ineligible for sick bay. Every man was needed. Redheaded Sam Griffith, then Edson's executive officer and later my commanding officer, remembers: "In the South Pacific the navy was no longer scraping the bottom of the barrel. That had been done." In any event, that was the explanation of the navy brass. Actually Fletcher had idle Wildcats in the New Hebrides. He just didn't believe in reinforcing failure. The enemy seemed to know that the embattled Marines had been all but disowned. Admiral Mikawa was assembling Jap aviation ground crews to be landed on Henderson as soon as the island had been surrendered by the Marines. Major General Kiyotake Kawaguchi, leading a brigade ashore west of the Matanikau, had drawn up the instrument of capitulation for Vandegrift's signature. He had brought a dress uniform to be worn at the ceremony. Even the date had been set: September 13, 1942. The Marines didn't know the size of the forces being moved from New Guinea to the Canal, but some canisters dropped from Zeroes for enemy infantry fell within our lines. All bore the same message: "Help is coming, coming, coming."

Meanwhile our force was shrinking, shrinking, shrinking. It is somehow unfair that only those disabled by wounds were eligible for Purple Hearts. Victims of malaria suffered just as much —

some writhed through recurring attacks until the early
1950s — and there were two of them for every one who fell in
battle. But if it came to that, every Marine on the island deserved a
decoration just for being there. Those spared by malaria and Jap
guns and bombs were afflicted with other fevers and with dysentery, virulent fungus infections, and malnutrition. The corpsmen
did what they could. Marines lined up for emergency rations, salt
tablets, quinine, and, starting on September 10, the malarial sup-
pressant Atabrine. Everyone was ordered to swallow Atabrine tablets daily. Many mutinied at this; the drug left its takers sicklied
o'er with a pale yellow cast, and scuttlebutt had it that it made men
impotent. In the end the pills were doled out in chow lines. A
corpsman popped a tablet on your tongue, then peered down your
throat to be sure you had swallowed it. Still, there were those who
managed to avoid it, and those who gulped it down and then worried about it. Personally I wasn't troubled by the pills. Being potent
hadn't done me much good.

The typical Marine on the island ran a fever, wore stinking
dungarees, loathed twilight, and wondered whether the U.S. Navy
still existed. He ate moldy rations and quinine. He alternately shiv-
ered and sweated. If he was bivouacked near Henderson, he spent
his mornings filling in craters left by enemy bombers the night
before. If he was on his way back to the line, he struggled through
shattered, stunted coconut trees, scraggy bushes, and putrescent
jungle, clawing up and down slopes ankle-deep in mud, hoping he
could catch a few hours of uninterrupted sleep in his foxhole.
Usually he was disappointed. Even when there were no Jap bayonet
charges, every evening brought fireworks. One night Nip bombers
hit a Marine ammunition dump; another night Pepper spent over
an hour trying to hit Charlie with AA fire; at dawn on a day which
came to be known as "Dugout Sunday," enemy six-inch guns tried
to pin down Grumman pilots long enough for a fleet of bombers
from Rabaul to arrive overhead unchallenged. The Jap tin cans
were silenced by counterbattery fire, thanks to information about
their location brought through the lines by natives, striking men
who wore only the lavalava and whose frizzled hair rose eight inches

above their forehead. The battle couldn't have been won without these islanders. Virtually every report from them was reliable. There were, however, exceptions.

On the first Wednesday after the landing an English-speaking Japanese seaman was captured alive. Plied with medicinal alcohol, he disclosed, apparently with reluctance, that hundreds of other Japs, starving in the bush, were ready to quit. A native guide and several termites entering the perimeter confirmed this, and a young Marine officer returning from patrol reported that a white flag was flying over an enemy camp near the Matanikau. That was good enough for Vandegrift's G-2, Lieutenant Colonel Frank Goettge. He told the general he wanted to board a Higgins boat with a patrol of his own and land beyond the Matanikau. Vandegrift agreed, though not without misgivings. Goettge picked his patrol — the prophetically named Stephen A. Custer, a sergeant, and twenty-five other intelligence men, among whom, I am glad to report, I was not.

It was a trap. Goettge, Custer, and their men left Kukum after night fell that same day. At midnight they landed somewhere west of the big river — no one knows just where, for the survivors were in deep shock. The enemy had a reception committee on hand. After a firefight which lasted less than five minutes, the patrol was overwhelmed. Three Marines escaped by swimming away from the beach and then crawling back to our lines over cruel coral. They reached our outposts at daybreak, bleeding and exhausted. Before they lost sight of the shore, they said, they had seen samurai swords flashing in the moonlight, beheading their comrades. This was the Marines' first encounter with Bushido, "the way of the warrior." After several other examples of it, Vandegrift wrote the Marine Corps Commandant in Washington: "General, I have never heard or read of this kind of fighting. These people refuse to surrender. The wounded will wait until men come up to examine them . . . and blow themselves and the other fellow to death with a hand grenade." Having been introduced to the enemy's code of total resistance, defiance to the last man, the Marines had no choice; they had to adopt it themselves. From then until the end of the war, neither side took prisoners except under freakish circumstances. It was combat without quarter: none was asked, none was given.

After the ambush of Goettge's patrol, the first major clash between the Japanese and the Americans occurred at the mouth of a stream on the other side of the perimeter. It is characteristic of our grasp of the island's geography that we called the creek the Tenaru; later we found that it was the Ilu. Most of the battle was fought on a ninety-foot sandspit where the Ilu flows into the Sound, and the first warning of what lay ahead came at midnight on August 18, when Marines ashore heard the splash and hiss of phosphorescent surf — evidence that a warship was racing past their beach, just beyond shoal water. By dawn, everyone within the perimeter had heard the scuttlebutt: the Japs were making night landings. It was true; the first thousand Nip troops had already been put ashore from destroyers. Martin Clemens told one of his natives, Jacob Vouza, to patrol the coconut groves east of the perimeter. Vouza was to become one of the battle's heroes. Before the enemy arrived on Guadalcanal, he had been the island's chief of police; his first impulse, when the Nips had come on June 29, was to arrest them, but Clemens told him to hole up and wait for the friendlier Americans. A powerfully built islander, absolutely fearless, Vouza had been quickly accepted by the Marines as one of them. They had given him an American flag (until Pearl Harbor he had never heard of either Japan or the United States) to show as his safe-conduct when he returned to their outposts from his scouting expeditions. Now, paddling his canoe toward Koli Point, he found that there were, in fact, strong new Japanese forces. Unfortunately he was caught by them on his next patrol. Finding the Stars and Stripes in his pocket, they demanded information about the Marine strongpoints. He wouldn't tell them. Furious, they tied him to a tree with straw ropes, bayoneted him seven times in the chest and throat, and left him for dead. But Vouza, no ordinary man, bit through his ropes and crawled nearly three miles on his hands and knees, bleeding all the way, into our lines. He was near death when brought in, but he refused treatment until he reported all he had seen. Miracu-

The Ilu sandspit, 1978

lously, navy doctors brought him back from the brink of death. Vandegrift awarded him a Silver Star and made him a sergeant major in the Marine Corps.

Fully alerted now, the Second Battalion of the First Marines, entrenched on the west bank of the Ilu, turned Japanese rice bags into sandbags and strengthened their line with barbed wire taken from the Lever Brothers plantation. A battalion of the Eleventh Marines arrived with 75-millimeter pack howitzers and short-barreled 105s. In the last hour of daylight they registered on the sandspit and the black, muddy east bank of the Ilu. Wildcats and Dauntless dive-bombers raked the enemy positions. From their deep foxholes the Marines checked their weapons. Some prayed. Some watched the crocodiles sliding in and out of the stream. Most, however, simply felt defiant. Their blood was up. After twelve days on this miserable island, they were about to justify their presence here. One of them yelled, "Now let the bastards come!"

They came. They were, we now know, supremely confident. Colonel Kiyono Ichiki, their leader, had already written in his diary: "21 August. Enjoyment of the fruits of victory." After nightfall he began moving his troops through the coconut trees, toward the Ilu. It was in just such situations as this that listening posts were invaluable. In the early hours of Thursday, August 20, they reported hearing Japanese voices and "clanking noises." They were drawn back behind our wire, and shortly before 3:00 A.M. the Nips struck. Their sickly green flares burst overhead, followed by the chatter of Nambu light machine guns, the *bup-bup-bup* of their heavy machine guns, and the explosion of their mortar shells among the Marine foxholes. The light from the flares disclosed a frightening horde of Japs in battle dress on the far side of the sandspit. Screaming, "Banzai!" they charged. Riflemen of the First Marines picked them off while our 37-millimeter canister shells exploded on the sandspit. The enemy's first wave faltered; then a second wave came on, and then a third. Because the wire was inadequate — thousands of spools had left with Fletcher's ships — some of the attackers got through. Three of them rushed the foxhole of a corporal firing a BAR. The BAR jammed. Shouting, "Maline, you die!" one Nip jumped into the hole. The corporal grabbed his machete and cut the Nip down; then he jumped the other two Japs and hacked them, too, to death. One Marine machine gunner was killed; his rigid finger remained locked on the trigger, scything the enemy. Blinded by a grenade, Al Schmid, another machine gunner, continued to fire, directed by his dying buddy. At daybreak nearly a thousand Jap corpses lay on the sandspit. The surviving Marines, still in combat shock, stared down at them. Most of the bodies looked alike. There is little variety in the postures of violent death. When the end comes instantaneously, the rag-doll effect is common. If there are a few moments of awareness between the wounding and the dying, muscular spasms draw up the legs and arms in the fetal position, and hands are clenched like boxers' fists. Somehow cadavers always seem smaller than life. The Nips were smaller than we were anyway; their dead looked like dwarfs.

One reason the Ilu battle had been a Marine victory was that

Vandegrift had the advantage of interior lines. The enemy had to move around our perimeter, through the worst of the jungle, but our men could be moved swiftly to any threatened link in our semicircular chain. Because of this, the position was ideal for Edson's Raiders. His battalion had first fought on Tulagi. Then it moved to Savo. Now, in the aftermath of the Ilu, Red Mike shrewdly guessed that the Japanese would try the Ilu approach again. He put one company on Yippie-towed Higgins boats which were then tugged to Tasimboko, twenty miles east of the Ilu, where, as Mike suspected, the Japs were regrouping. Startled, they fled. The Raiders spiked the enemy's guns, loaded tins of crab meat on the boats, dumped rice bags into the water, and disposed of Jap rations which had to be left behind by pissing on them.

Back within the perimeter, Edson reported to Vandegrift's G-3 (operations officer), bringing with him a half-gallon of captured sake and a warning. "This is no motley of Japs," he said in his throaty voice, predicting another major attack soon. Native scouts bore him out; thousands of enemy troops were moving inland. Mike turned to an aerial photograph of the beachhead. He put his finger on the irregular coral ridge which meandered south of Henderson. He said, "This looks like a good approach." Back with his men, he grinned his evil grin and rasped, "Too much bombing and shelling here close to the beach. We're moving to a quiet spot." That Saturday afternoon he and his Raiders, joined by parachutists, intelligence sections, and other miscellaneous troops, started digging in on the bluff, the last physical obstacle between the southern jungle and the airfield. Thus the stage was set for the most dramatic fight in the struggle for the island. Later it would be remembered as Bloody Ridge, Edson's Ridge, or simply the Ridge. Foxholes were dug on the spurs of this long, bare-topped height whose axis lay perpendicular to the airfield's. High, spiky, golden kunai grass feathered the slopes of the rugged hogback, leading down to heavily wooded ravines and dense jungle.

It is Saturday, September 12, 1942. Some eight hundred miles to the west, MacArthur's Australians have stopped the enemy's New Guinea offensive at Ioribaiwa, within sight of Port Moresby. In

Vandegrift's pagodalike headquarters Admiral Turner, visibly embarrassed, has just handed the besieged general a message from Ghormley informing him that because the enemy is massing fleets at Rabaul and Truk, and because Ghormley is short of shipping, the U.S. Navy "can no longer support the Marines on Guadalcanal." And south of Vandegrift and Turner, a twenty-minute walk away, Red Mike is preparing for the stand which will win him the Congressional Medal of Honor and, infinitely more important, will convince Washington that the Canal can be saved after all. It is sad to note that this tormented, highly complex man, a victim of satyriasis, will one day find death, not in battle, but by locking himself in a garage and running his motor until carbon monoxide kills him. Yet nothing can tarnish his successful struggle for the Ridge. He correctly guessed that the Nips' supreme effort would come here, he marked out the Raiders' positions on the brow of the hogback, and by sheer force of will he kept them from breaking.

Because Edson had called this "a quiet spot," and because they had seen so much combat in the past month, most of the Raiders and their hodgepodge of reinforcements were under the impression that they had been sent here to rest. That evening, when enemy warships entered the Sound, Edson's men assumed that the Japs' mission was a routine shelling of the airfield. Instead, the ships shelled the Ridge. Then twenty-six Bettys arrived overhead to drop five-hundred-pound bombs and daisy cutters on the Raiders. "Some goddam rest area!" a corporal yelled. "Some goddam rest area!" At 9:00 P.M. Edson pulled the Marines back to the southern crest of the hogback. There were still two knolls to fall back on. If they were thrown off those they faced annihilation. He told his men: "This is it. There is only us between the airfield and the Japs. If we don't hold, we'll lose the Canal." Within an hour battalions led by Major General Kiyotake Kawaguchi moved up the east bank of the Lunga, pivoted toward the Ridge, and cut a platoon of Marines into little pockets. Japs who spoke broken English led chants of "U.S. Maline be dead tomorrow." A Raider shouted, "Hirohito eats shit!" After a quick conference with his comrades, a Nip yelled back, "Eleanor eats shit!" Edson picked up his field telephone and told the beleaguered platoon commander to disengage. A precise voice replied: "Our situation here, Colonel Edson, is excellent. Thank you, sir." Edson knew his men didn't talk like that. He was speaking to a Jap. He picked a corporal with a voice like a foghorn and told him to roar: "Red Mike says it's OK to pull back!" The platoon retreated to the next spur, moving closer to Henderson but keeping the Marine line intact.

Enemy flares burst overhead. Moving by their light, massed Japs with fixed bayonets swarmed up the slopes of the Ridge. "Gas attack!" they shrieked. A Raider yelled back: "I'll gas you, you cocksucker!" Major Ken Bailey, who would also win a Congressional Medal of Honor in this action, crawled from foxhole to foxhole, distributing grenades. Raider mortars were all coughing together. All machine gunners were trained to fire in short bursts — hot barrels became warped and had to be replaced — but that night you heard no pauses between the flashes from the Brownings. The gunners cried, "Another belt, another barrel!" Palms were scorched in the barrel changing; tormented cries went up: "My fucking hand!" And during lulls you heard the sergeants bellowing: *Raiders, rally to me! Raiders, Raiders, rally to me!*

As daybreak crayoned the eastern sky red and yellow, Edson assembled his officers for a breakfast of dehydrated potatoes, cold hash, and sodden rice. He told them: "They were testing. Just testing. They'll be back. But maybe not as many of them. Or maybe more." He smiled his smile. He said, "I want all positions improved, all wire lines paralleled, a hot meal for the men. Today dig, wire up tight, get some sleep. We'll all need it. The Nip'll be back. I want to surprise him." His surprise was a slight withdrawal along the hogback, improving fields of fire and tightening his rewired lines. Now Japanese assault troops debouching from the bush would have to cover a hundred yards of open grass before reaching the Marines, and as they ran up the slope they would be a naked target for grazing fire from the battalion's automatic weapons. Actually, we learned after the war, Kawaguchi hadn't been testing at all. He had expected to overwhelm the Americans that first night. Later he wrote that now, "because of the devilish jungle, the

Bloody Ridge, 1978

brigade was scattered all over and completely beyond control. In my whole life I have never felt so helpless." Lacking interior lines, he couldn't match Edson's move. He had to do exactly what Red Mike wanted him to do: attack over a no-man's-land, and without his best men, who had been slain in that Saturday charge.

Now it was Sunday. The oppressive tropical night enveloped the Ridge and all through the early evening there was no sign of movement in the jungle below. At 9:00 P.M. Louie wheezed over Kukum, cut his engine, coasted over Henderson Field, and released a parachute flare. Simultaneously, over two thousand Japs charged up the slippery slopes of the Ridge. Edson's flanks were forced back until his position resembled a horseshoe. After an hour of fighting, the Japs withdrew to reform. The Raiders' mortars hadn't stopped many of the assault troops, so Edson called on heavier artillery sited near the airfield. Then, when another enemy wave appeared at midnight, the Long Toms' shells met them with blinding salvos. Edson told his FO (forward artillery observer): "Bring the fires in." Then: "Closer." And again: "Closer." Terrified by the huge shell bursts, Nips tried to hide from them by jumping into Marine foxholes. Marines hurled them out. At 2:00 A.M. the enemy charged again. Now flares showed them to be within sight of the airfield. Edson stood a few feet behind the Marine line. When stunned Raiders staggered toward him, he turned them around and shoved them back, rasping, "The only thing they've got that you haven't is guts." At 2:30, however, both sides fell back. Edson was now on the Ridge's northernmost knoll. If that was lost, all was lost. But he sent word back to Vandegrift: "We can hold." And the general, heartened, began to feed in his precious reserve, the Second Battalion of the Fifth Marines, a company at a time. The enemy was running out of men when, at first light, P-38s from Henderson swooped in, flying just twenty feet above the ground, strafing and firing 37-millimeter shells into the Nip reserves. Kawaguchi ordered a retreat. The Japanese dead littered the Ridge, their bodies already swelling in the heat. The Ridge was saved.

In our island war the fighting never really ended until all the Japs had been wiped out. That morning the enemy was still trying to force a passage across the mouth of the Ilu, and when five American tanks tried to descend the slopes of the Ridge, all were knocked out by Jap antiaircraft guns which had remained behind for just that purpose. During the confusing night melee, individual Nips had found their way through our lines. A jeep inching back toward Henderson and carrying five wounded Marines, one of them Red Mike's operations officer, was raked by a Nambu; there were no survivors. But the outcome of the battle was unchanged, and the losers faced a terrible prospect. Kawaguchi had to lead his men, staggering under their packs, back through the dense rainforest to the headwaters of the Matanikau, into deep, humid ravines and over towering cliffs, accompanied all the way by swarms of insects. Japs had malaria, too. They had also run out of food. And no doctors or rice awaited them. They fed on roots, leaves, and grass; they tore bark from trees; they chewed their leather rifle straps, and some, delirious, raved or stumbled into the swamps to die. "The army," a Japanese historian sadly notes, "had been used to fighting the Chinese."

Slowly the Marine perimeter grew, until it was seven miles wide and four miles deep. Now American ships brought men and supplies every day; since the Canal lacked a harbor, dock complexes were built at Kukum and, to the west, Point Cruz. The sensible course for the Japanese would have been to throw in the towel then and evacuate the Canal. But having won so much in the early bloodless months of the war, they simply could not believe that they must forfeit this island where they had spent so many lives. So they kept withdrawing troops from Papua to strengthen the forces here. Now that Henderson had become a hive of U.S. warplanes, including F4U Corsairs, the Tokyo Express no longer dared to venture out in daylight. Jap transports lay up in New Georgia and the Shortlands between dawn and dusk, bringing in reinforcements and heavy artillery each midnight and returning to Rabaul with the wounded and sick. One week a full division was landed at Cape Esperance, accompanied by ambitious battle plans from Tokyo. On paper they were impressive, but they were too complicated for the climate and the terrain. In heavy rains the jungle was completely impassable. Regimental commanders lost battalions, battalions lost companies, companies lost platoons, platoons lost squads. Lacking Atabrine, their quinine requisitions were huge. They ran out of it. Then they began running out of everything.

Meanwhile the Seabees completed another airstrip, "Fighter Two," at Kukum. Tulagi became a base for PT boats, including the boat that had brought MacArthur out of his Corregidor trap and PT-109, skippered by young Lieutenant (j.g.) John F. Kennedy. Carlson's Raiders arrived, spreading their gospel, then new, of "Gung Ho" ("Work together"). Carlson recommended long patrols, to be conducted, of course, by intelligence men. Ultimately his Raiders circled the entire island. The Second Marines landed, then the Eighth Marines, and then — the first affirmative action by the U.S. Army here — the Americal Division. The doggies were rich in candy bars; the Marines were rich in souvenirs. Bartering began, with so many Hershey bars or Butterfingers exchanged for a samurai sword or a Rising Sun battle flag. Later I acquired a little cache of mementos: a Jap helmet, a sword, and a meatball banner. I mailed them home in the only wooden box I could find; it was an awkward size, so I used packs of Chesterfields as ballast. The box reached my mother at the height of the home front's cigarette shortage, and she, thinking that was why I had sent it, merely acknowledged the souvenirs while enthusiastically thanking me for the Chesterfields.

Though Vandegrift eventually commanded forty thousand U.S. troops, though U.S. air power reduced the Express's flow to a trickle, and though Jap artillery was overwhelmed by our batteries of 75s, 105s, and Long Toms, the enemy clung stubbornly to the west bank of the Matanikau. Four separate battles were fought for this awful river. The most memorable fight was over a log crossing called the "Jap Bridge." Major Bailey was killed there, and Sam Griffith was wounded in the shoulder by a Jap marksman. (As he staggered and fell, Griffith, ever the professional, shouted, "Good shot!") Finally, on November 1, three Pioneer bridges were thrown over the river, and after that, attrition slowly sapped Japanese force and whatever morale was left. By the first week in February that was zero. In a three-night minor Dunkirk, the last eleven thousand Nips were evacuated from Cape Esperance. The long Japanese southward drive had been stopped. Between New Guinea and the Canal the myth of Jap invincibility had been gutted. And the price paid for Guadalcanal had not been excessive by standards of the Pacific war. During the six-month struggle for the island, 4,123 Americans had fallen. On Iwo Jima 25,851 Marines would be lost in less than four weeks, and the price of the eighty-two-day fight for Okinawa, the greatest bloodletting of all, would be 49,151 Americans. Vandegrift's casualty lists were less than half of MacArthur's on Papua. Papua was MacArthur's bloodiest campaign in the battles which led him back to the Philippines; after Buna, his nimble genius began to bypass enemy strongpoints, leaving them to wither on the vine. The real ordeal on the Canal had been psychological and malarial; when the army relieved the Marines, 95 percent of the original landing force was *hors de combat*, mostly by fever.

After the battle, Guadalcanal became a staging area for other troops. By then the island's name had entered the mists of legend. The *New York Times* called the Canal "one of the decisive struggles of the war in the Pacific," and after the battle Hanson Baldwin, the paper's military analyst, wrote jubilantly: "The future is ours to make." One of Hirohito's ablest strategists, Captain Toshikazu Ohmae, concluded that the situation had become "very serious." Guadalcanal met the standards, set by Winston Churchill, for great battles which, "won or lost, change the entire course of events, create new standards of values, new moods, new atmospheres in armies and in nations." President Roosevelt, citing the First Marine Division, said that its men "not only held their important strategic positions despite determined and repeated Japanese naval, air, and land attacks," but also drove the Japanese "from the proximity of the airfield" and "inflicted great losses on them." FDR concluded: "The courage and determination displayed in these operations were of an inspiring order."

But Southey may have been right: all famous victories may be meaningless. One difficulty is that, in looking back through the lens of time, we are constantly revising the definitions of proper nouns, both history's and our own, giving more weight to this battle, less weight to that. We balkanize the past, too; my recollections of the Canal are as fragmented and jumbled as the jungle I toiled through. And if you were hit in the skull, like me, you are never going to get the shattered pieces of remembrance just right. In addition, I have repressed what war memories I do have for so long that I have no way of knowing how distorted they are now. That, of course, is why I have come back to the islands.

It is the early evening of November 19, 1978, and I am hiking from Henderson Field to the Ridge, wearing khakis and my old Raider cap and carrying a flashlight, my notebook, and a small pick. I pause at a large sign:

LEVER PLANTATIONS
NO TRESPASSING

Behind the sign is a barbed-wire fence — better barbwire than the Marine Corps had then — but part of it is flattened by twisted, rusting old Marsden matting, easily stepped over. A slope of three-foot-high kunai grass, caressed just now by the rough hand of a rising wind, leads me to the ultimate knob on the Ridge. There a simple bronze plaque marks the site of Red Mike's command post. Running through my mind is the tune of "Remember Pearl Harbor," but the words are the words we sang then:

We'll remember Colonel Edson, how he led us to the fight,
We'll remember Major Bailey, how he fought with all his might . . .

Overhead the sky is a gunmetal gray. A light rain is falling. The Ridge curves southward like an incomplete question mark. Beyond it, the blue-green heights of the Grassy Knoll are shadowed by patches of fog, while on each side of me, the Ridge's slopes lead down to the rainforest where the Japanese massed for their attacks. Tropical trees there stand at least 150 feet tall. Smaller bushes lurk around them, like shrunken whores in doorways.

We'll remember the sergeants, 'cause they always led the way,
And we'll remember Pua Pua, when we're back in the U.S.A. . . .

I spit on my hands and swing the pick, once more mutilating this little acre of God. Presently I have hacked out a foxhole. It is shallow but snug; a fallen log bars the wind, the hip hollows fit, and the prospects for a comfortable night are a distinct improvement over those in the last hole I gouged out on this island, on a similar ridge three miles west of here. I had never spaded earth so easily. In a few minutes I had a deep, wide shelter, large enough for me and my gear with room to spare. I fell asleep feeling smug, sublimely unaware of catastrophe ahead. The reason the earth had been so soft was that I had been burrowing into the natural drainage line of the slope. At 3:00 A.M. a deluge awakened me, and I nearly drowned. In fact, I almost lost my weapon. Now, over a third of a century later, I avoid gullies. A man my age must be cautious, and I have decided to spend the night on the Ridge, listening once more to the sounds of the rainforest.

We'll remember the Raiders, how we marched into the fray,
Yes, we'll remember Pua Pua, when we're back in the U.S.A.

Mosquitoes appear. This time I am protected from diseases by hypodermic shots, and once I have smeared Cutter ointment on my skin the bugs withdraw. The rain stops, then the sun vanishes behind an archipelago of crimson clouds, leaving the hogback to darkness and to me. There is a stillness without echo. The night is soft, the stars slightly misty. But then, almost abruptly, the Ridge becomes a noisy place. Sound travels far here; I can hear the cries of children in a distant village, though I cannot tell from which direction they come. A dog yelps. Nearby, crickets and tree frogs chirp, and the medleys of birds grow and grow louder. They run up and down the scale, jabbering a double-quick cadence.

And then it starts to happen. Quietly, stealthily, imperceptibly, terror begins to creep across my mind so that, poring over my notebook by flashlight, I am taken quite unawares. New sounds, just now penetrating my consciousness, are impossible to identify. Down below, where the Japs formed for their assaults up the slopes, something is going *huk-huk-huk*. Something else is whickering, like the braying of a gigantic donkey. Most disconcerting is a kind of cosmic gasping. Its breath goes *hhhhhhh hhhhhhh hhhhhhh* and then *hhhhh hhhhh hhhhh*, and it is coming up after me.

Raiders, rally to me!

A nearby twig snaps. Common sense tells me it can only be a land crab, a lizard, or a wild rabbit, but my whole body goes rigid. The panting is coming closer. I want to flee, but my muscles won't respond. The thing is down there in the kunai grass, temporarily muffled by a rock. The gasping has stopped, to be replaced by a snuffling, a squeal, and sucking sounds. Now it is thumping to one side and then the other, trying to smell me out, whining impatiently.

Raiders, Raiders! Rally to me!

In that instant the thing catches my scent and I catch *its* scent. The malevolent panting has begun again, *hhh hhh hhh hhh hhh*, and it reeks of sweat, cordite, urine, and old leather. Then it arrives, clawing at the edge of my foxhole. I cannot look up. I can feel it hanging over me. My eyes are squeezed shut when a flash of light, bright enough to reach my pupils through my eyelids, pinks them. My lids flip open. There is nothing there. And there is no sound. Then the birds resume their crying, the dog barks, the children shout. Nothing has happened. Doubtless I am the victim of a nightmare. Yet my khakis are soaked with perspiration.

I am past shame, grateful for deliverance, but baffled by what to do. Returning to Henderson in the dark is out of the question. So, I think, is sleep. But I am wrong about that. I am fifty-six years old, this has been a strenuous day, and I have just had a strange shock. I roll over on my back and study the Southern Cross, its stars partly obscured by tattered clouds. I drop off. This time my dream is familiar. It is of the old party and the Sergeant. There is a difference, however. When the old man arrives he finds that the Sergeant has been there some time — his boondockers have plowed the mud — and he ignores his visitor's presence. He has the half-pathetic, half-comical look of a concentration camp victim, bereft of dignity. Atabrine has turned his skin yellower than a Jap's. His uniform is just hanging on his emaciated frame, and it is stained with what, at a closer look, turns out to be blood. He is in a towering rage, though clearly not at the old man; he doesn't even glance in that direction. Glaring elsewhere, he shakes his fist at the darkness in pitiful fury and swears savagely. At first he appears to be angry with himself. Then the truth becomes clear. I know his problem. He is furious at Lefty Zepp, the first of the Raggedy Ass Marines to die.

Of *course* I was pissed off. Zepp had been inexcusably insubordinate. I had ordered him to avoid high ground and especially to stay away from Easy Company. Forgiveness is very hard when someone you love gets killed doing what he has been expressly told not to do. Everybody in the line companies knew Zepp had been at Harvard. They all resented his sleepy, amused, almost insolent eyes, and the way he looked at you when he had scored a point: as though you had just said something disgusting, or had what was then called B.O. But Easy Company's Topkick was among those who had been suckered by Zepp's swagger stick, binoculars, handmade boondockers, and fancy pistol. Back at New River the Top had been flimflammed into saluting him, and when he found out Lefty was only a Pfc, he was furious. That wasn't my problem, and at the time it didn't seem to be much of a problem for Zepp. But in combat dislikes can be mortal. Easy Company wasn't going to look out for Zepp's ass. And in his distinctive outfit he was sniper bait anyhow. Our officers wore no insignia of rank. They knew enemy marksmen would be looking for our leaders. If a Pfc could dupe a First Soldier, he could certainly gull the Japs and draw fire. I made this point a hundred times with Zepp, but he either promised to leave the Abercrombie and Fitch gear behind when he went on the line, and then forgot to do it, or he gave me a tortuous legal argument about an enlisted man's right to private property. It was what you would expect from a Harvard man.

Later I wondered whether Easy Company knew that Lefty was a Jew. I don't think so. He didn't look Jewish, or what we thought looked Jewish. His black hair was thick and curly, but he had kept his boot-camp crew cut; it just looked like a tight cap. His eyes were slanted, his lips were thin, and his cheekbones were high, almost oriental. He was also wiry and well muscled. The race question had been raised point-blank in the section — by Bubba — and Lefty had flatly denied being Jewish. He said he was Armenian. He told Izzy Levy the truth but swore him to secrecy. Izzy didn't relay it to me until over thirty years later, when we ran into each other in Chicago. I was surprised. I had thought deception beneath Zepp. Except for his adolescent voice he emanated an invulnerable aura of self-confidence. His movements were always economical and precise; I was sure he would be an impressive physician. And his mind was first-rate. Neither Barney nor I ever beat him in chess, not once. He had joined the Marines on impulse after seeing John Payne, Randolph Scott, and Maureen O'Hara in *To the Shores of Tripoli*, a gung-ho movie that conned a lot of guys into boot camp. He wrote his father every day, and every day he got a letter back, despite the fact that doctors on the home front, with most of the younger physicians in uniform, were carrying enormous practices.

To civilians, men in combat dress look as alike as weeds in a patch, but a botanist can sort out the weeds, and a sergeant, if he is any good, should be able to sort out his people. This is something training cannot teach. It must be intuitive. The best NCOs are sensitive to the peculiarities in each rifleman's character, how he will react under pressure, what can be expected of him and what can't. To my surprise, I had found that I could do it. I could even make a fair guess about the special skills of men in other outfits — from the crouching walk of a machine gunner, for example, or the crablike movements of a mortarman. In the jungle I also learned that my timidity was actually an asset. Because of the beatings I had taken as a boy, I had become a master of evasion. And I was seldom startled. If I was about to be cornered, if danger was close, I knew it before anyone else. Most wounded infantrymen experience a lull, a dead instant between the time they are hit and the moment the shattered nerves and torn muscles catch up and start shrieking, but with me it was the other way around. I was like the White Queen in *Through the Looking-Glass*, who began to feel pain before she was hurt. And because I was young and frightened and had youthful reflexes, I responded instantly to those flickers of warning. It was a sense I cannot define, a kind of pusillanimity on a subliminal level.

My instincts told me that Lefty Zepp was a poor insurance risk, and that the open ground below Yaetake was to be avoided at all costs, particularly by him. I had made that clear. He had stared moodily over my head. We had often argued about courage. I told him that short of turning my back on the Japs and showing a clean pair of heels, which would merely make me a more conspicuous target — in combat he who fights and runs away may not live to fight another day — my actions would be governed solely by determination to survive the war. He said he wanted to live through it, too, but he wouldn't mind coming home with a Silver Star or even a Navy Cross. I quoted someone to the effect that a man wouldn't sell his life to you, but he will give it to you for a piece of colored ribbon. The whole panoply of military glory, I argued (and still argue), is a monstrous deception. I felt (and still feel) that one of the most effective ways to end war would be to strip the military of its anachronistic ribbons, uniforms, and titles. Ban medals, I said; put infantrymen in blue denim, make generals "superintendents," colonels "supervisors," and sergeants "foremen." Then, I said, the martial drive would slacken everywhere. Lefty was beguiled but unconvinced. I could see that he still wanted to greet his father as a certified military hero. So I ordered him to lie low at Yaetake, avoiding, above all, Easy Company's sector. And the son of a bitch double-crossed me.

The rest of us were huddled around a situation map in the ravine below our main line of resistance, trying to match the map's coordinates with a new batch of aerial photographs for a group of officers. The diversion was welcome. For over four hours we had been toiling like convicts in a Georgia chain gang, straining to haul heavy mortars and 37-millimeter guns up an almost perpendicular slope of shale and scree and small rocks, all unstable and treacherous. The few patches of earth were muddy and slippery: more dangerous, really, than the stones. At one point Horse Goltz — his full name was Horst von der Goltz, and I've never met an unlikelier Prussian — had clumsily skidded above me, and his bayonet scabbard had opened a nasty gash on my cheek. Now I was up to my stacking swivel with officers waving glossy pictures at me and demanding that I tell them what this lump and that line meant. Dusty Rhodes was my most skillful interpreter of aerial photographs, and I had just begun to wonder where he was when I heard a thin, breaking, unmistakable shriek from above: "Corpsman!" The word was voided into the hush. Rip looked at me. His face was fisted. He breathed: "Lefty!" Then Dusty came scuttling down wide-eyed. I asked shakily, "What's the word?" He said, "Lefty's hurt bad, they said a sniper."

At that time wounds, not to mention deaths, were still a novelty for us, and we didn't know what to do. In fact there was nothing we could have done. We stood around, hands on hips, avoiding each other's gaze and peering up to where, we knew, Easy Company held the line. They handed Lefty down, their hands held high to pass him overhead, but we heard him before we could see him. I had read an article about how the wounded never cry. It was a lie. Zepp was sobbing. Whatever his wound, I couldn't believe it was mortal. If it was, I thought, there would be no point in moving him. I didn't know then that our line had just pulled back to the reverse slope, that it was move him or leave him, and there was no choice there, because the Marine Corps always recovers its dead and dying, not for their sakes but to hearten the living.

The sobbing stopped, and then we saw him. The back of his blouse, splotched with great batwings of sweat, looked normal, but his legs were spread as wide as the hoist allowed, and his groin was one vast bloodstain, crimson bubbles forming and breaking on his thighs. Then I saw the loose lolling of the head, and I knew. As he came closer I saw that his features were untouched. The lips were parted, almost swollen; the neck heavy. His eyes looked astonished: how could they do this to a Harvard man? I felt a surge of pain, grief, shock, loss. My wrath came later, when Barney found out that Lefty had been standing in full view of the enemy, studying the Jap lines through his binoculars. But there was no rage at the time. I thought of four things all at once: he was nineteen years old, he would never sing "Fair Harvard" again, I would have to write his father, and I didn't have his father's address. But just then I couldn't move. I thought: *Dulce nec decorum est pro patria mori.* If anyone had hummed the "Marines' Hymn" then I would have pistoled him.

Two mortarmen laid Lefty's body under a grubby little tree apart from the map conference, which, to my amazement, was still going on. Then, as naturally as though we had planned it, we went over one by one to say goodbye. Pip was wiping his eyes on his cruddy sleeve. Knocko Craddock looked like a movie drunk, his every movement exaggerated, the arm-waving, falling-away motions of a man pretending to be plastered. Barney had a heartbreak look, his face in shadow. The rest followed, all in or near tears. If Samuel Eliot Morison had seen us then, he certainly wouldn't have thought of us as "tough guys" who "asked for nothing better than to come to grips with the sneaking enemy who had aroused all their primitive instincts."

I was last. I didn't know what to do, so I walked over and knelt on one knee. Lefty's skin, normally olive, looked like ivory. I remembered the words of Gustavo Adolfo Bécquer: "Oh God, how alone the dead are left!" though I thought how lonely the survivors were, too. Eventually, I realized, a chaplain would arrive, but Zepp had had no religion, or had renounced the one into which he had been born. The best I could do was a few lines from A. E. Housman's "To an Athlete Dying Young":

> To-day, the road all runners come,
> Shoulder-high we bring you home,
> And set you at your threshold down,
> Townsman of a stiller town. . . .
> And round that early-laurelled head
> Will flock to gaze the strengthless dead . . .

I couldn't remember the rest of it. I leaned over and kissed him full on the lips. Then I looked down at his gory crotch. In some obscene, unspeakable, vicarious but identifiable way, I felt that I had lost my virginity after all.

Descending the Ridge now in 1978, I maneuver my rented four-wheel-drive Toyota eastward on the island's one road — it was dirt in 1942, is paved now, but is as bumpy as ever — and park beside the Tenaru. Walking along the stream's bank, I catch a sudden glimpse of Jacob Vouza, who, thanks to Queen Elizabeth II, will soon become *Sir* Jacob Vouza. He sees me coming, and we trot awkwardly toward each other, two old warriors spavined in every joint. We embrace; he leads me to his village, and I wait outside while he changes clothes in his thatched hut — he insists he must don his uniform for the occasion. Overhead a flag ascends a flagpole. It is the same flag which he carried as his safe-conduct thirty-six years ago and which nearly cost him his life. If it is floating over the village, Vouza is home. When the British returned to the Solomons after the war, this custom annoyed them, but no one dared tell the old hero to replace the Stars and Stripes with the Union Jack. Sir Jacob was, and remains, the most popular man on the island.

Our reunion is no stroke of fate. An old-boy network still operates in the islands, mostly comprised of Australians, and Martin Clemens, now retired and living in Melbourne, has sent word to other former coastwatchers and senior islanders that I will be coming. Vouza is in his late eighties, and I decide it would be unwise to ask him to accompany me during my entire tour of the Canal. Instead, another native, Jackson Koria, will accompany me. Like Vouza, Koria worked for the Japanese as a laborer during the fighting and relayed information to Vandegrift's G-2.

It is difficult to describe the adoration these men feel for the United States. Several months earlier, when the Solomon Islands archipelago became the one hundred fiftieth member of the United Nations, with its own flag (bright blue, green, and yellow), motto ("To lead is to serve"), and national anthem ("God Bless the Solomon Islands"), the British ceremoniously handed the reins of authority to the prime minister of an elected legislature. A British band played "God Save the Queen." There was a ripple of polite applause. Then a native band played their new anthem. The applause was louder. Finally a band of American bluejackets swung into view playing the "Marines' Hymn." Every Solomon Islander was on his feet, roaring approval.

Vouza emerges from his hut. He wears a skirt instead of trousers; otherwise he is attired in the dress uniform of a Marine Corps sergeant major. His Silver Star is pinned to his blouse. He carries an engraved sword presented to him by the Marine Corps. As I photograph him, he asks me where I keep my dress blues. It is an embarrassing question; how can I tell him that long ago I discarded my blues, my khakis, and my greens — that my faded Raider cap is the only piece of uniform I kept? I change the subject. Elsewhere

Sergeant Major Jacob Vouza, 1978

I have been told that there is now a strong Japanese presence in the islands, and that one Japanese, a Captain Honda, is particularly enterprising. I ask Vouza about all this. He stiffens; the Nips are here, all right, but he never speaks to them. So I change the subject again, suggesting that we revisit the mouth of the Ilu. That pleases him. After lunching on cool, delicious chunks of papaya, we stroll along the river's bank, watching cattle and children bathe. Surprisingly, one of the children is wearing a pair of *tabi*, those World War II Jap sneakers which separated the big toe from the others, like the thumb in a mitten. It is incredible that they should still be in use; my boondockers didn't make it past the fifteenth year. I start to ask Vouza about them, then remember that the Japs are still a touchy subject with him. We arrive at the sandspit where so many men died and stand in silence. I think of Private Schmid, fighting on though blinded. I also think of Vouza and what he did that terrible night. Beside me he is erect, at attention. I compliment him on his military bearing and promise to remember him to his friends in the States. He says, "Tell them I love them all. Me old man now, and me no look good no more. But me never forget." I say, "You no old man, Vouza. You healthy, strong. You live long time." He relaxes and smiles.

In the Toyota, Koria and I cross a new, 150-foot bridge across the Lunga and another, longer span across the Matanikau. In 1942 it took two months for nineteen thousand Marines, with Chesty Puller cracking the whip, to reach the far bank of the Matanikau. Today it is a ten-minute ride from the airfield, now called Henderson International Airport. The bridge is one-way because, you are told, the Marines only went in one direction — forward. This harmless fiction is succeeded by surprises on all sides. A Catholic cathedral stands on one bank, a Chinatown on the other, and, in the place of Kukum's Fighter Two airstrip, a nine-hole golf course. That is only the beginning. The end is the town of Honiara. No Guadalcanal veteran will recognize the name. Honiara rose after the war, and takes its name from the native *naho ni ara*, meaning "facing the east and southeast wind." It occupies the site of Point Cruz, a complex of concrete docks we built to replace a coconut plantation. (More money for the soap company.) The town is now the capital for the Solomon nation's fifty thousand citizens. In it are two air-conditioned hotels, one of them owned by Chinese; there is another Chinatown in the capital; and the Chinese restaurant Lantern serves the best food on the island.

But it is the Nipponese who are most conspicuous. Young Japanese who hadn't even been born when the battle raged here come on economic missions, examining the Solomons' rich mineral deposits, testing its palm oil, netting its skipjack tuna, bargaining for the Canal's rice, sugarcane, cattle, papaya, and pineapple, and asking penetrating questions about the threats of natives on Malaita, one of the richer islands, to secede from the federation. Older Japanese arrive each year to pray at small shrines for the souls of their husbands and brothers who died in the fighting. Executives from huge Nipponese conglomerates sit around tables in the hotels, drinking cold Kirin beer and studying maps of the islands. They make me feel uncomfortable. But then, so does the sign reading "Jackets and Neckties," the menus printed in Japanese as well as English, the taxi stand, and the well-stocked bar. Heavy with survivor's guilt, I tell the waiter: "You catchum me one fella Scotch on rocks."

The following morning I call on Captain H. Honda in his office at the Taiko Fisheries Company. He is younger than I am, and looks younger still, a short, slender, but sinewy man with neatly parted black hair and eyes like green marbles. But he was old enough to volunteer for the kamikaze corps in 1945. He was turned down, and I, hoping to find common ground, congratulate him on his failure to pass the kamikaze examination. It doesn't work. His smile is so thin that he stops just short of baring his teeth. And to my surprise, after all these years I find my own hackles rising. The sad truth is that there can never be peace between men like this man and men like me; an invisible wall will forever separate us. To make the interview as short as possible, I confine myself to one bland question, asking whether he thinks that the new Solomons nation can become economically independent. He shakes his head. Papua, yes; the Fijis, yes; the Solomons, no. The problem, he says, is oriental imperialism. Bougainville, the richest of the islands, has been annexed by the Papuans. But the Papuans are victims, too; West Irian, the western half of their island, has been seized by the Indonesians. These issues have never been raised in the United Nations. Imperialism, it seems, is a crime in the UN only when the imperialists are white.

Returning to my hotel, I pass the local movie theater, a converted Quonset hut — the current flick is "It Happened One Night" — and meet Bill Bennett, an old coastwatcher wearing a First Raider Battalion T-shirt. Bennett and another Australian at the bar don't share Honda's pessimism, though they warn me not to be fooled by Honiara's fashion shops and the current island craze for Adidas footwear. Outside the city, Guadalcanal is still primitive. Although there is electricity here in the town, elsewhere, save for a few generators, light is provided by kerosene lamps. To be sure, the Seventh-Day Adventists have built a high school, Planned Parenthood has established a lively chapter, and the local hospital — still called Hospital No. 9, as it was in 1942, for sentimental reasons — is first class. But the government is weak and few islanders are interested in, or even aware of, their independence. "Oh, yes," says Bill's friend. "I forgot to mention that before leaving the British built a mental hospital." I say, "We could have used it."

My tour of the island convinces me that the Canal is still essentially pristine. On Red Beach I find the remains of a floating pier and two amphibian tractors, overgrown by vines and covered with nearly four decades of rust. Otherwise the fine-grained gray beach and the stately palms are much as they were on August 7, 1942. At Henderson Field the black skeleton of the old control tower is untouched. Cassia grows in a half-track near the airstrip. Since the field is now surfaced with concrete, natives have liberated strips of Marsden matting and use them for fences. To the west are the Japanese shrines — they are the same, I shall find, on all the islands: six feet high, four sided, with Japanese characters on all sides. I also discover several U.S. Army markers, but almost none erected by the Marine Corps. Here and there one comes across the fuselage of a downed World War II plane; invariably the interiors reek of urine. Near the Kokumbona River I trace the contours of old trenches and foxholes wrinkling the ground, though my own elude me. Except on the Ridge and the Ilu sandspit, all other landmarks of the past, including the Jap Bridge, have been reclaimed by the jungle. This is even true at Hell's Point, a stockpile of unexploded ammunition still marked out-of-bounds for anyone straying near it. There are overgrown Hell's Points all over the Pacific; they are the war's chief legacy to natives. I point to the warning sign, nearly obscured by vines, and tell Koria that this is a barren wasteland, that is will always be dangerous. He nods grimly and replies, "Mi save gut": he understands it well.

After the Allied victories on Papua and Guadalcanal, Japan's great 1942 offensive spluttered and died. In Tokyo Hirohito's generals and admirals assured him that they could hold the empire they had won. Until now American strategists in Washington had tacitly agreed; their plans for the Pacific war had been defensive; they had wanted only to hold Australia and Hawaii until the war in Europe had been won. But MacArthur, Halsey, and Nimitz were aggressive commanders. They had shown what their troops could do. In the southwest Pacific they were determined to seize, or at least neutralize, Rabaul. MacArthur could then skip along New Guinea's northern coast, moving closer to his cherished goal, the recapture of the Philippine Islands. And the U.S. Navy could open another offensive in the central Pacific. The split command worried the Joint Chiefs, and to this day historians wonder whether it was wise. MacArthur wasn't interested in the central Pacific, while Admiral King was convinced that Japan could be defeated without an American reconquest of the Philippines.

Actually the two drives became mutually supporting, each of them protecting the other's flank. Nimitz, King's theater commander, diverted enemy sea power which would otherwise have pounced on MacArthur from the east, while MacArthur's air force took out enemy planes which could have driven the Marines from their island beachheads. Their strategies differed — MacArthur's was to move land-based bombers forward in successive bounds to achieve local air superiority, while Nimitz's was predicated on carrier air power shielding amphibious landings on key isles, which then became stepping-stones through the enemy's defensive perimeters — but that was because they were dealing with different landscapes and seascapes. For a man in his sixties, MacArthur was extraordinarily receptive to new military concepts. Not only could he adopt the amphibious techniques developed by the Marine Corps; he went one step further by waging what Churchill later called "*tri*phibious warfare"— the coordination of land, sea, and air forces. At West Point the general had been taught army doctrine: rivers are barriers. At Annapolis, midshipmen are told that bodies of water are highways. MacArthur combined the two brilliantly.

His GIs never liked him, of course. He was too egotistical, they thought, and too unappreciative of them. He was that and more — perhaps the most exasperating general ever to wear a uniform. But his genius quickened the war, foiled the enemy, and executed movements beyond the imagination of the less gifted soldiers who scorned him.

Perhaps his two most famous battles were fought at Hollandia, now the Indonesian capital of Djajapura, and the island of Biak, between New Guinea and the Philippines. You can reach Djajapura's Senatai Airport on a weekly Air Niugini flight from Port Moresby; daily DC-9 flights leave Senatai for Biak. Hollandia, as those who served there know, has one of the world's finest natural harbors. Wartime warehouses and Quonset huts can still be found along the water, but most of the city's buildings date from the 1950s. Between Senatai and Cendrawasih University and the northwestern edge of the bay a large cement memorial marks the site of MacArthur's headquarters. Senatai is one of the Pacific's few international airports, but shipping in the harbor is scarce, and the government does not encourage visitors. Except for missionaries and an occasional businessman or tourist, one rarely sees a white face. The population is roughly half Indonesian and half Irianese. The fashionable suburb on Angkasa Hill offers a superb view of the harbor, and the governor's new office building (*Gubernuran*) is handsome. Otherwise, Hollandia is a disappointment. The city itself is built around a market and a central plaza. You find a couple of movie theaters there and a shocking stench of fish, garbage, and dog excrement.

Biak is more interesting. It, too, has its forlorn sights, notably railroad tracks which emerge from the bush, cross a crumbling dock, and vanish into the sea, but wartime memorabilia are easy to find. You arrive at Mokmer Airfield, the only one of MacArthur's huge runways there which still exists. Across from the field stands the old Bachelor Officers' Quarters, now a hotel run by the Merpati Nusantara Airways. And north of there you can explore what the natives call the "Japanese Caves" area — a complex of natural caverns in which Colonel Naoyuki Kuzumi holed up with his men for their last stand in June of 1944. When they refused to surrender, GIs dynamited the roof of the main cave. The roof collapsed, killing the defenders, and you can peer down at the debris of defeat: canteens, ammunition boxes, bits of uniforms, rifles, and the rusting skeletons of Jap vehicles.

Biak was a key battle, because Kuzumi had made the most murderous discovery of the war. Until then the Japs had defended each island at the beach. When the beach was lost, the island was lost; surviving Nips formed for a banzai charge, dying for the emperor at the muzzles of our guns while few, if any, Americans were lost. After Biak the enemy withdrew to deep caverns. Rooting them out became a bloody business which reached its ultimate horrors in the last months of the war. You think of the lives which would have been lost in an invasion of Japan's home islands — a staggering number of American lives but millions more of Japanese — and you thank God for the atomic bomb.

Back on Guadalcanal, I leave on an early morning call. Bob Milne, a local pilot, has invited me to fly up the Slot tomorrow in his little twin-engine, orange-and-white Queenair DC-3. In 1943, when MacArthur slowly approached the Philippines, we were inching up the ladder of the Solomons. Today we can fly to Bougainville and back in a day, but over a year passed between the Bloody Ridge battle and the Third Marine Division's landing at Bougainville's Empress Augusta Bay. In between we had driven the enemy from the islands of Pavuvu, Rendova, New Georgia, Vella Lavella, Kolombangara, Choiseul, Mono, and Shortland. This was Halsey's job. He was one of the few admirals who could work in tandem with MacArthur; between them they isolated the great Jap stronghold at Rabaul, where over 100,000 of Hirohito's infantrymen, who asked only to die for their emperor, were bypassed and left to bitterness and frustration. After the conquest of the Slot the Pacific war was divided into its two great theaters, MacArthur's and Nimitz's.

At daybreak Bob races us across Henderson's concrete and we soar over the Matanikau, Honiara, and Cape Esperance. Presently

Santa Isabel looms to starboard and then New Georgia to port. Peering down from my copilot's seat I see the islands on either side of the Slot as huge, green, hairy mushrooms dominated by volcanic mountains, of which 8,028-foot Pobomanashi is the highest. Here and there a clump of thatched roofs marks the site of a village, but these are few; in this part of the world there are more islands than people. As we lose altitude in the shining morning air, Bob points at crocodiles dozing in the sun and then toward Lolo, the largest lagoon in the world, over sixty-eight miles long. Rising once more, we pass over an enormous coconut plantation and then over more familiar terrain: hummocks of ascending hills with valleys, alternately jungle and kunai grass. On the dim horizon I spot Bougainville, that large, mountainous island of spectacular volcanoes and trackless rainforests where bulldozers can, and did, sink in the green porridge of swampland without leaving a trace.

Nothing historic is happening here now. The islands haven't changed since a million men altered the course of the war in countless local engagements. Bob points down at the remains of one of them, a shadow beneath the water which, he tells me, is the sunken hull of John F. Kennedy's PT-109. Once these skies belonged to Pappy Boyington. Now we refuel at a base Boyington used, Munda, on New Georgia, bulldozed and surfaced by Seabees long ago and now a carpet of weed-splotched coral. At Kieta, our turnabout field — this is on Bougainville, under the Papuan flag — I stretch my legs and drink 7-Up in a tiny tin-roofed terminal building which the Australians erected in 1970. It is modest, even shabby: linoleum on the floor, a figured-calico-covered table, broken wicker chairs. Like most airports in this part of the world it is usually crowded, mostly with natives there to see friends off or welcome them back. Some of them stare at me. One tells me in pidgin that Caucasians are rare here — so rare in the hills inland that when one of them appears the native girls open their thighs for him out of gratitude for the comic relief.

Elsewhere, in the Palaus and Marianas, ecology is shaping up as a public issue. Not in the Solomons; one doubts that it can ever be raised here. The jungle, allied with the climate, seems too strong ever to be threatened by man. The war was a major assault on the rainforests. It is scarcely remembered now. Nature holds all the cards. People can live on the forest's fringes, but only at its sufferance. In a sense the fighting in this theater was a struggle between man and the primeval forest. The forest won; man withdrew, defeated by the masses of green and the diseases lurking there. That awesome power still lies in wait, ready to shatter anyone who defies it. If you want to live in the jungle you must treat it with great respect and keep your distance. Maugham saw that, Gauguin saw it, and so did Robert Louis Stevenson. Even I, cosseted now by all the achievements of modern technology, know that this trip, like my last one here, will alter me in ways I cannot now know. Yet you cannot resent nature. It is too enormous. Besides, it didn't *ask* you to come. You are here because the Japanese brought you the first time and left wounds which cannot heal without this second trip. You can, of course, resent the Japanese. I did. I still do.

Our trip back to the Canal is hurried. Landings after dark are forbidden in the islands; there are no runway lights, no navigational aids to guide fliers, only the bush and the glaucous, phosphorescent sea waiting to swallow you below. Bob puts us down neatly in a thickening twilight, and a friend drives me over the Matanikau to Honiara. The hotel pool is lighted, and several middle-aged Japanese men are leaping in and out of it, enlivening their horseplay with jubilant shouts. As I pick up my key the clerk genially suggests that I join them. A dip would be refreshing, but I shake my head. I need rest. Tomorrow I fly to an island whose very name evokes terror. It is Tarawa.

Les Braves Gens

AMERICANS AT HOME THOUGHT ALL THE ISLAND BATTLEFIELDS IN the Pacific were pretty much alike: jungly, rainy, with deep white beaches ringed by awnings of palm trees. That was true of New Guinea and the Solomons, but most of Admiral Nimitz's central Pacific offensive, which opened in the autumn of 1943, was fought over very different ground. Only the palms and the pandanus there evoke memories of the South Pacific, and the pandanus do not flourish because rain seldom falls. A typical central Pacific island, straddling the equator, is a small platform of coral, sparsely covered with sand and scrub bush, whose highest point rises no more than a few feet above the surf line. Tarawa (pronounced *TAR-uh-wuh*), like most of the land formations in this part of the world, is actually an atoll, a triangular group of thirty-eight islands circled by a forbidding coral reef and sheltering, within the triangle, a dreamy lagoon. The fighting was on one of Tarawa's isles, Betio (*BAY-she-oh*), because that was where the priceless Japanese airstrip was. Betio is less than half the size of Manhattan's Central Park. No part of it is more than three hundred yards from the water. A good golfer can drive a ball across it at almost any point.

Tarawa is in the Gilbert Islands. Nimitz's real objective was Kwajalein, in the Marshall Islands, over five hundred miles to the northwest. The largest atoll in the world, sixty-five miles long, Kwajalein would provide the Americans with an immense anchorage and a superb airdrome. But Tarawa and its sister atoll Makin (pro-

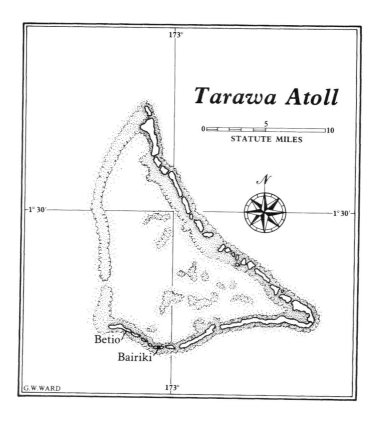

Tarawa Atoll

0 — 5 — 10
STATUTE MILES

N

1° 30'   1° 30'

Betio
Bairiki

G.W.WARD   173°

nounced *MUG-rin*) had to fall first. Unlike the Marshalls, which
had been mandated to Japan in the Treaty of Versailles, and which
Hirohito's troops had spent twenty years arming to the teeth, the
Gilberts, where Tarawa was, had been a British crown colony. The
Nips had arrived there two days after Pearl Harbor. Colonel Vivien
Fox-Strangeways, the resident British administrator, had fled
Tarawa in a small launch, dashing from island to island by day and
holing up in coves by night until a British ship picked him up in
the Ellice Islands, to the south. Since then the only Allied contact
with the Gilberts had been the ineffectual foray by Carlson's Raiders on Makin. Carlson reported that he hadn't encountered much
resistance. By the autumn of 1943 that was no longer true. Carlson,
ironically, had been the agent of change. Warned by his strike, the
enemy had strengthened the defenses of the Gilberts, particularly

those on Tarawa's Betio. The Japanese needed that airstrip there. It is a sign of their determination that they had chosen Betio's beach to site the British coastal defense guns they had captured at Singapore.

Before the war these islands had been as insignificant as Guadalcanal — remote, insular, far from the Pacific's trade routes. The islanders lived in thatched huts, harvested copra, fished for tuna, and watched the tides alter their shoreline from year to year. A schooner arrived once every three months to exchange tobacco and brightly colored cloth for copra. The Gilbertese were living over valuable phosphate deposits, but in the 1940s no one was aware of it. Indeed, few outsiders even knew or cared about the islands' existence. Christian missionaries were exceptions; by the time of Pearl Harbor half the natives were Catholics and the other half Protestants. They paid a price for their devotion when the Nips landed. Under threat of death Gilbertese men were forced to defecate on their crude altars; Gilbertese women had to perform obscene ceremonies with crucifixes. It was the same old story: islanders who had little stake in the war, and might have been befriended by their conquerors, were alienated by a barbarous occupation policy. Long before the fall of 1943 the Japs were thoroughly hated throughout the Gilberts.

In planning the seizure of Makin and Tarawa, Nimitz chose as his commander Rear Admiral Raymond A. Spruance, who had performed superbly at Midway seventeen months earlier. Spruance divided his armada of over a hundred warships into three task forces, one for Makin, one for Tarawa, and one to throw up an umbrella of fighter planes from seventeen carriers, challenging Jap fliers from Kwajalein who tried to disrupt the two operations. In the event, enemy warplanes were intimidated. Hirohito's troops were not. Makin, which was supposed to be easy, wasn't. GIs didn't take it until the fourth day of fighting. Here, for the first but not the last time, a basic amphibious issue arose between U.S. Army and U.S. Marine Corps generals. Soldiers moved slowly to keep casualty lists short. Marines lunged at the enemy, sometimes at reckless speed, because they knew that until the fighting ended the fleet which had landed them would be vulnerable to enemy attack. They believed that Makin vindicated them. While GIs crawled ashore there, a Nip sub torpedoed an American carrier, drowning ten times the number of men who died fighting on Makin.

Tarawa was to be a tragedy for different reasons, which, seen through the telescope of hindsight, seem incomprehensible. Everyone knew that Tarawa — which is to say Betio — would be tough. The reef was formidable. The enemy had mined it. The beach bristled with huge guns, concrete obstacles, and barbed-wire concertinas designed to force invaders into the fire zone of cannon and machine guns. That was only part of the problem, but it was the part known to Spruance and his staff before the first wave of Marines went in. The greater problem was the reef. The only craft which could cross a jutting reef, even after the mines had been defused, were what we called "amphtracs" — amphibious tractors. Driven by propellers, they could move through water at four knots; their caterpillar tracks would carry them over land, including the reef ledge, at twenty miles per hour. Twenty Marines could ride in each amphtrac. The landing force needed all it could get. But there were few available, and Spruance's staff, notably Rear Admiral Turner, took a sanguine view of the tidal problem anyway. Using 1841 charters, they assured the Marines that at H-hour the reef would be covered by five feet of water, which meant that a loaded Higgins boat, drawing between three and four feet, could cross it. Therefore there would be enough amphtracs for the first wave, though, they conceded, there would be none for those following.

This defies understanding. A landing in spring would have been another matter, but Fox-Strangeways had described Betio's low, dodging autumn tides to the Americans. Major F. L. G. Holland, a New Zealander who had lived on Tarawa for fifteen years, said the tide might be as little as three feet. And the night before the Betio attack Rota Onorio, now Speaker of the Gilberts' House of Assembly and then a fourteen-year-old boy, paddled his dugout out to the Allied fleet and told naval officers that tomorrow the reef would be impassable, even at high tide. He, Fox-Strangeways, and Holland were ignored. Then, in the morning, the situation worsened when the fleet's timetable began to come apart. The transports carrying the Marines were trapped between Spruance's battleship bombardment and the replying fire from the enemy's shore guns. They moved, delaying the landing and missing the tide. Next it was discovered that the battleship captains and the carrier commanders had failed to consult one another; the ships' thirty-five-minute salvos ended to permit the carrier planes to come in, but the planes, whose pilots had been given another schedule, were a half hour late. That permitted the Jap batteries to open up on the transports, further delaying the landing waves. The air strike was supposed to last thirty minutes. It lasted seven. Finally, everyone awaited what was supposed to be the last touch in softening up the beach defenses, a massive B-24 raid from a base in the Ellice Islands. They waited. And waited. The B-24s never arrived. H-hour was delayed by forty-three more precious minutes.

After the battle Seabees built more than nineteen miles of roads on Tarawa and erected piers, observation towers, and radio towers; installed a fuel pipeline; and gave the islands electricity, refrigeration, mosquito control, water purification, and a twenty-four-hundred-foot mole. The atoll's Australian nuns were presented with new blue-and-white habits. Then the war ended and the Americans left. Most of the technological marvels were ruined by the weather. The Gilberts once more became backwaters. Today Tarawa is less lonely than it was before the war, but by the standards of the rest of the world it is still remote. The atoll may be reached by air twice a week from Nauru, itself obscure, or every other week from Fiji. I choose to come via Nauru Airways. Peering down from my lazy flight — we are over an hour late — I see the twenty-two-mile reef first, a lopsided horseshoe containing the beautiful pink isles, each with its umbrella of palms twisted by centuries of typhoons. Sturdy Seabee rock-and-coral causeways still connect some of the islands in the atoll, though not Betio, which since 1943 has been regarded as the pariah of the Gilberts. As we enter our glide pattern I look down on the shore, four thousand yards within the reef, and see the horizontal rippling of the sand where the sea has ridged it. Here and there on Betio, rusty hulks are visible, though there is no way of telling whether they are the remains of boats, tanks, or shore batteries. The waters are placid. The islets are like stones in a delicate necklace. The trees lean indolently. It seems inconceivable that what happened here happened here.

We land on Bairiki, the islet closest to Betio. The runway ("Bairiki International Airport") is there. So are the government's offices; so is the atoll's tiny, whitewashed cinder-block Otintai Hotel. The airfield's tin-roofed, open-sided terminal building is about the size of a Beverly Hills carport. Outside are little rustlings and stirrings among the palms, as though they were whispering among themselves, but inside the terminal one's senses are assaulted by a shouting, sweating, colorfully dressed crowd. Sometimes, in a paranoid mood, I wonder whether these mobs at Pacific airports aren't always the same mob, a troupe that flies ahead of me to block my way. They all look the same, sound the same, smell the same. Abruptly the chaos thins and I am confronted by a black giant wearing Her Britannic Majesty's white tropical uniform — white short-sleeved blouse, white shorts, white pith helmet. He studies my passport, stamps it, rummages through my B-4 bag, and waves me on.

Outside I board a minibus. One by one, then two by two, other passengers join me, until the bus resembles one of those Barnum and Bailey circus cars packed with flesh, or the Marx Brothers' stateroom in *A Night at the Opera*. But I have a window. It provides an astonishing glimpse of one of those high, old-fashioned London taxis which were replaced by smaller, sleeker cabs years ago. The taxi bears Elizabeth II's coat of arms on its doors. Within, a pukka sahib — later I learn he is Governor the Honourable Reginald Wallace — is waving cheerily. No one waves back, or even glances in his direction. Thus, as in India, the British Raj ends with neither bang nor whimper but merely with massive indifference among its former, or soon-to-be former, subjects. In a few months, one of my fellow passengers tells me, the Gilbertese will become independent. He proudly shows me the new nation's flag: a yellow bird and sun on a red background, with wavy blue and white stripes below. It is vaguely suggestive of Arizona's state flag.

Here in the far reaches of the Pacific there is a kind of camaraderie among Europeans, a generic term which includes Americans, and within an hour I am lunching at the Otintai with four new acquaintances, all British, one of whom, a stocky woman who works for the World Health Organization, recently spent a week crossing the mountainous spine of Guadalcanal, a feat which has been matched by few, if any. My friends are all hearty, jolly, and blessed with that English love of incongruity which makes the eclipse of British power almost droll. A slender Welsh economist married to a Polynesian girl has discovered that one of the old Japanese blockhouses on Betio is precisely the size of a squash court; he is using it as such. Tony Charlwood, a chief master in the Royal Navy and an ordnance expert — his last assignment was defusing IRA bombs in Belfast — has just finished a three-month job here, removing from the beaches, at low tide, seventeen tons of live ammunition, including several eighteen-inch shells. He makes it sound like a parlor game.

The most interesting of the four is Ieuan Battan, deputy secretary to the Gilbertese chief minister, a handsome, husky man who just now has a grisly problem, though he speaks of it lightly. He has to handle the delicate consequences of finding the skeletons of fighting men, which are discovered from time to time when new sewer lines are laid, say, or when children are building sand castles around old spider holes. Last week a group of little boys unearthed the fleshless corpses of four Japanese and one American. How, I ask Ieuan, can he tell the four from the one? It is easy, he replies; the American was wearing dog tags and a Swiss watch, and Japanese femurs, teeth, and skulls are microscopically different from ours. At the moment it is the Nipponese skulls which are worrying him. A nineteen-man delegation is on its way from Tokyo to cremate what is left of their countrymen. But the children who found the craniums are exhibiting them on their windowsills, and he must persuade the boys to relinquish them. If this is black humor, there is worse to come, though I suspect it may be fictive. One of my companions insists that recently two couples were making love on a sand dune known to be littered with old artillery duds. One couple, still in the prelims, heard the other man shout, "I'm coming!" The girl cried, "I'm close!" Then they blew up.

Most of Ieuan's tasks are duller. He is masterminding the transfer of power from British colonial rule to Gilbertese independence. He deals with the islands' elected officials and such issues as water tables, natural resource development, and fishing rights off Christmas Island, one of the Gilberts. The main problem, he says, is that natives on outlying Gilbert islands are moving to Tarawa Atoll. Their expectations were raised during the years of the American occupation — they were given room and board, and paid twenty-five cents a day — and now they want cash wages, dance halls, and a consumer society. Before the war they didn't know that appliances, movies, and private cars existed. Now they do, and they are determined to have them, despite the meager yields of their primitive economy. Had they known I was coming, Ieuan tells me, they would have greeted me at the airport with tawny girls dancing the exotic *maneaba*, because they know visitors expect that of them. But they prefer the Twist. Chubby Checker is their idol. They are addicted to filter tips. On Betio, where young lovers couple in positions described by Masters and Johnson, their slogan is "Betio Swings!"

I decide to nap after lunch. Tropical evergreens decorate the hotel entrance; Christmas is a month away, but already the merchants are psyching up customers who really can't afford their wares. A few skilled workers can; outside my hotel door, interrupting my afternoon nap, are two islanders jabbing at coral with a jackhammer. I think of the Marines who tried to dig in here with entrenching tools. At dusk, as the sky deepens with a lovely flush — "Out here the sun," Bob Trumbull told me, "sets on the British Empire with style" — I slip into swimming trunks and dive from a coral ledge into the sea. The water is warm, sensual, but when I climb out I am reminded how vicious coral can be. I nick an elbow and open a nasty gash above a knee. Neither is disabling, however; tomorrow I shall take the ferry to Betio. Already the

Sergeant in me is brooding about it; I know I can expect a hilltop nightmare tonight. The Twist. Chubby Checker. Betio Swings. Is that why 3,381 Marines of my generation fell here thirty-five years ago?

Both the American *and* the Japanese troops were commanded by admirals — the defenders of the atoll were members of the Japanese Special Landing Forces: Japanese Marines, wearing the distinctive crysanthemum-and-anchor emblem on their helmets — and confidence was high, both on the flagship offshore and in the beach's headquarters bunker. The admiral commanding the American bombardment told Marine officers: "Gentlemen, we will not neutralize Betio. We will not destroy it. We will obliterate it!" A Marine general, Julian C. Smith, replied: "Even though you navy officers do come in to about a thousand yards, I remind you that you have a little armor. I want you to know that Marines are crossing that beach with bayonets, and the only armor they will have is a khaki shirt." But despite scheduling blunders the warships and warplanes seemed to be doing their best to prepare the way for the landing force. Three U.S. battleships, five cruisers, and nine destroyers had plastered the shore with three thousand tons of high explosives — roughly ten tons per acre. Yet the Japanese admiral remained confident. He had said that "a million men cannot take Tarawa in a hundred years." Each of his underground pillboxes was built with steel and reinforced concrete, covered with coconut logs and coral, invisible to the American bombers and warships. Underground tunnels, invulnerable even to direct hits, connected the pillboxes and blockhouses. Fourteen huge coastal guns, including the eight-inchers from Singapore, led an orchestra of fifty fieldpieces. Over a hundred machine-gun nests were zeroed in on the lip of a four-foot coconut-log and coral-block seawall. The Japs doubted that any of the U.S. assault troops would ever reach the beach, however. The reef standing between them and the Allied fleet was wider than Betio itself. And the Japanese, unlike the Americans, possessed accurate tide tables.

The struggle for the island began in the early hours of Saturday,

November 20, 1943. By 4:30 A.M. the Marines assigned to the first wave had descended their cargo nets, jumped into Higgins boats, and transferred to amphtracs, which began forming for the assault. Japanese ashore were aware of dark hulks in the night but were waiting until the Americans committed themselves to the isle's sea beach or its lagoon side. At 4:41 A.M. a Nip coastal defense gun fired a red-star cluster over the six U.S. transports. Now they knew: it was to be the lagoon side. Our naval gunfire had been stunning — one Marine said, "It's a wonder the whole goddam island doesn't fall apart and sink" — but it had ended an hour earlier. Two U.S. destroyers laying down a smoke screen for the Marines were shelling the beach, but against such defenses tin-can fire was ineffectual. Japs who had been braced for an approach from the sea leapt into prepared positions facing the lagoon. Now the American Marines would confront 4,836 Japanese, most of them Jap Marines.

Amphtrac coxswains found the seventeen-mile-long, nine-mile-wide lagoon choppy, its current strong, and their screws baffled by a riptide, a tug created by large volumes of water being sucked through underwater gaps in the reef. Instants later, they discovered that the Japs had somehow survived the bombardment. At three thousand yards from shore enemy artillery opened up on them; at two thousand yards they came under fire from long-range machine guns, and at eight hundred yards, as their awkward vehicles, half tanks, half boats, waddled over the reef, they were greeted by everything the enemy had, including sniper fire and heavy mortars. The amphtracs, performing as expected, came on. The Higgins boats behind them were stranded on the reef. They lowered their ramps, and the Marines stepped into chest-deep water. Robert Sherrod, then a *Time* war correspondent, has recalled: "It was painfully slow, wading in such deep water. And we had seven hundred yards to walk slowly into this machine-gun fire, looming into larger targets as we rose onto high ground." Aboard one of the American warships a naval officer wrote in his log: "The water seemed never clear of tiny men . . . slowly wading beachward. . . . They kept falling, falling, falling . . . singly, in groups, and in rows." Yet they trudged on, keeping their formations, "calm," in Sherrod's words, "even disdainful of death . . . black dots of men, holding their weapons high above their heads, moving at a snail's pace, never faltering." At Balaklava Pierre Bosquet had said of the Light Brigade: *"C'est magnifique, mais ce n'est pas la guerre."* And at Sedan in the Franco-Prussian War, where the French cavalry charged the Krupp guns again and again, until the last of them lay writhing in their own blood beside the carcasses of their slaughtered mounts, the King of Prussia had lowered his spyglass and murmured: *"Ah, les braves gens!"* Tarawa was more ghastly than magnificent, and it was certainly war, yet after all these years the bravery of its men is still wondrous.

There was a ramshackle, cribwork pier, long and narrow, jutting out from the beach. As shelters the pier's coconut stanchions were pitifully inadequate, but they were better than nothing, and those who reached them unwounded thought themselves lucky. There they crouched, with shellfire pealing in their ears, amid geysers of water from new shells and the smaller splashes from machine guns in the bunkers and Jap snipers tied in the trees overhead, while the precise American invasion plan fell apart. The troops in the amphtracs were luckier than those jumping from the Higgins boats stranded on the coral-reef apron, but in this fire storm danger was merely relative; there was no real safety for anyone. Unprotected by counterbattery fire from the U.S. fleet, which could not risk hitting Americans, five out of every six amphtracs were destroyed or disabled. Some reached the wrong beaches. Some, their coxswains dead, ran amok, spinning crazily and hurling seasick men into the surf. Some toppled into shell holes. And some blew up when enemy bullets pierced their fuel tanks. A survivor of the first wave remembers: "Amphtracs were hit, stopped, and burst into flames, with men jumping out like torches." Craft which survived were shuttling back and forth from the reef, carrying the wounded out and reinforcements in. The commander of the assault, Colonel David M. Shoup, a bullnecked, red-faced fighter who was also a scholar and poet, was wading toward shore when he hailed an amphtrac, ordered its crew to help him toss the Marine corpses in it overboard, rode in, and then set his command post in the shadow of the pier

Wading ashore at Tarawa

The author by the pier

Enemy guns overlooking Tarawa beach, 1978

pilings, issuing orders while standing waist-deep in water with two other officers and a sergeant. Shrapnel riddled Shoup's legs; he winced and then braced himself, waving away a corpsman. Other drenched Marines who had made it ashore huddled, terrified, beneath the four-foot seawall. Two brave amphtrac coxswains punched a gap in the long wall. Marines following them actually established a precarious toehold at the edge of the airstrip, about fifty yards inland, but their waterlogged radios didn't work and so Shoup was unaware of their position. Closer to him, another coxswain trying to climb the wall succeeded only in jamming his amphtrac treads against it. The men who had reached the beach alive seemed doomed. One later said that it felt "like being in the middle of a pool table without any pockets."

It was now noon. Because the tide had been misjudged, the Higgins boats couldn't even mount the reef now. Most of the amphtracs had been destroyed. One of them completely disappeared in a shell burst. "It had been there," recalls a Marine who was nearby, "and then suddenly it was not. In its place, for a split second, there was a blur in the air, and then there was nothing." One horrified coxswain lost his mind. On his way in, with bullets rattling on his hull, he screamed, "This is as far as I go!" He dropped his ramp and twenty Marines bowed by weapons and ammunition drowned in fifteen feet of water. A battalion commander elsewhere raised his pistol as he waded in and cried to the men behind him: "Come on, these bastards can't stop us!" A Nambu ripped open his rib cage, killing him instantly. Another battalion commander, gravely wounded in shallow water, crawled on top of a pile of dead Americans to avoid drowning in the incoming tide. He was found there the following afternoon, still alive but raving.

Enemy fire, writes Morison, "was horribly accurate; several times it dropped a shell right on a landing craft just as the ramp came down, spreading a pool of blood around the boat." The Marine dead became part of the terrain; they altered tactics; they provided defilade, and when they had died on barbed-wire obstacles, live men could avoid the wire by crawling over them. Even so, the living were always in some Jap's sights. There were many agents of death on Tarawa: snipers, machine gunners, artillery shells, mortar bursts, the wire, or drowning as a result of stepping into holes in the coral. As the day wore on, the water offshore was a grotesque mass of severed heads, limbs, and torsos. If a body was intact, you could tell which wave it had been in; the freshly killed were limp, with only their scalps and arms visible in the swells, but those who had died in the first hour floated stiffly, like kayaks, showing faces, or pieces of faces. If they had lost all their blood they were marble white, and the stench of their putrefaction soon hung over them. Most of those still alive cowered where they were. One who didn't, a corporal and a professional baseball pitcher in civilian life, crouched beside an amphtrac that Japs were trying to stop with hand grenades. As the grenades sailed in, he fielded them and flung them back as fastballs. Then one took a home-team bounce. Before he could grab it, it exploded. Later his hand was amputated. His example awed his men but did not inspire them. Real leadership was impossible. In a typical company, five of six officers were dead and all the sergeants dead or wounded. The survivors were bunched in little groups of three or four, trembling, sweating, and staring the thousand-yard stare of combat.

By early afternoon, with the tide falling, virtually all in the fourth wave, including 37-millimeter guns and their crews, were blocked by the reef. Some coxswains found holes in the coral; the others would be unable to move until night fell and the tide rose. The fifth wave landed its Sherman tanks on the reef; they plunged into four feet of water on the lee side and churned gamely on. Ashore, the survivors of four assault battalions held a lumpy arc about 300 yards wide which at places, owing to individual acts of heroism, reached a maximum depth of about 150 yards. Shoup had moved his command post fifteen yards in from the surf. His legs streaked with blood, he was standing exactly three feet from a Japanese blockhouse, but owing to the angle of its gunports, he couldn't reach the enemy and they couldn't reach him. Here and there officers and NCOs were shoving and kicking — literally kicking — dazed Marines inland. All the news was bad. The most dismaying reports came from the west, or right, of the island. The seawall was useless in the cove there; a sweeping cross fire enfiladed our riflemen. The battalion commander in the cove, seeing that his men ashore were being scythed by machine gunners, held the rest of them on the reef. He radioed Shoup: "Unable to land. Issue in doubt." After a silence he radioed: "Boats held up on reef of right flank Red One. Troops receiving heavy fire in water." Shoup replied: "Land Red Beach Two" — to the left — "and work west." Another silence from the battalion commander, then: "We have nothing left to land." The officers around Shoup stared at one another. There had been seven hundred men in that battalion. How could there be *nothing* left?

In fact about a hundred of the men were still alive, but in the chaos on the beach, with most radios still sodden or jammed, no one, including Shoup, knew of local successes. There was that tenuous hold on the end of the runway. It lay on the left flank of the assault, east of the pier. There was also the battalion of Major Henry P. "Jim" Crowe, a redheaded mustang, and it had landed intact, thanks to the covering fire of two destroyers. Except for the force on the runway tip, Crowe's men were pinned down on the beach by fire from Jap pillboxes, but he could have silenced them with flamethrowers and TNT satchel charges if he had had enough of them. Chagrin yielded to alarm when an enemy tank appeared, clanking toward the battalion. Two U.S. 37-millimeter antitank guns were offshore in a sunken landing craft. The men hauled them through the languid surf and then, with all hands lifting, the two nine-hundred-pound guns were thrown over the seawall just in time to drive the tank back. On the other end of the Marine position, Major Michael P. Ryan, leading a ragtag force of men who had made it ashore and supported by the 75-millimeter guns of two tanks, overran several enemy positions. But Ryan, too, lacked flamethrowers and TNT. Finding that he couldn't reach Shoup to call for reinforcements, he pulled back to a defense perimeter about five hundred yards deep. On Tarawa that was a victory.

Messages between the troops ashore and the hovering fleet also went astray. In desperation, Shoup sent out an officer (Evans Carlson) in an undamaged amphtrac to beg for men, water, and ammunition. Carlson didn't reach the battleship *Maryland* until late in the evening. By then, however, the plight of the force ashore had become obvious to General Smith, who had been anxiously following the sketchy reports from his CP on the battleship. Smith radioed his senior, Marine General Holland M. Smith, who, aboard the *Pennsylvania*, was commanding both the Makin and Tarawa assaults. His message to Holland Smith was: "Issue in doubt." He wanted the Sixth Marines, which were being held in reserve. Meanwhile he was organizing cooks, field musics, typists, motor transport men, specialists, and staff officers into an improvised battalion which he intended to lead ashore if reinforcements were denied him. But he got the Sixth Marines. At the time it was thought they might just swing the balance, but Shoup's position was at best precarious, and the Japanese were by now notorious for their night counterattacks.

As darkness fell, five thousand Marines on the beach awaited death or terror. Ryan's and Crowe's men were wired in and Shoup held a shallow, boxlike perimeter at the base of the pier. Everything, including ammunition, was in short supply. The beach was covered with shattered vehicles, the dead, the dying, and the wounded awaiting evacuation. Five 75-millimeter pack howitzers were ashore and a few medium tanks; that and the 37-millimeter guns was about it. The tropical moon was only a quarter full, but fuel dumps burning all over Betio provided a lurid, flickering light. Corpsmen worked through the night, ferrying casualties to the reef in large rubber rafts; other rafts brought water, blood plasma, ammunition, and reinforcements to the pier. The men on the perimeter, who thought they were ready for anything, were shocked to find their foxholes raked by machine-gun fire from the sea. Japs had swum out to disabled amphtracs abandoned there and were firing at the Marines' backs. To the Americans that seemed the ultimate blow. Demoralized, they expected a banzai charge at any moment. To their astonishment it didn't come. The night passed quietly. The Japanese had problems, too. Naval gunfire hadn't obliterated the island, but it had inflicted heavy casualties on Nips outside their bunkers. And it had destroyed their communications. Great as

Shoup's radio problems were, the Japanese commander's were worse. He couldn't get *any* messages through.

Seawalls are to beachheads what sunken roads — as at Waterloo and Antietam — are to great land battles. They provide inexpressible relief to assault troops who can crouch in their shadows, shielded for the moment from flat-trajectory fire, and they are exasperating to the troops' commanders because they bring the momentum of an attack to a shattering halt. On Tarawa the survival of the American force depended upon individual decisions to risk death. Wellington said, "The whole art of war consists of getting at what is on the other side of the hill." If no one vaulted over the wall, no Marine would leave Betio alive. Naturally everyone wanted others to take the chance. In the end, some did — not many, but a few — and they were responsible for the breakthrough. In defense of those who chose to remain until the odds were shorter it should be said that Tarawa was exceptional. In most instances frontal attacks are unnecessary. Cunning is more effective than daring. Even on Betio, even after the reef blunder and the failure to bombard the enemy until the last possible moment, permitting the shift of defenders to prepared positions on the lagoon side, there was a way out. Ryan provided it. He had turned the Jap flank. If Shoup's radio had worked he would have known that and could have strengthened Ryan, rolling up the Nip defenses from the rear. So the instincts of the rifleman who hides behind the wall are usually sound. At least that is what I tell myself whenever I think of Tubby Morris.

My seawall was on Oroku. There was no reef to speak of, and though enemy fire was heavy as the Higgins boats brought us in — we were soaked with splashes from near misses, and we could hear the small-arms lead pinging on our hulls — we lost very few men in the landing. Then we saw the seawall and thanked God for it. It was built of sturdy logs and stood over five feet high. Incongruously, an enormous scarlet vine rioted over the lower half of it. Between there and the surf line the beach was about ten feet deep. It looked wonderful. I was prepared to spend the rest of my life on those ten feet. A braver man, I knew, would try to skirt the wall and find Jap targets. But enemy machine gunners knew where we were. Nambus were chipping at the top of the wall; you could see the splinters. Even if I hadn't been determined to save my own skin, which I certainly was, there were other reasons for staying put. I was surrounded by the Raggedy Ass Marines, the least subordinate of fighters. I knew that if I went up I would be alone. Furthermore, it seemed possible, even probable, that the First Battalion, on our extreme right, could envelop the Nips. The seawall tapered off in that direction, and the map showed an inlet where our men had room to move around. Anyhow, I was going to give them their chance and all the time they wanted.

That was when Tubby arrived in the third wave. He had been in my officer candidate class at Quantico, and unlike me he had been commissioned. Now he was a second lieutenant, a replacement officer making his debut as a leader, or presumed leader, of seasoned troops. If there is a more pitiful role in war, I don't know it. Troops are wary of untested officers, and the Raggedy Ass Marines were contemptuous of them. Some of them, like me, remembered him from Quantico. He hadn't changed since we had last seen him; he was a stubby, brisk youth, in his early twenties but already running to fat around the jowls and belly. He had the sleek peach complexion of a baby and a perpetual frown, not of petulance but of concentration. I hadn't known him well. He had the megalomania of undersized men. He was like one of those boys who always do their homework at school and never let you copy. He had been an overachiever, determined to please his superiors, but there had been many like him at Quantico. Here, however, he was unique. Among men who prided themselves on the saltiness — shabbiness — of their uniforms, his was right off the quartermaster's shelf. I wondered whether he had been disappointed when they told him not to wear his bars in combat, for whatever his other failings he was, and was soon to prove, courageous.

He caught his breath, looked around, and said, "I'm your new officer." I grinned, held out my hand, and said, "Hi, Tubby." That was stupid of me. He glared and kept his own hand on his trouser seam. Standing cockily like a bantam rooster — the wall was just high enough to let him stand — he crisply asked, "Sergeant, are these your men?" The Raggedy Asses grinned at one another. The very thought of belonging to *anyone* amused them. I felt cold. This wasn't the good-natured Tubby I had known. This was trouble. I said, "Tubby —" and he cut me off: "Slim, I am an officer and I expect to be treated with proper military courtesy." That broke the men up. He heard their stifled chuckles and looked around furiously. It was an insane situation. Here we were, in the middle of a battle, and Tubby seemed to expect a salute, if not homage, from me. There wasn't much room, but I said in a low voice, "Let's talk this over," moved away a few feet, and knelt. He bridled, but came over and squatted beside me. I told him that I didn't want to undermine him, that I hadn't meant to sound familiar, and that I was sorry. His jaw muscles were working. He said, "You should be." Anger stirred in me. Looking back, I see that my motives were less selfless than I thought then. My sympathy for his position, though genuine, was tainted by resentment at taking orders from this little man whose background was no different from mine, by irrational scorn of junior officers who hadn't yet proved themselves, and by the arrogance which combat veterans feel toward all green replacements, especially platoon leaders. At that moment, however, all I saw was that there was bound to be a certain stiffness between us which we would probably work around in time. Then I learned that for Tubby there wasn't much time. He said, "Don't tell me. Show me. I'm going to lead these people over the top, and I want you with me."

He actually said "over the top." We didn't talk like that. He must have heard it from his father. World War I soldiers left their trenches to go over the top, over the parapet, into no-man's-land. Then the implication of what he had said hit me. I whispered, "You mean over this wall?" He nodded once, a quick little jerk of his head. He said, "That's where the Japs are. You can't kill them if you can't see them." I felt numb. I said, "Look, Tubby — Lieutenant — I think —" He snapped, "You're not paid to think. You're paid to take orders." I considered saying the hell with it. But this was literally a matter of life or imminent death. I tried again, earnestly: "Going up there would be suicide. The First Bat's down there," I said, pointing. "Give them a chance to turn the Nips' flank and roll up those machine-gun nests." He growled, "What's the matter with *this* battalion?" I said, "We're pinned down, so the action is on the flanks." I could see I wasn't convincing him, and I said hoarsely, "Tubby, I know they didn't teach you that at Quantico, but that's how we do it here. You're not on some fucking parade ground. You can't just pump your fist up and down and expect the men to spring up. They won't do it. *They won't do it.* I've been out here a long time, Tubby. I *know.*"

He stared at me for a long time, as though waiting for me to blink first. I blinked and blinked again. Letting his voice rise, he said, "You're scared shitless, aren't you?" I nodded emphatically. His voice rose higher. All the guys could hear him now. He said, "That's why I put up bars and you're just an NCO. They could tell the difference between us in O.C. I've got balls and you haven't." There was just a tremor in his voice, and it dawned on me that he himself was petrified — he was masking his fear with his rudeness to me. But what he said next smothered my compassion. He sneered, and keeping his voice in the same register, he said: "I know your kind, Bub. You think we couldn't hear you back there in the squad bay, masturbating every night? Did you think they'd give a Marine Corps commission to a masturbator? Only thing I couldn't make out was how you dried the come. I figured you had a handkerchief." I heard a titter from Bubba. I'm sure Bubba had never masturbated. His father, the Alabama preacher in whose steps he hoped to follow, had shown him the way to what he called "Nigra poontang" when he reached adolescence. But I wasn't interested in Bubba's good opinion. What Tubby had done, and it was unforgivable, was make me look ridiculous in the eyes of all my men. He knew that was wrong. They *had* taught *that* at Quantico. By mocking me he had contaminated both of us. I thought: *Since I am a dog, beware my fangs.* He and I were through. He was past saving now. His longevity would be less than a Jap's. No one could lengthen it for him. I've kept telling myself that all these years, but there will always be a tug of guilt.

Rising in one swift motion, he wiped his hands on his sturdy thighs, stood with arms akimbo, and barked: "Men, I know you'd like to stay here. I would myself. But those yellow bastards down the beach are killing your buddies." He didn't even realize that a combat man's loyalty is confined to those around him, that as far as the Raggedy Ass Marines were concerned the First Battalion might as well have belonged to a separate race. He said, "Our duty lies up there." He pointed. He went on: "That's what we call a target of opportunity, lads." He paused, and his pouter-pigeon breast swelled. I wondered if he was trying to imitate Chesty Puller, that legendary Marine hero who is said to have boasted that he would win a Medal of Honor if he had to bring home a seabag full of dog tags. Tubby said, "I'm not going to ask any of you people to do what I don't do. I'm going up first. Your sergeant will —" He checked himself. "It's your sergeant's job to see that every man follows me." I was still down on one knee, eyes averted, running sand through my fingers. I wanted no part of this. He asked, "Any questions?"

They looked up at him glassily. He hesitated, probably wondering whether he should threaten them with courts-martial. Then he turned and sprang at the seawall. He was too short. He couldn't get a footing. He tried to stick one boondocker in a vine crotch, but the V was too tight. He could only wedge his toe in sideways, and that didn't give him the right leverage. Panting, he tried again and again. He turned to me, his face flushed. He said, "Help me." He must have hated to ask. I certainly hated his asking. I felt an insane urge to laugh, which I knew would turn into weeping. I looked into his wide eyes and said, "My legs are too shaky." It was true. He said between his teeth, "I'll take care of you later." He turned, pointed to Bubba, and said, "You, over here." Bubba came over and linked his hands. Tubby put in a foot, as if into a stirrup, swung up, rolled atop the wall, and rose till he stood sideways. Both his hands were pointing. His left forefinger was pointed down at us, his right forefinger at the Japs. It was a Frederic Remington painting. He breathed deeply and yelled, *Follow me!*"

The men's faces still were turned up, expressionless. Nobody moved. I stood beneath the wall, my arms outstretched, waiting to catch what would be left. At that moment the slugs hit him. It was a Nambu; it stitched him vertically, from forehead to crotch. One moment he was looming above us in that heroic pose; in the next moment red pits blossomed down him, four on his face alone, and a dozen others down his uniform. One was off center; it slammed into the Marine Corps emblem over his heart; the gunner knew his job. Blood had just begun to stream from there, from his face, from his belly, and from his groin, when he collapsed, tottering on the edge and falling and whumping in my arms face up. His features were disappearing beneath a spreading stain, and he was trying to blink the blood out of his eyes. But he could see. He saw me. He choked faintly: "You . . . you . . . you . . ." Then he gagged and he was gone.

I looked away, feeling queasy. My blouse was wet with gore. Mo Crocker and Dusty Rhodes took Tubby from me and gently laid him out. There was no malice in the section. They mourned him as they would have mourned any casualty. They — and I above all — had merely been unwilling to share his folly. It was followed by savage irony. We had scarcely finished trussing him up in a poncho when we heard the sound of cheering to our right. The First Bat had turned the Jap flank. You could just see the bobbing of the camouflaged helmet covers and the moving line of smoke, and you could hear the snuffling of the tanks as their drivers shifted gears. I raged as I had raged over the death of Zepp. It was the sheer futility of it which was unbearable. Then I was diverted, as death in its grisly mercy diverts you, by the necessity of disposing of the corpse. I said to Knocko, "Pass the word to Buck Rogers —" Suddenly I realized that Buck might not still be alive, and that because Tubby had arrived so recently, his name might be unknown at the CP anyhow. Instead, I said, "The new lieutenant is dead. Pass the word to the nearest officer."

One of the problems at Tarawa was the uniforms. When General Smith said the Marines' armor would be limited to khaki, he was speaking figuratively. The men actually wore new jungle suits, camouflaged green on one side and brown on the other, presumably for use if the Marine Corps found itself fighting in the Sahara Desert. But the designers of the suits had neglected to make them porous. Wearing them was like being wrapped in plastic. The men would have sweated that first night on Betio whatever they wore — they were just ninety miles from the equator — but in those suits they lost pounds, and greeted the dawn gaunt and shrunken. In the early light, they saw that their lines were intact. That heartened them, and led many to conclude that the crisis was past. They were wrong. As the struggle resumed its ferocity, Sherrod heard on all sides the *pi-ing* of enemy rifles rippling the air and the *ratatatata* and the *brrrp* of their machine guns. In five minutes he saw six Marines die. He wrote: "This is worse, far worse than it was yesterday." The battleship *Maryland*, with communications restored, radioed Shoup, asking him if he had enough men. He said he didn't and added: "Imperative you land ammunition, water, rations and medical supplies. . . . Imperative you get all types of ammunition to all landing parties immediately." The corpsmen ran out of bandages. Shoup ordered them to wade out to the reef and strip dead Marines of first-aid kits that all men carried on their belts. At midmorning he told Sherrod: "We're in a mighty tough spot." At 11:00 A.M. he radioed General Julian Smith: "Situation doesn't look good ashore."

The immediate problem was bringing in reinforcements from the Sixth Marines. They had been waiting in Higgins boats for nearly twenty hours, trying to find a way past or over the reef. The Japs on the stranded amphtracs were still in position, firing seaward now, their .303-caliber copper bullets hitting with remarkable accuracy whenever men on the landing craft peered over their bulkheads. Nambus seemed to be firing on all sides. One was set up on a Jap privy built over the water. The greatest danger, however, came from the hulk of an old freighter to the right of the pier, about seven hundred yards out. From here the enemy could smash the fuel tanks of landing craft, exploding them, and zero in on the Sixth Marines as they jumped out into the water and started trudging in. There were 800 Marines when they started; 450 made it to the beach.

Marines already ashore rocked the freighter with 75-millimeter pack howitzers and 81-millimeter mortars, and dive-bombers from U.S. carriers tried to take it out, but it seemed indestructible. A naval officer on one Higgins boat suggested to debarking men that they keep the boat between them and the hulk, as a shield, but, as the officer recalls, "They told us to follow the plan and retire so other waves could get to help them." It was at this point that the erratic Betio tide began to rise, threatening the wounded men lying on the reef with drowning. A salvage crew from the transport *Sheridan*, rescuing them, encountered about thirty-five Marines, unharmed but lacking weapons. The skipper offered to evacuate them. They shook their heads, asking only that the crew "bring back something to fight with." During the five hours needed to land the First Battalion of the Eighth Marines — the last of the reinforcements — its casualties were greater than those of any battalion reaching shore the day before.

The survivors strengthened Ryan's end of the beachhead. At daybreak, his communication with the fleet reestablished, he had called in a barrage of five-inch shells from a destroyer offshore. With those salvos and fire from two tanks, he recovered the ground that he had yielded the previous afternoon; pushing on, he crossed the airfield and established an anchor on Betio's south shore. This time Shoup learned of Ryan's progress and altered his tactics to exploit it. As Tarawa's tide turned, the tide of the battle was at last turning with it. The freighter hulk was annihilated by concentrated fire. Jim Crowe's mortars and a seemingly invincible tank christened "Colorado" were cracking pillboxes open. Flamethrowers, suddenly plentiful, licked at spider holes and bunkers. One two-story concrete blockhouse, intact despite point-blank fire from a destroyer, was knocked out when a Marine tank crawled up to the entrance and blasted away. Over three hundred charred corpses were later found inside. The western half of Betio was now in American hands. Shoup radioed the fleet: "Casualties many; percentage dead not known: we are winning."

The Japanese didn't think so. They laid down such heavy howitzer fire on Shoup's left flank, resting on a Burns-Philip Company wharf, that any U.S. advance there was out of the question. The enemy didn't know about the cargoes of equipment, supplies, and plasma coming in over the now-submerged reef, or that another battalion had reached Ryan — the first to stream ashore with few casualties and dry weapons. The Nips' will to resist was as inflexible as ever. As American firepower drove them back and back on the eastern half of the island, their snipers scampered up palm trees or lay among their dead comrades, feigning death until they could leap up and attack Marines whose backs were to them. Monday night they launched three vicious counterattacks against the Marine line, which now lay athwart the entire island. Despite naval gunfire and Marine artillery, some Japs penetrated the American perimeter. Hand-to-hand fighting followed, with Kabars and bayonets. A Marine lieutenant sent back word: "We're killing them as fast as they come at us, but we can't hold much longer. We need reinforcements." He was told: "We haven't got them to send you. You've got to hold."

They did; Tuesday morning they counted 325 Jap bodies around their foxholes. At the time it was impolitic to pay the slightest tribute to the enemy, and Nip determination, their refusal to say die, was commonly attributed to "fanaticism." In retrospect it is indistinguishable from heroism. To call it anything less cheapens the victory, for American valor was necessary to defeat it. There were brave Marines, too, men who didn't commit suicide, as Tubby did, but who knew the risk, decided an objective was worth it, and never looked back. There was Jim Crowe, charging and shouting over his shoulder, "You'll never get the Purple Heart a-laying in those foxholes, men!" There was Lieutenant William "Hawk" Hawkins, who knocked out machine guns by standing in full view of the gunners and firing into pillbox slits, then tossing in grenades to finish off the Nips inside. He was wounded by a mortar burst and told a corpsman: "I came here to kill Japs, not to be evacuated." Still erect in the terrible heat, Hawk blew up three more pillboxes before a shell killed him. And there was Lieutenant Alexander Bonnyman, an officer of engineers who could have left the fighting to the infantry but who chose to attack the enemy's huge headquarters fortress bunker with five of his men. They climbed up the tough, stringy weeds of the slope outside to reach the roof, the highest point on the island. A door opened and a horde of Japanese poured out to drive him off. Bonnyman remained standing for thirty seconds, firing a carbine and then a flamethrower before he fell, mortally wounded. He had held the erupting Nips off just long enough for his men to drop grenades into the strongpoint's ventilation system. When the grenades exploded, more Nips swarmed up. Shells and small-arms fire drove them back. A bulldozer sealed the entry. Gasoline was poured in vents still open and ignited by TNT. The Marines heard the blasts, then screams, then nothing. Inside were nearly two hundred Japanese corpses.

One of them was that of the Jap admiral commanding Betio's defenses. His faith in Tarawa's impregnability had been based on the assumption that if he were attacked, Tokyo would send him warships, warplanes, and more troops. His superiors had assured him that Tarawa would be "a hornet's nest for the Yankees." He couldn't imagine what had gone wrong. We know now. Because of America's twin-pronged drive, the men and equipment which had been earmarked for him had gone to Bougainville, under assault by the Third Marine Division, and to MacArthur's objectives in New Guinea. Shortly before Bonnyman's feat, the doomed admiral had radioed Tokyo: "Our weapons have been destroyed, and from now on everyone is attempting a final charge. . . . May Japan exist for ten thousand years!" Leaderless now, the remaining Nips formed for the first of those suicidal banzai charges or took their lives in a sick ritual which would soon be familiar to American assault troops all over the Pacific: lying down, jamming the muzzle of an Arisaka rifle in the mouth, and squeezing the trigger with the big toe. By Tuesday Japanese resistance had collapsed. Except for seventeen Nips who surrendered, all were dead or fugitives, running across the reef to other islands in Tarawa's atoll, where they were soon pursued and shot. Tokyo's commentators eulogized them as "flowers of the Pacific" and quickly turned to other news, as well they might. Tarawa had been a Nipponese disaster. Already Hellcats were landing on Betio's airstrip, named Hawkins Field for Hawk. At 1:10 P.M. Tuesday the battle was officially ended. It had lasted seventy-six hours, and the only dispute about it now was whether the island's bird-shaped fragment of coral was worth the price the Americans had paid.

In Washington's new Pentagon building, officers studied the pictures of dead Marines on Tarawa, debating whether to release them to the press. They decided to do it; it was time, they felt, to shock the home front into understanding the red harvest of combat. The published photographs touched off an uproar. Nimitz received sacks of mail from grieving relatives — a mother wrote, "You killed my son" — and editorials demanded a congressional investigation. The men on Tarawa were puzzled. The photographers had been discreet. No dismembered corpses were shown, no faces with chunks missing, no flies crawling on eyeballs; virtually all the pictures were of bodies in Marine uniforms face down on the beach. Except for those who had known the dead, the pictures were quite ordinary to men who had scraped the remains of buddies off bunker walls or who, while digging foxholes, found their entrenching tools caught in the mouths of dead friends who had been buried in sand by exploding shells.

Time trumpeted the defense of the American tactics: "Last week some 2,000 or 3,000 United States Marines, most of them now dead or wounded, gave the nation a name to stand beside those of . . . the Alamo, Little Big Horn, and Belleau Wood. The name was Tarawa." That made everyone on Betio stand tall, but it deserves second thoughts. The Alamo and Little Big Horn were massacres for Americans, and the Fifth and Sixth Marines had been cut to pieces in Belleau Wood. *Time*'s comment may be attributed to a curious principle which seems to guide those who write of titanic battles. The longer the casualty lists — the vaster the investment in blood — the greater the need to justify the slain. Thus the fallen are honored by hallowing the names of the places where they fell; thus writers enshrine in memory the Verduns, the Passchendaeles, the Dunkirks, and the Iwo Jimas, while neglecting decisive struggles in which the loss of life was small. At the turn of the eighteenth century the Duke of Marlborough led ten successful, relatively bloodless, campaigns on the Continent, after which he was hounded into exile by his political enemies. In World War I Douglas Haig butchered the flower of England's youth on the Somme and in Flanders without winning a single victory. He was raised to the peerage and awarded 100,000 pounds by a grateful Parliament. Every American child is taught how Jackson's brigade stood like a stone wall against the waves of Union assault troops at Bull Run, but only the most zealous Civil War votaries know how, husbanding his strength, Jackson flashed up and down the Shenandoah Valley in 1862 with brilliant diversionary tactics, preventing the dispatch of reinforcements to McClellan, who, had he had them, could have taken Richmond. Similarly, in World War II Anzio and Peleliu are apotheosized, though neither contributed to the defeat of Germany and Japan, while the capture of Ulithi, one of the Pacific's finest anchorages, is unsung since the enemy had evacuated it, and Hollandia, MacArthur's greatest triumph in that war, is forgotten because the general's genius outfoxed the Japanese and limited his losses to a handful of GIs.

In the Pacific we received "pony" editions — reduced in size, with no ads — of *Time* and the *New Yorker*. The comparison of Tarawa with great battles of the past didn't impress most of us; we saw it for what it was: wartime propaganda designed to boost the morale of subscribers, a sophisticated version of rhapsodies about the Glorious Dead who had Given Their All, making the Supreme Sacrifice. Our sympathies were with those who protested the high casualties. Even so, neither we nor they were prepared to answer the ultimate question: What happens to the dead? Death's shadow falls on every man in combat, but he is, almost without exception, blind to it. If one is brave enough to try facing it, his mind comes to a shattering stop. Hemingway believed he knew what lay ahead: "*Nada, nada, nada.*" He was in his forties then, however. Youth who haven't reached their twenty-fifth birthday seldom grasp the concept of their own mortality. Like eternity and infinity, it is beyond them. They think: "It will happen to you, and you, and you, but not me." Indeed, virtually no one can come to terms with his own extinction until the very end, if then. This is especially true of fighting men. The mystery of war enshrouds the deeper mystery of death. And they are in no hurry to solve it. Yet its fascination lurks just outside the perimeter of their consciousness, as it has throughout the history of the human race.

Possibly prehistoric man first became aware of the puzzle when he saw that some sleepers never awoke and that their bodies subsequently underwent unpleasant transformations. We know that man, the only creature to bury his dead, began to do so before 50,000 B.C., and that Stone Age corpses were given food and interred in the fetal position, possibly to prepare them for rebirth, or possibly to shackle them, for a recurring theme in the history of thanatophobia is the belief that the dead may become possessed by evil and thus become a threat to all who are still alive. Over two thousand years before Christ strong stone coffins were pieced together for interments. At the same time, despite the horrors of rotting flesh, survivors were convinced that the dead lived on in one form or another. Two traditions evolved. Zoroastrianism, Judaism, Christianity, and Islam have held that souls carry on elsewhere, in *sheol*, hell, or heaven, and that all will be judged one day; Buddhists, Orphics, Pythagoreans, and Platonists, on the other hand, have believed in reincarnation. Egyptians, among others, went to great lengths to provide cadavers, particularly if they had been powerful in life, with meals and equipment to see them through to the other world. Since we are not dealing with reason, it is unsurprising that few cultures have looked upon death as natural. Usually it has been attributed to a demon. In Etruscan sepulchral art a terrible god called Charon is the slayer; in the Dark Ages the skeletal figure of Death was armed with a dart; Christians believe that Cain, the farmer son of Adam and Eve, committers of the original sin, introduced death into the world. Sinners, all agreed, are dealt with harshly after their demise. Judaism's Last Judgment is largely a vindication of Israel; Arabs, for example, are treated mercilessly in Jewish apocalyptic literature.

The geography of the next world varies from one creed to another. In Athens and Rome a coin was placed on the tongue of the corpse as payment for a dark guide waiting near the grave to lead him over a barrier. In ancient Egypt dead pharaohs flew up to join the sun-god Ra, but later Egyptians discovered the idea of passing across an infernal river on the way to the afterlife, with a fearsome ferryman at the tiller. Ancient Greeks and Romans, following suit, thought their dead crossed the Styx, or the Acheron, carrying with them delicious cakes to give Cerberus, the three-headed dog who guarded the entrance to the hereafter. But since corpses have usually been interred, most peoples have believed that the dead lived somewhere under the earth. In ancient Crete, graves were provided with pottery pipes from above, so that rainwater could slake the corpses' thirst while they awaited passage to the underworld. The Scandinavians envisaged a huge pit, ruled by a dreadful king. Others followed pretty much the same line: the awful sovereign was called the Yama by Buddhists and Hindus; Nergal in Mesopotamia; and Hades in Greece. As epoch succeeded epoch, the inevitability of hell, a joyless, gloomy underworld, became too terrible to contemplate, and the Buddhists, Hindus, Gnostics, and Christians conceived of a way station, a purgatory, where good souls could pay the price for excusable misdeeds before ascending into a divine realm. The form in which the human spirit expressed itself is conceptualized in Saint Paul's use of the Greek word *soma,* which might be roughly translated as gestalt, and Dante's account, in his *Purgatorio,* of the trials *somata* must endure as preparation for paradise.

The twentieth century has extended these threads. The followers of now-forgotten death cults, with their devotion to iconography (Etruscan effigies, early Christian art in the catacombs), would understand, and approve of, Moslems' deification of Mecca, Israel's enshrining of the ashes of those who died in the Holocaust, and Communists who make pilgrimages to the tombs of Marx and Lenin. A majority of mankind, which does not necessarily rule, is still convinced that there must be a life after death. In today's sophisticated cultures, however, there seems to be a silent but concerted effort to hide man's grief for the departed and his apprehension over his own eventual departure, as if both were shameful, or at least in poor taste. Deaths occur in hospitals, where children are "shielded," or "protected," from them. Undertakers disguise corpses to make them as lifelike as possible. Heaven, hell, and eventual judgment are rarely mentioned, even by clergymen. Funerals are almost stealthy. Mourning is seldom worn. Graveyards are landscaped, like parks. None of this is helpful to those who must do the dying, which, of course, means, sooner or later, everyone. The mortally ill must still pass through the five final stages of natural death: disbelief, rage, prayers for postponement of the end, depression, and acceptance. Modern society even deprives the dying of their final solace, when those breathing their last want their families gathered around the deathbed.

Violent death, including death on the battlefield, is unsparing on next of kin. The man killed in action cannot observe the five stages, so those who loved him must do it for him, or at least try to. Those who succeed are fortunate, and few. I wrote many letters to the parents of Marines who had died in my section. One came from the mother of an Iowa horticulturist. She was furious with me because I was alive and her son was not. I envied her; she was passing through a strengthening catharsis. Most relatives could not. They repressed their anguish, at great cost to themselves. We on the line did the same. It was bad form to weep long for a fallen buddy. We moved on, each of us inching along the brink of his own extinction, never speaking of what we considered the unspeakable. Today's children are baffled by our acquiescence then in what, to them, appears to have been a monstrous conspiracy against our lives. They are bewildered by those waves of relentless young men who plodded patiently on and on toward Betio's beach while their comrades were keeling over on all sides. They ask: Why? They are convinced that they couldn't do it.

And they are right. The United States was a different country then, with half today's population, a lordly father figure in the White House, and a tightly disciplined society. A counterculture didn't exist, as a word or as a concept. The thought of demonstrating against the war, had it crossed anyone's mind, would have been dismissed as absurd. Standards were rigid; everyone was determined to conform to them because the alternatives were unthinkable. Girls who became pregnant, or boys who cheated on examinations, were expelled from school and cast into outer darkness. Their only hope lay in moving to another part of the country, where they were unknown. Social criteria had to be met, and the Protestant work ethic was very strong. Although the Great Depression was plainly a national disaster, social workers had repeatedly observed that the jobless were suffering from feelings of guilt. "I haven't had a steady job in more than two years," a man facing eviction told a *New York Daily News* reporter. "Sometimes I feel like a murderer. What's wrong with me, that I can't protect my children?"

The bastion of social stability was the family. Children were guided, not by radar beams picking up trends and directions from other children, but by gyroscopes built into their superegos at home. Parents had a tremendous influence on them. If adolescents wanted to read pulp magazines, or smoke, or listen to Ben Bernie or the Lucky Strike Hit Parade on the radio, they needed parental permission; if they wanted to see *The Philadelphia Story*, their fathers decided whether or not it would be bad for their morals; if they made money shoveling snow or cutting lawns, their fathers, again, told them whether they should save it for college, or, if it was to be spent, what they could buy. (Usually it was clothes.) There was no teenage ethos; indeed, "teenage" meant "brushwood used for fences and hedges." Young people were called "youngsters," and since the brooding omnipotence of the peer group had not yet arrived, children rarely felt any conflict between their friends and their families. No youngster would dream of discussing familial conflicts with other youngsters. An insult to either parent had to be avenged. The master bedroom, in upper-middle-class homes, was off limits. Fathers had always ruled homes like sultans, but the Depression had increased all family activities over which patresfamilias reigned; a study of over a hundred families in Pittsburgh discovered that a majority had increased family recreation — Ping-Pong, jigsaw puzzles, checkers, bridge, and parlor games, notably Monopoly. There was also plenty of time for the householders, the doughboys of 1918, to explain to their sons the indissoluble relationship between virility and valor.

Sheathed in obedience, reinforced by Marine Corps pride and the

conviction that the war was just, the men wearing green camouflaged helmets could outfight the Japanese, and they did it again
and again. Home-front America was shocked by Jap kamikazes, but
its own sons were capable of similar sacrifices, and not just
Marines; the Devastator torpedo bombers who crashed Nip warships at Midway knew they were diving to certain death, and so did
Air Corps pilots over Ploesti. Today their sons wonder why. *I*
wonder why. The chasm between generations is one explanation.
Perhaps it is the only one. Yet on one level of the subconscious, too
deep for me to reach it, I am unsatisfied. So I have nightmares, and
so I have returned to the islands to exorcise my inner darkness with
the light of understanding.

But not on Tarawa. This visit in the fall of 1978 is my first here;
like the journeys to the Philippines and New Guinea, it is useful in
re-creating the Pacific war, but since I left none of myself here,
there is nothing of me to find. Yet it has one advantage; I
come without bias. Leaving the cinder-block hotel after breakfast, I
cross from Bairiki to Betio on the 8:15 A.M. ferry. Next to Guadalcanal, Tarawa is the battle natives remember best, and on the opposite shore I question islanders until I find Itaaka Bamiatoa, who
was here during the battle and whose capped teeth give him a glittering plastic smile. Bamiatoa, in turn, takes me to Taute Takanoi, a handsome, immaculately groomed native police officer.
Takanoi has just what I want: a Land Rover. Idle at the moment —
the chief local offense now is drunkenness, and all the local topers
are in jail — he agrees to chauffeur us, creeping along at twenty
miles per hour, the local speed limit, taking little side trips for my
benefit. Because of its isolation, the isle has changed little in a third
of a century. There are two stone moles, one of them built by
Seabees before they left. Hawkins Field, the battle's prize, no
longer exists, and erosion has revealed sunken wrecks which were
formerly invisible. It is a balmy, calm day. Under a canopy of coconut trees we pause at the Nano-Lelei supermarket for Australian
soft drinks, my treat — nagged by my *déjà vécu* thirst, I gulp down
two — and as we finish them Bamiatoa tells me that the historic

beach is within strolling distance. We pass a silvery British Petroleum storage tank, several sago-leaf-thatched huts, and the wreckage of the *Saeda Maru*, an abandoned Japanese freighter which
island women are using as a clothes rack. Then, suddenly, we are
on the shore. The scene has appeared in a hundred photographs of
Tarawa, but like the Berlin Wall it must be seen to be believed.

The debris of battle is all around us: rusting tanks and
amphtracs, artillery pieces twisted into grotesque shapes, coconut
bunkers, bent armor plate blackened by flamethrowers, shattered
landing craft, concrete pillboxes, and, under the coconut fronds,
the Japanese admiral's command post and a cement blockhouse
shaped like a double Quonset hut, looking much as it did when
Bonnyman stood defiantly on top of it. The blockhouse now serves
as a social club for native officials; another bunker nearby has become a meeting hall for Rotarians. Altogether, there are over five
hundred fortified positions on Betio, many of them intact. Here and
there, stepping on the thousands of cartridge cases underfoot, you
can see a Nip coastal gun which was actually pulled out of its moor-
ing by American naval shells. At first glance the famous pier seems
largely demolished, but it isn't; beyond its stump, if you peer
down, you can see the rest of it under water, submerged by half a
lifetime of wave action. Takanoi remarks that the tide is now high.
Looking seaward, I realize that the only way I can grasp what the
assault was like for those first three waves of Marines is to get my
feet wet. Leaving my camera with the policeman, to photograph
me, I trudge out and don't reach landing-craft depth until I have
gone over a thousand yards. Looking shoreward from that distance, seeing the bunkers and pillboxes, I feel anger roaring in my
chest, and I think of the men who fell in the surf, sprawled like
priests at high mass. Suddenly the most important thing in the
world for me is to leave Betio.

At the ferry slip I find Tony Charlwood, the ordnance wizard.
He has finished defusing shells and will return to Belfast and the
IRA on tomorrow's plane. As we wait for the boat he talks about
the battle here and says bluntly, "It was a bloody crime." In his
opinion even the coming of the white man was tragic for the islands

because the natives adopted the worst of the newcomers' ways. Pointing toward a litter of Australian beer cans and discarded filter-tip packs, he says scornfully, "Look at that. The people here have no respect now. And look at *that*." I am already looking at it: a monument to the Marine dead defaced by graffiti. But perhaps the memorial deserves no better, for as we read it together we see that it is clearly self-serving. "Tarawa," the plaque reads, "was the testing ground for Marine amphibious doctrine and techniques. It paved the way for the island campaigning that followed and provided answers that saved thousands of American lives along the road to victory in the Pacific." Tony turns away. He mutters, "That's what the British said about Dieppe."

Now Nimitz's central Pacific drive, like MacArthur's in the southwest Pacific, began to pick up speed. MacArthur had left Rabaul to rot and was in the Admiralty Islands. Meanwhile, less than three months after Betio, GIs of the Seventh Division and Marines in the newly formed Fourth Marine Division had taken Kwajalein Atoll, next on Nimitz's hit list, 718 miles beyond Tarawa. Eleven days after that they plunged ashore on Eniwetok Atoll, another 575 miles closer to Tokyo. These islands shared with Betio one advantage for attackers: no high ground. If one assumes that the men at Betio had to serve as guinea pigs — that admirals could learn only through blunders — then these relatively bloodless assaults were a partial justification of Tarawa. Battleships and cruisers coordinated their salvos with the landing timetable; there were more amphtracs, carrying heavier armor; and carrier pilots took out the great Jap base at Truk in the nearby Caroline archipelago, destroying two hundred enemy planes and sinking forty-two ships. Unfortunately, as we shall see, Tarawa was not the last botched landing.

Approached by air, Kwajalein, or "Kwaj," as it is now known, resembles every other atoll: low, flat, and verdant, with a tan prayer rug of a beach. This is one of the loneliest parts of the world. The 1,335 square miles of Micronesia, half the size of Rhode Island — including the Gilberts, Palaus, Carolines, Marshalls, and Marianas

— comprise 2,141 islands, of which only 96 are populated. The natives on all of them would fit in the Rose Bowl. Typically, there is no heavy surf at Kwaj; the beach is a strip of unvexed sand behind which pandanus, royal palms, and Samoan palms conceal the community inland. As we fasten our seat belts and I knock out my pipe, I see all of Kwaj below, serpentine and green in the placid dark blue water, supreme and magnificent. The plane touches down beside a sign: BUCHOLZ ARMY FIELD. All around the enormous airport are the varied pleasures of a remote U.S. military base: TV aerials, a movie theater, tennis courts, golf courses, swimming pools, bicycle racks — the twenty-eight hundred people on Kwaj own five thousand bikes — and a tax-free supermarket.

Consternation greets my arrival. Civilian planes are allowed to refuel here, but passengers may not wander off the runway. This rule, when written, was understandable; the Pentagon built a billion-dollar missile base here, and real military secrets cannot be reasonably challenged. I am an exception to the rule, however; I carry papers from the Department of Defense permitting me to roam. These are carefully examined. Officers huddle by the control tower and come up with a bureaucratic solution: twenty copies of my orders are Xeroxed, so everyone is covered. But they are still uneasy, and I am puzzled; the most sensitive missile equipment, I have been told, has been moved elsewhere. Then I come upon a likelier explanation for their touchiness.

It is the outrageous discrepancy between conditions on Kwaj and those on Ebeye, a much smaller island in the atoll, less than a mile long and nowhere more than 650 feet wide, where nine thousand native laborers live, six and seven to a room, in rat-infested shacks. The men are unskilled or semiskilled workers earning $2.10 to $2.40 an hour, and their wives are paid $5 to $6 a day as maids. Each morning all are boated to Kwaj and at the end of the day they are boated back. They may not stay on the main island overnight or shop in the supermarket there, though powdered milk, which must be imported, costs $4 a box on Kwaj and $10 on Ebeye. They cannot send their children to Kwaj's high school. Nor can they swim in its pools, eat in its restaurants, see its movies, use its hospital and dental facilities, or even borrow books from its library. This is what is called a Trust Territory of the United States. In an aside an American official tells me, "I hope the UN never hears about Ebeye." I reply that if it doesn't it won't be my fault. That night, I know, the Sergeant in my dream will be bitter.

Kwaj is depressing. On all sides are radar domes, sinister square towers, and curious contraptions fashioned of steel tubing which project antennae at awkward angles. Until recently, strategists in what are euphemistically called war games fired nuclear rockets from here, knocking down other rockets coming from Vandenberg Air Force Base in California, five thousand miles away. Today Kwaj's great radar systems, with walls thick enough to absorb atomic blasts, have become empty monuments to advancing technology. If *they* are obsolete, what can be said of the weapons in *my* war? In the opinion of military historians, the decisive tactical innovation of World War II was the amphibious landing, developed by the Marine Corps in response to a 1927 directive from the Joint Army-Navy Board. Its doctrines were used successfully, not only in the Pacific, but in Morocco, Algeria, Sicily, Italy, Normandy, and southern France. Today, however, in a major war, landing operations would be as useless as flintlocks. This is hardly cause for sentimental regret, but when a man reaches his late fifties almost any change empties him a little. It is disconcerting to feel quaint.

After the conquest of the atolls, Nimitz, still driving hard, took dead aim on the Mariana Islands, a thousand miles closer to Tokyo. First would come the turn of Saipan, to be attacked nine days after D-day in Normandy, and then Tinian. Saipan would be our first battlefield to be inhabited by a large number of Japanese civilians who, since the Versailles treaty gave the island to Tokyo, had established a substantial colonial presence among the Chamorro natives. Next we would take Guam, the only American possession to have been seized by the enemy in the great offensive that followed Pearl Harbor. Guam had a good image; the Chamorros there liked us, and we knew it. Saipan — where I would almost bleed to death later in a receiving hospital — was less popular. "Men," a sergeant told his people aboard ship before our invasion of the island, "Saipan is covered with dense jungle, quicksand, steep hills and cliffs hiding batteries of huge coastal guns, and strongholds of reinforced concrete. Insects bear lethal poisons. Crocodiles and snakes infest the streams. The waters around it are thick with sharks. The population will be hostile toward us." There was a long silence. Then a corporal said, "Sarge, why don't we just let the Japs keep it?"

HOW

We Are Living Very Fast

GENERAL EISENHOWER ONCE SAID THAT HE DOUBTED MARINES were better fighters than his own army Rangers. In a sense he was probably right; if you tell picked men they are crack troops, they are likely to fight like an elite. The difference is that Ike's Rangers were small bands of commandos, while the Marine Corps, a *corps d'élite,* fielded six divisions in the Pacific — three corps, a whole army. Their élan helped shape the character of the war and determined the course of Nimitz's great drive across the central Pacific. It is, for example, a military maxim, repeated down the ages, that casualties of 30 percent are usually the most a fighting unit can endure without losing combative spirit. Tarawa, where over 40 percent fell, proved that wasn't true of the Marine Corps. And as we approached Japan, the casualty rates of our rifle regiments rose higher and higher. On Peleliu the First Marines lost 56 percent of its men; on Iwo Jima the Twenty-sixth Marines lost 76 percent; on Okinawa the Twenty-ninth Marines lost 81 percent. Thus they seized islands whose defenders would have flung other invaders back into the surf. Whether the gains were worth the price is another matter; what cannot be disputed is the boldness and audacity of young Marines in the early 1940s. I recalled, from the days when I had been keelhauled through schoolboy Greek at Classical High, Simonides' epitaph at Thermopylae:

> *Go tell the Spartans, thou who passest by,*
> *That here, obedient to their laws, we lie.*

In the twenty-five centuries since Thermopylae, war has been variously described as an art, a profession, and a science, but the Marine infantryman of World War II was more a skilled blue-collar workman. His weapons were his tools, and even after he had become a journeyman he worked ceaselessly to improve his mastery of his craft. To this day I could, if called upon, pull the pin on an Mk. II hand grenade, release the safety lever, giving me four seconds before it will explode, count, "One Mississippi, two Mississippi," and then hurl it and hit the deck. The Raiders on Edson's Ridge could rapidly replace warped machine-gun barrels in the dark because they had done it a thousand times blindfolded. Not only blindfolded, but also working against the clock, between battles we fieldstripped and reassembled rifles, carbines, heavy and light machine guns, BARs, and 60-millimeter and 81-millimeter mortars, the artillery of the infantry. The BAR was a bitch. There were bolts and firing pins, extractors and receiver groups, a sliding leg assembly, a flash hider, a bipod bearing, and a recoil spring and guide. I lack small-muscle skills, and I have a mechanical IQ of about 32, but I became adroit with all infantry arms. I had no choice. It was that or my ass. The tricky part of the BAR, I remember, was putting your index finger on the checkered surface of the recoil spring guide, turning and pressing until the ends of the guide were clear of the retaining shoulders, and then carefully removing the spring and guide. You never hurried that part. If you let that spring get away from you, the guide would rip right through your throat.

Except for his helmet cover, the globe, eagle, and fouled-anchor emblem on the breast of his light-infantry-green uniform, and his profile — he tended to be tall and seldom wore glasses — the Marine Corps foot soldier in combat was indistinguishable from the average GI. Certainly John Payne, wearing his smart dress blues in *To the Shores of Tripoli*, would never have recognized him as a comrade. Mud-caked, unshaven, his uniform greasy and torn, he resembled a hobo, which in a way he was. Like tramps we smoked incessantly, carrying cigarettes in the cartridge pouches on our web belts (where they fitted perfectly), and stooped beneath the weight of our equipment, we looked both crippled and middle-aged. Grenades hung from our straps by the handles, a practice not likely to be recommended by insurance actuaries, but we knew that when we needed them, we would need them fast. If marching, we preferred to walk in ditches, which could provide instant defilade. We were given a ten-minute break every marching hour, and during it we lay collapsed on our backs. Then we sergeants ripped out the command "Saddle Up!" and all hands staggered to their feet and lurched on. Our feet dragged; often we appeared to be unconscious, and there were men who swore they could sleep while staying in column. The prescribed distance between marching Marines was five yards — "Don't bunch up, men!" — to keep casualties from an enemy shell or bomb at a minimum. You could always tell whether men were moving up or coming off the line. Usually those coming off had samurai swords jutting from their packs. And they had a different look — dull, sightless eyes showing the strain, misery, shock, sleeplessness, and, in veteran fighters, the supreme indifference of young men who have lost their youth and will never recover it. The Spanish poet Federico García Lorca caught their expressions. They had "sad infinite eyes, like those of a newborn beast of burden."

At the end of a day's movements, no matter how weary you were, you dug a foxhole, usually with a buddy. I struck big rocks and thick roots with discouraging frequency, but I never broke out my canned C rations (usually beans) or boxed K rations (cheese, crackers, ersatz lemonade powder, and "Fleetwood" cigarettes, a brand never heard of before or since) until I had a good hole. There was no hot food if you were on the line; fires were naturally forbidden there. Most of us carried cigarette lighters made by the Zippo Manufacturing Company of Bradford, Pennsylvania; before the war they had been nickel-plated and shiny, but now they were black with a rough finish, and if you were careful you could light a butt without drawing fire. Sometimes you could get away with heating soup or coffee in a canteen cup over a "hot box," a square of paraffin. But the cups were a problem. Their rolled-over rims collected so much heat that they burned your lips, so you had to wait until the contents were tepid. On the line you were seldom hungry, yet few escaped diarrhea. *Bon appétit.*

At night you kept watch-on-watch in two-man foxholes — four hours alert, four hours of sleep. When your turn to watch came you lay huddled in the darkness, listening to the distant rumblings of armored vehicles, straining to hear counterattack giveaways: the whiplike crack and shrill hissing of streams of sleeting small-arms red-tracer fire, the iron ring of ricochets, and the steady belch of automatic fire. Now and then a parachute flare would burst overhead, and you could see the saffron puffs of artillery in the ghostly light. It was a weird, humiliating, primitive life, unlike anything in my upbringing except, perhaps, the stories of Jules Verne. You learned to explore the possibilities of the few implements you had, and some discoveries were ingenious; behind the front, in reserve, you could use your steel helmet for digging, cooking, bathing, and, in the jungle, for gathering fruit. But it would be wrong to infer that the cheerful foot soldier solved all his wretched little problems. For example, if rain was falling, which it seemed to be most of the time, you were fully exposed to it, and helpless in deluges. By the time you had a hole dug, a couple of inches of rain had already gathered in it. Tossing shrubs in didn't help; their branches jabbed you. You wrapped yourself in your poncho or shelter half, but the water always seeped through. You lapsed into a coma of exhaustion and wakened in a drippy, misty dawn with your head fuzzy and a terrible taste in your mouth, resembling, Rip once said, "a Greek wrestler's jockstrap." Then, like any other worker tooling up for the day, you went about your morning chores, making sure that machine gunners were covered by BAR men, that the communications wire strung along the ground last night was intact, that the riflemen had clear fields of fire and the flanks were anchored and secure.

The Marine in a line company earned a very hard dollar. Unless be became a casualty, lost his mind, or shot himself in the foot — a court-martial offense — he stayed on the line until he was relieved, which usually happened only when his outfit had lost too many men to jump off in a new attack. Behind the lines his unit absorbed replacements (who always got a chilly reception; they were taking the places of beloved buddies) or attended to details which had to be postponed in combat. Some of these could be grueling. Once, my jaw throbbing with an impacted wisdom tooth, I hitchhiked back to a dentist's tent. There was no anesthetic. Lacking electricity, the dentist powered his drill by pumping on an old-fashioned treadle with his right foot. He split the tooth into three pieces and succeeded in extracting the last of them only after I had been in his chair six hours. Luckily, when I got back to the section I found the guys had scrounged some jungle juice produced by the Seventh Marines. The Seventh had built a Rube Goldberg still with old brass shell casings and copper tubing from wrecked planes, and sometimes ladled out a canteen cup of the result to sick outsiders, which, God knows, included me. Lieutenants fresh from Quantico tried to close the still down, but experienced officers called them off. In combat minor infractions were overlooked. Once the Raggedy Ass Marines even enlisted Colonel Krank as an accessory after the fact in a conspiracy against the Army Quartermaster Corps. Discovering that GIs had all been issued new combat boots, which could be quickly strapped on, while we still wore the old prewar lace-up leggings, Rip and Izzy plotted a raid. Acquiring an army requisition form from a sympathetic black corporal, they drew up a directive for the issuance of fifty pairs of boots and took it to the quartermaster dump. They were wearing the thin windbreakers which then passed for field jackets; there was nothing to indicate that they were Marines or identify their ranks. Rip represented himself as a first lieutenant; Izzy said he was a sergeant. When the NCO at the dump hesitated, Izzy took him aside and warned him that too much fighting had made the lieutenant triggerhappy; if they didn't get the boots fast, somebody might get shot. So they got the boots. Before they drove off in a liberated jeep, Izzy, in the finest tradition of the Raggedy Ass Marines, left his spoor, countersigning the requisition "Platoon Sergeant John Smith." Since there were no platoon sergeants in the army, within a few hours angry army officers realized what had happened and demanded that the Marine Corps produce the thieves. You can't hide fifty pairs of combat boots in a cramped reserve area. Krank knew exactly what had happened. The price for his silence was one pair for himself.

Izzy and Rip were heroes, not so much for their loot as for their triumph over "the rear echelon." It is a blunt statistic that for every man who saw action during the war, nineteen men, out of danger, were backing him up. But in practice "rear echelon" was the most relative of phrases. Your definition of it depended on your own role in the war. To the intelligence man out on patrol near the Jap wire, the platoon CP was rear echelon; to the platoon it was the company CP; to the company it was the battalion CP; to the battalion it was the regimental CP; to the regiment it was the divisional CP, and so on, until you reached the PX men who landed at D-plus-60 and scorned the "rear echelon" back in the States. The term was sensitive and was often misunderstood by civilians. Bing Crosby told reporters that it was the morale of the gloomy rear echelon troops which needed boosting; up on the line, he said, "morale is sky-high, clothes are cleaner, and salutes really snap." Of course, Crosby hadn't been near the front; virtually no USO shows and Red Cross girls reached us up there, uniforms were filthy, and any rifleman who saluted an officer on the line, targeting him for an enemy sniper, would have been in deep trouble. The men there would have settled for a Coleman stove and a hot-mess line, but the greatest contribution to their spirits, plus or minus, was mail call. Once the adjutant had been left with the tragic problem of letters whose addressees had been killed in action, individual Marines wandered off alone to read and reread every line from home. Usually they returned looking brighter, though there were exceptions. Some of their correspondents were unbelievably stupid. They complained about gas shortages, or rationing points, or income taxes, or problems with their Victory gardens — this to men who would have swapped places with them under almost any terms. The mail call I remember best came at Christmas, 1944. Pip got a present from his mother in Indianapolis. We all hovered over him when he unwrapped it. It was a can of Spam.

To us the dividing line between the front and the rear echelon was measured by the range of enemy artillery, which, for Japanese 150-millimeter guns, could be 21,800 yards, their maximum, though they had a 24-centimeter railway gun which could throw a shell 54,500 yards. Ordinarily you were relatively safe if you were two miles from Nip batteries. Inside that perimeter, however, you knew you could be hit at any time, and you developed a professional interest in all enemy weapons. During a crashing barrage, with Jap artillery raging and thundering all over the horizon, with as many as a dozen enemy shells (incoming mail) overhead at one time, you hugged the ground, which began to tremble when American guns (outgoing mail) replied. Under close, flat fire the projectiles whipping in were no more identifiable to the veteran than to the greenest replacement. But most of the time you had some warning, and you became familiar with the acoustics of the big cannon. Given a little time in combat — the first days were dangerous for the newcomers — you could sort out the whines of 75-millimeter, 105-millimeter, 24-centimeter, and 30-centimeter howitzers; coastal guns as large as 8-inchers (203 millimeters); 120- and 150-millimeter siege guns; rocket bombs; and huge, bloodcurdling 320-millimeter mortars.

Some shells moaned. Some chug-chug-chugged like a laboring locomotive. Some knocked rhythmically. Others chirred loudly throughout their flight, or rustled tonelessly, or sounded like a stick being jerked through water. There were shells that fizzled like sparklers, or whinnied, or squealed, or whickered, or whistled, or whuffed like a winter gale slamming a barn. The same principle governed all these sounds: the projectile's blast created a vacuum into which air rushed. But various sizes, shapes, and trajectories produced different effects. Howitzers had a two-toned murmur. HE (high-explosive) and phosphorus shells came with a whispering whoosh. Flat-trajectory mail was delivered with a noise like rapidly ripped canvas, and if fired at close range it neither whistled nor whined; it just went *whiz-bang*. There were those who preferred flat-trajectory fire, because if it missed you it kept right on going, leaving only the echo of its *yeeeooowww*. Those who favored howitzers and mortars argued that since they lobbed their mail in, you had a few moments' notice. The bad news was that if one missed you by ten yards it could still kill you. Eventually you reacted intuitively, knowing that you could never achieve complete mastery of the subject: there were shells that warbled after they exploded, shells that warbled and never exploded, shells that exploded without any warble at all.

If a shell landed within a hundred yards you had about one second to hit the deck. There were some Marines who affected indifference to mortars bursting nearby. This was usually a symptom of inner despair, of the terrible need to show contempt toward inhuman missiles which were so contemptuous of them. But it was foolish; even tiny fragments from a shell were white-hot and could kill you. And shrapnel could create new perils from harmless stone. On Okinawa General Simon B. Buckner, the American commander, was standing beneath a granite bluff when a Jap projectile hit the cliff. Buckner got a piece of rock and it killed him. I usually treated ominous sounds in the sky with great respect. Once I even dove into a slit trench — a latrine — to escape a 105-millimeter shell homing in on me. Nobody approached me for several hours, but I didn't apologize. Arriving mail always turned my joints to jellied consommé. The fear continued after the war; the sudden zip of a heavy zipper made me jump for a year after I discarded my uniform, and it was late in the 1940s before I could walk near New York's old Third Avenue El without trembling.

Such was our trade and our Stone Age life: knowing our weapons and how to use them, knowing the enemy's weapons and trying to avoid them, bitching about those behind our lines who didn't have to fight, dreaming of home, fantasizing about girls, controlling our terror, bathing when we could, if only in a water-filled shell hole, and blessing the corpsmen with their morphine syringes, plasma, and guts in risking death to bring back the wounded. Our vision of the war was largely tunnel vision. To each of us the most important place in the world was his foxhole. The impact of MacArthur's and Nimitz's twin offensives was lost on us. Most Marines were as ignorant of Pacific geography as their families at home. Yet it would be wrong to infer that they were wholly ignorant of strategy and tactics. They knew, as even wild animals know, the tactical advantages of deception and surprise. The value of the information brought back by the Raggedy Asses' reconnaissance patrols was obvious. More or less by instinct every fighting man in the Corps came to understand the advantage of attacking troops, who could pick the time and place of assault, and the defenders' advantage, that of fortifying likely targets. Some men even grasped the evolution of amphibious warfare, a combination of strategic offense and tactical defense — once a beachhead had been taken, the invaders could form a perimeter and await the Jap counterattacks. Success in amphibious offensives clearly turned on coordination. Everyone knew when synchronization went wrong. It had happened on Tarawa. It happened again on Saipan.

At dawn on June 13, 1944, as President Roosevelt prepared to run for a fourth term, the mightiest fleet in history till then steamed into the Philippine Sea: 112 U.S. warships, led by 7 battleships and 15 flattops carrying nearly a thousand warplanes. In their midst were 423 transports and freighters bearing 127,571 fighting men: the Second, Third, and Fourth Marine divisions, the First Provisional Marine Brigade, and the Twenty-seventh Army Division. The overall commander was a Marine general, Holland "Howling Mad" Smith. The commander of the Twenty-seventh Division was an army general, Ralph Smith. (The two Smiths cannot be confused, as we shall see.) The task force's mission was the capture of the three great Marianas islands — Guam, Saipan, and Tinian — each almost completely encircled by coral reefs. The prize was to be Guam, with its magnificent anchorage and many airstrips, but Saipan was to be seized first. Saipan was closer to Tokyo and therefore a better base for the new B-29 Superfortresses, which, using Aslito air base, at the southern end of the island, could fly daily raids over Tokyo. Tinian, lightly defended, would fall almost of its own weight. Meanwhile, three days after the landing on Saipan, the Marines were scheduled to hit Guam. Actually they didn't wade ashore on Guam until over a month later. Saipan, like Tarawa — like all the Marine battles which were to follow — was far tougher than anyone had expected.

Seahorse-shaped Saipan is a tropical isle of luxuriant beauty, rippling green ridges, and big rawboned valleys. The island is about as far north of the equator as the Virgin Islands, with the same matted, overgrown brush, and it is roughly the size of Saint Croix. A spine of volcanic mountains, topped by Mount Tipo Pale and the 1,554-foot crag of almost unscalable Mount Tapotchau, dominates the interior. To the north and east, rugged country — angular, flinty, and gnarled with precipitous gorges — pitches and yaws until it reaches steep limestone-and-coral cliffs, as sheer as Dover's, overlooking the sea at Marpi Point. South and west of Tapotchau the land is gentler. Terraced hills and fields of sugarcane glide gracefully toward a long, level plain. The waters over the reef are emerald; in the harbor they are sapphire blue. Lovely beaches fringe them. The Japanese knew that this was where the Americans would come when they came.

At that point in the war, the enemy was still committed to defending its islands at the waterline. Kuzumi's Biak tactics had not yet been wholly accepted in Tokyo as army doctrine. Not an inch of Saipan would be yielded without a fight, whatever the strategic logic. Phony lighthouses had been built near the shore and stocked with ammunition. (One of them still stands across the road from a rusty jail cell where, say some, Amelia Earhart was imprisoned and decapitated in 1937; forced down, so the story goes, she had seen the island's fortifications, already formidable and a violation of the League of Nations mandate, and therefore she and her copilot were executed.) Long before the American armada approached, Yoshitsugu Saito, the Jap commander, had impressed Chamorro and Carolinian natives as laborers to build concrete blockhouses, pillboxes, and ammunition bunkers. Then the islanders and imported Okinawan conscripts had spent eight back-breaking months constructing a new coral airstrip at Marpi Point. Overlooking the beaches, Saito's men sited 5-inch, 5.5-inch, 6-inch, and 8-inch coastal guns. Spider holes were dug, backed by earthworks, trenches, and, in the limestone heights, intricate networks of caves. Inside these warrens were 29,662 enemy soldiers and 6,100 Japanese Marines. All muzzles were trained on the reef.

On the clear, bright morning of June 15 Admiral Turner hoisted the traditional signal, "Land the Landing Force," and set H-hour at 8:40 A.M. As the first amphtracs bellied over the reef, the coral seemed to erupt in a curtain of flame. Officers aboard the U.S. fleet, seeing it, assumed that the reef had been mined. In fact every explosion was a mortar or artillery shell. Two Marine divisions (the third was in reserve) were landing on eleven beaches coded Red, Green, Blue, and Yellow. Those who made it over the reef formed shallow, vulnerable beachheads, where they were pinned down by machine-gun fire in front and shelling on their flanks. They were, for the moment, as helpless as those — some of them the same Marines — who had had to endure the calvary of Tarawa seven months earlier. Five battalion commanders were wounded on Saipan's first day; one battalion in the Sixth Marines lost three commanders before night fell. Some lessons had been learned at Betio. Working under fire, U.S. underwater demolitions teams, who surely had the war's most dangerous job, had breached the beach obstacles the night before, and the timetables of our bomber pilots had been improved. But the interdictive power of naval gunfire and blockbuster bombs had again been miscalculated. Our navy's broadsides simply couldn't reach the big blockhouses on so large an island. Older but more experienced battleships were allowed just one day to hit their shore targets, and gunnery officers on new battleships, untrained in amphibious bombardments, were wildly inaccurate. Amphtrac coxswains fought a strong sea current which had been mentioned in none of the intelligence reports, delivering some companies to the wrong beaches, where they milled around in confusion. By nightfall 1,575 men had fallen. Nevertheless, over 20,000 were ashore, and during that first night they hurled back two banzai charges.

In a war that was being fought on the sea and in the air, as well as on land, news of pivotal developments elsewhere often reached riflemen slowly. The youths on Saipan's gently sloping beaches were unaware that their landing had set off a chain of events which would lead to a tremendous engagement in the skies over the Marianas. The Japs hadn't expected the U.S. tide to lap at Saipan, a thousand miles from the nearest Allied base, so soon. They had, however, been gearing up for a decisive, do-or-die battle. Their warships were plowing toward Biak, where MacArthur's men were still fighting, when they learned of this new blow, with far graver strategic consequences for them. So they headed for the American armada off Saipan with nine of Hirohito's carriers, five battleships, thirteen cruisers, and twenty-eight destroyers. Unfortunately for them, they had lost most of their experienced pilots in earlier engagements; the new fliers were green and ill trained, and Nip warplanes on Saipan, Tinian, and Guam, essential to their battle plan, had been wiped out by U.S. carrier strikes in the days before the Saipan landing.

The result was the Battle of the Philippine Sea, or, as we came to call it, the "Great Marianas Turkey Shoot." As the first Zeroes and Nip torpedo bombers appeared on American radar screens, the old circus rallying cry, "Hey, Rube!" was radioed to all U.S. fliers already airborne, while their carriers began rotating landings and takeoffs to keep umbrellas of fighters overhead throughout the daylight hours. At 10:36 A.M. on the crucial day the first American pilot cried, "Tallyho!" and the slaughter, as it became, was on. By dusk 346 Nip aircraft had been flamed or splashed at a cost of 30 U.S. planes. The enemy's naval air arm had lost 75 percent of its force. Only thirty demoralized Jap fliers had survived. In addition, American submarines had sunk two Rising Sun carriers. The decisive battle had in fact been fought — and the Japs had lost it. In the mournful words of a Japanese historian, "The garrison on the Mariana Islands resembled fish caught in a casting net." Saito radioed Tokyo: "Please apologize deeply to the Emperor that we cannot do better than we are doing." Then he began burning his secret papers.

Saito's defeatism was unknown to the embattled armies on Saipan. All Holland Smith knew was that his troops were in the thick of a desperate battle. On the second night of the struggle the Japanese launched their first large-scale World War II tank attack against Marines: forty-four steel Goliaths hit the left flank of the Second Marine Division at 3:30 A.M. The American riflemen stood in their foxholes, throwing grenades and firing bazookas as the Nip tanks cruised among them, and U.S. warships offshore, guided by a Marine colonel — he sat on a stump in the middle of the melee, tranquilly puffing a cigar — laid heavy shells on the enemy position. At dawn the colonel was still on the stump, still puffing, with thirty-one derelict Jap tank hulks around him.

Holland Smith's plan was to send the Fourth Marine Division straight ahead, taking the big airfield, while the Second Marine Division wheeled northward toward the town of Garapan and the high ground. Then Ralph Smith's Twenty-seventh Army Division would be brought ashore, and the three divisions would sweep northward, the two Marine divisions on the flanks and the army division in the center, pushing the enemy troops toward Saipan's northern tip. By the fourth day of fighting, the island had been cut in two; by the eighth day, the lower half of it had been cleared of Nips. A battalion of my regiment, the Twenty-ninth Marines, was assigned the cruel job of seizing Mount Tapotchau's crest. It seemed impossible then; it seems so now. A heavy Toyota truck with four-wheel drive will take you halfway to the summit over a new, if unpaved, road. You cover the rest on all fours. Even Tapotchau's foothills are awesome. It was all you could do to climb them, let alone fight your way to the top.

On Friday, June 23, the ninth day of the struggle, Holland Smith ordered the great three-divisional sweep northward. Both Marine divisions moved well; Mount Tipo Pale was taken, riflemen began their agonizing ascent of Tapotchau, and the Second Marines battled their way into the outskirts of Garapan. But Ralph Smith's GIs seemed impotent. Their jump-off was fifty-five minutes late; they edged forward cautiously, then stopped altogether. Because the Marines continued to pick up momentum, fighting the Japs in caves with grenades and pole charges and the terrain with bulldozers, the American front formed a shallow U, exposing the Marines' flanks. Ralph Smith reprimanded his regimental commanders. He himself received a gruff message from Holland Smith informing him that Howling Mad was "highly displeased" with the GIs' performance. The next day was worse. The two Marine divisions continued to move forward on the flanks while the army division dug in, deepening the U. Holland Smith took a long look at his situation map and blew his top. He told Admirals Turner and Spruance: "Ralph Smith has shown that he lacks aggressive spirit, and his division is slowing down our advance. He should be relieved." He was, whereupon it developed that others, admirers of Ralph, also had tempers. The Hearst press was enraged. In Washington George Marshall swore that he would never again agree to put his soldiers under Marine officers, and the senior army general in Nimitz's theater arrived on Saipan with blood in his eye. Convening an inquiry (for which he had no authority), he yelled at Holland Smith and his staff: "We've had more experience in handling troops than you've had, and yet you dare remove one of my generals! You Marines are nothing but a bunch of beach runners anyway. What do you know about land warfare?"

Howling Mad, though he bit his lip till it bled, refused to pick up the gauntlet. He didn't have to; events on the front were vindicating him. In retrospect the Twenty-seventh appears to have been a jinxed outfit; it had fought poorly at Makin, would fail again on Saipan, and would disgrace itself the following year on Okinawa. Yet with Ralph Smith's departure its spirits momentarily rose. The GIs began to move in step with the Marines. June 25 was the turning point. Ably supported by the Eighth Marines, the men of the Twenty-ninth Marines executed an intricate maneuver behind a smoke screen and seized the pinnacle of Tapotchau. Half the attackers fell — overall casualties for the two-week-old battle had reached 9,762 — but now, for the first time, it was the Americans' turn to look down upon the enemy's rear. Saito radioed Tokyo: "There is now no hope for victory." He then drew his hara-kiri knife. Unfortunately, he hadn't told his troops that he was resorting to seppuku. His last message to them was: "I advance to seek out the enemy! Follow me!" To them there was only one possible interpretation of this. He wanted them to launch a tremendous banzai charge. Their sheer numbers worried Holland Smith. He wondered whether the GIs could stand up to such an onslaught. Already there had been a sign that they were unprepared for one. In southern Saipan a Japanese captain had led five hundred of his men through the soldiers' lines — "in column of twos," as Howling Mad had biliously reported — and burned U.S. planes on Aslito Field until aircraft mechanics wiped them out. Howling Mad warned all troops to expect a suicide attack, and the following day he made a special trip to the Twenty-seventh's new commander, predicting that hordes of Nips might come surging down the Tanapag Plain at any moment.

At 4:45 the next morning they emerged from the bush, fueled with sake, some merely armed with cudgels, some with a grenade or two, some with bayonets wired to the end of sticks, all of them determined to wreak havoc before they fell. It was the most spectacular banzai of the war. Two army battalions were immediately overwhelmed, cut off, and carved into bewildered pockets. Despite Holland Smith's exhortation, Ralph Smith's replacement had left a five-hundred-yard gap between two GI units. The Japs poured through it and fell upon the Tenth Marines, artillerymen behind the lines. Marine officers couldn't believe it. Infantrymen are supposed to protect artillerymen, or at the very least give them time for maneuver. But here swarming, screaming Japanese, racing four abreast, were descending on the dumbfounded gunners. The artillerymen responded by cutting their fuses to four-tenths of a second: muzzle bursts. They blew off the turret of the attackers' one tank and then leveled the barrels of their 105s at massed Japs who were now just fifty feet from them. Fusillade followed fusillade. The Japs still came on and on. Sometimes they had to climb over heaps of their comrades' corpses to keep their momentum. They did it, while hurrying Marine machine gunners arrived on the scene and flung aside Nip bodies to give themselves fields of fire. At dawn, when the last assault wave peaked and fell away, the artillerymen were wading through the slime and detritus of entrails, gore, splintered bones, mangled flesh, and brains. An exact count of the Jap dead was impossible. The figure agreed upon was 4,311 Japanese bodies. In Tokyo Hirohito said, "Hell is on us." Premier Tojo proclaimed "an unprecedentedly great national crisis." Then he resigned.

The Battle of Saipan officially ended on July 9, three days after the fall of Garapan, but the worst was to come. In a way, the Pacific war until now had been the cleanest in history. Typically, the two armies would meet on an island and fight until the Japanese had been annihilated. The natives melted into the hills or, in the case of atolls, sailed to nearby islands, returning once the shooting had stopped. But since Saipan had become a part of Hirohito's domain in 1919, over eighteen thousand Japanese civilians had settled there. Tojo's propaganda officers had been lecturing them since Pearl Harbor, describing the Americans as sadistic, redheaded, hairy monsters who committed unspeakable atrocities before putting all Nipponese, including women and infants, to the sword. As the battle turned against Saito's troops, these civilians, panicking, had fled northward to Marpi Point. After the great banzai obliterated their army, depriving them of their protectors, they decided that they, too, must die. Most of them gathered on two heights now called Banzai Cliff, an eighty-foot bluff overlooking the water, and, just inland from there, Suicide Cliff, which soars one thousand feet above clumps of jagged rocks.

Japanese-speaking islanders with bullhorns assured them that they had nothing to fear, but the broadcasters were ignored. Saito had left a last message to his civilian countrymen, too: "As it says in the *Senjinkum* [Ethics], 'I will never suffer the disgrace of being taken alive,' and I will offer up the courage of my soul and calmly rejoice in living by the eternal principle." In a final, cruel twist of the knife he reminded stunned mothers of the *oyaku-shinju* (the parents-children death pact). Mothers, fathers, daughters, sons — all had to die. Therefore children were encouraged to form circles and toss live grenades from hand to hand until they exploded. Their parents dashed babies' brains out on limestone slabs and then, clutching the tiny corpses, shouted, "*Tenno! Haiki! Banzai!*" (Long live the Emperor!) as they jumped off the brinks of the cliffs and soared downward. Below Banzai Cliff U.S. destroyers trying to rescue those who had survived the plunge found they could not steer among so many bodies; human flesh was jamming their screws. Still, they saved about one out of every five Japanese. The rest died of shock or drowning. But Suicide Cliff was worse. A brief strip of jerky newsreel footage, preserved in an island museum, shows a distraught mother, her baby in her arms, darting back and forth along the edge of the precipice, trying to make up her mind. Finally she leaps, she and the child joining the ghastly carnage below. There were no survivors at the base of Suicide Cliff. To this day this mass self-immolation retains a powerful grip on the imagination of the islanders, who, though 90 percent Christian, cherish local superstitions. Before the sacrifices, you are told, there were no white birds on Saipan. Now they drift serenely over the cliffs, containing, according to legend, the souls of those who died there.

Because my eardrums had been ruptured and I was partly blind, my memories of my first brief visit to Saipan are fragmentary. I remember the taste of the tiny, delicious Micronesian bananas and a blur of the lovely flame trees which were trumpeting their annual June flowering, and the superb army nurses who consoled

Suicide Cliff, 1978

Banzai Cliff, 1978

me while the doctor dug out shrapnel. Navy nurses were relatively rare in the western Pacific; scuttlebutt had it that the navy thought depraved Marines might rape them. We believed the story. We knew, from our pony editions, that there was some concern at home over how to handle trained killers like us when the war ended. One prominent New York clubwoman suggested that we be sent to a reorientation camp outside the States (she suggested the Panama Canal Zone) and that when we were released there, we be required to wear an identification patch warning of our lethal instincts, sort of like a yellow star. She thought the Raider patch, a skull, might be appropriate. We didn't know how navy nurses felt about this issue, not having encountered any at the front, but those we saw later treated us like *Untermenschen*. They wore heavily starched white uniforms with their ensigns' bars prominently displayed; as officers, they let it be known, they expected deference. The army nurses, on the other hand, tended to be freckled rangy tomboys in baggy dungarees who laughed a lot, kidded us, and, most important, knew when to say absolutely nothing. Mostly it was a time of healing for me, a time of serenity, of quiet: a nothing time.

My second visit, as an aging writer, is far more spectacular. As our plane skies in from Kwajalein in a raging storm, all the lights on the island, including the terminal's, suddenly go out. Figures with flashlights stand at the bottom of the ramp to direct us. But there are not enough of them. Surrounded by yelling Japanese, I am borne inside the building, down endless passageways, and into the presence of a customs officer, who, despite the blackout, insists on poking his own flashlight through all my possessions. I am hot, filthy, and weary. Abruptly the figure of a lanky, grinning young American looms and confronts me. He tells me that I am the guest of honor at a dinner party, already in progress. I beg off; he understands and offers to drive me to my hotel. The storm is at its height. He deposits me at the hotel and drives off. Unfortunately, the clerk at the reception desk informs me, I am in the wrong hotel. The right one is a quarter-mile away. I cannot find anyone, at any price, who will help me carry my luggage, so I stagger off through the jungle in the driving tropical downpour, and when I reach my destination I am given a candle to light my way to bed. By this single flame I shakily find my hypertension pills and a water tap and then collapse across my bed. But I cannot feel wrathful. After all, this is the Pacific. And I have spent worse nights on this island.

Over four thousand Japanese fly here from their homeland each month. Some are demolitions experts; before Hiroshima this was the chief U.S. ammunition dump for the scheduled invasion of Japan, and no one has found a safe way to defuse the tons of explosives. Some are businessmen; Nipponese commerce has thrived here since the early 1950s, when salvage teams from Tokyo reclaimed their rusting guns and tanks, using the metal to manufacture new guns and tanks for the South Korean army. Many visitors are honeymooners; Saipan and Guam have become the Nipponese equivalents of Niagara Falls. Morbid though it sounds, few of them can resist explorations of Banzai and Suicide cliffs, where the human Niagaras poured down on that hot, long-ago summer day. Two years ago the islanders began erecting bilingual signs, English and Japanese, to accommodate the multitude of tourists from Dai Nippon. One of the most popular attractions is billed as Saito's last command post, a picturesque park between the two cliffs, displaying tanks, planes, and artillery in remembrance of the fallen hero. Unfortunately the memorial is a fraud. It is a romantic scene — it *looks* like the proper setting for a general's seppuku — but the event actually occurred forty yards inland, among boulders and twisted reeds. The area was crowded that morning with other officers polishing off a last meal of crab meat and sake. Saito's hands were trembling; he tripped over a creeper, botched the act, and had to be finished off, like an old horse, by an aide with a pistol. Even in death the jungle robs men of dignity.

Apart from that lapse, the Japanese shafts reminding passersby of what happened to their men here are accurate and in excellent taste. There are ten of them. Chamorros like to raise monuments, too; one commemorates the 490 islanders who died during the battle, a second is a bust of President Kennedy, a third is dedicated to world peace, and last Easter they raised a fourth, a cross atop Mount

Tapotchau to honor those who died there. Everyone with reason to erect a pillar has done so, with one exception. The United States suffered 16,525 casualties on Saipan and commemorates none of them. There is a baffling stump which resembles the bottom of a flagpole and bears on its base three moss-covered letters: USN. No one on the island seems to know what it was meant to be. And on Beach Road a group of U.S. coastguardsmen have erected a column with a GI steel helmet, painted white, on top. They wanted to flank it with U.S. artillery pieces but were told they were unavailable, so they substituted two heavy Japanese guns. Cigarettes and empty liquor bottles litter the ground around it. This is odd, for Americans are very popular on the island. In a 1975 plebiscite 78.8 percent of the islanders voted to become an American commonwealth. President Ford signed the necessary papers — setting off a tremendous celebration on the island — and in 1981 Saipan will become a U.S. possession, like Puerto Rico and Guam.

Each autumn since 1968, when the U.S. government first permitted it, a delegation has arrived from Tokyo for a grisly but moving event. They are bone collectors. Having gathered the skeletal remains of thousands of their countrymen, they assemble in a jungly thicket near Marpi Point, where the old Japanese fighter strip is overgrown with tangantangan. A bonfire is ignited, and while the bones are cremated on it, and widows and orphans weep quietly, Buddhist priests chant their monotonous prayers — a final farewell to those whose gray-white bones have lain quietly here all these years. The ashes from the pyre are then boxed in eighteen-inch-square cartons, wrapped in white cloth, and returned to Japan the following spring. Thus far, about twenty-eight thousand skeletons have been reclaimed, the larger part being those who fell in that last mighty banzai charge. Photographs taken shortly after the battle ended show the bulldozed trenches where the fallen Japs were buried, but despite repeated test digs, the interred remain elusive.

During my recent visit, the bones of 1,128 Japanese were gathered in the thicket for cremation. All the skulls were put on top of the heap — you could identify the children by the skulls' sizes — and at first it was like a bad horror movie. But then I realized that the rite had a noble goal, a dramatic demonstration of the continuity of generations, which applies to the vanquished as well as the victors. Yet it seems more reasonable to bury the remains here. Since death lurked all around us, my section often talked of what should be done if we were killed in battle. The unanimous conviction was that our bodies ought to be spaded under out here on the islands. But survivors at home, like those in Dai Nippon, held another view, and virtually all the U.S. corpses were eventually shipped back to the States in body bags. Of course, there is no way of knowing what the Japanese dead would have wanted. The missions from Tokyo do add one touch which would be meaningful for any old infantryman, however. Before their departure each fall, they sprinkle fresh water from home around their monuments and in the thicket, because the greatest hardship in the last days of the fighting was the lack of drinking water. Obviously the annual sprinklings are too few to slake the greenery, yet at Marpi Point, it seems to me, the tangantangan is the most vivid on the island.

"Boonie-stomping" — prowling the bush in search of relics of the battle — is a popular sport among Americans on the isle, most of whom live on Capitol Hill, an affluent community originally built by the CIA to house important Kuomintang officials from Taiwan. (The Saipanese are selective stompers; they prowl around five huge Jap concrete bomb shelters, but never enter the caves — another island superstition.) I join several new friends for a day of roving, accumulating a clutter of gas masks, helmets, canteens, rifle stocks, rotten leather, and spent cartridges. Wandering off from the others I come upon a new Japanese shrine, dedicated the previous April 16 to "Major H. Kuroki and 289 men of the 2nd battalion, 9th Field Artillery Regiment." A lovely Japanese girl in a red brocade kimono, with exquisitely slanting gray eyes and a pink flower in her hair, is placing a wreath in front of a varnished Nipponese howitzer there. She looks up; our glances meet. It is an awkward moment. In halting English she explains that Major Kuroki was her grandfather. She catches her lower lip in her teeth and smiles tentatively. So do I. Our smiles broaden, and as we bow and part I look off toward Suicide Cliff, where a flock of white birds appears and rises higher and higher until it forms a great fluttering fan overhead, a deep white V blending into the enamel blue of the overarching sky.

Of Tinian, three miles across the water from Saipan, it can be said that the battle was a military gem which led to global angst. The neat, green, symmetrical, ten-mile-long isle was ideal for maneuvering. Dug in, the 9,162 Japanese defending it thought they could hold it. Camouflaged coastal cannon ranged from captured British 6-inchers to 75-millimeter flak guns. Leaving the shamed GIs of the Twenty-seventh behind, the Second and Fourth Marine divisions, preceded by 7,571 rounds of artillery fire from Saipan, feinted toward one beach while three reinforced companies of riflemen landed on another. Admiral Turner had predicted that the battle would last two weeks. It took just nine days. The cost was 328 Marines killed and 1,571 wounded — fewer than D-day's casualties on Saipan. But the aftermath was ominous. Tinian-based U.S. pilots flying P-47s first experimented with napalm, one of the cruelest instruments of war, and Tinian's five forty-seven-hundred-foot runways dispatched B-29s toward their fire-storm raids on the Japanese homeland. Finally, it was from here that the B-29 *Enola Gay* took off in the late afternoon of August 6, 1945, to drop the first atomic bomb on Hiroshima.

Today the island's eight hundred Chamorros are largely isolated from a world still struggling with the specter of nuclear weapons. Once a week a supply ship steams over from Saipan, docking beneath a sign which ironically proclaims WELCOME TO TINIAN: GATEWAY TO ECONOMIC DEVELOPMENT. Mail arrives twice a week, on a boat which takes three hours to cover the three miles from Saipan. A chartered motorboat with twin engines does the job quickly, but once you land you wish you hadn't bothered. There is an air of forbidding stillness on the isle, a desolation unmatched in, say, rebuilt Hiroshima. This is where the nuclear shadow first appeared. I feel forlorn, alienated, wholly without empathy for the men who did what they did. This was not my war. In my war a single fighter with one rifle could make a difference, however infinitesimal, in the struggle against the Axis. It was here that the role of men as protectors began to fade until women, seeing how much it had diminished, left their own traditional roles behind and shouldered their way upward.

Today the coral airstrip from which the *Enola Gay* took off is abandoned. Dense shrubs grow along its edges. On the runway itself, frogs and snails crawl among broken coconuts and the shells of dead crabs. The pit from which the first nuclear bomb was hoisted into the B-29's bomb bay has been filled in. Rising from it are a single stark coconut tree and a shrub bearing yellowish blossoms which emit a cloying, sickening odor. A nearby plaque on a three-foot stone marker tells the Superfortress's tale, though it does not, of course, note its implications. Standing there, notebook in hand, you are shrouded in absolute, inexpressible loneliness. You can hear nothing; there is nothing to be heard. The sky is implacable. No white birds hover overhead.

At the time of my return to the Pacific the governor of Guam was Ricardo J. "Ricky" Bordallo, a leonine, intense man, whose face seems riven with lines of passion. Ricky is an insomniac. One night in Washington on official business, he abandoned hope of sleep, switched on his hotel television set, and beheld me babbling on a talk show, mentioning, among other things, my forthcoming visit to Guam. Next day he phoned me, inviting me to be his houseguest, during my journey, in the governor's mansion, overlooking the Plaza de Español, which has been the seat of Guam's government since Spanish rule. Thus, when I land on the island, Ricky is at the gate to welcome me and introduce me to Laura Souder, his aide for cultural affairs. I am touched, and touched even more deeply when Laura whispers to me that yesterday Ricky lost his reelection campaign by the narrowest of margins. Over dinner that first evening the governor doesn't even mention his disappointment. He is too proud. Like the Philippines, Guam is largely ruled by patricians of Spanish descent who have dominated the islands for thirteen generations. They grow up together, attend the same schools, intermarry, and, in times of grief, mourn together.

Ricky's defeat at the polls hurts him, but it actually affects few Guamanians, for he and his successor are cut from the same bolt of damask and have known each other all their lives. The new governor's father was chairman of Guam's lower legislative house while Ricky's father, Baltazar Jerome Bordallo — known throughout the Marianas as "B.J." — chaired the upper house.

The island was inhabited as early as 500 B.C. by Malayans and Polynesians from Southeast Asia, but a synoptic history of modern Guam begins in 1521, when Ferdinand Magellan set foot on what later became known as Asan Beach and is called today, in honor of the Marines who recaptured it, Invasion Beach. (The Japanese arrival after Pearl Harbor is the "Unfriendly Invasion"; the Marines' reconquest, the "Friendly Invasion.") Magellan despised the Chamorro natives. They pilfered his stores, so he christened the island and those around it the "Ladrones," *ladrón* being Spanish for thief. Over the next three centuries Guam became a provisioning stop for galleons carrying gold bullion between Manila and Acapulco, and a hideout for pirates, mostly Englishmen. In 1868 missionaries arrived from Madrid. They rechristened the archipelago the "Marianas" in honor of Queen Maria Anna of Spain. Padres rolled up their sleeves and began proselytizing and catechizing. On Guam, as on Saipan, they converted 90 percent of the native population.

That is, they converted 90 percent of those who were *left*. For Magellan to rage over Chamorro larceny was chutzpah, since his countrymen were exterminating them. After a ruthless, successful campaign of genocide on Saipan and Tinian, they gathered the surviving Chamorros on Guam. There they married them to Spaniards, Mexicans, Filipinos, Polynesians, Micronesians, and Melanesians. Although most of the natives still call themselves Chamorros, the last full-blooded Chamorro died around 1900. Their language lingers — your greeting to full islanders is "*Hofi adoi*"; you say "*Carmen shino hara?*" to ask how they are — and their island retains its original name, a derivative of the Chamorro *guahan* ("we have") and a sign of their abiding love for their home isle. But you also hear Spanish, Tagalog, Malayan, Chinese, and Japanese. This tends to produce a state of linguistic vertigo.

The United States acquired Guam as part of the Spanish-American War settlement. At that time its chief value was as a coaling station, but like so many other Pacific isles it acquired new significance with the growth and power of air warfare. Unlike most of those outside the Marianas and the Philippines, however, it was inhabited by people who were fiercely loyal to the United States. Guam, in their view, was American soil. The Japanese knew of this allegiance and were determined to exorcise it. On the morning of December 9, 1941, two days after Pearl Harbor, stunned Guamanians learned that five thousand Japanese troops were ashore all along their island's west coast, at Piti, Asan, Agana, Tumon Bay, Merzio, and Tamung, where McDonald's golden arches now blemish the sky. The islanders had always assumed that American naval might would protect them. President Roosevelt had in fact wanted to arm the defenders to the teeth, but Republican congressmen, led by Joseph W. Martin of Massachusetts, had argued that reinforcing Guam might be interpreted in Tokyo as provocative. After the final vote, 205 to 168, congressman-adman Bruce Barton had merrily cried: "Guam, Guam with the wind!" Guam was gone, all right. On that December 9 its only weapons were four machine guns manned by 153 Marines and 80 Chamorros led by Marine sergeants. The only American to escape into the boondocks was a naval enlisted man named George R. Tweed. His memory is not revered there. The natives were willing to hide him, but their leaders rightly feared Japanese reprisals. Tweed promised Monsignor Oscar Calvo, Guam's ranking priest, that he would surrender to the Japs if his presence endangered those who had sheltered and fed him. Then the fugitive broke his promise, holding out in the bush while his samaritans were slain.

Naïveté best describes the mood on that Tuesday when the Nips seized the island. Guam's teenagers, who had only the vaguest concept of war, were excited, and Ricky, then one of them, led a band to Asan's Saint Nicholas Market, where they slithered through thick ipil shrubbery to see what they could see. Their first bizarre sight was the corpse of a Guamanian, spread-eagled in the middle of the street. They were astonished, never having seen a cadaver before, but the man was a stranger; they couldn't identify with him. Inside the market it was different. Ricky drew a canvas curtain aside and saw the bodies of twelve of his high-school classmates who had been lined up and machine-gunned. One of them was his steady girl friend, who, ironically, was a nisei. He ran home to tell his father what he had seen, and B.J., who knew opposing the invaders here was hopeless, told him to help establish links with guerrilla camps in the hills. Ricky did, and he wasn't caught, but the Bordallo family's troubles had just begun. Indeed, their ordeal typifies the fate of the island's leaders. Because of a trivial offense — he had failed to report that he knew how to drive a truck — Ricky was forced to beat a dog to death, skin it, quarter it; then to eat it in front of his friends. And that, too, was only a forerunner of what was coming.

Time has blurred the jagged contours of the Greater East Asia Co-Prosperity Sphere, but it should be remembered that the Nipponese were a savage foe, at least as merciless and sadistic as the Spaniards. In Manila they slew nearly 100,000 civilians; hospital patients were strapped to their beds and set afire; babies' eyeballs were gouged out and smeared on walls like jelly. On Guam they began with insignificant things. Children were taught to speak Japanese. Guamanians had to bow deeply to Japs. The Bordallos and other prosperous families were curtly informed that their farms and cattle had been confiscated. Then bewildered public figures were used for target practice. Next, others were ordered to dig their own graves and then shot down. But B.J.'s lot was harder. Arrested at two o'clock one morning, he told the Japanese police that he knew nothing about guerrilla sanctuaries, which was then true. He was imprisoned, tortured, flogged, then released. His flesh hanging in bloody shreds, he crept home on his hands and knees from the Español to the Plaza de Mangena — eleven miles — and found, when he reached his house, that his family had been taken into custody by the *kempei-tai*, the Nipponese gestapo, and locked in a damp cellar.

By the time they were set free, the family baby, Franklin Delano Bordallo, was desperately sick. B.J. sent Ricky to a Japanese

woman who had lived on Guam before the war and who now con-
trolled the conquerors' food stocks. Behind her he could see cases
of condensed-milk cartons. He begged for some for his little
brother. She gave him an open can, less than half full. It wasn't
enough; the baby died. Ricky first told me this story, and his father, after confirming it, burst into tears. In this barbarous century
the incident in itself is unremarkable. The Germans did it; so did
the Russians. What is extraordinary about the Bordallo experience
is that neither they nor their fellow Guamanians bear any grudge.
The Japanese woman still lives on the island and is unmolested.
And this is not exceptional in the Marianas. The islanders do draw
a line. A recent appeal from the Guam Tourist Commission for
families willing to house visiting students from Tokyo was answered by only one household. But visitors from Dai Nippon are
not only safe; Tokyo businessmen are the chief investors in the
island's thriving tourist business. With the round-trip fare from
Honshu only $130, three-fourths of arriving passengers at the air-
port are Japanese. They have no interest in war relics; they seem
unaware that there was a war here. Wearing ten-gallon hats, they
feast on thick sirloin steaks in Agana's nightclubs and enthusiastically applaud go-go girls. This offends the pious islanders —
nowhere in America's Bible Belt have I seen so many road signs
reading TO HEAVEN, TURN RIGHT, GO STRAIGHT — but the Nipponese visitors are safe from harm, and are always treated with civility. I know of no European nation lashed by the Nazi whip
which is so generous to Germans.

For the first two years of the war occupied Guam was little more
than a penal colony. Yet as long as Hirohito's empire seemed safe,
or at least defensible, the Nip guards confined their atrocities to the
island's elite. Then, as MacArthur's offensive crossed the equator
and the Marines approached the Marianas, the occupiers grew
edgy. All schools and churches were closed; forced labor increased;
civilians were put on starvation rations. A beloved Guamanian
priest, thirty-eight-year-old Jesús Baza Dueñas, was publicly beheaded. The island's most successful businessman, Pedro Martinez,

was emasculated and executed as his petrified family, bayonet points at their backs, looked on. Over eighteen thousand Japanese troops landed to strengthen Guam's defenses; then all the natives were cooped in six *kempei-tai* concentration camps. This proved a blessing in disguise, for the camps, identified on U.S. aerial photographs, were spared by American bombers, whose sorties were increasing each day. The prisoners' morale soared. Their confidence in the United States was intact. It had, in fact, never waned. During the first two weeks of the war they had expected the Marines back by Christmas. Chagrined then, they nevertheless continued to follow grapevine reports of struggles on other islands with high hopes. A surviving testament to their loyalty is a crude U.S. flag, sewn in Yono concentration camp. There are but twelve stars and nine stripes — the seamstress had no more cloth — but it is all the more stirring for that. In the camps they sang:

> *Oh, Uncle Saum,*
> *Oh, Uncle Saum,*
> *Won't you please come back to Guam?*

By the third week in July 1944 the Americans were pounding the island night and day, first with B-24s and then with naval gunfire; they wanted no second Saipan. Guamanians to this day cannot understand why Agana, their capital, had to be leveled. One reason is that the American commanders wanted no repetition of the house-to-house fighting in Garapan. The other reason is that the battleships and cruisers, and the air fleets overhead, had nothing better to do. Guam couldn't be invaded until Saipan was secure, so the U.S. armada cruised back and forth — Marines and GIs had to sweat out seven weeks aboard their crammed transports — while the navy gunners targeted 28,761 heavy shells on the island. Down in the holds the fighting men, nursing headaches, swore vengeance on the bluejackets, but the consequence of the long preliminary bombardment was the saving of thousands of infantrymen's lives. The gunners' broadsides on Tarawa and Saipan had been inadequate. This time the Japs waiting on the beaches would be in a state of shock, their intra-island radios demolished and half of their eight-inch coastal batteries shattered. They were too dazed to notice the navy frogmen slithering about offshore. By W-day, as Guam's D-day was encoded, their teams had blown up nearly a thousand mines, tank traps, and other island defensive obstacles. Then, in the flamboyant style of those years, the frogmen left a sign on the reef: WELCOME MARINES.

Guam, the largest of the Marianas, was expected to be tougher than Saipan. It resembled Saipan without cane fields: limestone cliffs in the north were cleft by ravines and clothed with thick rain-forests, and in the south jungly tableland was checkered by rice paddies. Despite forty-three years of U.S. occupation, the task force's topographical maps of Guam were astonishingly imprecise. Since the island is thirty miles long, the Americans had hoped to repeat their Tinian maneuver, faking a landing at one end while coming ashore elsewhere. Here that was impossible. Aerial photographs showed that the jungle along the coast was impenetrable everywhere except on a short stretch of coast on the western shore. Everything we wanted was there: the airfield on Orote Peninsula, Apra Harbor, and Agana. Rear Admiral Richard L. Conolly decided to send in two forces. My outfit, the First Provisional Brigade, later the Sixth Marine Division, would hit the neck of Orote Peninsula with the army's newly arrived Seventy-seventh Division — a fine body of troops, everything the Twenty-seventh was not. The mission of the brigade and the Seventy-seventh was to choke off the isthmus and then link up with the Third Marine Division, which would land beneath frowning bluffs north of Apra Harbor and take the Japs' navy yard. Altogether, 54,891 Marines and GIs would sprint ashore on W-day, Friday, July 21, 1944. On Guam the night before, a group of teenagers, led by Jesús Meno, defied Nip threats of swift retaliation and repeated Rota Onorio's Tarawa feat, slipping out to a U.S. warship in two outriggers to pinpoint Jap strongpoints. Unlike Onorio, they were believed. If the Americans made any mistakes on W-day, they have been forgotten. Guam, like Tinian, was to be a tactical jewel.

The landings were set pieces. The Third Marine Division es-

Guam

0 ⟨═══5═══⟩ 10
STATUTE MILES

Tumon Bay

CHONITO CLIFF

Apra Harbor

●Asan ●Agana
●Piti ✿*Nimitz Hill*

Orote Peninsula

✿*Mt. Alifan*

—13° 20'

●Merizo

144° 45'

144° 45'

G.W.WARD

𝒩

13° 20'—

tablished a beachhead beneath an eminence known as Chonito
Cliff; five miles to the south, the Marine brigade puffed to the top
of Mount Alifan while, on the shore below, GIs of the Seventy-
seventh held the perimeter the brigade had taken at daybreak.
Then Lemuel C. Shepherd, Jr., the Marine general commanding
the force, ordered an attack across the swamp ahead. By Monday
his troops had seized the base of the peninsula, isolating over three
thousand Japanese Marines on the tip.

Discovering that the only road was in our hands and that they
could not perforce escape, the defenders staged one of the most extraordinary performances of the Pacific war. They were bottled up
in more ways than one. Orote, it developed, was the central liquor
storehouse for all Japanese in the central Pacific. There was enough

alcohol in its godowns to intoxicate an entire army. The sealed-off troops had no intention of letting it all fall into American hands. Instead, they planned to tie one on and stage the jolliest of banzais.

As night fell Wednesday they assembled in a mangrove swamp a few hundred feet from our lines. Not only our listening posts but our entire front line, including the Seventy-seventh's artillery forward observers (FOs) heard the gurgling of sake and synthetic Scotch, the clunk and crash of bottles, the shrieking, laughing, and singing. It sounded like New Year's Eve at the zoo. So noisy was the din that artillerymen could calculate the range of imminent targets at the edge of the swamp. At 10:30 P.M., as heavy rain began to fall, the first wave of drunks lurched toward the American lines — stumbling, brandishing pitchforks and clubs; some with explosives strapped to their bodies; others, officers, waving flags and samurai swords. Shells from the Seventy-seventh's Long Toms landed in their midst. Arms and legs flew in all directions; momentarily there was more blood than rain falling in Marine foxholes. Screaming and milling around, these groggy warriors staggered back into the swamp. A second wave hit shortly before midnight. This time some of the souses penetrated the outposts of the Twenty-second Marines and were thrown back only after hand-to-hand struggles. At 1:30 A.M., with every American infantry weapon hammering at them, the third wave reached our trenches before being driven back. In three hours U.S. artillerymen had fired over twenty-six thousand rounds. The crisis here was over. The next morning, Shepherd examined hundreds of the enemy bodies. He recalls: "Within the lines there were many instances when I observed Japanese and Marines lying side by side, which was mute evidence of the violence of the last assault."

Meanwhile, five miles away, the Third Marine Division was fighting what Samuel Eliot Morison later called "a miniature Salerno" — a desperate fight to avoid annihilation. Here the enemy had no alcohol. Preparing for a counterattack, Japs patrolled our lines under cover of darkness and found a gap between two rifle regiments. The Americans had little room for maneuver. They were perched on the brink of Chonito Cliff, an almost perpendicular drop of scree and shale and small boulders, treacherous and unstable to a frightening degree, the whole dangerous slope broken only by small ledges of rock about halfway down. Engineers at the base of the cliff had rigged a wire trolley to haul up ammo and rations and to lower casualties down, which illustrates the precariousness of the American position. At 4:00 A.M. Wednesday the Nips launched a ferocious, carefully coordinated assault: seven battalions determined to throw the Marines over the cliff. Hurtling over no-man's-land they yelled, "Wake up and die, Maline!" (One of the leather-necks shouted back: "Come on in, you bastards, and we'll see who dies!") It was touch and go; our men were down to two clips of ammo per rifleman and six rounds per mortar. The most dangerous point was the gap. Here the Nips penetrated to the rear echelon, on the cliff's edge, before engineers, truck drivers, Seabees, members of the navy's shore party, and walking wounded — sometimes crawling wounded — threw them back with small-arms fire and showers of grenades. At that, the Japanese would probably have won if all their officers hadn't been killed. Confused, they lost their momentum and contact with one another. Pocket by pocket they were wiped out. In the morning nearly four thousand enemy bodies were counted on the bluff and its approaches.

Appropriately, the Japs then made their last stand astride the prewar rifle range of Guam's old Marine Corps barracks. Here the conflict was very different, U.S. tanks versus Japanese pillboxes. GIs of the Seventy-seventh played the key role. Friday afternoon nearby Orote Airfield fell, and on Saturday, with the enemy in full flight, an honor guard of the Twenty-second Marines presented arms still warm from fighting while the Stars and Stripes was hoisted to the top of the Marine barracks flagpole. The issue had been decided, though the fighting was far from over. Surviving Nips crept off through dense thickets of bonsai, those dwarf evergreens which, revealing the oriental gift for miniaturization, mimic great gnarled trees in every detail, down to the writhing angles of limbs twisted in their joints by the rheumatism of time. At bay in their *bokongo,* as the Chamorros called the island's caverns, the enemy shouted abuse at their tormentors and fired out at anything that moved. But they were quickly flushed, completing a clear triumph for the Americans. The cost was 7,081 U.S. casualties — half Saipan's. The friendly population had helped. So had the frogmen, a sign of the navy's growing wisdom in the ways of amphibious warfare. Had the enemy commanders continued their stop-them-at-the-waterline tactics, the Marine Corps would now have had the bloodiest of its World War II battlefields behind it. But the Japanese didn't oblige. Tokyo was beginning to learn the lesson of Biak. Though the Nipponese were losing the war, they vowed to kill as many of the foe as possible before falling themselves. Thus the war's greatest slaughters lay in the future.

Not all Japanese liquor was stashed away on Orote, as we discovered our first day ashore on Irammiya. We were digging in for the night when little Mickey McGuire's entrenching spade hit a wooden box. "Buried treasure," he panted, unearthing it. "Bullshit," Horse said excitedly. "That looks like schnapps!" We counted twenty-four bottles, each in its cardboard compartment. Herr von der Goltz, having advertised himself as Maine's finest epicure, was permitted to uncork the first of them and sip it. "Rice wine," he said, smacking his lips. "Marvelous. Absolutely terrific." This presented me, for the thousandth time, with the problem of leadership. I never tried to inspire the section by example. Never did an NCO run fewer risks than I did, except, perhaps, on Sugar Loaf Hill, and that came later. In the words of Walter Affitto, a Marine sergeant on Peleliu, "I was not very military. I tried to lead the men by being a prankster, making jokes." Obviously, turning the box in wouldn't tickle the Raggedy Ass Marines. The only sidesplitting would come at our expense, from the rear-echelon types who would dispose of it. Since any SOP order I gave would have been ignored by the Raggedy Asses, since we were already dug in, and since I was thirsty myself, I told each man that he could drink one bottle. Straws would be drawn for the five remaining bottles. What no one had noticed was that the labels were not quite identical. We couldn't read the complicated *kanji* characters; it didn't seem to matter. Actually it mattered a great deal. Twenty-three of the bottles, bearing white labels, were wine, all right, but the label on the twenty-fourth was salmon colored. Doubtless this had been reserved for an officer or senior NCO. It contained 110-proof sake. And I drew the straw for it.

Because my taste buds had been dulled by the wine, or my throat dried by the fear that, in combat, never lay more than a millimeter from the surface of my mind, I gulped the sake down chug-a-lug, like a beer. I remember an instant numbness, as though I had been hit by a two-by-four. Then suddenly I felt transported onto the seventh astral plane, feasting upon heaven on the half shell. I recall trying to sing a campus song:

> *Take a neck from any old bottle*
> *Take an arm from any old chair* . . .

Suddenly I was out, the first and oddest casualty of Irammiya. I lay on my back, spread out like a starfish. Night was coming swiftly; the others had their own holes to dig; there seemed to be no Japs here, so I was left in my stupor. Despite intermittent machine-gun and mortar fire throughout the night, I was quite safe. Around midnight, I later learned, the heavens opened, long shafts of rain like arrows arching down from the sky, as was customary when I arrived on a new island, but I felt nothing. One of our star shells, fired to expose any infiltrating Japs, burst overhead, illuminating me, and Colonel Krank, dug in on the safest part of the beachhead (like the Raggedy Ass Marines), saw me. He asked an NCO, "Is Slim hit?" By now everyone else in the company knew what had happened. Krank, when told, erupted with Rabelaisian laughter — nothing is as funny to a drunk as another drunk — and dismissed the adjutant's proposal for disciplinary measures, explaining that I would be punished soon enough. Since I was comatose, I felt neither embarrassed nor threatened then. The next day, however, was another story. The colonel was right. I regained consciousness when a shaft of sunlight lanced down and blinded me through my lids. After a K-ration breakfast, in which I did not join, we saddled up and moved north with full field packs on a reconnaissance in force. I wasn't fit to stand, let alone march. My heartbeat was slower than a turtle's. The right place for me was a hospital, where I could be fed intravenously while under heavy sedation. I felt as though I had been pumped full of helium and shot through a wind tunnel. It was, without doubt, the greatest hangover of my life, possibly the worst in the history of warfare. My head had become a ganglion of screeching, spastic nerves. Every muscle twitched with pain. My legs felt rubbery. My head hung dahlialike on its stalk. I thought each step would be my last. During our hourly ten-minute breaks I simply fainted, only to waken to jeers from the colonel. I needed an emetic, or, better still, a hair of the dog. Knowing of the colonel's fondness for the grape, aware that he carried a flask which would have brought me back from this walking death, I prayed he would take pity on me. When he didn't, I prayed instead that Jap bullets would riddle his liver and leave him a weeping basket case. They didn't, but after the war I learned, with great satisfaction, that one of his platoon leaders, by then a civilian, encountered him in a bar and beat the shit out of him.

As we advanced, opposition continued to be light. The next day we reached the village of Nakasoni. There was still no sign of enemy formations, so we were told we were being held there in temporary reserve. The Raggedy Asses, always adept at scrounging, bivouacked in a spacious, open-sided, pagoda-roofed house whose furnishings included phonograph records and an old Victor talking machine with a brass horn. Because I was blessed with the rapid recuperative powers of youth — and because by then I had sweated out every drop of the sake — I felt rid of the horrors. Rip and I waded across to the adjacent island of Yagachi. We had a hunch there were no Nips there, and we were right, but we had no way of making sure; it was one of the foolish risks young men run, gambles in which they gain nothing and could lose everything. When we returned to our oriental villa we brightened upon hearing dance music; Shiloh, the officer-hater, had liberated several records and cranked up the Victrola. One tune, which haunts me to this day, was Japanese. The lyrics went: *"Shina yo, yaru. . . ."* Two of the records were actually American: "When There's Moonlight on the

Blue Pacific (I'm All Alone with Only Dreams of You)," sung by
Bea Wain or some other thrush, and Louis Armstrong belting out
"On the Sunny Side of the Street":

> *Grab your coat and get your hat,*
> *Leave your worry on the doorstep,*
> *Life can be so sweet*
> *On the sunny side of the street*

Wally Moon, he of MIT, had quickly put the record player in A1
shape, and as we came up Pisser McAdam of Swarthmore was extracting a case of Jap beer from beneath a trapdoor. The sergeant
who commanded these fine troops instantly appropriated two bottles and, using his Kabar knife as an opener, beat his closest rival
by three gulps. Even Bubba was enchanted with Armstrong. He
said he always liked to hear darkies sing.

> *I used to walk in the shade,*
> *With those blues on parade*

The light was beginning to fail. I made my usual footling attempt
to impose discipline, reading orders on sanitation from field man-
uals ("Men going into battle should wash thoroughly and wear
clean clothing to prevent the infection of wounds"), and they, as
usual, responded with "Heil Hitler!" I shrugged. I think we were
all feeling the first moment of tranquillity since the death of Lefty.
We were on a lee shore and about to break up fast, but we didn't
know it then; there was a kind of sheen about us: the glow of health
and wit and the comfort of knowing that we were among our peers.
Except for Wally, the prewar physicist, and Bubba, who at the time
of Pearl Harbor seemed to have been studying some kind of KKK
theology, we were mostly liberal arts majors from old eastern col-
leges and universities. We looked like combat veterans and that, on
the surface, is what we were. But we knew campuses and professors
better than infantry deployments. We belonged to the last generation of what were once called gentlemen. In our grandfathers' day

we would have been bound by a common knowledge, of Latin and Greek. Several of us had indeed mastered the classics, but what really united us was a love of ideas, literature, and philosophy. Philosophically we had accepted the war, and we could still recite, sometimes in unison, the poets who had given us so much joy, ennobling sacrifice and bravery. In time disenchantment would leave us spiritually bankrupt, but for the present it was enough to just loll back and hear Armstrong, croaking like Aristophanes' frogs, telling us to:

> *Just direct your feet*
> *To the sunny side of the street*

On the landward side of our little villa, a rock shaped like a griffin loomed over us like a misshapen monster, grimacing down. Little patches of fog, like gray suede, flecked the view of Yagachi; a mackerel sky foretold rain. But we were too grateful for the present to brood over the future. And in fact the sky cleared briefly for a splendid moment, revealing a carpet of damascened crimson mist suspended among the stars and the moon sailing serenely through a long white corridor of cloud, setting off the villa's flowering quince against a background of mango, jacaranda, and flamboyant trees.

In the absence of the enemy we freely lit up our Fleetwoods, talking among ourselves, the talk growing louder as the various conversations merged into a full-blown bull session, our first and last of the war. There was a little talk about combat, quickly exhausted when Swifty Crabbe said that true steel had to be tempered in fire. (Hoots silenced him.) Inevitably we also expatiated on quail, though not as coarsely as you might think. My generation of college men, I've been told over and over, enjoyed clinical discussions of coitus — "locker-room talk" — in which specific girls were identified. I never heard any of it, with one exception: a wheel in my fraternity who described foreplay with his fiancée and was therefore and thenceforth ostracized. He married the girl, stayed married to her, and is a major general today, but he is still remembered for that unforgivable lapse. I wouldn't have dreamed of mentioning

Taffy to the section. I might have told them about Mae, had not the denouement been so humiliating, but that would have been different, partly because she advertised her horizontal profile but also because no one there knew her. Descriptions of vague, even imaginary, sexual exploits were OK; the important thing was never to damage the reputation of a girl who would be vulnerable to gossip.

We kept beating our gums by candlelight hour after hour, looking, I think now, for some evidence that one day the human race was going to make it. Somebody, Blinker, I think, said that war was a game of inches, like baseball; the width of your thumb could determine whether you were killed, wounded, or completely spared. I remember sprawling on my left hip, looking almost affectionately at my gunsels, one by one. There was Barney, of course, closer to me than my brother, and whippy Rip, who had almost broken my record on the Parris Island rifle range. Either of them, I believed, would have made a better sergeant than I was; I think they both knew it, but they rarely argued with me unless a life was at stake. Others in the section approached mutiny from time to time but were absolutely dependable in a crisis: Knocko, Horse, Mickey, Mo Crocker, who was always "Crock," Swifty Crabbe, Pip, Izzy, Blinker, Hunky, Pisser McAdam, Killer Kane, and Dusty, a dark, animated youth whose quick eyes were useful on patrol. I could always count on lard-faced Bubba, despite my dislike of his racism and despite his bulbous head, which was shaped exactly like an onion. I felt protective toward Beau Tatum, Pip, Chet Przyastawaki, and Shiloh. Pip was just a kid, Beau was married, and the other two were engaged. Emotional attachments complicate a man's reactions in combat. Only two men really troubled me: Pisser and Killer Kane. Pisser was a biologist who resembled a shoat; he covered his lack of moxie, or tried to, with an aggressive use of slang which was already passing from the language: "snazzy," "jeepers," "nobby," "you can say that again," and "check and double-check." Kane was fearsome only by name. He was a thin, balding radish of a youth with watery eyes; loose-jointed, like a marionette; who shuddered at the very sight of blood. Neither Pisser nor Kane had developed that ruthless suppression of compassion which fighting men need to endure battle. Neither, for that matter, had Wally Moon, but with Wally you couldn't be sure; none of us understood him; he played the absentminded scientist with brio. Wally was always wise about mechanics — cams, cogs, flanges, gaskets, bushings — but I knew he had been taught more than that at MIT. To me his outer man was rather like an unoccupied stage, with the essence of his character invisible in the wings. I had long ago forsaken hope of seeing him perform. But that night in Nakasoni the curtain parted a little.

He said crisply: "War has nothing to do with inches, or millimeters, or anything linear. It exists in another dimension. It is time. Heraclitus saw it five hundred years before Christ, and he wasn't the only one." Wally talked about the Chinese yin and yang, Empedocles' Love and Strife, and, shifting back, Heraclitus's belief that strife — war — was men's "dominant and creative force, 'father and king of us all.' " Hegel, he continued, picked this up and held that time was an eternal struggle between thesis and antithesis; then Marx, in the next generation, interpreted it as an inevitable conflict between the bourgeoisie and the proletariat. Jews, Christians, and Moslems all agreed that time would reach its consummation in a frightening climax. Before you could understand war and peace, Wally said, you had to come to grips with the nature of time, with awareness of it as the essence of consciousness. He said that the passage of time was probably the first phenomenon observed by prehistoric man, thus creating the concept of events succeeding one another in man's primitive experience.

Then the mechanic in Wally reemerged in what at first seemed an irrelevant tangent. Once men had perceived time as a stream of experience, he said, they began trying to measure it, beginning with the sun, the stars, the moon, the two equinoxes, and the wobbly spinning of the earth. In 1583 Galileo discovered the pendulum; seventy-three years later a Dutchman built the first pendulum clock. Splitting the day into 24 hours, or 86,400 seconds, followed. A.M. (ante meridiem, "before noon") and P.M. (post meridiem, "after noon") became accepted concepts on all levels of society — the week, having no scientific validity, varied by as much as three days from one culture to another — and in 1884 the world was divided into twenty-four time zones. The International Date Line, electromagnetic time, confirmation of Newton's laws of motion and gravitation, and the transmission of time signals to ships at sea, beginning in 1904 as navigational aids, united the civilized world in an ordered, if binding, time structure.

Thus far Wally had held us rapt. There were four Phi Beta Kappas in the section; he was talking the language we knew and loved. He hadn't come full circle yet — the pendulum clock's relationship to the battlefield was unclear — but that was the way of college bull sessions in my day, leading the others through a long loop before homing in on the objective. Unfortunately the loop sometimes went too far into uncharted territory and the speaker lost his audience. For a while there Wally was losing his. Chronometers and the value of rational time for navigation and geodetic surveys were understandable; so was Parmenides' argument that time is an illusion; so were the conclusions of Alfred North Whitehead and Henri Bergson that passing time could be comprehended only by intuition. But when Wally tried to take us into the fourth and fifth dimensions, citing Einstein's theory of special relativity and William James's hypothesis of the specious present, we began to stir and yawn. Like the old vaudeville act of Desiretta, the Man Who Wrestles with Himself, Wally was pinning himself to the mat. In my war diary I retained, but still do not understand, his equation for Minkowski's clock paradox:

$$ds = \sqrt{c^2dt^2 - dx^2 - dy^2 - dz^2}$$

It meant nothing then; it means nothing now. But bull sessions rarely ended on boring notes. Either someone changed the subject or the man with the floor, sensing the lethargy of the others, took a new tack. Wally quickly tacked back to his original objective. I had read Heraclitus and remember best one fragment of his work: "No man crosses the same river twice, because the river has changed, and so has the man." Now Wally was reminding us that Heraclitus believed that the procession of time is the essence of reality, that there is only one earthly life. The riddle of time, Wally said, was baffling because no one knew whether it flowed past men or men passed through it — "If I fire my MI, does that mean that firing it is what the future was?" The point was not picayune; it was infinite. Either life was a one-way trip or it was cyclical, with the dead reborn. The life you lived, and the death you died, were determined by which view you held. Despite all evidence to the contrary, most thinkers, with the exception of the Egyptian era and the twentieth century, had come down hard on the side of rebirth. Plato, Aristotle, the fourteenth-century Moslem Ibn Khaldun, and Oswald Spengler believed men and civilizations were destined for rehabilitation. So did the biblical prophets: Abraham, Moses, Isaiah, and Jesus. All used the same evidence: the generational cycle and the cycle of the seasons.

It was at this point that Bubba astounded everyone by speaking up. He recited: "Unless a grain of wheat falls to the earth and dies, it remains alone; but, if it dies, it bears much fruit." He trumpeted: "John 12:24." There was a hush. Into it he tried to introduce certain observations of Robert Ingersoll, Dale Carnegie, and Emanuel Haldeman-Julius. Then Knocko — to my regret — turned him to dusky vermilion by saying gently, "Bubba, this is too deep for Dixie. The day they introduce the entrenching tool in Alabama, it'll spark an industrial revolution." I should have said something, because Bubba was a fighter and therefore valuable to me, but I was eager to hear Wally's windup. And here it came. He said: "Like it or not, time really is a matter of relevance. We all have rhythms built into us. It wouldn't much matter if all the timepieces in the world were destroyed. Even animals have a kind of internal clock. Sea anemones expand and contract with the tides even when they are put in tanks. Men are a little different. John Locke wrote that we only experience time as a relationship between a succession of sensations. No two moments are alike. Often time drags. It dragged for most of us toward the end on the Canal. I think it won't drag much here. I have a feeling we are going to be living very fast very soon."

Events confirmed him, though he didn't live to know it. He was right about the unevenness of the time flow, too. Time really is relative. Einstein wasn't the first to discover it — the ancients knew it, too, and so did some of the modern mystics. In our memories, as in our dreams, there are set pieces which live on and on, overriding what happened afterward. For some of my generation it was that last long weekend in Florida before Kennedy went to Dallas; Torbert MacDonald, his college roommate, was there, and afterward he said of that Palm Beach weekend that it reminded him of "way back in 1939, where there was nothing of any moment on anybody's mind." History has other bittersweet dates: 1913, 1859, 1788 — all evoking the last flickering of splendor before everything loved and cherished was forever lost. That lazy evening in Nakasoni will always be poignant for me. I think of those doomed men, tough, idealistic, possessed of inexhaustible reservoirs of energy, and very vulnerable. So was I; so was I. But unlike them I didn't expect to make it through to the end. Thomas Wolfe, my college idol, had written: "You hang time up in great bells in a tower, you keep time ticking in a delicate pulse upon your wrist, you imprison time within the small, coiled wafer of a watch, and each man has his own, a separate time." Out here in the Pacific, I thought, my time was coming; coming, as Wally said, very fast.

On Guam my dreams of the Sergeant begin to change. Color is returning; the sky is cerulean, the blood crimson; various shades of green merge in his camouflaged helmet cover. He himself, viewed now as through a prism, is subtly altered. His self-assurance has begun to ebb. And now, for the first time, there are intruders in the nightmares, shadowy figures flitting back and forth behind him. They seem sexless. I'm not even sure they are human. But on Guam, and in the nights to come elsewhere, they are always in the background — a chorus of Furies, avengers, whatever — and they have begun to distract the young NCO. He is becoming confused. He hesitates; his attention is divided; every third or fourth night I sleep through without any sign of him.

On the eighth day of the battle for Guam, Takeshi Takeshina, the Japanese commander, was killed in action. His army was finished, but those people never gave up. Organized resistance continued for two weeks; then the surviving Nips slipped into the hills to wage guerrilla warfare. Skirmishes continued until the end of the following year — seventeen weeks after Hirohito had surrendered to MacArthur — and even then diehards remained in the bush. Nine of them emerged from the jungle in the mid-1960s, and on February 9, 1972, a Nipponese soldier named Shoichi Yokoi ended his twenty-eight-year green exile and surrendered to amazed Guamanians, some of whom hadn't even been born when he disappeared from civilization. One by one the comrades who had shared his hideout had died. For the last nine years he had been alone, living on breadfruit, fish, coconut milk, and coconut meat. He had woven clothes from coir, and rope matting from shrubs, and he had fashioned implements from shell cases, coconut husks, and his mess gear. In Tokyo he was greeted as a national hero. It is sad to learn that he was deeply disappointed in what postwar Japan had become. I wonder if he had nightmares like mine.

Ricky Bordallo thinks there are more stragglers out there. He predicts they will come in from the hot in 1994, the fiftieth anniversary of the battle. If so, their artifacts, like Yokoi's, will be preserved in Guam's museum, whose most enthusiastic patroness is Ricky's Minnesota-born wife, Madeleine. The museum is an archaeologist's paradise: prehistoric mortars and pestles; ancient pottery shards fashioned from the island's thick red clay; a *belembautuyan*, which is a stringed instrument startlingly like those found in the interior of Brazil; huge stone *rai* disks, some of them twelve feet in diameter, once used for money on the Yap Islands, which lie five hundred miles to the southwest — the *rai* have holes in the center to permit them to be strung on poles and carried on men's shoulders — and blubber pots brought in 1823 by British whalers. Outside the museum is the Kiosko, or "Chocolate House," a gazebo where upper-class Chamorro women once gathered each afternoon to eat sweets and gossip. Nearby a handsome young priest, Thomas Devine, has rebuilt a primitive Guamanian village, an exact replica of those found by the first Spaniards four and a half centuries ago. It is seductive; my New England drive flags; I find my mind drifting, wondering what it would be like to be a beach-

The author with the relic of an enemy tank

A cave with Japanese gun emplacement

comber, wondering, like Captain Cook, whether Magellan's arrival has been good for the Guamanians or bad for the Guamanians.

Guam's architecture, like its history, reflects a hodgepodge of influences: Spanish, English, Chinese, German, Filipino, and Dutch. But the prevailing influence is American. Mustard-colored stucco walls are flimsy carbons of Beverly Hills originals. Orote's airfield has been cleared of bamboo clumps which sprang up after the war and is now used by local teenagers as a drag strip. The outskirts of Agana, which has never really recovered from its wartime devastation — 90 percent of its prewar population never returned; it looks like a ghost town — are cultural atrocities: junk-food stands, supermarkets, bars, filling stations, discount houses. Partly because taxi fares are exorbitant, there are over forty thousand Detroit gas-guzzlers on the island. Unless you are lucky enough to have a friend who will put you up, you stay at the Guam Hilton Hotel on Tumon Bay.

Looking up from the hotel pool you can see Nimitz Hill, the admiral's headquarters in the final months of the war and still a treasured property of the U.S. Navy. One source of abrasion, were the islanders less complaisant, would be this huge U.S. military presence on the island. Erwin Canham, whose siesta I interrupted on Saipan, confirmed their tolerance of it. The Canhams chose to live in the Marianas after he had retired as editor of the *Christian Science Monitor*. Over and over they express astonishment that the Saipanese and the Guamanians, who have much to be bitter about, are unresentful, though clearly they were pawns in a titanic quarrel, victims because they happened to be bystanders. Guamanians have erected war memorials for their sons lost in battle, and not just in the battle of 1944. They cannot participate in American presidential elections. Their representative in Congress can vote in committee but not on the floor. They couldn't even choose their own governor until 1970. Yet islanders of military age were drafted and sent to Vietnam.

Guam was a major staging area in that hopeless war; over 100,000 U.S. GIs passed through here. Since Okinawa was returned to Japanese rule in 1972, Guam has become the chief U.S. base in the western Pacific. Nearly 20,000 uniformed Americans are stationed on the island, and it is the home of a B-52 fleet. The navy owns a third of the isle — all of it prime real estate, with vast tracts where officers hunt wildlife and where one finds lovely beaches for wives and children. The navy opposes first-class citizenship for the islanders because they still read, speak, pray, and are taught Chamorro. The Guamanians reply that linguistic differences haven't crippled Puerto Ricans, that the Viet Cong didn't spare them because they hadn't mastered the English. In the islanders' opinion, the admirals regard Guam as the navy's paradise and intend to keep it as such.

Yet all this is low-key. Guamanians are proud of their relationship with the United States. They have built an unknown soldier a memorial: "Here lies in honored glory an American soldier known but to God." The length of shoreline where our Orote force came ashore is called Invasion Beach; the coast below Chonito Cliff is Nimitz Beach. On the first, near two rusting Jap warships, are gazebos for family picnics; an elementary school has been built near the second, and a spent artillery shell is cemented there into a stone marker. Every July 21 the island celebrates "Liberation Day," in remembrance of the Marines and GIs who retook Guam. Schools are out, shops are closed, and community leaders deliver eloquent patriotic speeches pitched on an emotional level unheard in the United States for at least a generation. American visitors find them embarrassing, which perhaps says more about them than about the rhetoricians. Veterans' Day is similarly observed. On a cloudless November 11 I found myself in a packed square, sitting in the front row with Ricky, a U.S. general, and two flag officers of the navy. Toward the end of the ceremony the band played a medley of U.S. military songs. There is a tradition that anyone who has served in the Marine Corps must stand when he hears the "Marines' Hymn." I hadn't been in that situation since my return to civilian life, but I was in it now. Somewhat to my amazement — for I am not that kind of man, and I scorn the sequins of militarism — I found myself rising and standing there, the only spectator on his feet, until the band switched to another tune. As the program ended and the crowd broke up, I was surrounded by islanders who wanted to embrace me. It was embarrassing, but it was moving, too. I still don't understand why I did it. But I'm not apologizing.

My last evening on Guam is spent with Ricky and Madeleine atop Oksu Jujan, Chamorro for the heights upon which the governor's mansion stands. Lights play upon a lovely fountain, through the mists of which lighted buildings below us gleam and winkle. Ricky's defeat at the polls overshadows my thoughts. Eviction from high office is always hard, but especially so for the imperious, and Ricky is very much the aristocrat. Yet he is philosophical about his discomfiture. He has lost, he says, but the people haven't; the people never lose a free election. And Guam's devotion to democracy lies as deep as in any of the United States. A clock booms deep within the mansion, and we head for the hay. Checking my watch — I keep zigzagging from one time zone to another — I remember one official here pointing out to me shortly after my arrival that because of the International Date Line, Guam's dawn arrives when it is still early afternoon of the day before in mainland America. Indeed, the local newspaper here carries a front-page ear: "Guam: where America's day begins." It sounds like one of those old FitzGerald Traveltalks, but it is literally true. The first rays of each sunrise first touch the Stars and Stripes here. It's not a bad start for a day.

I Will Lay Me Down
for to Bleed a While...

THE PALAU ISLANDS, ABOUT HALFWAY BETWEEN THE MARIANAS
and the Philippines, are so remote that none of the European colonial powers had bothered to develop them. Indeed, except for a
party of sixteenth-century conquistadores led by Ruy López de Vi-
llalobos, few outsiders were even aware of the mini-archipelago until the autumn of 1944. Peleliu is the southernmost isle in the Palau
group. Roughly speaking, it was to the Palaus what Betio was to
Tarawa — the key to the Japanese defense of the surrounding atolls
and volcanic land masses. Today it is the least accessible of the central Pacific's great battlefields, hidden away in the trackless deep
like a guilty secret. And that is altogether appropriate. It was a bad
battle, fought at a bad place and a bad time, with an enemy garrison that could have been left to wither on the vine without altering
the course of the Pacific war in any way.

To grasp what happened on Peleliu, or what ought not to have
happened, you need only glance at a map of the Pacific. America's
two enormous pincers — the drives of MacArthur and Nimitz —
were swiftly approaching one another. In the Pentagon, Peleliu
seemed necessary to protect MacArthur's flank when he invaded
Mindanao, the big island at the bottom of the Philippines. But then
Halsey, cruising off the Philippines, launching carrier strikes at
Japanese bases, concluded that Leyte, farther up the Filipino island
chain, was held by far fewer enemy troops than had been thought.
He radioed Nimitz, suggesting the canceling of all other operations,

especially Peleliu, which, he had already predicted, would become another Tarawa. In their place he urged the swift seizure of Leyte.

Nimitz relayed the proposal, accompanied by recommendations of his own, to Quebec, where the Combined Chiefs of Staff were attending a formal dinner as guests of Prime Minister W. L. Mackenzie King. Admirals King and Leahy and Generals Marshall and Arnold excused themselves, read the message, and told a staff officer to cable their approval. There was one small difficulty. In Nimitz's endorsement of Halsey's message he insisted that the convoy of Marines steaming toward the Palaus, which was two sailing days from its objective, steam on and take Peleliu anyway. This defies understanding. The island's only strategic value was that it lay 550 miles east of Mindanao, which, under the new plan, would be bypassed.

Part of the problem lay in U.S. ignorance of the Palaus and the assumption that Peleliu would be easy to take. There were no coastwatchers and therefore no information on what was happening there. Intelligence came from navy frogmen demolishing beach obstacles, submarine shore parties, and aerial photographs. Since the frogmen and the submariners could not see inland, they could not contradict the conclusions of those who had analyzed the aerial photographs and said Peleliu was flat. None of them suspected the presence of jagged limestone ridges overlooking the island's airfield, heights which had been turned into fortresses of underground strongpoints shielded by cement, sand, and coral, all connected by tunnels and virtually impervious to air and naval bombardment. One hulk of rock, later to be christened "The Point" by the Marines who had to take it, rose thirty feet above the water's edge, a bastion of huge fractured boulders, deep gorges, and razor-sharp spikes, the entire mass studded with pillboxes reinforced with steel and concrete. It was Tarawa, Saipan, and Guam in spades.

During the preinvasion bombardment, a gunnery officer on the heavy cruiser *Portland* glimpsed what lay ahead. Focusing his field glasses on a Peleliu slope, he saw a coastal gun emerge from a coral fissure. Shells were rapidly fired at the U.S. warships and then the gun was dragged back out of sight. The gunnery officer ordered his crews to hit the coral with five salvos of eight-inch shells. It was done. The gun, untouched, repeated its act. Frustrated, he said, "You can put all the steel in Pittsburgh onto that thing and still not get it." But he was a junior officer, and in a minority. Admiral Jesse Oldendorf ordered his batteries to cease firing. He said he had run out of targets; the Jap defense had been annihilated. William Rupertus, the Marine commander, told his officers: "We're going to have some casualties, but let me assure you this is going to be a short one, a quickie. Rough but fast. We'll be through in three days. It might take only two." Company K of the First Marines climbed down the cargo nets singing, "Give my regards to Broadway." The captain of a transport asked the First Marines' CO, Chesty Puller, "Coming back for supper?" Chesty asked, "Why?" The captain said, "Everything's done over there. You'll walk in." Puller said, "If you think it's that easy, why don't you come on the beach at five o'clock, have supper with me, and pick up a few souvenirs?"

Later, after the First Marines had suffered over seventeen hundred casualties, another naval officer asked an evacuated Marine if he had any souvenirs to trade. The Marine stared at him and then reached down and patted his butt. "I brought my ass out of there, swabbie," he said. "That's my souvenir of Peleliu." Painfully aware that they continued to carry prewar equipment, priority still being given to the ETO, and learning that the bombardment had been entrusted to inexperienced naval commanders, the men who suffered on this ill-starred island became bitter. A Marine officer later said: "It seemed to us that somebody forgot to give the order to call off Peleliu. That's one place nobody wants to remember." Oldendorf conceded that if Nimitz had realized the implications of his decision, "undoubtedly the assault and capture of the Palaus would never have been attempted." *Time* called it "a horrible place." Few Americans at home even knew of the ferocious struggle there. When President Truman pinned a medal on a Peleliu hero, he couldn't pronounce the island's name. Samuel Eliot Morison, rarely critical of U.S. admirals, wrote that "Stalemate II," as the operation had been prophetically encoded, "should have been counter-

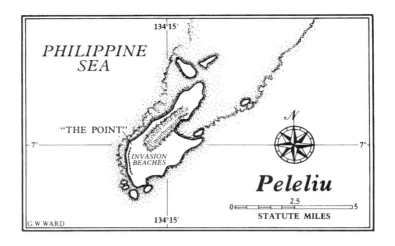

manded," being "hardly worth" the price of over ten thousand American casualties — three times Tarawa's.

The target island, seven miles long and two miles wide, lies within the coral reef which surrounds most of the Palaus. Peleliu is shaped like a lobster's claw. The Jap airstrip had been built on a level field south of the claw's hinge. North of the hinge a spiny ridge of rock dominates the battlefield. Steep, heavily forested, and riddled with caves, it was known as the Umurbrogol until the Marines rechristened it Bloody Nose Ridge. The enemy knew that any assault on the Palaus would have to hit Peleliu's mushy white sand coast because the airfield was there, and because the reef there was closest to the shore. The island's postwar population is about four hundred. In the summer of 1944, over twelve hundred natives had been living here. Most of them left before the battle because U.S. planes, in one of those humane gestures which fighting men will never understand, had showered Peleliu with leaflets warning of the coming attack. Undoubtedly that saved the lives of many islanders, but it cost American lives, too, because the Japanese also read the pamphlets and made their dispositions accordingly.

It was the misfortune of the attackers — the First Marine Division, followed by the Eighty-first Army Division — that their landings coincided with a revolutionary change in Japanese tactics. The murderous doctrine of attrition, which had first appeared as a local commander's decision on Biak, and which would reach its peak in the slaughterhouses of Iwo Jima and Okinawa, became official enemy policy in the weeks before the Battle of Peleliu. There would be no more banzai charges. Tokyo knew the war was lost. The Japanese garrisons in the Palaus were written off; their orders were to butcher Marines and GIs, bleeding them white before falling themselves — to dig deep, hold their fire during bombardments and preliminary maneuvering, and infiltrate and counterattack whenever possible. Thus the Peleliu gunports with sliding steel doors; thus the blasting of more than five hundred cunningly located coral caverns, one of them large enough to hold a thousand Japs, well stocked with food and ammunition. Most of the caves were tiered, with laterals, bays, and alternate entrances. Some were six stories deep, with slanting, labyrinthine entrances to deflect flamethrower jets and satchel charges of TNT. Camouflaged so that Americans would unwittingly advance beyond them, these fortresses held Nips drilled to emerge and attack from the rear following seven separate counterattack plans, each to be triggered by a signal flag or flare. On September 14, 1944, there were 10,700 such Japanese waiting, all prepared to die, all aware that the survivors among them would make their last stand on Bloody Nose Ridge. The terrain was their ally. Mangrove swamps, inside the reef, encircled the entire island. Steep-sided ravines — often more like chasms between cliffs — made progress difficult. Finding the fire zones of pillboxes and caverns would be even harder.

This, then, was the ghastly stage which awaited three regiments, veterans of Guadalcanal, who had been recuperating in the Solomons. They landed abreast: Puller's First Marines on the left, the Fifth Marines in the center, and the Seventh Marines on the right. The instant they reached the reef it burst, as Saipan's had, in a sheet of fire, steel, and lead. Only the Fifth landed more or less intact, threw a loop over the southern runways on the airfield, and, crossing the island, anchored on the far shore by evening. For the other regiments the landing was Tarawa without a seawall. To the right of the Seventh, obstacles which had eluded the frogmen marooned blazing amphtracs on the reef and forced the rest to come in single file, each in succession a lonely target, so that Marines jumped off and waded in instead. But the First Marines, moving under the muzzles of the largest pillboxes, faced the hardest task of all. Those who reached the beach were trapped by enfilading fire from the Point. One company was down to eighteen men. In a co-conut grove near the water's edge the dead and dying, furled in bloody bandages, lay row on row, the corpses grotesquely trans-fixed in attitudes of death and those still alive writhing and groan-ing. Ahead, in craggy jungle laced with enemy machine-gun nests, lay knobs and wrinkles of stone which, as the riflemen ap-proached them, were christened Death Valley, the Horseshoe, the Five Sisters, the Five Brothers, and Walt Ridge.

At 5:30 P.M. of the first day, the Japanese counterattacked across the airfield from a wrecked hangar, led by thirteen light tanks. With Nip infantry clinging to them at every possible place, the tanks raced, their throttles open, like charging cavalry. The Marines fired back with everything they had: bazookas, 37-millimeter antitank guns, pack howitzers, Sherman tanks armed with 75-millimeter guns, and, at the moment of collision between the two forces, a well-timed lunge by an American dive-bomber. One man rushed a Jap tank with his flamethrower and was cut down when a burst of machine-gun fire ripped open his chest. Marine infantry held fast; several Nip tanks reached our lines, prodding with their grotesque snouts, but their skin of armor was too thin to withstand the concentrated fire, and Marines standing in full view of their gunners, some even perched on rocks, blazed away until the last tank blew up.

Digging foxholes on Peleliu, as on so many islands, was impos-sible. Beneath the dense scrub jungle lay solid limestone and coral. At midnight the Japanese opened fire with heavy mortars; then their infiltrating parties crept close to Marine outposts. The cruiser *Honolulu* and three destroyers sent up star shells, exposing the infil-trators to our small-arms fire. Fire discipline had to be tight; amph-tracs were bringing in ammunition as quickly as possible, but some units ran out of it; one company commander led his men in throw-ing chunks of coral at the Nips. Sniper fire, the scuffling of crawling Japs, and the wounded's cries for corpsmen continued until dawn, when the enemy mounted new mortar and grenade barrages. Marine radios had been knocked out and were useless for calling in supporting fire from our artillery and mortars, and some companies had lost two men out of every three, but the American lines held fast and the airfield was seized by the Fifth Marines. With the Seventh Marines driving south, the first assault on Bloody Nose Ridge fell to Puller's regiment, which had already suffered the heaviest losses in the attacking force.

They confronted an utterly barren land. Naval gunfire had denuded the Umurbrogol, leaving naked mazes of gulches, crags, and pocked rubble which became coral shrapnel as the enemy artillerymen found their range. The sharp rock underfoot sliced open men's boondockers and, when they hit the deck as incoming shells arrived, tore their flesh. They mounted the first scarp and found another, higher, rising beyond it; thirty-five caves had to be blown up before they could advance further. Then a ferocious counterattack threw them back. This went on, dawn to dusk, with hand-to-hand struggles in the dark, until, on the sixth day, the First Marines' three companies, 612 men, had been reduced to 74. Platoons of the Seventh Marines were fed into the lines and immediately pinned down. GIs of the Eighty-first Division arrived while the Fifth Marines attacked the Umurbrogol from the north. Everyone was waiting for the banzai charge which had ended other battles. Slowly they grasped the enemy's new tactics. A Marine company would scale a bluff unmolested; then the Japanese would open up on three sides with infantry fire, mortars, and antitank guns, killing the Americans or throwing them to their death on the floor of the gorge below.

The Ridge had become a monstrous thing. Wounded men lay on shelves of rock, moaning or screaming as they were hit again and again. Their comrades fell and tumbled past them. Some men committed the ultimate sin for Marines, throwing away their rifles and clawing back down the slopes. Down below, a shocked company commander yelled, "Smoke up that hill!" Under roiling clouds from smoke grenades, those not hit tried to lead or carry the

Bloody Nose Ridge, 1978

wounded down. One infantryman, bleeding badly, cried, "You've done all you could for us. Get out of here!" The company commander ran up, carried one casualty down, and laid him in defilade beside a tank hulk. As he straightened, a mortar shell killed him. His exec, a second lieutenant, sprinted up to help; he was killed by an antitank shell. The company was down to eleven men, finished as a fighting unit.

Now the slow, horrible slugging of attrition began. Hummocks of shattered coral changed hands again and again. Cave entrances were sealed with TNT; the Japs within escaped through tunnels. Corsair fighters dove at pillboxes; their bombs exploded harmlessly. Tongues of wicked fire licked at Nip strongpoints from flamethrowers mounted on Shermans; Japs appeared in ravines and knocked the Shermans out with grenades. Using the airfield was impossible; cave entrances overlooked it. Slowly, moving upward in searing heat — the thermometer seemed stuck at 115 degrees in the shade — Marines rooted out enemy troops or sealed them off, hole by hole. The island was declared secure on September 30, but eight weeks of desperate fighting lay ahead. By the end of October, when GIs arrived in force, the defenders had been reduced to about seven hundred men. The Japanese commander burned his flag and committed hara-kiri. Yet two months later Japs were still killing GIs poking around for souvenirs. The last of the Japs did not surface until eleven years later.

We used to say that the Japanese fought for their emperor, the British for glory, and the Americans for souvenirs. One wonders how many attics in the United States are cluttered with samurai swords and Rising Sun flags, keepsakes that once seemed so valuable and are worthless today. I collected them like everyone else, but I shall never understand men whose jobs kept them away from the front, who could safely wait out the war — "sweat it out," as we said then — yet who deliberately courted death in those Golcondas of mementos, the combat zones. You heard stories about "Remington Raiders," "chairborne" men ready to risk everything for something, *anything*, that would impress families and girls at home. I didn't believe any of them until I saw one. Even then I wondered what he was looking for. I suppose he was partly moved by a need to prove something to himself. He succeeded.

Our war, unlike our fathers', was largely mobile. It was just as bloody and, because of such technological achievements as napalm and flamethrowers, at least as ugly, but we didn't live troglodytic lives in trenches facing no-man's-land, where the same stumps, splintered to matchwood, stood in silhouette against the sky day after desolate day, and great victories were measured by gains of a few hundred yards of sour ground. Nevertheless, there were battles — Bloody Nose Ridge was one — where we were trapped in static warfare, neither side able to move, both ravaged around the clock by massed enemy fire. I saw similar deadlocks, most memorably at Takargshi. It wasn't worse than war of movement, but it was different. Under such circumstances the instinct of self-preservation turns the skilled infantryman into a mole, a ferret, or a cheetah, depending on the clear and present danger of the moment. He will do anything to avoid drawing enemy fire, or, having drawn it, to reach defilade as swiftly as possible. A scout, which is essentially what I was, learned to know the landscape down to the last hollow and stone as thoroughly as a child knows his backyard or a pet a small park. In such a situation, certain topographical features, insignificant under any other circumstances, become obsessions. At Takargshi they were known as Dead Man's Corner, Krank's Chancre, the Hanging Tree, the Double Asshole, and the End Zone. It was in the End Zone that I met the souvenir hunter. We were introduced by a Japanese 6.5-millimeter light machine gun, a gas-operated, hopper-fed weapon with a muzzle velocity of 2,440 feet per second which fired 150 rounds a minute in 5-round bursts. Its effective range was 1,640 yards. We were both well within that.

At Takargshi, as so often elsewhere, I was carrying a message to the battalion operations officer. All morning I had been hanging around Dog Company CP, content to lie back on the oars after a patrol, but the company commander wanted heavy mortar support and he couldn't get through to battalion. The Japs had jammed the radio; all you heard was martial music. So I was drafted as a runner. If there had been any way to shirk it I would have. There was only one approach from here to battalion. I had come up it this morning, at dawn. The risk then had been acceptable. The light was faint and the rifles of the section covered me on the first leg, the one dangerous place. Now, however, the daylight was broad, and since I wasn't expected back until dusk, I couldn't count on covering fire from anybody. Still, I had no choice, so I went. I remember the moment I took off from the Dog CP. The stench of cordite was heavy. I was hot and thirsty. And I felt that premonition of danger which is ludicrous to everyone except those who have experienced it and lived to tell of it. All my senses were exceptionally alert. A bristling, tingling feeling raced up my back. Each decision to move was made with great deliberation and then executed as rapidly as a Jesse Owens sprint. I had that sensation you have when you think someone is looking at you, and you turn around, and you are right. So I made the ninety-degree turn at Dead Man's Corner, stealthily, dodged past Krank's Chancre, burrowed through the exposed roots of the Hanging Tree, bounded over the Double Asshole — two shell holes — and lay in defilade, gasping and sweating, trying not to panic at the thought of what came next. What came next was the End Zone, a broad ledge about thirty yards long, all of it naked to enemy gunners. Even with covering fire three men had been killed and five wounded trying to cross the Zone. But many more had made it safely, and I kept reminding myself of that as I counted to ten and then leapt out like a whippet, my legs pumping, picking up momentum, flying toward the sheltering rock beyond.

On the third pump I heard the machine gun, humming close like a swarm of enveloping bees. Then several things happened at once. Coming from the opposite direction, a uniformed figure with a bare GI steel helmet emerged hesitantly from the rock toward which I was rushing. Simultaneously, I hit the deck, rolled twice, advanced four pumps, dropped and rolled again, felt a sharp blow just above my right kneecap, dropped and rolled twice more, passing the shifting figure, and slid home, head first, reaching the haven of the rock. My chest was pounding and my right knee was bloody and my mouth had a bitter taste. On my second gulp of air I heard a thud behind me and a thin wail: "Medic!" My hand flew to my weapon. Infantrymen are professional paranoiacs. Wounded Marines call for corpsmen, not medics. As far as I knew, and it was my job to know such things, there wasn't supposed to be a GI within a mile of here. But as I rose I saw, crawling toward me, a wailing, badly hit soldier of the U.S. Army. His blouse around his stomach was bellying with blood. And he wasn't safe yet. Just before he reached the sanctuary of the rock, a 6.5-millimeter burst ripped away the left half of his jaw. I reached out, grabbed his wrist, and yanked him out of the Zone. Then I turned him on his back. Blood was seeping through his abdomen and streaming from his mangled chin. First aid would have been pointless. I wasn't a corpsman; I had no morphine; I couldn't think what to do. I noticed the Jap colors sticking from one of those huge side pockets on his GI pants. It wasn't much of a flag: just a thin synthetic rectangle with a red blob on a white field; no streaming rays, no *kanji* inscriptions. We'd kept these thin, unmarked little banners earlier in the war and thrown them away when we found that the Japs had thousands of them, whole cases of them, in their supply dumps.

The GI looked up at me with spaniel eyes. One cheek was smudged with coral dust. The other was dead white. I asked him who he was, what he was doing here. Setting down his exact words is impossible. There is no way to reproduce the gargling sound, the wet sucking around his smashed jaw. Yet he did get out a few intelligible phrases. He was a Seventy-seventh Division quartermaster clerk, and he had been roaming around the line searching for "loot" to send his family. I felt revulsion, pity, and disgust. If this hadn't happened in battle — if, say, he had been injured at home in an automobile accident — I would have consoled him. But a foot soldier retains his sanity only by hardening himself. Though I could still cry, and did, I saved my tears for the men I knew. This GI was a stranger. His behavior had been suicidal and cheap. Everything I had learned about wounds told me his were mortal. I couldn't just leave him here, but I was raging inside, not just at him but he was part of it, too.

The battalion aid station was a ten-minute walk away. This trip took longer. I had slung him over my shoulders in a fireman's carry, and he was much heavier than I was. My own slight wound, which had started to clot, began bleeding again. Once I had him up on my back and started trudging, he stopped trying to talk. I talked, though; I was swearing and ranting to myself. His blood was streaming down my back, warm at first and then sticky. I felt glued to him. I wondered whether they would have to cut us apart, whether I'd have to turn in my salty blouse for a new one, making me look like a replacement. I was wallowing in self-pity; all my thoughts were selfish; I knew he was suffering, but his agony found no echo in my heart now. I wanted to get rid of him. My eyes were damp, not from sorrow but because sweat was streaming from my brow. Apart from unfocused wrath, my strongest feeling was a heave of relief in my chest when I spotted the canvas tenting of the aid station on the reverse slope of a small bluff.

Two corpsmen ran out to help me. He and I *were* stuck to each other, or at least our uniforms were; there was a smacking sound as they swung him off me and laid him out. I turned and looked. His eyes had that blurry cast. There we were, the three of us, just staring down. Then one of the corpsmen turned to me. "A dogface," he said. "How come?" I didn't know what to say. The truth was so preposterous that it would sound like a desecration. Fleetingly I wondered who would write his family, and how they would put it. How *could* you put it? "Dear folks: Your son was killed in action while stupidly heading for the Double Asshole in search of loot"? Even if you invented a story about heroism in combat, you wouldn't convince them. They must have known he was supposed to be back in QM. I avoided the corpsman's eyes and shrugged. It wasn't my problem. I gave a runner my message to the battalion CP. My wound had been salted with sulfa powder and dressed before I realized that I hadn't looked at the corpse's dog tags. I didn't even know who he had been.

Today Peleliu can be reached only from the Palauan island of Koror, itself no hub of activity, though powerful interests would like to make it one. Robert Owen, district administrator for the Trust Territory, tells the sad tale. Owen is one of those tireless American advisers who serve in the tropics much as Englishmen served a century ago: underpaid, overworked, and absolutely devoted to the islands. But after twenty-nine years here he has decided to quit. His whole career has been a struggle for Palauan ecology, and he has just about lost it. Fishermen smuggle in dynamite, devastating the waters; the streams are contaminated with Clorox; the topsoil, already thin, is vanishing because of inept use of chemicals that create erosion.

But the real rogues, in Owen's opinion, are a consortium of Japanese and Middle East petroleum titans, led by an American entrepreneur, who want to build a superport here to service supertankers. "The Japanese," he says, "want to export their pollution." Every supertanker eventually defiles the water around it — recently twenty-three hundred tons were spilled in French waters — and Owen predicts the end of the Palaus' delicate environment, the destruction of irreplaceable flora and fauna. The natives approve of superport plans because they think their standard of living will rise, but in Puerto Rico, he has tried to tell them, it was the wealthy, not the poor, who reaped the profits of a similar project. He is appealing to the U.S. Army Corps of Engineers, which has the power to reject the plans. He doubts it will.

Although I am sympathetic, my contract is with the past and his with the future. We glide past one another like freighters flying the same flag of convenience but bound for very different destinations. Yet I know he is right; it would be tragic to lose the Palaus. That thought may startle those who fought here, who remember only the horror and the heat. In peacetime, however, the islands' aspect is altogether different, and you become aware of it long before you reach Peleliu. Checking in at the thatch-roofed hotel, you rent a Toyota Land Cruiser and drive to the ferry slip. The ferry — actually a small launch powered by twin 85-horsepower Johnsons — takes you past the breathtaking Rock Islands, which resemble enormous green toadstools, narrow at the bottom, because of erosion and sea urchins, and swelling into dark green caps of vegetation above. Some of the islands have natural caves. The Japanese used these for storage; deteriorating wooden boxes and corroded tin containers may still be found there, and one cavern, which was used to stockpile Nipponese ammunition, is black where an American demolitions team blew it up. These are great waters for snorkeling, clear and abundant with life. Tuna are thick, and so are mackerel, bonito, marlin, sailfish, and flying fish. But there are also sharks and barracuda, and, most menacing of all, giant tridacna clams, some four feet across, whose traverse adduction muscles can grip divers and carry them to a drowning death. Before the battle, the great clams were a special threat to navy frogmen, who carried long knives to cut the creatures' muscles.

Once you have reached Peleliu, you are on your own, unless, as in my case, you have a native acquaintance. My friend is Dave Ngirmidol, a short, swart, powerfully built history major from California State University in Northridge and now a Trust Territory employee. Dave is waiting for me at the island's only dock with a

Dave Ngirmidol and the author alongside an abandoned American tank

Mazda pickup truck and three islanders: Hinao Soalablai, the island's young magistrate; Ichiro Loitang, an elderly Papuan who ran the island after all the Japanese had been wiped out and before American Military Government arrived; and Kalista Smau, whose chief qualifications for this field trip are her beauty, her lovely smile, and the brightest green Punjabi trousers I have ever seen.

Miss Smau also carries, in a basket balanced on her head, box lunches and raspberry-flavored soda. She offers a bottle, and I boorishly drain it. I am apologetic, but she is delighted; Dave explains that I have paid her a great compliment. So off we go in the little truck, bouncing over deeply rutted paths and ducking to avoid tremendous swooping branches. In Koror I asked a botanist to identify Palau foliage. He threw up his hands; thirty or forty major genera have been classified, he said, and they haven't been able to explore beyond the outermost fringes of the rainforests.

The road becomes a sticky, humid trough, but if I am uncomfortable, my companions are not; they are eager to tell me what the war did to Peleliu. Regrettably, they are not always reliable. Every great battle becomes a source of apocrypha. Near the water we come upon a small beached yacht, the *Por Dinana*, once white but now rusted, and my guides tell me it was General MacArthur's headquarters, which is a geographic impossibility; MacArthur was never within a hundred miles of Peleliu. Still, they know what they actually witnessed. For ages the islanders had lived in thatched A-frame huts, eating coconuts, pandanus fruit, breadfruit, and taros, starchy tubers much like potatoes. Then the Japanese, their ostensible protectors, rounded them up, put them in camps, and assigned them to forced labor. There was a lot to do; Peleliu was being heavily fortified. Importing coastal defense guns, the Japanese sited them so they could dominate Toagel Mlungui Strait, the narrow channel through which American battleships would have to pass. They overlooked air power, even when U.S. planes were overhead every day dropping their leaflets, telling the natives to get out while the getting was good.

One reason so few of the evacuees returned after V-J Day was the postwar craze — it still flourishes — of Modekne, a nativist religion preaching a return to prewar simplicity. Modekne's center was and is Koror, where natives dispossessed by the fighting put down roots. On Peleliu there were more corpses than people, and very little activity. The Americans disposed of their Higgins boats by sinking them and then departed — that is, most of them departed; when we reach the serene invasion beach, rimmed by Samoan palms and conifers, I find near it an imposing fence bearing a sign informing me that this is a "Federal Program Campsite — CITA Project No. VIII." Dave explains that Americans are training islanders in new skills; he doesn't know which, and there is no one around to instruct us.

Trudging through the brush at the base of Bloody Nose Ridge, I find ten-inch Nip guns, oiled and ready for action. Who has been cleaning them? My companions seem as astonished as I am. The only possibility is the Japanese who arrive in the Palaus, as elsewhere, in large numbers, and who have erected two monuments to their dead. We speculate upon their motives and settle for the

A Japanese gun, mysteriously oiled and ready for action

cliché that Orientals (the islanders do not regard themselves as Orientals) are inscrutable.

Now I decide to ascend the ridge. My young companions are dismayed. At my age, they argue, the climb is folly, and I know they are right, but I have to do what I have to do. If the decision is irrational, so was my enlistment in the Marine Corps and all that followed. The girl and Loitang stay below, preparing our lunch. Dave ascends first, pulling me up over the huge stones, deep clefts, steep pinnacles, and beetling outcroppings while the magistrate propels me upward. I reach the crest filthy and bleeding from scratches. There I find the only American monument on Peleliu, or, to be more exact, what is left of the monument. It is a granite column with a white limestone inscription which reads:

<pre>
              LEST
              WE
          FO   ET
             THOSE
              WH
             DIED
              32
          NF   TRY
          S. AR Y
             1944
</pre>

Exhausted as I am, I feel a surge of fury. To commit brave men
to a needless struggle was criminal; to consign them to oblivion is
profane. Is this the apotheosis of our mourning? Can we FO   ET
them so completely? Are the Japanese prouder of their men than
we? Can't the Pentagon spare a few token dollars out of its billions
for a decent memorial? Can't the American Legion and the VFW,
so adept at lobbying for live veterans, pause to propose a suitable
tribute to those who, though they cannot vote, safeguarded our
right to do so? Back on the beach I nibble bleakly on a sandwich,
poking at driftwood and clots of seaweed with my field boot. There
are times when one understands the pull of primitive superstition.
A recent article in the *Marine Corps Gazette* complained that the
"American news media . . . contributed to the almost total neglect
of this historic battle by focusing the American public's attention
on events in Europe and in the Philippines as Peleliu dragged out
its bloody course." The press is, of course, everyone's scapegoat.
The fact is that the liberation of France, the Lowlands, and the
Philippines was more fascinating, and also more successful, than
this pointless hammering of American flesh on a distant anvil of
despair. No, Peleliu — like Arnhem, which was being fought simultaneously on the other side of the world — appears to have
been doomed from the very outset. It almost seems as though both
were hexed.

The American monument at Peleliu

A typical Japanese monument

On the map the island of Leyte, MacArthur's first Philippine target, resembles a molar tooth, its roots pointing downward. To the south lies Mindanao, as big as Ireland; to the north, Luzon, nearly as large as England. In the predawn hours of Friday, October 20, when fighting was still heavy around Peleliu's airstrip, MacArthur stood aboard the cruiser *Nashville,* waiting for the first waves of his 200,000 veteran GIs to leap ashore on Leyte's east coast, the last place the Japanese expected him. The vain, brilliant general had perfected a battle plan which he considered his best yet. After the war Vincent Sheean agreed: "His operations towards the end . . . were extremely daring, more daring and far more complicated than those of Patton in Europe, because MacArthur used not infantry alone but also air and seapower in a concerted series of jabbing and jumping motions designed to outflank and bypass the Japanese all through the islands." When all else is said about this baffling, exasperating man, the fact remains that in all his campaigns he was remarkably economical of human life; his total casualties from Australia to V-J Day (90,437) were fewer than the ETO's in the single Battle of the Bulge (106,502).

At daybreak the U.S. warships opened fire on the beach. The general watched from the *Nashville*'s bridge. The shore was dimly visible through a rising haze shot with yellow flashes; inland, white phosphorus crumps were bursting among the thick, ripe underbrush of the hills. As the first waves of American infantry hit Red Beach, MacArthur descended a ship's ladder to a barge. Fifty yards from shore they ran aground. That was unexpected. The general had counted on tying up at a pier and stepping majestically ashore, immaculate and dry. Most of the docks had been destroyed in the naval bombardment, however, and while a few were still intact, the naval officer serving as beachmaster — whom no one, not even MacArthur, could overrule –– had no time to show the general's party where they were. When he growled, "Let 'em walk," they had no choice. MacArthur, greatly annoyed, ordered the barge ramp lowered, stepped off into knee-deep brine, and splashed forty wet strides to the shore, eliminating the neat creases of his trousers. A newspaper photographer snapped the famous picture of this.

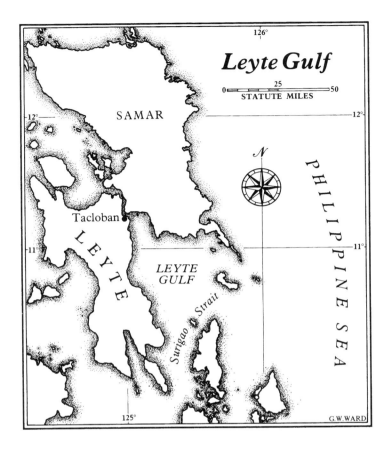

Leyte Gulf

25
0 — 50
STATUTE MILES

SAMAR

PHILIPPINE SEA

Tacloban

LEYTE

LEYTE GULF

Surigao Strait

G.W.WARD

MacArthur's scowl, which millions of readers interpreted as a re-
flection of his steely determination, was actually a wrathful glare at
the impertinent naval officer. When the general saw a print of the
photograph, however, he instantly grasped its dramatic value, and
the next day he deliberately waded ashore for cameramen on a safe
beach which had been secured by troopers of the First Cavalry
Division. Later the First Cavalry's troopers, seeing the photograph
taken the day before, condemned it as a phony. Another touch had
been added to MacArthur's antihero legend.

Standing in a rainstorm, holding a hand microphone, he broadcast to Filipinos: "People of the Philippines, I have returned. . . .
Rally to me. . . . As the lines of battle roll forward to bring you

within the zone of operations, rise and strike. Strike at every favorable opportunity. For your homes and hearths, strike! For future generations of your sons and daughters, strike! In the name of your sacred dead, strike!"

Now that the general had committed himself to Leyte, now that his men were pouring ashore, the Japanese navy and air force made their last great move of the war. Their commanders still cherished the hope of changing the fortunes of war at sea, preferably while our warships were covering a landing. This was the hour. Four separate Jap forces sailed against Halsey's powerful main fleet, which was protecting the operation, and Thomas Kinkaid's weaker group of old battleships and small carriers. The enemy admirals knew they could no longer match our power, so they hatched a brilliant plan. Leyte Gulf, where MacArthur was, could be reached through two straits, San Bernardino to the north and Surigao to the south. The Japanese center force was to head for San Bernardino while two southern forces steamed into Surigao. At the same time, a fourth force, acting as a decoy, was to lure Halsey away to the north. Kinkaid would be helpless. *Banzai.*

Salvo by salvo the two huge fleets roared away at one another over an area as large as France. Nippon's southern prongs had no luck. Torpedoes and gunfire wiped out the first of them; the second turned back after firing at radar pictures which were really islands. In the beginning the center force also seemed luckless. American submarines destroyed two of its cruisers; its largest battleship was sunk by planes. Actually these losses were a break for the enemy. Halsey, learning of them and assuming that the rest of that force was retiring, took out after the fourth force — the bait — leaving San Bernardino Strait unguarded. In the darkness the Japs slipped through unobserved. But the Nips milled around, confused by intercepted American messages, and turned back as U.S. destroyers made smoke. American warplanes flew in pursuit of the retreating enemy and Halsey returned at flank speed. Thus ended the Battle of Leyte Gulf. It had involved 282 warships, compared with 129 in the Spanish Armada and 250 at Jutland, until then the greatest naval engagement in history. And unlike Jutland, which neither side won, this action had been decisive. After the last distant broadside had been fired the Americans had lost one light carrier, two escort carriers, and three destroyers. They had sunk four carriers, three battleships, six heavy cruisers, three light cruisers, and eight destroyers. Except for sacrificial kamikaze fliers, who made their debut in this battle, Japanese air squadrons and naval strength would never again be serious instruments in the war.

MacArthur would tolerate no criticism of Halsey in his mess. He slammed his bunched fist on the table and roared, "Leave the Bull alone! He's still a fighting admiral in my book." Halsey had been loyal to him in earlier struggles, and he was reciprocating. Though both men were prima donnas, they remained on the best of terms, perhaps because each recognized himself in the other. Among other things, the admiral admired the general's courage. On Leyte MacArthur had chosen as his CP a two-story stucco-and-concrete mansion, previously owned by an American businessman named Walter Price, at the corner of Santo Niño and Justice Romualdez streets in the town of Tacloban. The home was the most spacious in the community — the Japanese had used it as an officers' club — and therefore a prime target. As he was striding back and forth on the wide veranda, MacArthur suddenly halted and pointed at the yard, saying, "What's that mound of earth there by the edge of the porch?" One of his men explained that it was an elaborate bomb shelter built by the Japanese. The general said, "Level it off and fill the thing in. It spoils the looks of the lawn." Though Radio Tokyo broadcast that they knew the general had established his "headquarters in the Price house, right in the center of town," and though Zeroes and Mitsubishis attacked Tacloban daily, often missing MacArthur by a few feet or less, he refused to move. This is the man we called "Dugout Doug."

His greatest problem was the wet weather, which erased the margin that superior air power should have given him. He had called Leyte a springboard, but it was proving to be a very soggy one. In forty days, thirty-four inches of rain fell, turning the island into one vast bog. Runway grading was impossible. GIs captured five airfields, but the island's drainage system was such that they had become useless mud flats. To top that, Leyte was struck by an earthquake and three typhoons during the fighting. The Japanese, with firm fields on surrounding islands, swooped in low over the hills, permitting their land commanders to reinforce Leyte easily. Yet the doubts of Tomoyuki Yamashita, the enemy commander, were growing daily. He knew that Leyte was a lost cause, that eventually the weather would improve. MacArthur extended his flanks in the first week of November, and by Thanksgiving he had the enemy garrison trapped. Fighting continued until Saint Patrick's Day, 1945, but long before then the general was plotting his invasion of Luzon and the recapture of Manila. For Dai Nippon, Leyte had been a catastrophe. Apart from the destruction of their planes and the backbone of their fleet, the Nips had lost sixty-five thousand front-line troops. Their supply lines to the Dutch East Indies, vital for raw materials they needed to survive, had been pierced. Even Hirohito despaired.

My arrival in Tacloban is both spectacular and disconcerting. At President Marcos's insistence, I am once more ensconced in a gleaming limousine, part of a cavalcade flanked by motorcycle outriders. Sirens scream again; red lights flash; a phalanx of Philippine generals and high officials accompanies me at every stop. The explanation, which I demand, is that guerrillas and Moro secessionists lurk in the rice paddies and among the hillocks in the countryside. That is hardly satisfactory for a knee-jerk FDR liberal, but I have no alternative. In time we draw up to the Price house under a hurriedly erected sign whose paint is still wet: DISTINGUISHED VISITORS — WELCOME TO LEYTE. The building is imposing, of white stucco with green trim surrounded by a fence of painted Marsden matting. It is also unoccupied. Until recently the mansion housed the offices of a Regional National Economic Development Authority — whatever that was; I am just reading my notes — and before that it was a school: "Notice: Undergraduate Students Are Not Allowed to Make a Research Here," reads a mysterious warning on one door. But none of the subsequent occupants have removed evidence of the Japanese determination to kill MacArthur here. Walls are pocked and pitted by machine-gun bullets, one wall is marred by a hole made by a 20-millimeter shell, and a .50-caliber slug is still embedded in plaster above the bed in which the general slept.

Outside, the brooding mass of Samar is visible on the left; Leyte's Red Beach is a short stroll from here, and I and my mob head for it. Various signs accost me along the way: the delights of San Miguel beer are described; a beverage called Miranda is advertised as "the Sunshine Drink"; Coke and Pepsi are available ("Have a Pepsi Day"); and a placard urges us to buy "Unisex Fashions," though how such clothing could achieve popularity in one of the world's most male chauvinistic countries I do not know. Presently the landscape becomes more attractive. Straw huts are tidy and picturesque, the shrubbery is riotously green, and amid its waxen leaves you see the red flowers of *santan* and the white blossoms of the *Doña Aurora*, named for the widow of Manuel Quezon, the Philippines' George Washington.

In a vast reflecting pool stand statues of MacArthur and the six men who trudged ashore with him. They are depicted exactly as they were in the famous photograph, but each is twice life-size. A three-tiered memorial carries inscriptions from the general's invasion speech and a tribute from Marcos. There is one peculiar error. MacArthur's collar bears five-star ornaments, but he didn't achieve five-star rank until December 16, 1944, nearly two months after he waded in. It is a small slip; pointing it out to my hosts now would be needlessly rude. Instead, I turn to a four-and-a-half-foot seawall beneath which the surf laps listlessly. I bound down. There can be no doubt that I am where I mean to be. The temptation to plunge in is irresistible. I wade out and back; the spectators, including several small children from the huts, watch solemnly, almost standing at attention. This ground is sacred to them. Like the Guamanians, they celebrate Liberation Day every October 20 by reenacting MacArthur's return with landing craft and fireworks simulating shellfire. In 1969, the twenty-fifth anniversary, they even dropped paratroopers. To me, however, peeling off my socks and wringing them out, the experience is flat. Unlike my feelings on the shores of the Canal and Tarawa, I cannot identify with what

The author at Leyte, where MacArthur waded ashore

The Filipino monument to MacArthur's landing party

happened here — cannot re-create it because I neither served here nor knew anyone who did. And my well-meaning escorts are no help. You cannot evoke the past in a crowd. I need solitude.

But I am not going to get it, not on this trip. By motorcade and then by air I am borne to Lingayen Gulf, 450 miles closer to Japan and thirty-five years after MacArthur landed here on Luzon and opened his drive toward Manila. In addition to my retinue, all the local officials turn out to welcome me — one suspects that Marcos would have their heads if they didn't — and after ceremonial bows and murmured greetings, we stroll along a strip of beach, though not all of it. This incomparable shore goes on and on, 124 miles of it, as though New York's Jones Beach extended southward to Wilmington, or Malibu Beach to San Diego. For the historian, however, the chief spectacle is near a monument to MacArthur's landing of January 10, 1945. Passing a graceful promenade, I stumble upon *dalakorak*, small creeping vines that seem to be underfoot everywhere, and come upon a playground. How often on this trip I have seen children romping beneath silent guns, I think, and how splendid a tribute that is. Rehearsing his invasion speech the night before the Leyte landing, the general had anticipated "the tinkle of the laughter of little children returning to the Philippines." His outspoken physician had said, "You can't say that." MacArthur said, "What's the matter with it?" The doctor said, "It stinks. It's a cliché." The general muttered but crossed it out. One wishes he had found another way of saying it. Continuity of the generations is, after all, the only bright sequel to war.

The general would have preferred to come ashore on Luzon almost anywhere but here. As early as 1909 an American writer had predicted that any invader of the island would have to hit Lingayen first. This was where Homma's Japanese had debarked on the fifteenth day of the war. MacArthur valued surprise, usually above all else, but after studying a half-dozen other beaches and searching his memory — he had first served in the Philippines forty-two years earlier — he reluctantly returned to this one. There was just no other way of manipulating the enemy into a series of in-

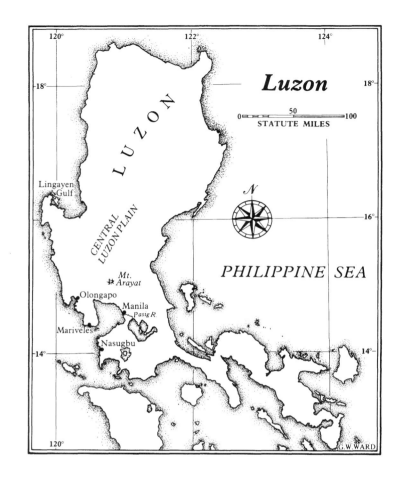

tricate maneuvers, where MacArthur's prodigious gifts could soar, on the Central Luzon Plain. You needn't be a strategist or even like the man (he wasn't very likable) to appreciate his subsequent feats there. His reconquest of Luzon was awesome. And the Filipinos were jubilant. They already knew of his triumph on Leyte. From the moment he landed at Lingayen and began moving inland by jeep, they decked the jeep with flowers, like a Roman chariot. They kissed his hand, pressed wreaths around his neck, and tried to touch his uniform.

This performance could have been shattered had Yamashita, who had become the legendary "Tiger of Malaya" in the opening weeks of the war, chosen to contest the beachhead. But drained of his best men on Leyte, where Tokyo had ordered him to fight despite his misgivings, he knew he could not expose his Luzon force to U.S. naval gunfire. Instead, he withdrew into the mountains, awaiting his opportunity to descend onto the central plain, the amphitheater both commanders needed to grasp the rainbow's end at the bottom of it: Manila. But the Tiger's chance never came. In a series of lightning thrusts MacArthur invested Clark Field, landed a corps above Bataan, took the invaluable port of Olongapo, put a regiment ashore at Mariveles, seized Nasugbu, south of Manila, without losing a man, and lost just 210 men in overpowering the 5,200 Japanese on Corregidor by landing an airborne regiment on Topside while an infantry battalion, with exquisite timing, leaped from Higgins boats to storm the Bottomside shore. Manila was virtually surrounded. The Tiger had been denied an opportunity to show his claws. He was trapped in a double envelopment, isolated and impotent. In the Pentagon George Marshall, who detested MacArthur personally, was rhapsodic. The outcome was, in fact, unparalleled in modern warfare. Never had such masses of superbly disciplined soldiers been so completely outwitted, foiled, and surpassed on every level. The most gifted officer Hirohito could put in the field was left with his army, tons of equipment — and no one to fight.

Yet every judgment of MacArthur, praising him or blaming him, has to be qualified. Flying in our small plane from Lingayen and its charming playground to Manila, we follow the same route taken by the Japanese Mitsubishi bombers in December 1941, nine hours after Pearl Harbor, when, incredibly, MacArthur's air force was caught on the ground at Clark Field and destroyed. Off the starboard bow lies Mount Arayat, once a stronghold of the Hukbalahaps, the Huk guerrillas who had fought the Japanese occupiers so steadfastly and were so shamefully ignored when the general restored power to the Spanish aristocrats, despite the fact that the most prominent of them had spent the past three years collaborating with the enemy. As we descend for our landing on what was once Nichols Field and is now Luzon's chief airport, the low-slung mountains of Bataan and the placid waters of the bay, with Corregidor at its neck, are on our right. I wonder whether the Mitsubishi pilots noticed them on that first morning of the war and pondered their military significance.

In the 1930s Japanese officers, disguised as bicycle salesmen, sidewalk photographers, and assorted tradesmen, appeared in the archipelago to survey Philippine defenses. Today 80 percent of the islands' tourists are Japanese, but here, as in the Marianas, this is another era; the tourist ministry estimates that three couples out of every four are honeymooners. The Manila they see is not prewar Manila. That city was virtually destroyed in 1945. Yet some landmarks remain. The ageless, gargantuan rubber tree still stands in front of the Army Navy Club. No. 1 Victoria Street, MacArthur's prewar headquarters, has vanished, and the Manila Hotel, just across the street, was leveled by the Japanese near the end of the war when MacArthur was within sight of it and preparing to retake it. Its facade was preserved, however, and a new hotel has been built on the site of the old one, with a MacArthur penthouse on top. Sugar and rice barges continue to drift between the ancient gray stone walls on either bank of the Pasig River, and on the shores jitneys weave in and out of the heavy traffic. Periodically Marcos threatens to abolish the vans, but they perform a useful service, skillfully cutting in and out of the flow of cars. Auto density is very high; Manila's population is now over seven million.

Both foreigners and Filipinos are drawn to the city's magnet for sightseers: Intramuros, the old walled city, with Fort Santiago and San Augustine Church within it. No one knows the exact age of Intramuros, but Magellan arrived in 1521, the Spaniards founded Manila in 1572, and everything within the ancient city had been built by the turn of that century, nearly four hundred years ago. In their last, drunken orgy of destruction, the Japanese tried to reduce Intramuros to ruins, but it was impossible; the stone walls are nineteen feet high and more than twice that thick. At one time they shielded within their triangular perimeter six churches and monasteries, hanging gardens, inner courts, and a maze of cobblestoned streets. Most of that is gone, though the Augustine church still

stands as it did when the Nipponese used most of Intramuros for
barracks and shawled Filipino women prayed in the church's pews
for the safety of their sons, fighting in the guerrilla bands in the
hills. Today lovers embrace in dark corners. Outside, one is depressed to see frolicking boys playing war with toy pistols.

As in most countries outside North America and Western
Europe, the gap between rich and poor here boggles the mind. It
shocks American newcomers, who do not grasp that anything above
bare subsistence for the masses hardly exists outside Western
Europe and their own fortunate oasis. Most wealthy Filipinos live
in Manila's Makati district, in sprawling villas hidden by ivy-
covered walls, each with its private police force and snarling Dober-
mans. In many ways Makati is redolent of San Juan's Condato, or
Nassau's Lyford Cay. The average Filipino earns a few pesos, less
than a dollar, a week. In Makati, a patrician bride may spend twelve
thousand dollars for her wedding dress. Polo is a popular sport among
the oligarchy, and although newspapers report some of the conspicuous consumption of the few, the many are not mutinous. Marcos
does suppress news of the most shocking extravaganzas. "We're too
close to the flames," he says elliptically, "to play with fire." Perhaps the most striking evidence of upper-class dominance is the
presence of the military cemetery in their midst. Surrounded by the
mansions of the aristocracy, the white crosses in Makati rise and
fall, in rhythmic undulations of the rolling topsoil, like whitecaps
fixed in time. Even the dead belong to the opulent. But the ironies
of the Pacific war are endless. Riding up to my room in the rebuilt Manila Hotel that evening, I glance casually at the elevator's
control panel. It bears the name of the manufacturer: Mitsubishi.

Once the Joint Chiefs had decided to retake the Philippines, instead of bypassing them, plans for driving toward Formosa or the
Chinese mainland were discarded, to be replaced by a direct lunge at
the Japanese home islands. Two more stepping-stones were needed:
Iwo Jima, in the Volcano Islands, and Okinawa, in the Ryukyus.
Iwo Jima was to be seized first, because it was considered easier —
which was true, in the sense that Buchenwald was less lethal than

The cemetery at Makati

Auschwitz — and because Iwo was a major obstacle for B-29 Superfortress fleets raiding Tokyo. The first Superfort attack on the Japanese capital had been staged from Saipan on November 24, 1944, but the results of the raids had been disappointing. Curtis LeMay, their commander, said, "This outfit has been getting a lot of publicity without having accomplished a hell of a lot in bombing results." Iwo Jima was the chief reason. Situated halfway between the Marianas and Japan, Iwo's radar sets gave Tokyo two hours' warning of approaching B-29s. Zeroes based on the island swarmed around the big bombers both coming up from the Marianas and then returning, when they had often been crippled by flak. Moreover, the Japs flew some raids of their own on our Saipan, Tinian, and Guam bases. Therefore in mid-February, when the house-to-house fighting in Manila was reaching its height, convoys bearing the Third, Fourth, and Fifth Marine divisions steamed toward Iwo.

B-24s had been flying high-level sorties over the island for six weeks, but aerial photographs showed negligible results. Now U.S. warships approached Iwo like hunters stalking a maimed but still vicious tiger. They moved slowly and deliberately, trying to test the enemy's strength and at the same time lure him into action. To the U.S. fliers and naval gunners, Iwo appeared absurdly small prey. The island was just four miles long — altogether, eight square miles — an ugly, smelly glob of cold lava squatting in a surly ocean. In silhouette it was shaped somewhat like the Civil War iron-clad *Monitor*, the "cheesebox on a raft," the raft in this case being the northern mass of the island and the cheesebox, on the southwest tip, the volcanic crater of 556-foot Mount Suribachi, *Suribachi* being Japanese for "cone-shaped bowl." *Iwo* is Japanese for "sulfur," and daring pilots who swept low over its three air-fields knew why; jets of green and yellow sulfuric mist penetrated the entire surface of the isle, giving it a permanent stench of rotten eggs. Essentially Iwo had changed little since it had risen, hissing, from the sea. Nipponese farmers had tried to grow sugar and pine-apples there, with little success; by late 1944 they had given up and returned home. And yet Iwo in some ways seemed quintessentially Japanese. It had the tiny, fastidious compactness of small Tokyo backyards, and its rocks resembled the wind-buffed, water-scoured stones Nips love to collect for their miniature gardens. There the similarity to any civilized community ended, however. Most of the isle was a desolate, barren wasteland of volcanic pumice, finer than sand; more like coarse, loose flour. The only landing beaches were below Suribachi, to the immediate left and right of its base. North of there lay a smoking, blasted wilderness of crags, caves, buttes, and canyons, ending in jagged ridges overlooking the sea.

Samuel Eliot Morison wrote: "The operation looked like a push-over. Optimists predicted that the island would be secured in four days." Some thought seventy-two hours would be enough. Here, as throughout the war, naval gunnery officers wildly exaggerated the effect of their preinvasion bombardment. One reported jubilantly that a fourteen-inch shell, scoring a direct hit in the mouth of a

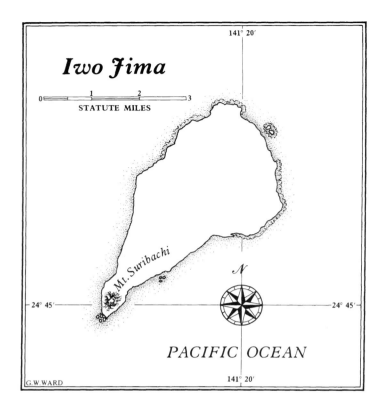

Iwo Jima

STATUTE MILES

Mt. Suribachi

141° 20'

24° 45'

24° 45'

𝒩

PACIFIC OCEAN

141° 20'

G.W.WARD

cave, destroyed a gun, leaving it to hang over the cliff below "like a half-extracted tooth hanging on a man's jaw." But hundreds of other guns were intact. Holland Smith, warning that "we may expect casualties far beyond any heretofore suffered in the Central Pacific," and estimating that we might lose fifteen thousand men — which was thought to be ridiculously high and proved to be ridiculously low — asked for a nine-day bombardment, like Guam's. The navy gave him three, explaining that they must depart to bombard the beaches of central Okinawa, where, ironically, there were no defenses. Our naval guns did rock Iwo Jima with more shells than those fired on Saipan, fifteen times as large as Iwo, but it wasn't enough, and even the frogmen, though now skilled and numerous, missed many underwater obstacles on Iwo. The fact is that nothing short of nuclear weapons could have left a serious dent in the enemy's defenses. Here, as in southern Okinawa, the new let-'em-come-to-us tactics approached perfection.

The defenders' CO, Tadamichi Kuribayashi — Holland Smith called him Hirohito's "most redoubtable" commander — had been among the first to conclude that banzai charges, once so effective in Japan's earlier wars with Russia and China, were futile against American firepower. Tokyo had warned him that he could expect no reinforcements. He replied that he didn't need them; the air attacks on Iwo had tipped off the coming invasion, and transports had beefed up his garrison to twenty-one thousand men, led by Japanese Marines. Kuribayashi turned his men into supermoles, excavating the hard *konhake* rock. They built 750 major defense installations sheltering guns, and blockhouses with five-foot concrete walls, strengthened, in some instances, with fifty feet of earthen cover overhead. Under Suribachi alone lay a four-story galley and a hospital cave. Southward from the volcano lay interweaving iron belts of defense. Altogether there were thirteen thousand yards of tunnels and five thousand cave entrances and pillboxes — a thousand on Suribachi alone. Once he learned of the force about to attack him, Kuribayashi had no illusion about his future. He wrote his wife: "Do not plan for my return." Rear Admiral Toshinosuke Ichimaru, who led the seven thousand Nipponese Marines, felt the same way. Awaiting the coming assault, he wrote a poem:

> *Let me fall like a flower petal*
> *May enemy bombs be directed at me, and enemy shells*
> *Mark me their target.*

Yet both the general and the admiral were burrowing in. They meant to make the conquest of Iwo so costly that the Americans would recoil from the thought of invading their homeland. They knew the island could be taken only by infantrymen; the U.S. warships' 21,926 shells and the six weeks of B-24 bombing didn't touch them; it merely rearranged the volcanic ash overhead and gave the invaders dangerous illusions of easy pickings. Those illusions were dashed on D-minus-2, when the Japanese mistook a deep reconnaissance by navy and Marine frogmen for the main landing; six-inchers embedded in the base of Suribachi and the face of a quarry to the north roared and quickly sank twelve small U.S. warships. So much for the high hopes. Everyone knew now that just as sure as God made little green Japs, the Higgins boats ferrying in the first Marine waves might as well be tumbrels.

On D-day Iwo seemed to lie low in the water, shrouded in dust and smoke. Two divisions were landed abreast, the Fifth's job being to knife across the isle's narrow neck and seize Suribachi while the Fourth turned northward. The moment they hit the shore they were in trouble. The steep-pitched beach sucked hundreds of men seaward in its backwash. Mines blew up Sherman tanks. Infantrymen found it impossible to dig foxholes in the powdery volcanic ash; the sides kept caving in. The invaders were taking heavy mortar and artillery fire. Steel sleeted down on them like the lash of a desert storm. By dusk 2,420 of the 30,000 men in the beachhead were dead or wounded. The perimeter was only four thousand yards long, seven hundred yards deep in the north and a thousand yards in the south. It resembled Doré's illustrations of the *Inferno*. Essential cargo — ammo, rations, water — was piled up in sprawling chaos. And gore, flesh, and bones were lying all about. The deaths on Iwo were extraordinarily violent. There seemed to be no clean wounds; just fragments of corpses. It reminded one battalion medical officer of a Bellevue dissecting room. Often the only way to distinguish between Japanese and Marine dead was by the legs; Marines wore canvas leggings and Nips khaki puttees. Otherwise identification was completely impossible. You tripped over strings of viscera fifteen feet long, over bodies which had been cut in half at the waist. Legs and arms, and heads bearing only necks, lay fifty feet from the closest torsos. As night fell the beachhead reeked with the stench of burning flesh. It was doubtful that a night counterattack by the Japs could be contained.

But there was none. Kuribayashi stuck to his battle plan, lying in wait. The next day the U.S. push northward began at an agonizingly slow pace and continued this, week after week, with heart-breaking engagements gaining as little as sixty or seventy yards a day. Curiously, the flag raising atop Mount Suribachi by the Twenty-eighth Marines, the most famous photograph of the Pacific war, was taken early in the struggle, on the fifth day of battle, before the Americans confronted the enormity of the challenge before them. Believing they had reached the first of their three main objectives — the others were conquering the island's backbone and seizing the high ground, sown with mines and pillboxes, between the two completed airstrips — they were unaware that the volcanic slopes beneath them swarmed with Japs, like mites in cheese. Before the annihilation of enemy troops in and around Suribachi — prophetically encoded "Hotrocks" — three of the six men who had anchored the pipe bearing the U.S. colors had been killed in action.

Now the long, bloody, painfully slow drive to the north began. It seemed inconceivable that the island's eight square miles could conceal so large a Nipponese army, but gradually, as the navy corpsmen carried the casualties away in mounting numbers, the Americans realized the scope of their peril. Until Marsden matting could be landed, tanks and trucks couldn't negotiate the pumice. One truck's wheel sank to the axle beside a fence post. Investigating, the driver found it wasn't a post at all; it was a ventilator shaft. Other posts — a long line of them — provided oxygen for Japanese below. *Time* reported: "On Iwo the Japs dug themselves in so deeply that all the explosives in the world could hardly have reached them." They were overcome in time, but in the process the Marines lost more men than the enemy. A pattern evolved. Each morning at 7:40 naval gunfire and Marine artillery opened a heavy bombardment. At 8:10 A.M. the Marine infantry jumped off. Tanks lumbered up. Offshore landing craft with their shallow drafts worked inshore, bearing mortars that blasted gullies the men on the island couldn't see. During the first week of the engagement the mortarmen fired over thirty-two thousand shells. But in the end it was the riflemen throwing hand grenades, engineers with satchel charges, and flamethrower teams that sealed off caves and demolished pillboxes. Every yard gained was an achievement in itself.

Nimitz later said of Iwo: "Uncommon valor was a common virtue." A Marine wrote in his diary: "It takes courage to stay at the front on Iwo Jima. It takes something we can't tag or classify to push out ahead of those lines, against an unseen enemy who has survived two months of shell and shock, who lives beneath the rocks of the island, an enemy capable of suddenly appearing on your flanks or even at your rear, and of disappearing back into his hole. . . . It takes courage to crawl ahead, 100 yards a day, and get up the next morning, count losses, and do it again. But that's the only way it can be done."

Motoyama Airfield No. 1, close to the beaches, had fallen on the second day, but No. 2 wasn't taken until March 1, and then only by three Marine divisions advancing abreast. There were eighty-two thousand leathernecks on the island now, all of them, because of the caves and tunnels, in constant danger. Two weeks of consolidation followed the capture of the second airstrip; then a full week was needed to take a rocky gorge similar to those on Peleliu. Kuribayashi's bunker was there. Hirohito promoted him to full general, but whether or not the promotion was posthumous is unknown. On March 24 he radioed his last message to the Japanese garrison on a nearby isle: "All officers and men of Chichi Jima" — the nearest Nip outpost — "goodbye." Then he and Admiral Ichimaru vanished. No trace of either was ever found.

But their men kept fighting. Instead of holing up and awaiting destruction, they donned Marine uniforms stripped from the American dead and crept out of their caves at night with rifles, swords, grenades, and knee mortars, so called because the tube was braced on the knee. (There were also wild stories about "ball mortars," which, fired from the crotch, emasculated the mortarmen. The myth is worth noting because it illustrates our conviction that the Japs would sacrifice anything for their emperor.) Iwo was declared secure on March 16 and the operation officially completed ten days later, but heavy ground fighting continued, with the Marines taking another 3,885 casualties before GIs arrived to garrison the island. Even then, the soldiers had to spend another two months mopping up. It was depressing; the closer we came to Japan, the more tenacious the defenders were. No one wanted to talk about, or even think about, what would happen when we invaded their home islands.

James Forrestal, secretary of the navy, said of Iwo: "I can never again see a United States Marine without feeling a reverence." The price of the little island had been 25,851 Marines, including 19 battalion commanders. Battle casualties in the rifle regiments had come to 60 percent in the Third Marine Division and 75 percent in the Fourth and Fifth divisions. But they had done the job. On March 4 the first crippled B-29 had wobbled into a crash landing on Airfield No. 1. Three weeks later, with the battle still raging in the northern pockets of the isle, Superfortresses began regular runs from Iwo's three fields to Tokyo. Before V-J Day, 2,251 B-29s, carrying 24,761 crewmen, had made successful landings on Iwo's airstrips. One Air Corps pilot who made three of them told a *Time* reporter: "Whenever I land on this island, I thank God and the men who fought for it."

Of the war's last two great battlefields, Iwo Jima and Okinawa, Iwo is far more difficult to reach today. Yokota, a remote American air base on Honshu, Japan, sends one Coast Guard plane there each week with provisions, but a civilian cannot board it without clearance from Washington. The aircraft is a Lockheed C-130, normally used as a cargo plane; there are no seats and no heat. It is uncomfortable and therefore suitable for your miserable mission. When you land on the seventy-five-hundred-foot jet runway and climb down the ramp, your first full breath is sulfurous. You can almost see the air you are inhaling, and for the first few minutes it is nauseating. Then you board a truck sent to pick up the provisions. Geodetic faults buckle and twist the roads, so that driving is a jarring experience, inducing motion sickness. And then there are the winds. This is a stormy climate. The shape of Iwo is in fact altered slightly by each typhoon. (Recently Suribachi's shape was also transformed by demolitions experts taking safety measures against further volcanic eruptions.)

Your first thought, upon reaching the island, is how to flee from it. Timid visitors may reach a pitch bordering on panic; for some inexplicable reason, newcomers are pursued by an irrational fear that the isle is about to sink into the sea. Actually it has risen thirty-four feet since the war, but it seems too small to survive. The whole of it, including the landing beach, can be seen from the top of Suribachi. Today Iwo is largely green, covered with a low, almost indestructible form of plant life. During the American occupation there was talk of using it as a missile base, but it came to nothing. Only flocks of wild goats share the island with the men stationed there. In 1968, when the United States formally returned it to the Japanese, Tokyo's diplomats expressed gratitude, but they couldn't have been serious.

One has the instinctive feeling that the raging past is very much present here. Japs were still emerging from the ground years after the war, and the number listed as missing is staggering. When intact corpses are found, the Japanese Graves Registration Commission sends its teams with tanks of fuel; the bones are burned, and if the body can be identified, the family is notified. There seems to be no limit to the foreign objects below Iwo's black silt surface. Thus far, 560 major pillboxes have been uncovered. Relatives of slain Japanese who are successful in wangling space on the weekly flight first climb on Suribachi, to view the island, the beach, and the surf. Then they visit the memorials. The chief American monument is a bas-relief of the Suribachi flag raising, and it is sad to note that it is marred by many graffiti. The names are both American and Japanese — A. L. Warren and R. H. Nakamura, for example — suggesting a diaspora of vandals, but the disfigurement is depressing all the same. Even Kilroy had the good taste to leave this place alone.

My flight back to Japan will leave in an hour or so, and I am standing outside a Quonset-hut barracks, talking to Lieutenant Julilo Oshikawa, one of the officers commanding the Japanese troops stationed here. *Japanese* troops? On *Iwo Jima?* Yes; and eventually this will be a base for more of Hirohito's soldiers than those who fought here under Kuribayashi. It is startling, but there is a benign explanation. Since 1945 Nippon's civilians have been so hostile

The author on the beach at Iwo Jima, with Mount Suribachi in the background

The view of the landing beach from Mount Suribachi

toward soldiers wearing their country's uniform that life in the home islands has become unendurable for their Japanese Self-Defense Force. So the government cast about for another depot. Through a bureaucratic freak, Iwo, which could not be accommodated elsewhere in the country's political system, was incorporated into the Tokyo prefecture. When you are on Iwo you are legally within Tokyo's city limits, 660 miles away. Therefore officials in the capital can determine your legal status and clear away batches of paperwork which antimilitarists could exploit. Putting Nipponese soldiers here was a clever solution to a vexing problem, though some Americans may regard it as almost sacrilegious.

Oshikawa, like his men, is wearing a red baseball cap with yellow felt *kanji* characters designating his rank and unit — a deliberately unmilitaristic hat — and the last thing he wants to discuss is World War II. Therefore I ask him how his men and the Coast Guard meteorologists get along. Pretty well, he says; they jog together, swap movies and girlie magazines, join in resurfacing the airstrip's tarmac when it becomes riddled by sulfur vents from below, and, until the recent completion of a quarter-mile-high radio tower to beam low-frequency weather and navigational messages to ships, gathered together to gawk at the workmen up there. The servicemen from the two nations have a baseball league, sprint against one another, and play tennis in one of the larger bunkers.

Nevertheless there is tension. The Nipponese are bound to resent the fact that every American has an air-conditioned room and, in most cases, his own stereo. On the other hand, the Japanese have access to an unlimited supply of sake, a drink of great authority, while the coastguardsmen are only issued beer. It has always been that way for U.S. troops, and it is stupid. Solace, *any* solace, seems the least that can be done for men marooned here. Yet they don't think theirs a hard lot. They like to jog. They like to roam around alone. They all feel attached to Iwo. It is, they say, so very peaceful. And they mean it; they are too young to remember Iwo's fiery hour in history. Men of my generation, of course, take an altogether different view. To us this battle was the latest in a series which began at Pearl Harbor and became worse and worse. Morison quotes a wounded Marine on Iwo: "I hope to God that we don't have to go on any more of these screwy islands." Morison then apostrophizes: "Only one more, Marine — the even screwier Okinawa — and the war would be almost over."

...Then I'll Rise
and Fight with You Again

IT IS TIME, ODYSSEUS SAID, THAT I TOLD YOU OF THE DI-
sastrous voyage Zeus gave me. On Saturday, March 24, 1945, with
heavy fighting continuing on Iwo and in the Philippines — and GIs
pouring across the Rhine — I was hopping around on the distant
island of Mog Mog, trying to dodge American baseball bats aimed
at my skull. Is this clear? Am I going too fast for you? Well, *nil
desperandum;* the facts are quickly told. Mog Mog is the chief island
of Ulithi Atoll in the western Carolines, where 1,457 Allied vessels
had assembled for the invasion of Okinawa. Each of the 182,112
U.S. fighting men heading into the battle was to be allowed two
hours ashore and all the beer he could drink while PA systems
belted out songs popular at home. It was a thoughtful gesture. Unfortunately, the picnic wasn't left at that. Some recreational officer
thought red-blooded American boys deserved another outlet. It was
his idea to issue us sports equipment, so we could burn up all that
energy accumulated during the long voyage here. It didn't work
quite as expected. He had no notion of what it meant to be psyched
up for combat. We quickly got loaded and called, like Cynara's
lover, for madder music and stronger wine. When none was forthcoming, we destroyed most of the sports gear, and the hard-
chargers among us began hitting people over the head with Louisville Sluggers. The officer was furious, but his threats were as futile
as a clock in an empty house. What could he do? Deprive us of the
privilege of getting shot at? It was reminiscent of the notorious

"Battle of Brisbane," earlier in the war, when a file of Australian soldiers leaving their country passed a file of arriving GIs, coming in the other direction. Imprudent GIs mocked the Diggers, promising to lay every Aussie woman, married or not. Shots were exchanged — some men were actually killed — and then the sad affair was quickly hushed up. That sort of thing happens in war, but civilians on the home front cannot be expected to understand it.

Officers and senior NCOs had been briefed earlier on our objective, and once we weighed anchor and left Ulithi on the way to battle, I put my men, as we said then, in the picture. We formed a semicircle on the fantail of our APA, the *George C. Clymer*, and I unrolled a map of the target isle. Okinawa, in the Ryukyu Archipelago, is a big island, sixty miles long and, on the average, eight miles wide, with a fringing reef which would have been dismaying a year earlier but was no problem for our fleets of new amphtracs. The island, lying exactly midway between Formosa and Japan, would be an ideal staging area for our invasion of Dai Nippon. In the north it is rugged and thickly forested; in the south it is rolling and farmed; the Ichikawa Isthmus separates the two. One way of visualizing Okinawa is to compare it to Walt Disney's dog Pluto. The northern two-thirds, the head and long neck, is largely barren; Motobu Peninsula, Pluto's uplifted ear, is mountainous and about the size of Saipan. In the south the small harbor of Naha, the isle's capital, is just forward of the tail. The southern side of that harbor, which would acquire special meaning for me, is Oroku Peninsula. Various other bays, isthmuses, capes, and promontories form the dog's short forelegs and hind feet. Off Motobu, looking like a bee, is the tiny isle of Ie Shima.

General Buckner, our overall U.S. commander, planned to land four divisions on L-day, or Love-Day: Easter Sunday, April 1, 1945. That would leave him with three more divisions for the follow-up and another in reserve. The first waves would hit the Hagushi beaches, just south of the island's midriff. Our immediate objective was the seizure of Yontan and Kadena airfields. The lineup, right to left, would be two army divisions, the Ninety-sixth and the Seventh, then the First and Sixth Marine divisions. Once

Okinawa

EAST CHINA SEA

IE SHIMA

Motobu
Peninsula
Mt.Yaetake
Mt.Katsu
Nago

Ichikawa Isthmus

Hagushi

Asa
Kawa
Machinato
Line

Oroku
Peninsula
Naha

Charlie Shuri
Hill Hill
Horseshoe
Ridge
Sugar Loaf
Hill
Naha
Half Moon Hill

G.W.WARD

the airstrips were in our hands, the GIs of the Ninety-sixth and Seventh would wheel south, while the two Marine divisions wheeled northward. The most ambitious goals, or so it then seemed, had been assigned to the Sixth, my division — an amalgam of smaller units, most of which had fought on Guadalcanal, New Georgia, Bougainville, Saipan, and Guam — because the assumption then was that the enemy was entrenched in the north. Aboard ship, sergeants were told to pass along the usual instructions: watch out for snipers, don't shout names (a Jap would shout the same name again a minute later and drill the poor jerk who stuck his head up), maintain fire discipline when the enemy screams to draw fire and thus spot automatic weapons, and if you face a banzai charge, stay loose: don't fire till you see their buckteeth. There was the usual crap about malaria, dengue, filariasis, typhus, leprosy, dysentery,

and jungle rot, and what were described as the world's two most
deadly snakes, the habu and the kufau. We were issued elaborately
printed scrip, as though we would have anything to spend it on.
Noncoms were also assembled for a weather briefing. The annual
rainfall, we were told, was 120 inches. I'm not sure I wrote that
down. I tried to check later, but those pages in my diary were
blurred beyond recognition by countless cloudbursts. I can't tell
you how much rain there actually was, but 120 inches wasn't even
close.

Our voyage to the island was smooth. We read about the natives
of Okinawa, a race with mixed Chinese, Malayan, and Ainu blood
who buried their ancestors in elaborate stone and concrete tombs.
The Japanese had encouraged this custom, our guidebooks said;
they could be expected to use these tombs as shelters from artillery
fire. (*Not*, I thought, *if I can get there first.*) In their bunks some of
the guys read armed services double-columned editions of the classics. Barney and I were absorbed in our endless chess tournament.
Others read, wrote letters home, shot the breeze, told sea stories,
played hearts, and sang songs based on awful puns: "After Rabaul
Is Over," "Ta-ra-wa-boom-de-ay," and "Good-bye, Mama, I'm Off
to Okinawa." I didn't feel particularly cheerful, but I do recall a
kind of serenity, a sense of solidarity with the Raggedy Asses,
which didn't fit with the instinctive aloofness which had been part
of my prewar character and would return, afterward, like a healing
scar. I had been, and after the war I would again be, a man who
usually prefers his own company, finding contentment in solitude.
But for the present I had taken others into my heart and given of
myself to theirs. This was especially true in combat. Once, when
we were treated to the exquisite luxury of riding to the front in six-
by trucks (six wheels, six-wheel drive), I was seized by a compelling
need to empty my bowels. Just then the line of trucks stopped
while the lead driver negotiated a way around a fallen tree, and I
took advantage of the pause to leap out and squat in full view of a
company of Marines. At the critical moment, all the truck motors
started up, and I yelped, "Wait for me!" I finished the job with one
convulsion and sprinted back in time, pulling up my pants as all

hands cheered. Before the war I wouldn't have dreamt of hurrying so personal an errand, let alone carrying it out in the full view of strangers. But it was essential then that I not be left behind by the Raggedy Ass Marines. I had to be with my own people. Like Saul on the road to Damascus, I had entered the true fold by turning all of my previous customs on their heads. I had no inkling then of how vincible that made me, how terrible was the price I might have to pay. Yet as a Christian I should have known how vulnerable love can be.

Holy Week ended on Saturday, March 31, when the fleet anchored off western Okinawa. We were awakened in the night by the shattering crash of broadsides from over a thousand Allied warship muzzles — the Royal Navy was there, too — and like the virtuous woman in the Proverbs, we rose while it was not yet light, worked willingly with our hands, squaring away our gear, and ate not the bread of idleness. We did, however, eat. Indeed, feast might be a better word. We lined up in the murky companionways for the only decent fare I ever saw on a troop transport: steak, eggs, ice cream, and hot coffee. I remember wondering whether this would be my last meal. This Easter happened to be my twenty-third birthday. My chances of becoming twenty-four were, I reflected, very slight. None of us, of course, had heard anything about the atomic bombs, then approaching completion. We assumed we would have to invade Kyushu and Honshu, and we would have been unsurprised to learn that MacArthur, whose forecasts of losses were uncannily accurate, had told Washington that he expected the first stage of that final campaign to "cost one million casualties to American forces alone." All we could be sure of was that Okinawa was to be the last island before that climax, and that the enemy would sacrifice every available man to drive us off it.

At 4:06 A.M. Admiral Turner's flagship signaled: "Land the Landing Force." We saddled up in darkness, groaning under the weight, and waited by the cargo nets, watching shells burst on a beach we could not yet see. Then dawn came rapidly, so fast you could almost watch it travel across the water. In the first dim light I could see that there was land there; there were clouds on the horizon and then a denser mass that was shapeless beneath the clouds. As the first shafts of sunlight arrived the mass became lettuce green, an isle floating in a misty haze, and in the distance you could see the torn, ragged edges of the ridges supporting the rice terraces. I hadn't expected such vivid colors. All the photographs I had seen had been black-and-white.

Now we descended the ropes into the amphtracs, which, fully loaded, began forming up in waves. Yellow cordite smoke blew across our bows, battleship guns were flashing, rockets hitting the shore sounded *c-r-r-rack*, like a monstrous lash, and we were, as infantrymen always are at this point in a landing, utterly helpless. Then, fully aligned, the amphtracs headed for the beach, tossing and churning like steeds in a cavalry charge. Slowly we realized that something we had anticipated wasn't happening. There were no splashes of Jap mortar shells, no roars of Jap coastal guns, no grazing Jap machine-gun fire. The enemy wasn't shooting back because, when we hit the beach at 8:27 A.M., there wasn't any enemy there. It was an unprecedented stratagem — the greatest April Fool's Day joke of all time. Sixty thousand of us walked inland standing up and took Yontan (now Yometan) and Kadena airfields before noon. A Japanese fighter pilot landed on Yontan, climbed down, and ordered a tank of gas in Japanese before he realized something was wrong. He reached for his pistol and was gunned down before he could touch the butt. Idly exploring the quaint, concrete, lyre-shaped burial vaults built on the slopes of the low hills, we felt jubilant. In our first day we had established a beach-head fifteen hundred yards long and five thousand yards deep. None of us could have known then that the battle would last nearly three months, becoming the bloodiest island fight of the Pacific war; that over 200,000 people would perish; that Ernie Pyle, the famous war correspondent just arrived from the ETO, would be killed on Ie Shima; and that both Buckner and Mitsura Ushijima, the Japanese general, would be dead before the guns were silenced.

There was an omen, had we but recognized it. At 7:13 P.M. a kamikaze dove into the *West Virginia*, erupting in flame. That should have been the tip-off to the enemy's strategy: sink the ships, isolating the Americans ashore. Ushijima had 110,000 Nips of his Thirty-second Army, all Manchurian veterans, concentrated in the southern third of the island. Tokyo's high command had decided to make Okinawa the war's greatest Gethsemane, another Iwo but on a much grander scale. The Americans would be allowed "to land in full" and "lured into a position where they cannot receive cover and support from the naval and aerial bombardment." Because of the tremendous U.S. commitment, there would be ten American soldiers for every foot of ground on Okinawa's lower waist, where Ushijima planned to make his stand. Thus wedged together, they would be like livestock in a slaughterhouse. Ushijima had studied the cable traffic from Iwo in its last days. Curiously, he found it encouraging. Pillboxes and blockhouses had been built here, too; but in addition, massive numbers of caves masked heavy artillery which could be rolled out on railroad tracks, fired, and rolled back in. Naha had been the site of Japan's artillery school for years. Every gully, every crossroads, every ravine in the south had been pinpointed by the defenders. It would be like an enemy attack on American infantry at Fort Benning. The Japs could target each shell within inches. Under these circumstances, Ushijima reasoned, Buckner's army could be "exterminated to the last man."

The Allied fleet, in this scenario, would be wiped out by the kamikazes. Even before L-day, these human torpedoes had begun their destruction of our ships. Zeroes, Zekes, Bettys, Nicks, Vals, Nakajimas, Aichis, Kagas — virtually every Nip warplane that could fly was loaded with high explosives and manned by pilots, some mere teenagers, who would dive to their deaths and take sinking Allied warships with them. In the Philippines, in the early stages of this airborne hara-kiri, fliers had operated individually. Now the American and British seamen would confront massed suicide attacks called *kikusui*, or "floating chrysanthemums." Ultimately they failed, but anyone who saw a bluejacket who had been burned by them, writhing in agony under his bandages, never again slandered the sailors who stayed on ships while the infantrymen hit the beach. Altogether, Nippon's human bombs accounted for 400 ships and 9,724 seamen — a casualty list which may be unique in the history of naval warfare.

Our first night ashore was interrupted only by fitful machine-gun bursts and the *wump-wump-wump* of small mortars — there were a few Japs beyond our perimeter, left behind for nuisance value — and during morning twilight, after breakfasting on K rations, we NCOs shouted, "Route march, ho!" starting the long push northward, the Marines loping along in the unmistakable gait of the infantryman, our muscles feeling as though they had been pulled loose from the joints and sockets they were supposed to control. In those first days we covered about twenty miles a day, an ordeal, since we were carrying all our equipment, but we were young and grateful to be still alive. The scenery was lovely. To the left lay the sea; to the right, the hills rose in graceful terraces, each supporting rice paddies. Our path was of orange clay, bordered by stunted bushes and shrubs, cherry trees, and red calla lilies; I had never seen red ones before. Even the remains of the bridges, which had been taken out by our bombers, were beautiful. The Okinawans, like the Japanese, believe that straight lines are harsh, while curved lines suggest serenity, and the sinuosity of these arches conveyed a calm and repose wholly irrelevant to, and superior to, our mission here. Especially was this true when we rounded a curve and beheld, on the beach, the sprawled body of a girl who had been murdered. I had never seen anything like that. The thought that an American man could commit such a crime in fighting a just war raged against everything I believed in, everything my country represented. I was deeply troubled.

Northern Okinawa, we found, was not defenseless. Motobu Peninsula, steep, rocky, wooded, and almost trackless, was dominated by two mountains, Katsu and fifteen-hundred-foot, three-crested Yaetake. Entrenched on Yaetake were two battalions under the command of a tenacious officer, Takehiko Udo. In the ensuing battle the Sixth lost 1,304 men, among them Swifty Crabbe, who took a rifle bullet below his right elbow which severed a nerve, rendering his thumb uncontrollable — a ridiculous wound, but he was delighted to leave the island. To these casualties must be added the professional reputation of our redundant commanding officer, Colonel Hastings, who was fired in the middle of the fight. I was present at the dramatic moment. Lem Shepherd, the divisional commander, asked where the regiment's three battalions were, and the Old Turk, highly agitated, confessed that he wasn't aware of, familiar with, or apprised of where nearly three thousand men might be located, found, or situated. So Shepherd sent him back to the rearest echelon and appointed Colonel William J. Whaling as our new CO. Whaling had fought well on the Canal; we had confidence in him.

And our confidence in ourselves was growing. The Raggedy Asses were always in their element off parade, with no saluting and little sirring, unshaven and grimy in filthy dungarees, left to do what they did best: use their wits. There was no role here for mechanized tactics; tanks were useful only for warming your hands in their exhaust fumes. This was more like French and Indian warfare. Each of us quickly formed a map of the peninsula in his mind; we knew which ravines were swept by Nambu fire and how to avoid them. (Beau Tatum was the exception. His sense of direction, or rather the lack of it, was still uncanny. If a company had let Beau direct them, they would have wound up on Iwo Jima.) Much of the time I kept the battalion situation map, drawing red and blue greasepaint arrows on Plexiglas to show, respectively, what the Japs and our forces were doing. The genial operations officer, an Irish major from the Bronx, never pulled rank on me, though he must have been tempted. It was interesting work; better still, it was comparatively safe. Unfortunately Krank found another job for me. Shepherd planned a viselike compression, an elaborate envelopment, with the Fourth Marines assaulting the face of Yaetake while we in the Twenty-ninth attacked the rear. A patrol was needed to link up the two regiments. The Raggedy Asses, it was decided, would provide the four-man patrol. Their craven sergeant was ordered to lead it.

I took Knocko, Crock, Pisser, and Killer Kane because they were immediately available and the afternoon was waning. The veins and arteries of the dying day streaked the horizon over the East China Sea. My throat was thick with fear. We moved silently down the path, half crouched, passing Japanese corpses on both sides, any of which could be shamming. Darkness began to gather. Now I was more worried about the Fourth Marines than the enemy. Because the Nips were so skillful at infiltration, the rule had been established that after night had fallen, no Marine could leave his foxhole for any reason. Anyone moving was slain. Two nights before, a man in our battalion had been drilled between the eyes when he rose to urinate. So I moved along the path as quickly as I could, and I recall ascending a little wiggle in the trail, turning a corner, and staring into the muzzle of a Browning heavy machine gun. "Flimsy," I said shakily, giving that day's password. "Virgin," said the Fourth Marines' gunner, giving the countersign. He relaxed and reached for a cigarette. He said, "You heard the news? FDR died." I thought: *my father*.

Resistance ended on Yaetake's peak after a hand-to-hand struggle; 347 Japs died. Since the Marines had killed nearly three thousand Japs and captured the northern two-thirds of the island — 436 square miles — we expected a respite, hot chow, and a few days in the sack. We didn't get any of them. For over a week we had heard ominous rumors of stiffening resistance in the south. GIs were encountering unprecedented concentrations of Japanese artillery fire. Progress was being measured in yards, then in feet. Regrouping, the GIs launched a massive attack and were stopped cold. It was Peleliu and Iwo all over again, but to the nth degree; because of it, Morison wrote, "the battle for Okinawa was the toughest and most prolonged of any in the Pacific war since Guadalcanal." Being Marines, and therefore arrogant, we assumed that the dogfaces simply lacked our spirit. What infuriated us, however, was the news that one of Buckner's chief problems lay on his right flank. The division stalled there was the infamous Twenty-seventh. They couldn't keep up with the other army outfits, couldn't even recover their own dead. So we were going to relieve them and they would move up here as garrison troops. Before boarding the six-bys for the trip south, the Raggedy Asses gave the children in the little town of Nago a lesson in elementary English. When the GIs came up to take our place, we told them, they should chant loudly: "Twenty-seventh Division eats shit! Twenty-seventh Division eats shit!" Later we were told they had performed superbly. It was probably the greatest event in the history of Nago. Doubtless it was unfair to some doggies. I'm sure there were brave men in the Twenty-seventh. But if anyone bleats to me about the division's reputation and asks for sympathy, I can tell him where to find it. In the dictionary.

Our movement into the southern line took two days. As we rode south, we became aware of a grumbling on the horizon, which turned into a thumping, then a drumming, then a rumbling, and then an enormous thudding, as though Fafner and Fasolt, the giants in the *Rhinegold*, had been let loose. The enemy's main line of resistance bore various names, depending upon what part of it faced you; to GIs it would be remembered as Skyline Ridge, or the Kakazu, or the Kochi, or the Maeda Escarpment. The First Marine Division, which moved up on our left flank, called it the Shuri Line, because their immediate objective was the ancient ruins of Shuri Castle. We named it the Machinato Line, after a village on our front. But it was all of a piece, all horrible. Counting both sides, the line represented an extraordinary concentration of 300,000 fighting men, and countless terrified civilians, on a battleground that was about as wide as the distance between Capitol Hill in Washington and Arlington National Cemetery. In the densest combat of World War I, battalion frontage had been approximately eight hundred yards. Here it was less than six hundred yards. The sewage, of course, was appalling. You could smell the front long before you saw it; it was one vast cesspool. My first glimpse of the line itself came when our truck was stopped by the convoy traffic and I jumped over the tailgate to climb a little hillock and see where we were heading. By sheer chance, I had chosen a spot from which the entire battlefield was visible. It was hideous, and it was also strangely familiar, resembling, I then realized, photographs of 1914–1918. This, I thought, is what Verdun and Passchendaele must have looked like. The two great armies, squatting opposite one another in mud and smoke, were locked together in unimaginable agony. There was no room for a flanking operation; the Pacific Ocean lay to the east and the East China Sea to the west. A landing behind Japanese lines would have been possible and would have relieved the pressure on the front, but despite the pleas of the Marine generals for an amphibious operation, Buckner insisted on fighting it out this way.

I lingered on that hummock, repelled and bewitched. It was a monstrous sight, a moonscape. Hills, ridges, and cliffs rose and fell along the front like gray stumps of rotting teeth. There was nothing green left; artillery had denuded and scarred every inch of ground. Tiny flares glowed and disappeared. Shrapnel burst with bluish white puffs. Jets of flamethrowers flickered and here and there new explosions stirred up the rubble. While I watched, awed, an American observation plane, a Piper Cub, droned over the Japanese lines, spotting targets for the U.S. warships lying offshore so that they could bring their powerful guns to bear on the enemy. Suddenly the little plane was hit by flak and disintegrated. The carnage below continued without pause. Here I was safe, but tomorrow I would be there. In that instant I realized that the worst thing that could happen to me was about to happen to me.

That afternoon we pushed ahead a thousand yards, retrieving the Twenty-seventh's fallen, but our optimism was premature. The Japs were giving us the ground. They knew who we were. They now had a word for American Marines — *kai-he-tai* — and had developed special tactics for us. These followed a pattern. Each line was held stubbornly until it was about to be overwhelmed; then the Japs withdrew to prepared positions, leaving snipers in coral grottoes to carve up our CPs. A truer sign of what lay ahead was a stark statistic from the Seventh Marines, who had preceded us into the line and held our left flank. In nine days of attacks on a little wrinkle of land called Wana Ridge, the regiment had suffered 1,249 casualties. Our own baptism in siege warfare came when we forced a passage across the Asa Kawa, or River. The Japs had burned the bridge behind them. In those days Americans still prided themselves on their knack for mechanical improvisation — one vehicle which had made its debut on L-day was a tank which actually swam — and our Engineer Battalion welcomed the Asa problem as a challenge. At night, moving like shadows in the slimy stream, they threw a footbridge across the river. Assault companies raced across it in the first moments of morning twilight. Japs wired dynamite to their bellies, darted out of tall grass, and blew up both the footbridge and themselves. Amphtracs ferried more Marines across the water until the following day, when the engineers built a Bailey bridge strong enough to bear the weight of tanks.

Meanwhile the spring rains had begun, coinciding, I might point out, with my own arrival on the line. Torrents blew in from the East China Sea for three straight weeks, day and night, and no one who has not fought under such conditions, or even worked under them, can possibly envisage how miserable they are. Plasma, for example, was usually fed into the veins of a wounded man by taping the plasma container to the stock of a reversed rifle with a fixed bayonet; the bayonet was driven into the ground, providing a post from which the plasma could flow downward. The gruel of Okinawa mud was so thin that it couldn't support a rifle bayonet; men had to be withdrawn from the line to hold the containers. On the other side of the globe Bill Mauldin was writing: "I'm sure Europe never got this muddy during peacetime. I'm equally sure that no mud in the world is so deep or sticky or wet as European mud." Mauldin should have seen what the Twenty-ninth Marines were up against. In places our muck was waist-deep. Jeeps, artillery pieces, even bulldozers — everything but amphtracs and DUKWs — sank in it. And there is one massive difference between peacetime mud and wartime mud. In peacetime it is usually avoidable. You can step around it, or take another route. In combat you fight in the mud, sleep in it, void in it, bleed in it, and sometimes die in it.

Your torment in combat is compounded by your utter ignorance of how the battle is going elsewhere. You know what is happening in this gully, or what lies behind that stump, but you have no idea of how things look back at the platoon CP, let alone the company, battalion, regimental, divisional, corps, or army CPs. As keeper of the situation map, I knew more than most. My map was gridded with numbered squares representing areas each of which was two thousand feet wide. Each of these was then divided into twenty-five lettered squares, A through Y, these being four hundred feet wide. In turn, the tiny squares could be further divided, for those who knew the gen, into 1, 2, 3, 4, and 5, indicating the four corners and the center. Thus the naval gunfire officer in every battalion headquarters could order gunfire from a warship offshore and put it within two hundred feet of the target. In addition, each battalion carried on its roster a full-blooded Navaho. He could talk to other Indians in other battalions over SCR-300 radios, confident that no Japanese eavesdropper would understand a word. But such information was fragmentary at best, and there was nothing from the regimental level or further up. The army divisions on the left were fighting just as hard as we were, but I don't recall any dope about how things were going for them.

I yearned for a better view. It did not seem to be an impossible dream. Before our invasion the island had supported 400,000 Okinawans, and a few relics of civilization had somehow endured. War which displaces civilizations always leaves a few odd reminders of the peaceful past — a half-demolished wall, say, or the front door of a home which no longer exists. Until L-day a large concrete sugar mill had flourished in western Okinawa, on what was now our end of the Machinato Line. Bombardments had destroyed all of it except two tall brick chimneys which overlooked the entire battleground. The Japanese were using these smokestacks for observation posts, and despite our naval gunfire, artillery, and aerial bombardment the chimneys had miraculously survived. If only I could get up there, I thought, I would know what was going on. I now know that was wrong. I would have seen the blackened ruins of Naha, still thickly toothed with Japs, to the southwest, and looking down on the line I would have had a stunning view of the fighting, emanating a sullen burning glow like a kitchen range. But the key features would have escaped me because their significance would have been invisible from the smokestacks. The whole history of war is a story of men moving closer and closer to the ground and then deeper and deeper in it. The anchor of the line, which Ushijima considered the key to it, was an undistinguished mound now known to history as Sugar Loaf Hill.

Sugar Loaf, which was actually shaped more like a bread loaf, was a height of coral and volcanic rock three hundred yards long and one hundred feet high. It was vital because it was almost impregnable. Not in itself; few summits are unscalable if attackers can reach their slopes. But this ugly hive was supported on the southeast by another mound, Half Moon Hill, and to the south by yet another, Horseshoe Ridge. Thus Sugar Loaf, a spear pointed at the advancing Sixth Marine Division, was merely the most visible feature of a triangular system connected by hidden galleries. Each of the three peaks could deliver murderous fire from heavy 15-centimeter guns on any other peak attacked by us. Moreover, a deep trough of ground within Horseshoe Ridge gave the Japanese mortar positions which could be reached only by grenades and small-arms fire, and our riflemen couldn't get that close because the three hummocks rose abruptly from a bare plain, providing no defilade. Assaulting troops charging one precipice would be cut down by converging interlocking fire from the rest of the triangle. In addition, the complex could be raked by Jap artillery, mortars, and machine guns emplaced in Shuri Hill, to the east, which had stopped the First Marine Division in its muddy tracks. Shuri was bigger, but it was the Sugar Loaf complex that cracked the whip of the Machinato Line. There the hills stood, piled in great, weighty, pressing, heaped, lethal masses, oppressive beyond words for us who studied the maps and knew that one way or another the peaks must be taken.

My first grasp of what the immediate future held for me, provided I had a future, came when my battalion relieved the battered Third Battalion, which had been fighting on a smaller mound called Charlie Hill. We were moving up in a coiling line, single file, as the Third, uncoiling, moved out. I was struck by the Third's faces: haggard, with jaws hanging open and the expressionless eyes of men who had left nowhere and were going nowhere. There was little conversation on either side, but in one of those lulls that come in any march, when there was no movement in either column, I found myself opposite John Baker. I knew Baker well. He was a former newspaperman, a cheerful, sturdy corporal whom I had never seen not chomping on an unlit cigar. In fact, I suspected it was always the same cigar. He had been stationed in San Diego at the time of Pearl Harbor, and his company had been detailed to dig trenches on the beaches because the Californians were convinced that an invasion armada was steaming toward them. I doubt that it disturbed him or even dislodged his cigar. He was a solid, imperturbable man, as steady as though he carried a binnacle in his chest. I had often wished I had him in my section, but he had remained in the Third Battalion, and now he was coming out of combat, and I asked him, "Baker, what's it like up there?"

I had thought he was looking at me. Now I realized that he was really looking through me in a thousand-yard stare. Slowly he focused on my face, removed the cigar, spat on the mud, replaced the cigar, and replied flatly: "You really want to know?" I turned away, and turned back. I noticed that this file was much shorter than ours. I asked him, "Where's the rest of your battalion?" In that same dull voice he said, "This isn't a battalion. These are the survivors of a battalion."

The two lines of men began to move again. We rounded a bend, and suddenly I understood Baker. On the right side of the path lay about a hundred dead Marines. Each had been wrapped in his poncho, now his shroud. These had been secured with communications wire and then the bodies had been stacked as you would stack cordwood. You could see the boondockers jutting out; the rest of the bodies were covered by the ponchos. The stack was neatly made, as though ready to pass inspection. Probably I knew some of the men, but covered as they were I couldn't identify any. Every pair of boondockers looked like every other pair. I looked down at my own. They were the same.

The sounds of enemy artillery were becoming louder and louder; we were well within mortar range. Once we were in position, on the reverse slope of Charlie Hill, I set up the Raggedy Ass base in one of the little courtyards that led to the lyre-shaped tombs; every courtyard was encircled by a three-foot wall, with an entrance at one end of it and the tomb itself at the other end. Blue ceramic jars, containing the ashes of ancestors, stood on shelves within the tombs. At night we moved the ancestors out and ourselves in — these mini-mausoleums made superb bomb shelters — and in the morning we moved the vases back. During the battle we changed tombs several times, but for the time being we weren't going anywhere, because the battle wasn't moving. The Japanese still had us deadlocked here, and had even regained some ground on the left with a fifteen-thousand-man counterattack. By the end of that first week on the line, we had begun to understand the maze of hills. Sugar Loaf had changed hands fourteen times. Every time we took it, the tremendous firepower from Half Moon, Horseshoe, and Shuri drove us off. The Japs would retake it, and our artillery would do the same to them. But we couldn't see how they could be completely dislodged. They always had men on some part of the hill. And they had others *in* the hill, because their sappers, starting with foxholes, had dug deeper caves and tunnels, all in our direction.

Now I enter a period of time in which a structured account of events is impossible. Continuity disappears; the timepiece in the attic of memory ticks erratically. These pages in my war diary are glued together with blood which hardened long ago. Certain incidents and impressions can be recalled, but only as a kaleidoscopic montage. Somewhere in here occurred the Truce of the Fucking Dogs; one of our war dogs got loose, ran out on the killing ground north of Sugar Loaf, somehow met an Okinawan pye-dog, and mounted her while both sides, astounded by this act of creativity in the midst of annihilation, held their fire. Then there was the Matter of the Everlasting D Ration, a chunk of bitter chocolate, supposedly packed with nutrition, which looked like and tasted like modeling clay and was all I ate for five days, combat having destroyed my appetite. More darkly I remember the Execution of the Two Pricks, a supercilious pair of junior army officers who were reconnoitering the front, addressing us as "bellhops," and ordering us to direct them to the best view of the battle. A gunny pointed toward the Horseshoe, and off they went, covering about thirty feet before they were slain. There was also the Great Helmet Debate between me and Bubba. Both of us were wearing our steel chamber pots at the time, facing each other, sitting on the reverse slope of a little rise overlooking no-man's-land. Bubba said helmets were an unnecessary encumbrance and dampened the offensive spirit. The Army of Northern Virginia hadn't needed them, he said. I was trying to introduce the subject of Appomattox when a large chunk of shrapnel whirred through the air and hit Bubba's helmet. He took it off and fingered the dent. No doubt about it; if he hadn't been wearing it, he would have been dead. He carefully put it back on, fastened the strap — and then took up where he had left off, his finger wagging and his voice rumbling, insisting that helmets were completely useless.

One of my clearest memories is of the Arrival of the Six Replacements. Rain was still pelting us mercilessly when we were taken off the line briefly, and I found us a dry cave near Machinato Airfield. The cave faced the shore. I was exhausted, and once inside my dry sanctuary I lay on my side for a few minutes, watching the kamikazes diving and exploding on our warships. It was one of the war's most extraordinary spectacles, but I was too weary to keep my eyes open. I took off my boondockers and lapsed into a coma of sleep without even removing my pack or helmet. Then I felt someone plucking at one of my leggings. A reedy, adolescent voice was saying urgently, "Hey, Sarge! Sarge!" I looked up and saw a half-dozen seventeen-year-old boys who had been brought here directly from boot camp. I vaguely remembered the Top having told me that they were on their way to me. We had heard that back home men were being drafted into the Marine Corps, which was outrageous, if true — *every* Marine had *always* been a volunteer — but sending these children was worse. Between Iwo Jima and Okinawa the Marine Corps was running out of fighting men, so these kids were here, disturbing (I was selfish enough to think of it that way) my siesta. They weren't much of an advertisement for the Corps. All of them looked pallid, mottled, and puffy. "What'll we do?" their spokesman asked anxiously in a voice which was still changing. He wanted orders, and I had none. I knew I should give them a full briefing; if they went into the line without one, they could die fast. It was my duty to protect replacements from that. That was what I was being paid for. I didn't do it; I turned over and again drifted off into deep sleep.

Then black comedy, whose role in war is rarely appreciated, solved the problem. Water was dripping on my face. Incredulous, I opened my eyes and realized that the cave was leaking. Over the past week the porous limestone overhead had become saturated. Now it was raining *indoors*. I ripped out all the filthy words I knew, repeated them, and then noticed that my new wards were still there, earnestly hoping that I could spare a few minutes of my valuable time for them. So I did. I told them how to learn about shellfire on the job, and the tricks of Jap snipers, and booby traps, and how doubt is more fatal than slowed reflexes, and where they might avoid being enfiladed on the line, adding, however, as gently as I could, that they would seldom be in a position to benefit from that information because they would spend most of their time as runners, and a runner is exposed far more often than a rifleman. Their boondockers, I said, were their best friends; they should dry them whenever possible. If they were overrun by a Jap charge they should play dead, affecting a grotesque pose of death; they would probably be bayoneted anyway, but there was always that chance they might be overlooked. They should be alert for the sharp click of steel on steel, which probably meant trouble, because that was how Japs armed grenades. If they heard it, they should move fast. (I should have told them to leap toward the sound, getting the Jap, but this was a lesson in survival, not heroism.) I saw they were beginning to tremble, but it was better to have it out here than there. Feelings of elation in the moments before combat were normal and OK as long as men didn't become suicidal; the moth-in-the-flame threat was always there. Also OK was the instinct to fantasize, to dramatize your actions to yourself. This was actually helpful and should, in fact, be encouraged. To be avoided, and if necessary ignored, were gung-ho platoon leaders who drew enemy fire by ordering spectacular charges. Ground wasn't gained that way; it was won by small groups of men, five or six in a cluster, who moved warily forward in a kind of autohypnosis, advancing in mysterious concert with similar groups on their flanks. These young Marines were going to lose a lot of illusions, but if they lost faith in everything else, including the possibility of winning this fight, including the rear echelon and even the flag, they should keep faith with the regiment. It had an outstanding record, and all its men were proud of it. If it was any comfort to them, I ended, they should know that unfounded fears were worse than founded fears and that this battle was the toughest struggle in the history of the Corps. They nodded dumbly, kneeling there like novitiates, steadied by hands grasping upright M1s propped on the wet cave floor. I wondered whether they had understood any of what I had said or whether I had become as sounding brass or a tinkling cymbal.

Had anybody told *me* all this on my first day, I would have thought he was Asiatic, snapping in for a survey, or, as it was sometimes put, one who had "missed too many boats." Since then I had become a disciplined fighter, however, though until now my own survival had been more a coefficient of luck than of skill. There was just one moment in the war when I saved my own life, and it came right after my soggy nap in that defective cave. Back on our own little amphitheater of war, still soaked to the skin, I started a routine tour of the line companies that afternoon, covering it much as a mailman covers his route, except that I had company, because, if possible, we always moved in pairs. My buddy that day was Chet Przyastawaki, the Colgate athlete with the shrill voice. We followed the embankment as far as it went and then moved from one local feature to another: the Long Square, the Blue Icicle, Grable's Tit, the X, the Iron Claw, Thurston's Trick, and the V, also known as the Hairless Pussy. This was a time when the Japanese were constantly challenging us, trying to infiltrate every night and sometimes, brazenly, by day. If their purpose was to keep us off balance, they were succeeding. This surging back and forth quickened the pulses of the Raggedy Asses. People like us, moving from one CP to another, could get caught by occasional Nips who were testing us, penetrating as deeply as they could and then, when found, trying to slip back.

Chet and I had covered the companies, Fox to Easy to Dog, as smoothly as Tinker to Evers to Chance. Positions around Sugar Loaf were in constant flux — at one time or another nine Marine battalions fought on the hill — and we had been told to skirt enemy lines on our way back, scouting every dip, crease, cranny, and rut in the ground that might be useful in combined attacks. The last leg of our journey, before we reached the lee side of the railroad embankment, took us past the crevice called McGee's Closet and down Windy Alley, a rock gulch which, like Sugar Loaf itself, had changed hands repeatedly. We arrived there at the worst possible time. The Japs had launched a reconnaissance in force; no sooner had we entered the lower throat of the alley than we heard the unmistakable sounds of an enemy patrol sealing it off behind us, closing our option of retracing our steps. Then we heard a familiar, husky sob in the air, directly overhead. We hit the deck, and a mortar shell burst a hundred feet away, followed by another, and then another. Silence followed. Chet crossed himself. Another shell burst. The stupid Japs were falling short of their targets, our lines, mortaring us in. When mortared, you are supposed to flee in almost any direction, but, as we were about to discover, it is not always that easy. As we rose cautiously, we heard jabbering on the opposite slopes of both sides of Windy Alley. So much for our flanks. We darted ahead, toward the embankment, and that was when the pneumatic whuff of the first bullet from that direction sang between us. It wasn't from an M1; it had that unmistakable Arisaka whine. We hit the deck again and rolled rightward together, toward the protection of a huge boulder, a rough slab of rock. Two more bullets whuffed past before we made it. Our problem now, and I cannot begin to tell you how much it discouraged me, was that a Nip sniper was in position at the alley's upper throat, behind another boulder, blocking the maze of intersecting paths there, cutting us off at the pass. We were trapped, the nightmare of every foot soldier. All I had going for me was sheer desperation. *Warning: this animal is vicious; when attacked, it defends itself.*

Lying in tandem, Chet and I exchanged wide-eyed glances. The coral had cut both his hands, but I was in no mood to comfort him. I felt a wave of self-pity. For several seconds I was completely mindless. Fear is the relinquishment of reason; we yield to it or fight it, but there are no halfway points. Then I struggled and shook off the panic. It was one of Napoleon's maxims that in war you must never do what the enemy wants you to do. This Jap expected us to stay put. So we wouldn't. Each of us had two grenades hooked on his harness. I hunched up and reached for one. Chet shook his head. "Too far," he whispered. If the range was too great for a Colgate halfback, a scrawny sergeant didn't have a chance, but I already knew the distance was too great; reaching the Nip with a pitch wasn't what I had in mind. I didn't tell Chet now what was there, because as I unlooped the grenade I had to think about a weapon which would reach our man. I was carrying a carbine and a .45, both useless in a sniper's duel. Chet had an M1. I asked, "Did you qualify?" He said, "Sharpshooter. Under three hundred." I shook my head. It wasn't good enough. For once I was going to do what the Marine Corps had taught me to do best. I said to Chet, "Give me your weapon and an extra clip."

My problems were complicated. I knew nothing, for example, of the Japs' timetable. If this was a quick in-and-out operation, the sniper might disappear, running back to his hole in Sugar Loaf. But that wasn't the way their snipers worked; if they had quarry, they usually hung around until they flushed it. And this one now confirmed his personal interest in us in a thin, falsetto, singsong chant, a kind of liquid gloating: "One, two, three — you can't catch me!" Chet muttered in an even higher register, "No, but he can catch us." I was looking up at the sky. The light was clouded. Soon waves of darkness would envelop us, and conceivably it could come to the knife. I couldn't even think about that. Instead, I asked Chet, "Is your piece at true zero?" He said, "It throws low and a little to the right." I took it, leaving him the carbine, and said, "His piece must throw high, and he probably doesn't know it. He

had three clear shots at us and drew Maggie's drawers every time."
Chet said, "But from where he is . . ." I nodded grimly. That was
the worst of it. An invisible line lay between his position and ours.
It was diagonal. The azimuth of his lair was about 45 degrees west;
mine was 135 degrees east. On a clock this would put him at eight
minutes before the hour and me at twenty-three minutes past —
northwest for him, southeast to me. Since both our slabs of rock
were set dead against the alley's walls, I couldn't use my weapon
and my right arm without stepping clear of my boulder, exposing
myself completely. All he needed to show was an arm and an eye,
unless, by some great stroke of luck, he was left-handed. I had to
find that out right now.

Peering out with my left eye I caught a glimpse of him — mus-
tard colored, with a turkeylike movement of his head. He was
right-handed, all right; he snapped off a shot. But he wore no harness, and I had been right about his rifle. It wasn't true; the bullet
hummed overhead and hit the gorge wall, chipping it. So much for
the marksmanship of the Thirty-second Manchurian Army. My job
was to beat it. Luckily Windy Alley was calm just now. I checked
the cartridge in the chamber and the five in the magazine. Now
came the harnessing. The full sling I had perfected during my Parris Island apprenticeship involved loops, keepers, hooks, feed ends,
and buckles. It took forever, which I didn't have just then, so I
made a hasty sling instead, loosening the strap to fit around and
steady my upper arm. My options were narrowing with each fading
moment of daylight, so I didn't have time to give Chet an explanation. I handed him the grenade now and said, "Pitch it at him, as
far as you can throw. I'm going to draw him out." He just stared at
me. What I loved about the Raggedy Ass Marines was the way my
crispest commands were unquestioningly obeyed. He started to
protest: "But I don't understa—" "You don't have to," I said.
"Just do it." I started shaking. I punched myself in the throat. I
said, "*Now.*"

I turned away; he pulled the pin and threw the grenade — an
amazing distance — some forty yards. I darted out as it exploded
and rolled over on the deck, into the prone position, the M1 butt

tight against my shoulder, the strap taut above my left elbow, and my left hand gripped on the front hand guard, just behind the stacking swivel.

Load and lock
Ready on the left   Ready on the right   Ready on the firing line
Stand by to commence firing

My right finger was on the trigger, ready to squeeze. But when I first looked through my sights I saw dim prospects. Then, just as I was training the front sight above and to the left of his rocky refuge, trying unsuccessfully to feel at one with the weapon, the way a professional assassin feels, the air parted overhead with a shredding rustle and a mortar shell exploded in my field of fire. Momentarily I was stunned, but I wasn't hit, and when my wits returned I felt, surprisingly, sharper. Except for Chet's heavy breathing, a cathedral hush seemed to have enveloped the gorge. I could almost hear the friction of the earth turning on its axis. I had literally taken leave of my senses. There remained only a trace of normal anxiety, the roughage of mental diet that sharpens awareness. Everything I saw over my sights had a cameolike clarity, as keen and well-defined as a line by Van Eyck. Dr. Johnson said that "when a man knows he is to be hanged in a fortnight, it concentrates his mind wonderfully." So does the immediate prospect of a sniper bullet. The Jap's slab of rock had my undivided attention. I breathed as little as possible — unlike Chet, who was panting — because I hoped to be holding my breath, for stability, when my target appeared. I felt nothing, not even the soppiness of my uniform. I looked at the boulder and looked at it and looked at it, thinking about nothing else, seeing only the jagged edge of rock from which he had to make his move.

I had taken a deep breath, let a little of it out, and was absolutely steady when the tip of his helmet appeared, his rifle muzzle just below it. If he thought he could draw fire with that little, he must be new on the Marine front. Pressure was building up in my lungs, but I thought I would see more of him soon, and I did; an eye, peering in the direction of my boulder, my last whereabouts. I was in plain view, but lying flat, head-on, provides the lowest possible profile, and his vision was tunneled to my right. Now I saw a throat, half a face, a second eye — and that was enough. I squeezed off a shot. The M1 still threw a few inches low, but since I had been aiming at his forehead I hit him anyway, in the cheek. I heard his sharp whine of pain. Simultaneously he saw me and shot back, about an inch over my head, as I had expected. He got off one more, lower, denting my helmet. By then, however, I was empty-ing my magazine into his upper chest. He took one halting step to the right, where I could see all of him. His arms fell and his Arisaka toppled to the deck. Then his right knee turned in on him like a flamingo's and he collapsed.

Other Nips might be near. I knifed another clip into the M1, keeping my eyes on the Jap corpse, and crept back to the boulder, where Chet, still breathing hard, leaned against me. I turned to-ward him and stifled a scream. He had no face, just juicy shapeless red pulp. In all likelihood he had been peering out curiously when that last mortar shell burst. Death must have been instantaneous. I had been alone. Nobody had been breathing here but me. My shoulder was all over blood. Now I could feel it soaking through to my upper arm. I shrank away, sickened, and the thing he had be-come fell over on its side. Suddenly I could take no more. I jumped out and dodged, stumbling, up the pitted, pocked alley. I braked to a halt when I came to the body of the dead sniper. To my aston-ishment, and then to my rage, I saw that his uniform was dry. All these weeks I had been suffering in the rain, night and day, this bastard had been holed up in some waterproof cave. It was the only instant in the war when I felt hatred for a Jap. I swung back my right leg and kicked the bloody head. Then, recovering my balance, I ran toward the safety of the embankment. Just before I reached it I glanced to my right and saw, on the inner slope of a shell hole, a breastless creature leaning backward and leering at me with a lipless grin. I couldn't identify its race or sex. It couldn't have been alive.

Back at battalion, the news of Chet's death deepened the sec-tion's numbness, but the days of cathartic grief, of incredulity and fury, were gone. One by one the Raggedy Ass Marines were disap-pearing. The Twenty-ninth was taking unprecedented casualties.

On April 1 the regiment had landed 3,512 men, including rear-echelon troops. Of these, 2,812 had fallen or would fall soon. The faces in the line companies became stranger and stranger as replacements were fed in. In our section we had already lost Lefty, of course, and Swifty; now Chet was gone, too. Death had become a kind of epidemic. It seemed unlikely that any of us would leave the island in one piece. The Jap artillery was unbelievable. One night Wally Moon was buried alive, suffocated in his one-man foxhole — he always insisted on sleeping alone — by sheets of mud from exploding shells. We didn't miss him until after the bombardment, when I whispered the usual roll call. Everyone answered "Here" or "Yo" until I came to Wally. There was no answer; we hurriedly excavated his hole, but it was too late. Wally, who had told us so much about time, was eternally gone.

Inside, though I was still scared, I felt the growing reserve which is the veteran's shield against grief. I was also puzzled. I wondered, as I had wondered before, what had become of our dead, where they were now. And in a way which I cannot explain I felt responsible for the lost Raggedy Asses, guilty because I was here and they weren't, frustrated because I was unable to purge my shock by loathing the enemy. I was ever a lover; that was what Christianity meant to me. I was in the midst of satanic madness: I knew it. I wanted to return to sanity: I couldn't. All one could do, it seemed to me, was to stop combat from breaking you in half, to keep going until you reached the other side of your immediate objective, hoping it would be different from this side while knowing all the time, with the weary cynicism of the veteran, that it would be exactly the same. It was in this mood that we scapegoated all cases of combat fatigue — my father's generation of infantrymen had called it "shell shock" — because we felt that those so diagnosed were taking the dishonorable way out. We were all psychotic, inmates of the greatest madhouse in history, but staying on the line was a matter of pride. Pride was important to young men then. Today it is derided as machismo. But without that macho spirit California and Australia would have been invaded long before this final battle.

Looking back across thirty-five years, I see the Raggedy Ass

Marines, moving in single file toward the front, glancing, not at their peerless leader, in whom they justifiably had so little confidence, but back over their shoulders toward all they had left on the other side of the Pacific. They are bunching up, enraging the colonel, and their packs are lumpy and their lack of discipline is disgraceful. Griping, stumbling, their leggings ineptly laced, they are still the men to whom I remain faithful in memory. And as I had pledged myself to them, so had they to me. In retrospect their Indian file tends to blur, like movie dissolves, each superimposed on the others, but they keep moving up and keep peering over their shoulders, their expressions bewildered, as though they are unable to fathom why they are where they are and what is expected of them; anxious, under their collegiate banter and self-deprecation, to remain true to the principles they have been taught; determined not to shame themselves in the eyes of the others; wondering whether they will ever see the present become the past. And then, as their single file disappears in the mists around the bottom of Sugar Loaf, I remember how they were hit and how they died.

Lefty had been Harvard '45 and premed; Swifty had been Ohio State '44 and an engineering major; Chet, Colgate '45, hadn't picked a major; Wally, MIT '43, would have become a physicist. The class dates are significant. That was our generation: old enough to fight, but too young for chairborne jobs. Most of us — I was an exception — had been isolationists before Pearl Harbor, or at any rate before the fall of France. Unlike the doughboys of 1917, we had expected very little of war. We got less. It is a marvel that we not only failed to show the enemy a clean pair of heels, but, on the whole, fought very well. Some were actually heroic. Knocko Craddock had quivered all over as we approached the line. But on Horseshoe Ridge he found a Japanese knee mortar and carried it to his foxhole. When the Nips rushed him, he fired eight rounds at them with their own ammunition and then stood erect in his hole, blazing away with a tommy gun until they cut him down. Knocko was Holy Cross '45. He would have become a lawyer.

Bubba Yates, Ole 'Bama '45 and a divinity student, spent his last night of combat on the forward slope of Half Moon. He fired BAR bursts at the enemy till dawn. Six Nip bodies were found around him. He was bleeding from four gunshot wounds; corpsmen carried him back to a field hospital. All the way he muttered, "Vicksburg, Vicksburg . . ." I heard he was going to be written up for a Silver Star, but I doubt that he got it; witnesses of valor were being gunned down themselves before they could report.

Barr — I never learned his first name — came up as a replacement rifleman and disappeared in two hours. He and Mickey McGuire went out on a two-man patrol and became separated. No one found any trace of him, not even a shred of uniform. He simply vanished. I don't even recall what he looked like. Our eyes never met. One moment he was at my elbow, reporting; an instant later he was gone to wherever he went — probably to total obliteration.

Killer Kane, autodidact, was dug in for the night near the crest of Sugar Loaf when a Jap loomed overhead and bayoneted him in the neck, left shoulder, and upper left arm. The Nip was taking off his wristwatch when Kane leapt up, wrapped him in the strangler's hold, choked him to death, and walked to the battalion aid station without even calling for help.

Pip Spencer, aged seventeen, who wanted to spend his life caring for handicapped children, had his throat cut one night in his foxhole. Nobody had heard the Jap infiltrators.

Mo Crocker, with an IQ of 154 but no college — scholarships were hard to come by in the Depression — had worked in a Vermont post office. He was deeply in love; his girl wrote him every day. He disintegrated after one of our own 81-millimeter mortar shells fell short and exploded behind him.

Horst von der Goltz, Maine '43, who would have become a professor of political science, was leading a flamethrower team toward

Hand Grenade Ridge, an approach to Sugar Loaf, when a Nip sniper picked off the operator of the flamethrower. Horse had pinpointed the sniper's cave. He had never been checked out on flamethrowers, but he insisted on strapping this one to his back and creeping toward the cave. Twenty yards from its maw he stood and did what he had seen others do: gripped the valve in his right hand and the trigger in his left. Then he pulled the trigger vigorously, igniting the charge. He didn't know that he was supposed to lean forward, countering the flame's kick. He fell backward, saturated with fuel, and was cremated within seconds.

Blinker Reid, Oberlin '45, a prelaw student as angular as a praying mantis, was hit in the thigh by a mortar burst. Two Fox Company men carried him to the aid station between them, his arms looped over their shoulders. I saw the three of them limp in, all gaunt, looking like Picasso's *Absinthe Drinker*. Blinker's face was a jerking convulsion, his tics throbbing like a Swiss watch. He wanted to talk. I tried to listen, but his jabbering was so fast I couldn't understand him. He was still babbling, still twitching, when a tank — no ambulances were available — carried him back to the base hospital.

Shiloh Davidson III, Williams '44, a strong candidate for his family's stock-exchange seat, crawled out on a one-man twilight patrol up Sugar Loaf. He had just cleared our wire when a Nambu burst eviscerated him. Thrown back, he was caught on improvised wire. The only natural light came from the palest wash of moon, but the Japs illuminated that side of the hill all night with their green flares. There was no way that any of us could reach Shiloh, so he hung there, screaming for his mother, until about 4:30 in the morning, when he died. After the war I visited his mother. She had heard, on a Gabriel Heatter broadcast, that the Twenty-ninth was assaulting Sugar Loaf. She had spent the night on her knees, praying for her son. She said to me, "God didn't answer my prayers." I said, "He didn't answer any of mine."

Barney, with his hyperthyroidism, hypertension, and the complexion of an eggplant — I had thought he would be our first casualty — became one of the section's survivors, which was all the more remarkable because after I had been evacuated on a litter, I later learned, he perched on a tank barreling into a nest of Japs, firing bursts on a tommy gun and singing:

> *I'm a Brown man born, I'm a Brown man bred,*
> *And when I die, I'll be a Brown man dead . . .*

Once the battle was over, once the island was declared secure, Barney hitchhiked to the cemetery near Naha where our dead lay. He was wearing dungarees, the only clothing he had. An MP turned him away for being out of uniform.

At various times Sugar Loaf and its two supporting crests, Half Moon and Horseshoe, were attacked by both our sister regiments, the Twenty-second Marines and the Fourth Marines, but the Twenty-ninth made the main, week-long effort. In one charge up Half Moon we lost four hundred men. *Time* reported after a typical night: "There were 50 Marines on top of Sugar Loaf Hill. They had been ordered to hold the position all night, at any cost. By dawn, 46 of them had been killed or wounded. Then, into the foxhole where the remaining four huddled, the Japs dropped a white phosphorus shell, burning three men to death. The last survivor crawled to an aid station." In another battalion attack, all three company commanders were killed. Now that Germany had surrendered, Okinawa had become, in *Time*'s phrase, "the vortex of the war."

Infantry couldn't advance. Every weapon was tried: tanks, Long Toms, rockets, napalm, smoke, naval gunfire, aircraft. None of them worked. If anything, the enemy's hold on the heights grew stronger. The Japanese artillery never seemed to let up, and every night Ushijima sent fresh troops up his side of the hill. We kept rushing them, moving like somnambulists, the weight of Sugar Loaf pressing down on us, harder and harder. And as we crawled forward, shamming death whenever a flare burst over us, we could almost feel the waves of darkness moving up behind us. In such situations a man has very little control over his destiny. He does what he must do, responding to the pressures within. Physical courage, which I lacked, fascinated me; I wanted to know how it worked. One of Sugar Loaf's heroes was a man I knew, a major named Henry A. Courtney, Jr., a fair, handsome man who looked like what we then called a matinee idol. No man bore less resemblance to John Wayne. There was something faintly feminine about Courtney, a dainty manner, almost a prissiness. Yet he rallied what was left of his battalion at the base of Sugar Loaf, asked for volunteers to make "a banzai of our own," and led them up in the night through shrapnel, small-arms fire from Horseshoe and Half Moon, and grenades from Sugar Loaf's forward slope. Reaching the top, he heard Japs lining up on the other side for a counterattack. He decided to charge them first, leading the attack himself, throwing hand grenades. His last cry was, "Keep coming — there's a mess of them down there!" He was awarded the Congressional Medal of Honor posthumously. After the war I called on his widow in Oklahoma. Apart from our shared grief, I was still trying to understand why he had done what he had done. I thought she might know. She didn't. She was as mystified as I was.

The odd thing, or odd to those who have never lived in the strange land of combat, is that I never had a clear view of Sugar Loaf. I was on its reverse slope, on the crest, and eventually on the forward slope, but there were always coral dust, high-explosive fumes, and heavy clouds of bursting ammunition on all sides. It would be interesting to see a study of the air pollution there. I'll bet it was very unhealthy. In that smog, grappling with whatever came to hand, we were like the blind man trying to identify an elephant by feeling his legs. After the war I saw a photograph of the hill, but it had been taken from a peculiar angle and was out of focus. That was also true of my memory, which was blurred because, I think, there was so much that I did not want to remember. There, as in the months following my father's death, I suffered from traumatic amnesia. Some flickers of unreal recollection remain: standing at the foot of the hill, arms akimbo, quavering with senseless excitement and grinning maniacally, and — this makes even less sense — running up the slope, not straight up, but on a diagonal, cradling the gun of a heavy machine gun in my left elbow, with a cartridge belt, streaming up from the breechblock, draped over my right shoulder. The gun alone weighed forty-one pounds. Nobody runs uphill with such an awkward piece of machinery. And where was the tripod? I don't know where I had acquired the gun, or where I was taking it, or why I was there at all.

Mostly I remember a lot of scampering about, being constantly on the move under heavy enemy fire, racing from one company CP to another, always keeping an eye open for the nearest hole. Usually I was with either Alan Meissner, skipper of Easy Company, or Howard Mabie, Dog Company's CO until he was hit. There were dead Japs and dead Marines everywhere. Meissner's company went up the hill with 240 men and came back with 2. On the slopes the fighting was sometimes hand-to-hand, and some Marines, though not I, used Kabar knives, the knives being a more practical implement for ripping out a man's guts than a rifle or bayonet. At close range the mustard-colored Japs looked like badly wrapped brown-paper parcels. Jumping around on their bandy legs, they jabbered or grunted; their eyes were glazed over and fixed, as though they were in a trance. I suppose we were the same. Had I not been fasting I'm sure I would have shit my pants. Many did. One of the last orders before going into action was "Keep your assholes tight," but often that wasn't possible. We were animals, really, torn between fear — I was mostly frightened — and a murderous rage at events. One strange feeling, which I remember clearly, was a powerful link with the slain, particularly those who had fallen within the past hour or two. There was so much death around that life seemed almost indecent. Some men's uniforms were soaked with gobs of blood. The ground was sodden with it. I killed, too.

By sundown of May 17 we had just about lost heart, ready to withdraw from the hill because we were running out of ammunition. There wasn't a hand grenade left in the battalion; E Company had used the last of them in two futile charges. As it happened, we not only stayed; we won the battle. That night Ushijima tried to reinforce his troops on the opposite slope, but our flares lit up his counterattack force just as it was forming, and twelve battalions of Marine artillery laid down so strong a concentration that he withdrew. Our battalion commander called Whaling on the field telephone and said, "We can take it. We'll give it another go in the morning." His faith was largely based on news that other Marines had captured Horseshoe Ridge, while our Third Battalion — Baker's, beefed up with replacements and back on the line — was digging in on the slope of Half Moon. At 8:30 A.M. on Friday, May 18, six U.S. tanks tried to reach the hill but couldn't; all were destroyed by enemy mines. New tanks arrived, however, and maneuvered their way through the minefield. At 10:00 A.M. a combined tank-infantry assault, half of Mabie's D Company swarming up one side of the hill while the other half lunged at the other side, sprang at the top. It worked. There was a terrific grenade battle at close quarters on the summit, and the Japanese sent a heavy mortar barrage down on our people, but the remnants of D Company, with the fire support from F Company, which was now on the forward slope of Horseshoe, didn't yield an inch. As night fell on the embattled army, the Twenty-ninth Marines held the hill. The Twenty-ninth holds it still.

Newsweek called Sugar Loaf "the most critical local battle of the war," but I felt no thrill of exultation. My father had warned me that war is grisly beyond imagining. Now I believed him. Bob Fowler, F Company's popular, towheaded commander, had bled to death after being hit in the spleen. His orderly, who adored him, snatched up a submachine gun and unforgivably massacred a line of unarmed Japanese soldiers who had just surrendered. Even worse was the tragic lot of eighty-five student nurses. Terrified, they had retreated into a cave. Marines reaching the mouth of the cave heard Japanese voices within. They didn't recognize the tones as feminine, and neither did their interpreter, who demanded that those inside emerge at once. When they didn't, flamethrowers, moving in, killed them all. To this day, Japanese come to mourn at what is now known as the "Cave of the Virgins."

So my feelings about Sugar Loaf were mixed. As I look back, it

was somewhere on the slopes of that hill, where I confronted the
dark underside of battle, that passion died between me and the
Marine Corps. The silver cord had been loosed, the golden bowl
broken, the pitcher broken at the fountain, the wheel broken at the
cistern. Half the evil in the world, I thought, is done in the name of
honor. *Nicht die Kinder bloss speist man mit Märchen ab.* I now
caught the jarring notes in the "Marines' Hymn" — which, after
all, was a melody lifted from an obscure Offenbach operetta — and
the tacky appeals to patriotism which lay behind the mass butchery
on the islands. I saw through the Corps' swagger, the ruthless
exploitation of the loyalty I had guilelessly plighted in that Springfield recruiting station after Pearl Harbor. On Sugar Loaf, in short,
I realized that something within me, long ailing, had expired. Although I would continue to do the job, performing as the hired
gun, I now knew that banners and swords, ruffles and flourishes,
bugles and drums, the whole rigmarole, eventually ended in squa-
lor. Goethe said, "There is no man so dangerous as the disillu-
sioned idealist," but before one can lose his illusions he must first
possess them. I, to my shame, had been among the enchanted fighters. My dream of war had been colorful but puerile. It had been so
evanescent, so ethereal, so wholly unrealistic that it deserved to be
demolished. Later, after time had washed away the bitterness, I
came to understand that.

On May 19 the Fourth Marines relieved the bleeding remnants of
the Twenty-ninth. Wet as it had been, it now became wetter; eighteen inches of rain fell in the next nine days, and twice the weather
was so poor that the fighting simply stopped. Nevertheless, the
Fourth mopped up Half Moon and Horseshoe and then moved on
Naha, or its ruins. Enemy artillery, even back where we now were,
continued to be heavy. One new piece was a mammoth eight-inch
rocket mortar whose shells shrieked when launched but approached
their targets silently. They were variously called screaming mee-
mies, box-car Charlies, and flying seabags, because if you happened
to be looking at the right place you could actually see one coming,
tumbling end over end. They were launched from crude V-shaped

troughs: the propelling charge was detonated by striking it with a mallet. We were told that they were wildly inaccurate, that their sole purpose was to damage our morale. In my case they were a stupendous success. Every time I heard the shriek I hit the deck. Most of the men ignored them, saying, as I'm sure fighting men have said in every battle since the arrows of Agincourt, "It won't hit you unless it's got your name on it, and if it does, you haven't got a prayer."

Having broken through the Machinato Line, we thought we had won. The Japanese, as usual, refused to concede. Six days after we took Sugar Loaf, Ushijima launched a daring airborne attack on Yontan and Kadena airfields, sending *giretsu* (paratroopers) tumbling down. Both sides suffered casualties; U.S. planes were destroyed. Two American fuel dumps, containing seventy thousand gallons of gasoline, were set off. Kamikazes, launching their seventh major *kikusui* assault, ravaged the Allied fleet and its shore stations. But the Fourth Marines had already waded through the waist-deep waters of the Asato Kawa and entered Naha. Okinawan bodies were everywhere — in shops, in gutters, hanging from windows. Once a city of sixty-five thousand, Naha now teemed with Jap mortars and machine guns. In Tomari, the city's suburb, white phosphorus was fired into the frame buildings to destroy enemy positions, and on May 30 the Twenty-second and Twenty-ninth Marines, strengthened by reinforcements, drove through the Shichina area to the Kokuba estuary, isolating the island's capital. Three days later, on Saturday, June 2, I suffered my superficial gunshot wound. I remember asking a corpsman, "Will I get a Purple Heart?" He nodded, and I thought of my father: *We're even.*

So I had my million-dollar wound, the dream of every infantryman. I was moved back to a field hospital where the only reminder of combat was the rumble of artillery on the horizon. I was served hot chow on clean plates, and even heard rebroadcasts of radio programs from the states, including, that Sunday, Jack Benny, Charlie McCarthy, and the Great Gildersleeve. Then I learned that General Shepherd, determined to avoid a repetition of Garapan and Manila, had decided to bypass the city and outflank the enemy with an amphibious landing on Oroku Peninsula, behind Japanese lines. So I left my dry bunk, went AWOL, rejoined what was left of the Raggedy Ass Marines, and made the landing on Monday. It went well. There were a few perilous moments at a seawall, but then the Japs pinning us down with Nambus were rolled up from the right, and we had our beachhead, which rapidly expanded during the day. In the late afternoon I, shamed by the example of others, temporarily abandoned my timidity and stayed on my feet when a screaming meemie screamed. The shell landed close enough to knock me down, thereby renewing my respect for the big mortars and, as it turned out, saving my life.

Early the next morning several of us were standing in a tomb courtyard when we heard the familiar shriek. We were on a reverse slope from the enemy; the chances of a shell clearing the top of the hill and landing on us were, we calculated, a thousand to one, and the Nips, we now knew, had no way of controlling the flight of these missiles. I crept into the doorway of the tomb. I wasn't actually safe there, but I had more protection than Izzy Levy and Rip Thorpe, who were cooking breakfast over hot boxes. The eight-incher beat the thousand-to-one odds. It landed in the exact center of the courtyard. Rip's body absorbed most of the shock. It disintegrated, and his flesh, blood, brains, and intestines encompassed me. Izzy was blind. So was I — temporarily, though I didn't know that until much later. There was a tremendous roaring inside my head, which was strange, because I was also deaf, both eardrums having been ruptured. My back and left side were pierced by chunks of shrapnel and fragments of Rip's bones. I also suffered brain injury. Apparently I rose, staggered out of the courtyard, and collapsed. For four hours I was left for dead. Then one of our corpsmen, Doc Logan, found I was still hanging on. He gave me two shots of morphine and I was evacuated to an LST offshore which served as a clearinghouse for casualties. All the beautiful white hospital ships — *Solace, Relief,* and *Comfort* — were gone. There were just too many wounded men; they couldn't handle the casualty traffic. So I sailed off for Saipan on an APA. Goodbye, Okinawa, and up yours.

The gravest Marine cases, of which I was one, were sent to Saipan by ship and then flown in stages to San Diego's Balboa Park. I was on and off operating tables, beginning in Hawaii, until mid-autumn, when the surgeons decided that some of the shrapnel was too close to my heart to be removed. It was safe where it was; they would leave it there. I remember wondering, one bad night, whether the old saw — that men were likeliest to succumb with the coming of dawn and at the turn of the tide — was true. For me the worst part of the day was the doctors' prodding and poking for the shrapnel. They gave me a piece of wood to bite while the long steel instruments probed around. I think I screamed just twice.

But that was the only bad part. In Honolulu's Aiea Heights Naval Hospital I even made a friend, a chief petty officer named Claude Thornhill, who had been a bandleader in civilian life and whose band had, in fact, played at my last college prom. I was still in an Aiea Heights ward when I first heard the voice of the new President, learned that Okinawa had been secured and that 207,283 people had died there. In San Francisco the news of the Hiroshima bombing was read to me. And I was napping in San Diego when I was awakened by church bells ringing all over the city. A nurse ran in, a starched white dragon of a woman. I asked what had happened. She cried, "The war's over! The Japs have surrendered!" I said, "Thank you." I meant it. I was really very grateful, though why, and for what, I didn't tell.

Returning to Okinawa today is like watching a naked priest celebrate mass. It is so incongruous, so preposterous, that indignation is impossible. Solemn memories suppress the urge to laugh, so you simply stand stunned and helpless, unable to respond or even move. Luckily, two Marine friends of friends, Lieutenant Colonel Jon Abel and his Top Sergeant, Arnold Milton, are there to assure me that I haven't lost my sanity, that there's no need for that stiff drink I've begun to crave. Of course, I could get it immediately. On today's Okinawa one quickly becomes accustomed to instant gratification. Everything on the island seems to be for sale, including female inhabitants. Thus, the greatest of the island battlefields, more precious than Gettysburg — or at any rate more expensive in American blood — at first glance appears to be covered with used-car lots, junkyards, stereo shops, pinball-machine emporiums, and vendors of McDonald's fast food, Colonel Sanders's fried chicken, Shakey's pizza, and Dairy Queen sundaes. All-night drive-in restaurants prosper, including one overlooking White Beach Three, where the Ninety-sixth Division landed that April 1. In an Apollo Motel you and a girl you've just met and will never meet again, with whom you have nothing in common but convexity, concavity, and a few dollar bills, can rent a bed for an hour. The Okinawans who once moved slowly and gracefully among their lovely terraced rice paddies now sweep around cloverleaf intersections in their souped-up Hondas and Toyotas, and race into neoned Naha — which has become a metropolis the size of Indianapolis — on a four-lane freeway. The Okinawan Expressway carries you from Motobu to the central part of the island in two hours. On the peninsula, by a seawall on the Ie Shima side, Top Milton says: "This is Route Fifty-eight. You probably knew it as Highway Number One." How can I explain that I knew it as an unnumbered path of earth a yard wide?

Off Motobu, Japanese scuba divers disappear under water and reappear triumphantly holding aloft exotic shells. The Americans have built two golf courses, countless tennis courts, and athletic fields. The Japanese enjoy them very much. Sometimes they play against Americans. When they win, they crow. The Americans are good losers, and they are acquiring a great deal of experience in that. Out in the boondocks you can still find rice paddies, but with rice selling at ten dollars for a twenty-five-pound blue plastic bag, the magnificent hillside terraces which once supported thousands of paddies have disappeared; sugarcane and pineapple plantations, which need far less irrigation, are far more profitable. And though many of the old lyre-shaped tombs still stand, the new mausoleums lack the lyre design. Instead they are small, and, being built of cinder blocks, cheap. One entrepreneur is erecting three hundred of them on Motobu. Reportedly he is giving serious consideration to a suggestion, made in jest, that he call it Forest Lawn East.

There are about thirty-five thousand Americans on the island, ten thousand of them in the Third Marine Division. Okinawa is considered good duty. Since Vietnam-bound B-52s are no longer serviced there, it is also light duty, and now that the old DUKWs have been replaced by the more efficient LBTP-7s as amphibious workhorses, landing maneuvers are far easier. The U.S. PX complex at Camp Butler, a small city in itself, is more impressive than any shopping center I've seen in the United States. Local entertainment is provided by bullfighting, sumo wrestling, and habu-mongoose fights. Bullfights aren't bloody. The matador carries a heavy rope. His job is to loop it around the bull's horns and pull, persuade, or trick the animal out of the ring. Sumo wrestling, subsidized by local businessmen, is very popular with GIs and Marines. It is more psychological than physical. Two grotesque, 350-pound Japanese men circle one another again and again, making little movements and twitches which, one is told, have enormous symbolic significance. The actual struggle, the period of contact, lasts no more than thirty seconds, and the wrestler, like the bull, loses when he is forced to leave the arena. The popularity of the fights between mongooses and habus — the habu is a poisonous snake, much feared — is peculiar, because the mongoose always wins. But the Americans love to watch them, too.

The more they like it, the more they try to integrate themselves into the local culture, the more the islanders exclude them. Before the war, Okinawa's inhabitants, like Korea's, were little more than colonial subjects of the emperor. Since the spring of 1972 the island has been the forty-seventh prefecture (*ken*) of Japan, with a bicameral legislature which swarms with political activity. Although the U.S. victory in 1945 paved the way for this, Okinawan politicians and intellectuals resent the American presence among them. When they say "Us," they mean themselves and the Japanese; when they say "Them," they are talking about Americans. From time to time they stage demonstrations to remind the world of their hostility toward Them, though they know, as everyone who has mastered simple arithmetic knows, that an American departure would be an economic disaster for the island, ending, among other things, the

$150 million Tokyo pays Okinawan property owners as rent for land occupied by U.S. forces. This paradox, of course, is not unique in history. The British learned to live with it, realizing that the world's most powerful nation is the obvious choice for anyone in need of a whipping boy. When I recall the sacrifices which gave the Okinawans their freedom, the slanders seem hard. Then I remember the corpse of the girl on the beach; our patronizing manner toward a little Okinawan boy we picked up as a mascot and treated like a household pet; the homes our 105-millimeter and 155-millimeter guns leveled; the callousness with which we destroyed a people who had never harmed us. The Americans of today may not deserve the slurs of the demonstrators, but the fact remains that more than seventy-seven thousand civilians died here during the battle, and no one comes out of a fight like that with clean hands.

That night in the Okinawa Hilton I dream of the Sergeant, the old man, and their hill. It is a shocking nightmare, the worst yet. I had expected irony, scorn, contempt, and sneers from him. Instead, he is almost catatonic. He doesn't even seem to see the old man. His face is emaciated, deathly white, smeared with blood, and pitted with tiny wounds, as though he had blundered into a bramble bush. His eyes are quite mad. He appears so defiled and so miserable that on awakening I instantly think of Dorian Gray. I have, I think, done this to myself. I have been betrayed, or been a betrayer, and this fragile youth is paying the price. *Mea culpa, mea maxima culpa.* And for this there can be no absolution.

But I cannot leave it at that. Despite my disillusionment with the Marine Corps, I cannot easily unlearn lessons taught then, and as the youngest DI on Parris Island can tell you, there is no such word as impossible in the Marine Corps. There must be more on this island than I have seen. And there is. Next morning I explore the lands beyond the neon and all it implies, and find that the island's surface tawdriness is no more characteristic of postwar Okinawa than Times Square is typical of Manhattan. Hill 53, for example, once an outer link in the coast-to-coast chain of the Machinato Line, is now shared by an amusement park and a botanical garden. The peak provides a superb view of modern Naha. Looking in that direction through field glasses, it is satisfying to see that the city's tidal flats, where we trapped a huge pocket of Nipponese after Sugar Loaf had been taken, have been filled in and are part of the downtown shopping center. The city's suburbs reflect quiet good taste: flat-topped stucco houses roofed with tiles and shielded for privacy by lush shrubs.

The pleasantest surprise is Shuri, the Machinato Line strong-point which was second only to Sugar Loaf in Ushijima's defenses. Japanese tourists seem to prefer visits to the Cave of the Virgins, or a descent of the 168 sandstone steps that lead to the Japanese com-manders' last, underground command post on the island's southern tip, but to me Shuri is more attractive and far more significant. Commodore Matthew C. Perry first raised the American flag over Shuri Castle on May 26, 1853; the Fifth Marines did it again on May 29, 1945. Since 1950 the ruins of the castle's twelve-foot-thick walls — some of which have survived, curving upward with effort-less grace — have enclosed the University of the Ryukyus, Okinawa being the largest island in the Ryukyu Archipelago, and dotting the ridges flanking the university are modest, immaculate, middle-class homes. The castle-cum-university is on Akamaruso Dori, or Street, on the opposite side of which are swings, jungle gyms, and sandboxes. Under the shade of a tree in one corner stands an old Japanese tank, rusting in peace. None of the children in the little park pay any attention to it, and neither, after all I've seen, do I.

Before leaving the island I want to pay my respects to scenes once vivid to me. This seems a recipe for frustration, because most of them are gone. Green Beach Two, where my boondockers first touched Okinawan soil, is remarkable only for a silvery petroleum storage tank and two fuel pumps. My leaking cave near Machinato Field is gone; so is the field; only a renamed village, Makiminato, remains, and there is nothing familiar in it. The seawall on Oroku Peninsula and the tomb where I nearly died have completely van-ished; a power station has replaced them. Motobu Peninsula, still clothed in its dense jungle, is the least-changed part of the island. The trouble here is not the absence of memorabilia. It is, once more, in my aging flesh. Precipices I once scaled effortlessly are grueling. Nevertheless I make it up the peninsula's peaks, Katsu and Yaetake. The pinnacles there provide first-rate views of the peninsula, and my presence on them attracts inquiring guards. I have been trespassing, once more, and I have been caught. But the guards are more curious than punitive, and presently I am talking to a voluble Japanese technician, Mr. Y. Fujumura. He explains that the peaks are used for Japanese and U.S. Signal Corps equipment which relays long-distance telephone calls, monitors radio traffic, and eavesdrops on phone conversations as far away as North Korea. He provides details. I understand none of them. We part, and on my way once more, checking my notes, I conclude that I have touched all bases on Okinawa.

I am wrong. I left the United States believing that a revisit to Sugar Loaf was out of the question because it had been bulldozed away for an officers' housing development. In La Jolla, General Lemuel C. Shepherd, Jr., the retired Marine Corps commandant, said he had been in the neighborhood recently; he assured me that the hill just wasn't there any more. But I ask Jon Abel and Top Milton to join me in a visit to the development anyway. There we pass a teen center, turn from McKinley Street to Washington Street, and, as I give a shout, come to a complete stop.

There it is, a half-block ahead. I am looking at the whole of it for the first time. It is the hill in my dreams.

Sugar Loaf Hill.

Jon and Top, almost as excited as I am, begin digging out old maps, which confirm me, but I don't need confirmation. Instinctively I look around for patterns of terrain, cover and concealment, fields of fire. To a stranger, noticing all the wrinkles and bumps pitting its slopes, Sugar Loaf would merely look like a height upon which something extraordinary happened long ago. That is the impression of housewives along the street when we ring their doorbells and ask them. They are wide-eyed when we tell them that they are absolutely right, that those lumps and ripples once were shell holes and foxholes. Now a mantle of thick greensward covers all. I remember Carl Sandburg: "I am the grass . . . let me work."

Up I go — no gasping this time — and find two joined pieces of wood at the top, a surveyor's marker referring to a bench mark below. I take a deep breath, suddenly realizing that the last time I was here anyone standing where I now stand would have had a life expectancy of about seven seconds. Today the ascent of Sugar Loaf takes a few minutes. In 1945 it took ten days and cost 7,547 Marine casualties. Ignoring the surveyor's marker, I take my own bearings, from memory. Northeast: Shuri and its university. Southeast: Half Moon; officers' dwellings there, too. South-southwest: one leg of Horseshoe visible, and that barren. Southwest: Naha's Grand Castle Hotel, once a flat saucer of black ruins. And beneath my feet, where mud had been deeply veined with human blood, the healing mantle of turf. "I am the grass." *I the Lord am thy Saviour and thy Redeemer.* "Let me work." *Sacred heart of the crucified Jesus, take away this murdering hate and give us thine own eternal love.*

And then, in one of those great thundering jolts in which a man's real motives are revealed to him in an electrifying vision, I understand, at last, why I jumped hospital that Sunday thirty-five years ago and, in violation of orders, returned to the front and almost certain death.

It was an act of love. Those men on the line were my family, my home. They were closer to me than I can say, closer than any friends had been or ever would be. They had never let me down, and I couldn't do it to them. I had to be with them, rather than let them die and me live with the knowledge that I might have saved them. Men, I now knew, do not fight for flag or country, for the Marine Corps or glory or any other abstraction. They fight for one another. Any man in combat who lacks comrades who will die for him, or for whom he is willing to die, is not a man at all. He is truly damned.

And as I stand on that crest I remember a passage from Scott Fitzgerald. World War I, he wrote, "was the last love battle"; men, he said, could never "do that again in this generation." But Fitzgerald died just a year before Pearl Harbor. Had he lived, he would have seen his countrymen united in a greater love than he had ever known. Actually love was only part of it. Among other

Sugar Loaf, then and now

things, we had to be tough, too. To fight World War II you had to have been tempered and strengthened in the 1930s Depression by a struggle for survival — in 1940 two out of every five draftees had been rejected, most of them victims of malnutrition. And you had to know that your whole generation, unlike the Vietnam generation, was in this together, that no strings were being pulled for anybody; the four Roosevelt brothers were in uniform, and the sons of both Harry Hopkins, FDR's closest adviser, and Leverett Saltonstall, one of the most powerful Republicans in the Senate, served in the Marine Corps as enlisted men and were killed in action. But devotion overarched all this. It was a bond woven of many strands. You had to remember your father's stories about the Argonne, and saying your prayers, and Memorial Day, and Scouting, and what Barbara Frietchie said to Stonewall Jackson. And you had to have heard Lionel Barrymore as Scrooge and to have seen Gary Cooper as Sergeant York. And seen how your mother bought day-old bread and cut sheets lengthwise and resewed them to equalize wear while your father sold the family car, both forfeiting what would be considered essentials today so that you could enter college.

You also needed nationalism, the absolute conviction that the United States was the envy of all other nations, a country which had never done anything infamous, in which nothing was insuperable, whose ingenuity could solve anything by inventing something. You felt sure that all lands, given our democracy and our know-how, could shine as radiantly as we did. Esteem was personal, too; you assumed that if you came through this ordeal, you would age with dignity, respected as well as adored by your children. Wickedness was attributed to flaws in individual characters, not to society's shortcomings. To accept unemployment compensation, had it existed, would have been considered humiliating. So would committing a senile aunt to a state mental hospital. Instead, she was kept in the back bedroom, still a member of the family.

Debt was ignoble. Courage was a virtue. Mothers were beloved, fathers obeyed. Marriage was a sacrament. Divorce was disgraceful. Pregnancy meant expulsion from school or dismissal from a job. The boys responsible for the crimes of impregnation had to marry the

The author in 1979

girls. Couples did not keep house before they were married and there could be no wedding until the girl's father had approved. You assumed that gentlemen always stood and removed their hats when a woman entered a room. The suggestion that some of them might resent being called "ladies" would have confounded you. You needed a precise relationship between the sexes, so that no one questioned the duty of boys to cross the seas and fight while girls wrote them cheerful letters from home, girls you knew were still pure because they had let you touch them here but not there, explaining that they were saving themselves for marriage. All these and "God Bless America" and Christmas or Hanukkah and the certitude that victory in the war would assure their continuance into perpetuity — all this led you into battle, and sustained you as you fought, and comforted you if you fell, and, if it came to that, justified your death to all who loved you as you had loved them.

Later the rules would change. But we didn't know that then. We didn't *know*.

My last war dream came to me in Hong Kong's Ambassador Hotel, in a room overlooking the intersection of Nathan and Middle streets. The dream began in a red blur, like a film completely out of focus, so much so that I didn't have the faintest idea of what I would see. Clarity came slowly. First: broad daylight, for the first time in these dreams. Second: the hill. No mystery about that now; it was Sugar Loaf down to the last dimple. The old man appeared on the right and began his weary ascent. But there was no figure rising on the left to greet him, though he didn't know that until, breathing heavily, he reached the summit and peered down the reverse slope. He saw nothing, heard nothing. There was nothing to see or hear. He waited, shifting slightly this way and that with the passive patience of the middle-aged. A cloud passed overhead, darkening the hill. Then the old man grasped what had happened. Embers would never again glow in the ashes of his memory. His Sergeant would never come again. He turned away, blinded by tears.

Author's Note

THIS BOOK IS LARGELY A MARINE'S MEMOIR, NOT A BALANCED HIStory of the war with Japan. Those who want versions of air and naval engagements during the conflict must look elsewhere; descriptions of Douglas MacArthur's campaigns, for example, may be found in *American Caesar*, my biography of the general.

That is the first breath. The second, which must quickly follow, is that my reminiscences are not chronological. Any attempt to impose structure upon the chaos of personal history, with the intent of attracting and holding the reader, necessarily involves some distortion. It may be as great as a Mercator projection's — for instance, Daniel Defoe's *Journal of the Plague Year*, a riveting account of a disaster which struck when the writer was five years old — or as slight as H. L. Mencken's genial caveat that his autobiography was "yarning" and "not always photographically precise," that "there are no doubt some stretchers in this book," though "mainly it is fact."

So here too. After thirty-five years, any man who suffered a head wound (my medical discharge papers note that, among other things, I had sustained "traumatic lesions of the brain") can never be absolutely sure of his memory. But everything I have set down happened, and to the best of my recollection it happened just this way, except that I have changed names to respect the privacy of other men and their families. But I have resorted to some legerdemain in the interests of re-creating, and clarifying the spirit of, the historical past. Here and there I use the pronoun "we" in its all-inclusive sense, as in "We won the war." More specifically, although I enlisted in the Marine Corps shortly after Pearl Harbor, I was ordered back to college until called up. Thus, although I spent seven months on Guadalcanal, I arrived after the Japanese hegira and saw no fighting there. No infantryman fought on all, or even many, of the Pacific islands. Deployment of troops, casualty figures, and tropical diseases laid down impossible odds against that. My own combat experience occurred on Okinawa, where I fought for over two months, during which I was wounded twice, was ordered off the line once, and was ultimately carried off the island and evacuated to Saipan. I have drawn from that bank of experience for flash-forwards in earlier chapters, introducing each episode at a point where it seems fitting. Writing them was extremely difficult. My feelings about the Marine Corps are still highly ambivalent, tinged with sadness and bitterness, yet with the first enchantment lingering. But by mining that tough old ore, and altering the order of those personal events, I have, I believe, been able to present a sequential account of a war which still confuses most Americans.

This, then, was the life I knew, where death sought me, during which I was transformed from a cheeky youth to a troubled man who, for over thirty years, repressed what he could not bear to remember.

Expressing gratitude to those who helped me along the way during this long journey into the past is an occasion for both pleasure and frustration — pleasure, because my memories of their kindnesses are still warm, and frustration, because my appreciation can never be adequate. I hope I have omitted no one. It is possible. Jungles are poor places to keep files. If I thus err in omission, I trust I shall be forgiven. Forgiveness is also asked for my failure to identify individuals by their military, diplomatic, civilian, tribal, and ecclesiastical titles. Generals are here, and monsignors, and ambassadors — all in different hierarchies, so varied and often so defiant of classification that I have resorted to that weak crutch, the alphabet. I honor each source; I thank each; I am deeply indebted to all; and I believe that they will share my doubt that rank will count for much when we cross that dark river to the far shore where all voyages end and all paths meet.

My samaritans, then, were: Jonathan F. Abel, Aguedo F. Agbayani, Consul Alberto, C. W. Allison, Norman Anderson, John A. Baker, Itaaka Bamiatoa, Kabataan Barangay, Carmelo Barbero, Susan Bardelosa, Ieuan Batten, Bill Bennett, Homer Bigart, Al Bonney, Baltazar Jerome Bordallo, Madeleine M. Bordallo, Ricardo J. Bordallo, Robert L. Bowen, Edward R. Brady, Margaret A. Brewer, Paul H. Brown, Stanley Brown, Robert Byck, George Cakobau, Oscar Calvo, Carlos S. Camacho, Anthony Charlwood, Donald Chung, Martin Clemens, Andrew W. Coffey, Jeremiah Collins, John P. Condon, Paul Cox, Elfriede Craddock, Jerry Craddock, R. Don Crider, Horace Dawson, Beth Day, Judy Day, John deYoung, Rodolfo L. Diaz, Mack R. Douglas, R. E. Duca, Rodolfo Dula, Jim Earl, Florence Fenton, Y. Fujumura, Robert B. Fowler, Jay Gildner, John R. Griffith, Samuel B. Griffith II, John Guise, James Gunther, Robert Debs Heinl, Jr., Ernest S. Hildebrand, Jr., Frank W. Ingraham, Osi Ivaroa, Sy Ivice, Emilie Johnson, Robert Jordan, Timothy Joyner, Bruce Kirkwood, Jackson Koria, Isirfli Korovula, Joiji Kotobalavu, Maura Leavy, Harland Lee, Theodore Lidz, Chester A. Lipa, Arthur C. Livick, Jr., Ichiro Loitang, Haldon Ray Loomis, Fijito Oshikawa, Howard Mabie, P. D. MacDonald, Luis G. Magbanua, Pio Manoa, P. F. Manueli, Ferdinand Marcos, Imelda Romualdez Marcos, Ann Marshall, Tim Mauldin, Alan Meissner, Mike Mennard, Ross Milloy, Robert Milne, Arnold Milton, Yoshida Mitsui, Ben Moide, George E. Murphy, Satendra Nandan, Beretitaro Neeti, Dave Ngirmidol, Praxiteles C. Nicholson, Homer Noble, Myron Nordquist, Russell E. Olson, Jeremiah J. O'Neil, Noah Onglunge, Hera Owen, Robert Owen, Ted Oxburrow, Katsy Parsons, Lester E. Penney, Harry W. Peterson, Jr., Raymond Pillai, Eugene Ramsey, Asasela Ravuvu, John E. Reece, Garth Rees, Thomas Remengesaw, Carlos Romulo, Tessie Romulo, Pedro C. Sanchez, Frank Santo, Frans Schutzman, Tom Scott, Charles S. Shapiro, Lemuel C. Shepherd, Jr., George Silk, Harry Simes, E. H. Simmons, Gus Smales,

Kalista Smau, Hinao Soalablai, Kerrie Somosi, Robert Somosi, Laura M. Souder, Patrick Spread, Taute Takanoi, Jay Taylor, John Terrance, Ian Thompson, Joe Tooker, Jean Trumbull, Robert Trumbull, Fred Turner, Richard Underwood, Mae Verave, Mariano C. Kersosa, Jacob Vouza, Mike Ward, R. J. Wenzei, Roger L. Williams, William Wilson, Adrian P. Winkel, Anne Wray, and Stanton F. Zoglin.

Although this tale is personal, certain books were useful in the telling of it and are recommended to those interested in reading more about the battlefields it cites. These are *Rust in Peace*, by Bruce Adams (Sydney, 1975); *The Pacific: Then and Now*, by Bruce Bahrenburg (New York, 1971); *A Complete History of Guam*, by Paul Carano and Pedro C. Sanchez (Rutland, Vermont, 1964); *History of the Sixth Marine Division*, by Bevan Cass (Washington, 1948); *The Battle for Guadalcanal*, a superb account of that struggle, by Samuel B. Griffith II (Philadelphia, 1963); *History of the Second World War*, by B. H. Lidell Hart (New York, 1971); *Soldiers of the Sea*, a history of the Marine Corps, by Robert Debs Heinl, Jr. (Annapolis, 1962); *The Long and the Short and the Tall*, by Alvin M. Josephy, Jr. (New York, 1946); *The Old Breed*, a history of the First Marine Division in World War II, by George McMillan (Washington, 1949); *The Fatal Impact*, by Alan Moorehead (Middlesex, England, 1966); *History of United States Naval Operations in World War II*, volumes III, IV, V, VI, VII, VIII, XIII, XIV, by Samuel Eliot Morison (Boston, 1948, 1949, 1949, 1949, 1951, 1953, 1959, 1960); *Untangled New Guinea Pidgin*, by Wesley Sadler (Madang, Papua New Guinea, 1973); *Tin Roofs and Palm Trees*, by Robert Trumbull (Seattle, 1977); *The Pacific Way*, edited by Sione Tupouniua, et al. (Suva, Fiji, 1975); *Tarawa*, by Robert Sherrod (New York, 1944); *World War II: Island Fighting*, by Rafael Steinberg and the Editors of Time-Life Books (Alexandria, Virginia, 1978); and *World War II: The Rising Sun*, by Arthur Zich and the Editors of Time-Life Books (Alexandria, Virginia, 1977).

Readers of Sean O'Casey's *Juno and the Paycock* may find the second italicized sentence on page 391 familiar. It is a paraphrase of two sentences appearing in different acts of that splendid play.

In this, as in previous books, the author is profoundly grateful to the staff of Wesleyan University's Olin Library, and in particular to J. Robert Adams, University Librarian, and William Dillon, Suzanne H. Fall, Peg Halstead, Alice Henry, Joan Jurale, Erhard Konerding, Steven Lebergott, Edmund Rubacha, and Elizabeth Swaim, for their generous help, thoughtfulness, and understanding. Once more my invaluable assistant, Margaret Kennedy Rider, has proved to be loyal, tireless, and understanding. And I am again indebted to Don Congdon, my literary agent; Roger Donald, my editor; and Melissa Clemence, my copy editor — three peerless professionals whose patience and counsel never failed, never flagged, and who saw to it that everything attainable was attained.

W.M.

Wesleyan University
May 1980